D1090739

ON GARDENS AND GARDENING

(Frontispiece) Geraniums in a happy clash of colour followed hyacinths
and lily-flowering tulips in the courtyard of a town garden.

ON GARDENS AND GARDENING

by Lanning Roper

HARPER & ROW, PUBLISHERS
New York and Evanston

On Gardens and Gardening. © 1969 by Thomas Nelson and Sons Ltd.
Printed in **Great Britain** for Harper & Row. All rights reserved.
No part of this book may be used or reproduced in any manner
whatsoever without written permission except in the case of brief
quotations embodied in critical articles and reviews. For information
address Harper & Row, Publishers, Incorporated, 49 East 33rd Street,
New York, N.Y. 10016.

First U.S. Edition

Library of Congress Catalog Card Number: 72–83976

Photoset in Malta by St Paul's Press Ltd, Malta

Contents

Acknowledgements

We would like to thank the following for the use of black and white photographs
and colour plates. *Amateur Gardening:* page 24: *J. E. Downward:* pages 7, 8, 13, 20,
26, 30, 32, 33, 34, 36, 40, 45, 46, 51, 52, 55, 68, 73, 76, 77, 86, 89, 94, 97, 98, 100,
101, 103, 104, 105, 106, 111, 112, 115, 119, 120, 122, 123, 125, 127, 131, 133, 134,
157, 161, 163, 164, 169, 171, 172, 173, 179, 182, 184, 190, 197, 199, 202, 203, 204,
208, 220, 222, 225, 226, 229, and colour plates facing pages 16, 92, 149, 181: *The Dutch
Bulb Growers' Association,* for colour plates facing pages 188, 224: *Miss Valerie Finnis,*
for the frontispiece: *Fisons' Studio,* page 215: *A. J. Huxley,* pages 187, 195: *H. Smith,*
pages 14, 18, 21, 42, 43, 47, 48, 50, 53, 58, 59, 61, 64, 66, 67, 69, 70, 74, 78, 80,
81, 82, 83, 84, 88, 90, 91, 93, 99, 110, 114, 124, 126, 130, 132, 135, 139, 141, 144,
148, 150, 153, 154, 155, 158, 160, 162, 166, 167, 168, 176, 177, 178, 180, 185, 189,
192, 194, 196, 206, 207, 210, 213, 216, 223, and colour plates facing pages 37,
44, 53, 60, 85, 133, 140, 156, 209: *Mrs Jocelyn Steward,* page 147: *Sutton and
Sons Ltd.,* page 45: *Sydney W. Newbery,* page 219: *Thomson Newspapers,* page 137:
Miss Mary Wellesley, pages, 11, 12, 15, 28, 57, 63, 75, 92, 138, 142: *Ian Yeomans,*
page 174.

1 Introduction

The aim of this book is to give encouragement, advice and assistance to those with some knowledge of gardening, but who would like to know more about the subject. It is based on forty years of practical experience of gardening in the diverse conditions of soil and climate that are to be found in the United States and Britain and of planning gardens in countries where the potentialities are as different as those of Long Island compared with southern Italy or Scotland with the Midi.

As experienced gardeners well know, gardening is not simply a natural gift that matures of its own accord. It is something that requires for its true success and enjoyment a considerable amount of study and hard work, as well as infinite patience and experimentation.

My love of flowers and my gardening career started at a very early age in northern New Jersey on the wooded slopes of the Palisades, overlooking the Hudson River. Fortunately this section of the Palisades Interstate Park was a rich hunting ground for wild flowers. With my two brothers I soon learned where to find the first Hepaticas, nestling among the dry leaves, Bloodroot with its fascinating curled sheath of silvery grey leaves from which emerged the snow-white flowers, and Dutchman's Breeches *(Dicentra cucullaria)*, which always proved a source of delight and amusement. Later there were violets – yellow, blue, white and purple – on special banks and in moist clearings, and the wild red columbines *(Aquilegia canadensis)* that grew with ferns in shady crevices of the grey rocks.

Alas, houses now stand on my two favourite spots for the pink Lady Slipper orchids *(Cypripedium acaule)* and moist fields near home, once starred with Field Lilies *(Lilium canadense)*, have shared a similar fate. In late summer the Cardinal Flower *(Lobelia cardinalis)* grew by the streams and the exquisite Fringed and Bottle Gentians could be visited on my walk home from school in the fall.

During summer holidays in New England and later when I was at Harvard, I roamed the woodlands to find trilliums by the thousands and Solomon's Seals nodding in the wind. The Arnold Arboretum with its fine trees and shrubs became an inspiration as had the other botanic gardens nearer home.

Later I made an annual spring pilgrimage to the great Charleston plantations including The Cypress, Middleton and The Magnolia Gardens with their undreamed-of masses of camellias, azaleas, spring bulbs and tumbling masses of wistaria intertwined with the creamy white Cherokee rose against the waving grey Spanish moss. This was also the moment for Red Bud *(Cercis canadensis)* and Dogwood *(Cornus florida)*. The latter is certainly one of the finest sights of the horticultural world.

The gardens at Williamsburg, Mt Vernon, Monticello and the James River plantations with their superb boxwood and strong sense of eighteenth-century design have proved a lasting influence. The late Mrs Robert Woods Bliss's remarkable garden, Dumbarton Oaks in Washington, D.C., and the great gardens at Longwood and Winterthur near Wilmington, the latter the lifetime creation of Mr Henry Francis du Pont, added to my determination for a gardening career, as did trips to California, Florida, and the West Indies, which opened up vistas of a vast, exciting, new flora.

I have perhaps been more fortunate than most in having had a long period of practical training, first in the Fine Arts at Harvard University with an eye to graduate-work in Landscape Architecture, then, at the end of the war, as a student at Kew, and afterwards at the Royal Botanic Garden in Edinburgh. This practical period of my training was followed by four years as assistant to the Editor of the Royal Horticultural Society.

As a landscape consultant, I have advised on gardens in various parts of the world, on soils ranging from rocky slopes in Italy to acid peaty bogs in Ireland and rich fertile valleys in England. Some are large country gardens, others small back gardens in urban areas, and I have also advised on the planning of town squares, as well as on hospital gardens and housing estates. Rose gardens, mixed borders, formal parterres, paved herb-gardens, and shrub and woodland gardens have all absorbed my interest in turn. All this has helped to give me a wider conspectus of the subject than is the lot of most writers. I have made it a rule to select personally the plants for my designs, and, whenever

Pale blue campanulas provide colour after the irises have finished blooming, yet in no way are they injurious to the rhizomes. Annuals such as Californian poppies and salpiglossis are also suitable.

possible, I supervise the planting and often do a good deal of it myself. In this way I get to know the problems and merits of the soil with which I work and keep in touch with new plants.

As a garden designer, I experience some of the same emotions as a nanny. Having made a garden, I always want to follow its development to maturity. If I plant an avenue of oaks or chestnuts, the well-being of each tree is my concern, as well as the avenue as a whole. I have my favourite plants, of course, and my anathemas, but the excitement of creating and planning for the future is stimulating and very satisfying.

It should not be thought this book will always provide an answer to the innumerable questions that must arise in a gardener's mind at all periods of the year. In short, it is not a gardening encyclopaedia, of which some excellent ones are already available. I have concentrated on hardy plants, shrubs, trees, roses and bulbs, with the emphasis on good plants and their cultivation. What I have set out to do is to write primarily about gardens and the plants with which they are made.

I hope you will enjoy what you find here and that it will help you with your own garden – be it patch, acre or park. Above all, I want to give pleasure and open up new vistas.

I am grateful to the Royal Horticultural Society for their many kindnesses, to Mr Patrick Synge, their Editor, for his wise counsel, and particularly to Mr Denis Hamilton, the former Editor of *The Sunday Times* (London), for allowing me to draw on my articles that appeared in that newspaper. To all my friends in the United States who have helped with this edition I express my heartfelt thanks.

2 Down to Earth

The Making of Gardens

As a garden designer I am lucky to follow a profession which is so absorbing, satisfying and pleasurable that at times it is not easy to decide where work ends and recreation begins. I want to emphasize this fact, as the making of gardens, whether your own or some-one else's, should be rewarding, as it is creative work and, one always hopes, enduring. That is why we plant yew hedges, avenues of oaks and trees that may take twenty years or more to flower, such as rare Asiatic magnolias and the Dove Tree, *Davidia involucrata*. A good gardener will usually take this long-term view. If the creators of the great plantations in the Southern States including Mount Vernon, Middleton, and Monticello, or the famous English parks such as those at Stowe, Levens Hall, Petworth, Stourhead and Castle Howard, coupled with the names of William Kent, 'Capability' Brown and Repton, had not adopted this attitude when planting, these gardens would be very different places today, as would the general aspect of this country and Britain. By the same token, in a few decades many of the famous old parks and gardens where replacements have not been planted over the years will be gravely altered, as so many of the trees have reached their life span.

First of all what is a garden? The Oxford Dictionary suggests as a first definition; 'An enclosed piece of ground devoted to the cultivation of flowers, fruits and vegetables'. This is a good one for my purpose as it at once puts a limit on the extent of the garden. I spend a great deal of my time, when not decreasing the size of gardens and simplifying them for some clients, persuading others not to go on expanding when they already are having difficulty in maintaining what they have.

A small herb garden with brick paths and box topiary, designed by the author. Fragrant pinks, purple fennel, golden marjoram and lots of silver foliage relieved the monotony of green.

A corner of the George Washington Garden at Claverton Manor, the American Museum in Britain, near Bath. This faithful reproduction of the garden at Mount Vernon was the gift of the Colonial Dames.

Everyone probably has a slightly different conception of a garden. To one it may be undulating park land with water and carefully planted groups of trees. To another it is a walled garden with borders of flowers, fruit trees and vegetables and to yet another it means a decorative garden of compartmentation with infinite variety of planting. To some it is a garden packed with rare plants, a collector's garden rather like a museum of living plants. To many it is a quiet secluded place in which to rest and work. To others it is a place for recreation, with swings, a barbecue, a croquet lawn, a tennis court or a pool. Alas, to a few it is a cruel battlefield with quickly growing lawns, rampageous weeds, and hungry insects.

The landscape designer, confronted with a new garden, is not unlike the general who, before entering a military engagement, must have a clear picture of the objective, a knowledge of the resources at hand including man-power, supplies and financial backing, as well as a thorough understanding of the terrain, the climate and the vagaries of the local weather.

In planning there is first the survey of the site. On the credit side there may be a fine view and this will help to determine whether the garden is to be outlooking or inlooking. A number in the first category have views to the sea, distant hills or mountains. In town gardens the object will probably be the reverse with an attempt to shut out the movement of traffic, the inquisitive eyes, the blank walls and the television masts. Also on the credit side is water in any form, whether a lake, a canal, a river or a gushing rocky stream. Running water will give movement to the landscape, and pools of still water reflect ever-changing patterns of trees and clouds.

Then there is the question of aspect, shelter from wind, depth of soil, and its composition. Let's hope it is not heavy clay. If in doubt as to whether soil is acid, alkaline or neutral, send a sample for analysis. Drainage is important, but this can be corrected in various ways, and poor light soil can be improved with manure, humus, compost and basic nutrients.

Trees are vital. Perhaps there are fine Lebanon cedars with wonderful horizontal branches, pines with red-brown stems and purple-green foliage, fine beeches, elms, lindens or oaks. Preserve the best at all costs and work them into your design as it evolves. With thinning and a little tree surgery, miracles can be accomplished. Save thickets, hedgerows, spinneys, old orchards and above all shelter belts near the sea or on windy ridges. They weren't grown there without good reason. What is more, they may provide containment for the garden, which is important. Additional trees can obviously be removed later.

If you are to build, make sure that the house is correctly sited in relation to the area destined for the garden, and give great attention to the lie of the land, the cross-falls and the levels. Architects and builders often determine the levels of the house with an eye to expense and to the location of damp courses but with little regard for the garden and its problems. If possible, the plans for the house and its garden should be developed simultaneously. I have worked closely with architects on different projects, with benefit to both.

If possible, visit a new site as often as possible at different times of day and at different seasons. In an established garden, try to visualize the design without the existing plan, stripping it of features and reducing it to the bare bones. This may be difficult for the layman. In almost every case gardens can be improved by simplification and by elimination. Remember that a great deal of the existing planting may have been afterthoughts when the scheme was more or less completed. As you are so accustomed to your own garden, you may find it difficult to see other possibilities, and that is why a fresh eye is useful.

A site survey with accurate measurements should be made, and if there is to be construction or contouring, levels should be taken at key points. Onto this survey plan the proposed layout can be imposed.

Cost is an important factor. It is always cheaper to complete a garden in one operation. For example, if you want a lily pond or a swimming pool, construct it initially so that the subsoil can either be utilized in contouring or removed. If you add them later, the lawns will be ruined, and you will be paying for much of the work twice over. This goes for construction work generally. Choose paving you like, and if you can't afford real stone, there are excellent composition substitutes. Go to the expense of setting the stone and mortaring the joints so that there is no subsequent weed problem, but leave pockets for planting as required.

Next, it must be decided what type of garden is wanted. Here is a matter of personal taste and a way of life. Tell me the hobbies of the family and I can surmise the garden. Do you want to include sculpture or a garden folly? Is the yearning for your own fresh spinach, sweet corn, asparagus, *courgettes* and *fraises des bois* irresistible? Is a tennis court or a pool more important? Do you want masses of flowers for cutting? Is it to be formal or woodland? What plants do you wish to grow? What can you spend? What are you prepared to spend to keep it up? Will you look after it yourself on the weekend, or will you be able to have a gardener? All these are vital questions. Having made these decisions, it is then a matter of adapting the site to accommodate the essential features. Some may go by the board because of lack of space and the lie of the land. A steeply sloping site can be enchanting with walled terraces, flights of steps and paved parterres, but costs will be very high. Grassy slopes are effective but they are difficult to mow. Perhaps ground covers are the answer on the steeper ones.

Contouring of the site is far easier than it used to be in the days when soil-shifting was a prolonged hand operation. Today with modern earth-moving equipment in a matter of a few hours it is possible to remove trees, alter levels and contour an area by shaping glades, throwing up mounds and hollowing out lakes and ponds. A skilful operator of a bulldozer who has a feeling for contours can perform miracles if there is depth of soil without rocky subsoil or outcrops. There are two things to remember during such operations – remove precious top soil from all areas to be excavated either for building or contouring as well as from depressions that are to be levelled or mounded with subsoil. The top soil can be spread over the area at the end. Secondly, have regard for trees. By raising the soil level around the boles or by disturbing the surface roots, fatal damage can be done. There are far too many unnecessary casualties to trees as a result of careless earth-moving operations.

Access to many gardens, both town and country, is difficult. Anyone with a city garden with no approach save through the house will understand. When planning your programme, be sure to consider this problem throughout the garden. Have convenient access so that soil, peat and manure can be easily delivered to the spot where it is needed and provide adequate storage facilities. Make all gates wide enough for garden equipment which you may eventually have. Plan so that the mower can be moved from area to area with ease, avoiding steps where possible. Provide adequate parking facilities with sufficient turning radius for cars and make sure the curves of the drive can be easily manoeuvred. Above all, arrange for water points or irrigation at convenient positions before paths and lawns are made as these can be expensive after-thoughts.

When planning paths, be sure that they are wide enough. Walking single file in Indian fashion is hardly sociable. The route will be controlled by the design. In formal geometric schemes this becomes obvious, but in the woodland garden, especially with banks and slopes,

Roses in profusion, whether bush or climber, are a part of many small gardens and combine with fragrant pinks, campanulas, bleeding hearts and lavender.

the solution of the natural route can best be determined by casually asking someone to walk from points A to B and by observing his route. The easy natural one is usually the answer.

Containment, which is so important, can be architectural with buildings or walls. It can be natural with formal hedges of yew, holly, hemlock, beech, pittosporum and other plants that lend themselves to clipping, or by loose flowering hedges or shrubberies. If there is room, planting in depth with shadows and the stems of trees is a happy solution. If labour is not a problem, pleached lindens or hornbeams make a superb aerial hedge or screen.

A sense of scale and proportion are fundamental to garden design. The relation of the width of a border or a terrace to the height of a wall must be carefully considered. Steps should be comfortable and inviting. Sculpture and garden ornament must be large enough to stand up to the scale of the garden or the landscape. Some of the most attractive gardens consist of a series of rooms each with a different treatment or theme and in each of these the scale may alter. Obviously the choice of trees and shrubs must be governed by the size of the garden. Thus we see that scale is connected with every aspect of design and planting.

The Influence of Cottage Gardens

Gardens, both large and small, are increasingly inspired by the cottage garden. The plants that are grown,

11

the informality of arrangement, and the combination of flowers and vegetables all find favour today. I have looked at cottage gardens in places as diverse as Cape Cod and Cornwall, and I am always impressed by the masses of colour, and by little touches so characteristic of cottage gardens, such as the charming use of parsley as a border along a path, the decorative effect of the tall white flower-stalks of rhubarb which have been allowed to seed, or an early Dutch honeysuckle, so covered with flowers that few leaves show.

Yet this inspiration of the cottage garden is not new. Miss Gertrude Jekyll, who had such a profound influence on both sides of the Atlantic, through her books and the gardens which she made over the years during her long association with Sir Edwin Lutyens, drew heavily for inspiration from cottage gardens. In *Wood and Garden*, she pays tribute: 'Some of the most delightful of all gardens are the little strips in front of roadside cottages. They have a simple and tender charm that one may look for in vain in gardens of greater pretension. And the old garden flowers seem to know that there they are seen at their best; for where can one see such wallflowers, double daisies, or white rose bushes; such clustering masses of perennial peas, or such well-kept flowery edges of pinks or thrift or London Pride?'

Cottage gardens in late June are so colourful that I find myself adding to the hazards on the road as I slow up to look at rainbow clumps of irises, the tall spires of lupins – pink, apricot, soft gold, but more probably blue – growing in the light shade of a pear or apple tree, huge blowsy poppies, dazzling pink and velvety red pyrethrums, yellow-eyed white daisies and enormous shaggy paeonies, fragrant and glistening. Big shrubs of philadelphus, when they come into full flower in June, fill gardens with their delicious scent, and everywhere in summer there are roses, tall arching shrubs, climbers and ramblers that festoon walls, arbours and fences, old hybrid teas and huge hybrid perpetuals that have grown larger with the years. Here we find the old-timers such as 'Albertine', 'Paul's Scarlet', 'Caroline Testout', 'Alberic Barbier', 'Paul's Lemon Pillar', 'François Juranville', and a number of others that turn country lanes, villa gardens and town doorways into a tumbling mass of colour. Journeys in early summer are exciting because of the wealth of colour, and I find myself thinking with wonder – yes, it's fair to use the word –

Pansies growing on top of a dry stone wall by a dog-run, with geraniums and snap-dragons, typify the unselfconscious planting of cottage gardens.

The bold glaucous leaves of hostas contrast effectively with feathery ferns, a creeping sedum and the dark gleaming leaves of ivy in the paving stones of a courtyard of a city house.

that so many gardens are so easily transformed by a few roses. There are, of course, always new varieties, some of them excellent, but old loves are not easily supplanted.

Ground-cover plants are noticeable in cottage gardens too, spilling on the paths or making pools of leaf and flower under the fruit trees. Like Miss Jekyll, I have a deep affection for London Pride *(Saxifraga umbrosa)*. The gleaming, dark green rosettes and the foam of tiny pink flowers will carpet a very dark corner or thrive in full sun, as long as the ground is sufficiently moist. It can be propagated from the smallest piece, and once you have a clump you can divide it in spring or early autumn to enlarge the planting. The feathery pink flowers are useful for cutting. In fact, it is one plant I could not be without. In the same category I put Lady's Mantle *(Alchemilla mollis)*, with its lovely light green foliage and acid-green flowers. In spite of the fact that this plant

seeds very freely, it is another 'must'. Both these plants are excellent in town gardens and for shade.

Add campanulas and pinks to the list of cottage-garden flowers. So many cottage paths are planted with groups of both. The first deserves a separate chapter. There are some tricky names such as *Campanula portenschlagiana* and *poscharskyana*, both vigorous spreading plants, particularly the latter, with masses of flowers over a long season. They will tolerate some shade and don't like too dry a root-run. I am particularly fond of *C. carpatica* and its many varieties and forms. The large, broadly bell-shaped, erect flowers are most effective and are very much a cottage-garden flower.

Pinks offer a vast field in themselves. I am particularly fond of the old-fashioned singles in a range of colours, with fringed edges and a strong clove scent. The clumps of blue-green foliage are an addition to the garden even in winter and give extra value. Then there are the old favourites 'Mrs Sinkins' and 'White Ladies', both wonderful for scent and cutting, but with rather a short flowering season. For a good garden pink the fully double, bright pink 'Doris' is hard to beat. Easy, free-flowering, a fine colour, scented and hardy, she really is a pretty good girl.

Valerian and cerastium are two other plants always associated with cottage gardens, and I use them a great deal in the making of gardens. The former seeds itself freely and will grow happily in pavements and walls. There is a lovely white variety that is effective in the border as well as the red. Cerastium, Snow in Summer, as it is called, is a ramper and spreads through paving and stone walls. Its grey foliage is good value all the year round. I know of a wall and old rock garden, abandoned for lack of labour, which are now completely smothered with it. The thick silvery mass covered with white flowers makes a fine contrast to the green lawns and yew hedges nearby. Both these plants can be weeds, so have a care unless you have a place in your garden where it doesn't matter if they spread.

Discrimination in Plants

A criticism occasionally heard of small gardens is that they lack plan and unity. This is often quite true, for some gardens have evolved by circumstance and are homes for a varied collection of plants which may at best be strange bedfellows. Heathers are not sympathetic to most conventional herbaceous plants; rhododendrons can look equally out of place in a simple cottage garden or in areas where the soil makes their cultivation incongruous. Today, with the miracles possible on alkaline soils, thanks to sequestrenes to release the locked-up iron and trace-elements, and to the liberal use of peat to correct further the composition and humus content of the compost, the range of plants that can be effectively used in a small garden is vastly expanded. We must make sure whether or not the plants now possible justify this yearly treatment with sequestrenes, which is expensive if many plants are involved, and even more important, whether they add to or detract from the total harmony of the garden.

Small gardens can easily become over-complicated. Several that I know look like gardens at a flower show, where the object is to display as much stock as possible to draw the eye of the public. This technique has its dangers, as too many eye-catchers in the same area will vie with each other and create clashes of colour. Many of the brilliant orange-red rhododendrons of recent development and the fiery-hued modern roses, though lovely in themselves if isolated with masses of green, silver or even blue as a foil, tend to upset the balance of harmony and repose in small gardens. In larger ones, where they can be massed with other plants in the same colour-range, splendid effects are possible. Every gardener must ask himself the overriding question when he sees a spectacular new plant, 'Does it belong in my garden, or will it be too much of a good thing?' Of course, some gardeners are collectors and want a plant for its own sake. Others – and there are an increasing number in this group – think in terms of flower-arrangements.

I am often greeted with the comment, 'I saw a new rose (or rhododendron or tulip) and I just had to have it'. But this is followed by the query, 'Where can I put it?' The answer is, of course, easier in a large garden than in a small one, but there are moments when I am hard put for an answer, even in the former. The problem is a little like the woman who buys a dress because she likes its vivid hue, but with no thought as to whether it harmonizes with the hats, shoes, coats and bags in her wardrobe. My comments about bright colours are not a condemnation – quite the contrary. There are lots of striking plants, including the fiery *Lychnis chalcedonica*, various border-phloxes, red-hot pokers, lilies, *fosteriana* hybrid tulips, with their dazzling glowing scarlet cups of enormous size, and a host of others which give character to gardens. These flowers are lovely, useful, dramatic and challenging. In the right place they can make a garden; in the wrong place they can wreck it. It's as easy as that. So, too, we must beware of the hard reds and magentas of some of

The fragrance of heliotrope is one of the delicious scents of summer. The uncommon white found in old conservatories is the strongest scented.

14

The large pink blooms of a climbing rose enhance the charm of an old cottage, filling the garden with fragrance. Older varieties have a particular appeal, although few are recurrent-flowering.

the Kurumes and other types of azaleas which spoil a harmonious effect.

With the steady influx of new hybrids, whether roses, bulbs, perennials, flowering shrubs or annuals, the gardener has an ever-increasing range from which to choose. He must visualize the picture which he is trying to create and get the best plants to carry it out. In theory, our gardens should be more beautiful as the years go by, but they will not be unless we are discriminating in our selection.

There is a charming and very accurate definition of a weed which I learned from the late C. P. Raffill when I was working at Kew as a trainee just after the War. The first week I was there he spotted me in the rock garden and popped the question, seemingly so easy, 'What is a weed?' After an embarrassed and rather hesitant attempt on my part, he turned on his heel and called back over his shoulder, 'A good plant in the wrong place. Don't forget it'. He was gone, but I pondered the remark for a long time and have never forgotten it.

As I look at my garden, I realize how right he was. The so-called weeds of other gardens such as the giant hemlock, Himalayan Balsam, Lady's Mantle and a host of others, are cherished for the beauty of their foliage. By the same token, many a modern hybrid tea or dazzling new annual has been given away because, in the light of Mr Raffill's definition, they were weeds in my garden, and expensive ones at that.

As we thumb the catalogues to prepare our seed- and plant-lists, let us be more discriminating. Let us try to keep in mind our goal and not rule out old, tried-and-true varieties for the sake of a novelty, unless it offers qualities we demand and because it is a good plant for the right place. Novelty in itself is not a guarantee of success.

An Emphasis on Fragrance

Gardens for the blind have become well known through gardens made specifically in public parks and hospital grounds in different parts of this country and Great Britain for those who have lost their sight. But these gardens for the blind are really not very different from other gardens, save that fragrance has assumed greater importance than colour. I am all in favour of this, for scent is one of the real delights of any garden, and not enough thought goes into the use that can be made of it. Raised beds, which are featured in gardens for the blind, are just as practical for others. They bring treasured small plants within reach and make it possible to work without bending, a feature appreciated equally by the blind and the old or the lame.

Fragrant plants fall into several categories. First, there are those which exude fragrance which is airborne. The best examples are the balsam poplars *(Populus trichocarpa, tacamahaca* and *candicans)* and the sweetbriar rose *(Rosa rubiginosa)* or its hybrids. The delightfully pervasive incense smell of the former hangs heavy on the air, especially in the early spring when buds are unfolding and then through the summer, particularly in damp weather. But, alas, these scented poplars form large trees with invasive roots and cast heavy shade. They definitely are not for small gardens and should always be planted at a distance from buildings, walls, and especially tennis courts. There are other plants that fall into this first category, including rhododendrons with delightfully aromatic foliage *(R. rubiginosum, saluenense, desquamatum,* etc.*)*, eucalyptus in variety for mild gardens, and the Incense Rose *(Rosa primula)*, which is deliciously aromatic on a moist day.

Our next category consists of scented flowers, which are legion. Mignonette, pinks, heliotropes, stocks, particularly the night-scented ones, the tall white tobacco *(Nicotiana affinis)* and sweet peas are outstanding among annuals, while pinks, border carnations, roses, daphnes, mock orange, viburnums and lilacs are noteworthy among hardy plants and shrubs. For climbers there are the richly scented honeysuckles, jasmines, wistarias and even some of the clematises, including the fragrant pink *C. montana* 'Elizabeth', the cowslip-scented pale yellow *C. rhederiana* and the free-flowering white *C. flammula*, the latter two in bloom at the end of summer.

Bulbs offer a very wide range of fragrant flowers, such as hyacinths, both Roman and Dutch, freesias, narcissus in variety, particularly the Poeticus group and the honey-sweet *N. jonquilla*, a treasure for a raised bed, and last the lilies, which come in such profusion.

For pleasure nothing can equal the large number of aromatic plants which are fragrant to the touch, as even brushing against them releases their pent-up fragrance. Again, this is not an enjoyment for the sightless alone, though probably the blind, through their sharpened sense of smell, are more keenly aware of sweet-smelling plants. The thyme family offers many possibilities, ranging from the lemon-scented *Thymus citriodorus* and the prostrate *T. serpyllum* in a variety of forms, to the grey, woolly *T. lanuginosus (T. pseudolanuginosus)*. All are delightfully aromatic. Then there are the various sages *(Salvia officinalis)*, rosemary, marjoram and endless mints, all of which have culinary properties as well, so

there is the pleasure of the identification of flavour as well as smell. Think of the variety of mints; they include *Mentha piperita*, which has a strong, astringent, peppermint scent, the delicate Apple Mint *(M. rotundifolia)*, the refreshing and well-named Eau de Cologne Mint *(M. citrata* 'Eau de Cologne'*)* and the Pineapple Mint *(M. citrata)*.

There are a number of silvery-leaved artemisias, including Old Man *(A. abrotanum)* and Wormwood *(A. absinthium)*, both of which have a strong odour, pleasant to some people but displeasing to others. Lavenders, too, are fragrant to touch and the flowers are scented as well, the oil being extracted from the latter when they are just opening. The Curry Plant *(Helichrysum angustifolium)* is a charming, small, grey-leaved shrub with a startling aromatic scent. In contrast, there is the dwarf Sweet Woodruff *(Asperula odorata)*, reminiscent of new-mown hay.

No garden should be without a few scented-leaved geraniums. Scents range from nutmeg *(Pelargonium fragrans)* and balsam *(P. filicifolium)* to peppermint *(P. tomentosum)* and rose ('Attar of Roses' and *denticulatum)*. Lemon scent is common to various species, including *P. crispum, citriodorum* and 'Mabel Grey'. The last is the best and is a close rival to the shrubby Lemon Verbena *(Lippia citriodora)*, which deserves a place by a sunny gate or doorway in every garden, so that we can easily pluck a leaf to crush and savour. The list of pelargoniums grows large, but alas, they are not very hardy, though most of them can be kept going by cuttings and they form good old plants.

Many fragrant plants have been omitted from this list. Winter Sweet *(Chimonanthus fragrans)* and *Mahonia japonica*, two of the most fragrant of winter shrubs, spring to mind. Then there is *Sarcococca*, an ugly name for a low-growing, sweet-scented, winter-flowering evergreen. You will, no doubt, have fun thinking of many I have forgotten, ranging from sweet alyssum and nasturtiums to buddleias and lilies of the valley. The important point is to concentrate on fragrance for our own pleasure and we will at the same time make a garden a delight for those whose eyesight is failing.

Sweet Scents of Summer

When flower-lovers describe the sort of garden they would like, there are always certain priorities, and while most people favour colour, fragrance is also given a high priority, as is evident from the demand for fragrant roses, sweet peas, honeysuckles, jasmines, hyacinths, lilacs and a host of others.

I have often been struck before by the wonderful perfume of linden trees (which are strangely referred to in Great Britain as limes) in early June in Italy, where they are planted in the squares to provide much-needed

Lilium auratum, the handsomest of summer-flowering lilies, combines happily with blue clematis in a mixed border. Lime-free soil and ample moisture are essential for successful cultivation.

shade from the scorching sun, and later in northern France and England. The scent of lindens is intoxicating, especially at night, along avenues and country roads.

Lindens are particularly satisfactory for streets or drives, as they are graceful in habit and can safely be cut back or pleached if necessary. They transplant easily, even when fairly large, because of their compact root-systems. For those who love fragrance a linden is a 'must' if space permits. This last 'if' is important, as they grow to be true forest trees. And as many of us have found, it is not easy to grow other plants under them, particularly the varieties which are prone to aphides, as these excrete a substance known as honey-dew, which coats the leaves of the herbage under the trees. This in turn serves as a culture medium for sooty moulds, which disfigure the foliage with a black film. Although this does no serious harm, it diminishes the sunlight available to the leaves and obviously causes more harm to young plants than to larger, well-established ones. I am sometimes asked about the sooty mould that is often seen under lindens. For this there is no cure except the eradication of the aphides which are the cause. *Tilia europea* and *T. cordata* unfortunately are subject to attack.

Certain varieties, however, are free of aphides and should therefore be planted in preference to some others. One of the best is *T. euchlora*, a tree of moderate size (forty to sixty feet), which has many merits, particularly its clean, gleaming foliage and its graceful, rather pendulous, compact habit. This is an ideal linden either for an avenue or a specimen tree, if a very large one is not required.

Silver lindens are beautiful with their silvery leaves, felted on the under-surfaces. *Tilia petiolaris*, the weeping silver linden, forms a large tree of up to eighty feet with quantities of richly fragrant, pendulous, whitish flowers. *Tilia tomentosa* is similar save for its more erect habit. When a breeze stirs the leaves, the flashes of silvery-white under-surfaces make a lovely sight. For street-planting the red-twigged species (*T. platyphyllos rubra*) is invaluable because of its neat, upright habit when young, its tolerance of harsh conditions in cities and industrial areas, its beautiful gleaming reddish-brown twigs in winter, which lend a warm patch of colour on a cold, grey day, its fragrant flowers in July, and its freedom from honeydew. Red-twigged lindens are also excellent for pleaching.

Another delicious fragrance which I have always loved is that of the flowers of vines. In sunny vineyards in southern California the scent of grape flowers, inconspicuous though they are, on a warm summer day is something never to be forgotten. A fruiting vine or even some of the decorative ones grown on a sunny wall will scent the air for quite a distance. I am also fond of the fragrance of the common privet *(Ligustrum vulgare)* which, when left unpruned, bears panicles of white flowers in July and August.

On walks in the hills of northern Italy the mingled fragrances of privet, linden, grape and Traveller's Joy *(Clematis vitalba)*, which even as early as June makes bowers of silvery-white in the trees, are a constant delight. Underfoot you will often find a carpet of aromatic plants, including the various thymes, mints, marjorams and sages.

In our gardens we should grow herbs and aromatic plants wherever we are likely to brush against them or tread upon them and so release their pent-up fragrance. Plant rosemary, scented-leaved geraniums and Lemon Verbena outside a door or along the edge of a path. Where I have done this I find myself automatically plucking a sprig of rosemary as I pass. On an established bush this pinching-out of the growing tips makes the stems branch below. We should all do far more pinching-back of plants at regular intervals to encourage a solid compact habit. Silver and grey plants such as artemisias, santolinas, *Cineraria maritima, Senecio greyi* and a host of others are also the better for it.

Garden Terms Simplified

There is nothing quite so frustrating as not comprehending the exact meaning of garden terms. Many of us have a vague idea about species, genera, clones and cultivars, but how many could really define them? Let us take roses, as they are in practically all our gardens. The genus is *Rosa*, and there are, of course, hundreds of other genera, such as *Lilium, Tulipa* and *Prunus*. These genera are in turn broken down into species, which are individual plants with constant and distinctive characteristics which breed true in successive generations. Thus *Rosa moyesii* always has blood-red single flowers and brilliant sealing-wax red flagon-shaped heps or fruits. This wonderful shrub-rose was introduced from North-west China by Reginald Farrer in 1894. There it was one of the wild species native to that locality, just as the lovely pink Dog Rose *(R. canina)* and the Sweet Briar *(R. rubiginosa)* are species native to European countries, including Britain. What, then, are roses which bear vernacular names such as 'Peace', 'Iceberg', 'Penelope' and 'Tropicana'? These are not species but cultivars, as these hybrid varieties are correctly called.

To take another example, the genus *Primula* is a large and varied one, divided up into sections. Species vary enormously in character from that pale yellow harbinger of spring, *P. vulgaris* (surely one of the loveliest in spite of its familiarity), the sweet-scented cowslip *(P. veris)*, the familiar candelabra *P. japonica* of bogs and water gardens, the endearing *P. denticulata* of early

The twisted, golden, strap-shaped flowers of *Hamamelis mollis* brighten the garden in winter, and withstand snow and frost.

'White City', 'Desert Song' or 'Jane Philips' are part of their original clones. The essential thing is vegetative propagation, whether by division, layering, cuttings, grafting, budding, etc.

Some of the terms I have used may sound mystifying: hep (hip), for example, or scape, or stolon. We automatically refer to hyacinth bulbs, crocus corms, iris rhizomes and dahlia tubers. Do you know how to differentiate bulbs, corms, rhizomes and tubers? With less well-known plants such as Solomon's Seal we may be in doubt. The root is, in fact, a rhizome. Then there are curious terms such as witch's broom, hose-in-hose, Irishman's cuttings, puddling and fairy ring. Can you picture the difference between flower racemes, cymes, spikes and umbels? Then there are tools such as a besom (for sweeping) and a dibber (for pricking out seedlings). On the technical side we talk about sports, new breaks, tetraploids, F_1 hybrids and chimaeras.

Turning to trees, do you know the meaning of the terms fastigiate, cordon, espalier, and pleached? We read constantly about standards and half-standards. The former means a tree with a six-foot stem; a half-standard is one with a three to four-foot stem. Standard roses are usually on five-foot stems. In a flower, a standard can mean something quite different. With irises it obviously is the three upright petals above the pendulous falls.

If we are to read gardening books and journals intelligently we require a handy reference book for all these terms. *A Gardener's Book of Plant Names*, by A. W. Smith (Harper and Row, New York, 1963) and the more technical *An Introduction to Plant Taxonomy*, by George H. M. Lawrence (Macmillan, New York, 1955), are both very helpful. I hope some day a slim little book *Garden Terms Simplified*, by A. J. Huxley, (Collingridge, London, 1962) will be republished and that it will find its way to this country. It is short, concise, heavily illustrated with line drawings and in every way ideal for the amateur as it combines the botanical terms with the common parlance of the down-to-earth gardener.

Gardens in Winter
THE IMPORTANCE OF EVERGREENS

Nothing looks quite so naked as a newly built house without foundation planting. It is a little like a face without eyebrows. Obviously our permanent home should have an attractive well-furnished look throughout the year while the summer cottage can be planted with roses, hollyhocks and morning glories for a happy burst of colour, or in milder districts you can ring the changes with bulbs and seasonal flowering plants. But in much of this country where winters are severe, obviously evergreens in some form are the solution. Not only are these always effective but they

spring with heads of mauve or purple closely-bunched flowers on a tall scape, to the dwarf bright pink *P. rosea*, one of the brightest coloured members of the family. Then there are the greenhouse species, such as *P. malacoides*, *P. obconica* and *P. sinensis*. In turn, there are cultivars of these, such as the bright mandarin-red 'Dazzler', derived from *P. sinensis*, or the charming hardy 'Garryarde Guinevere' with its purplish-bronze foliage and clustered, pale pink flowers, obviously of mixed parentage, probably including *P. juliae*. So much for genera, species and cultivars.

One other term needs definition, and that is clone. This is applied to the vegetative offspring of a given plant. In other words, if a runner is taken from a strawberry, the new plant is actually part of the parent clone. The same is true of an iris plant grown from a piece of a rhizome of the parent plant. In this way all plants of

18

have a solidarity and feeling of mass that is three-dimensional and appropriate to architecture. Furthermore evergreens are relatively labour-saving.

There is no country where more care is given to the planting of architecture to make a permanent all-the-year setting than the United States. As a building is completed, the landscape gardener or contractor moves on to the site to do the basic planting, and thanks to the availability of container-grown plants, this can be done at any season when the ground is open and frost-free. Spring, summer or autumn, it makes little difference, so long as planting plans are limited to the more conventional range of plants that are available. In the milder zones with open frost-free ground, winter is one of the most satisfactory planting seasons. It is strange that the British, good gardeners that they are, have not had the same instinct for the planting of architecture. Only now are they becoming fully conscious of this.

All-important is a sense of scale with a knowledge of rate of growth and ultimate size of each plant. How often have we seen homes with porches and windows blocked out by hemlocks, yews, thujas and cupressus or vigorous shrubs including mock oranges, forsythias and cotoneasters. Obviously, for the first few years all was well, but later the so-called 'dwarf' conifers and those of moderate growth turned out to be giants. Evergreens that are low and spreading such as dwarf yews, junipers, slow-growing small-leaved ilexes, box, dwarf rhododendrons and japanese azaleas are suitable.

Subjects that can be informally clipped to be kept within bounds are ideal but formal geometric shapes, save in unusual circumstances, are on the whole to be avoided, although pairs of clipped bays, box bushes, yews or ilexes can be attractive in simple pyramids, blocks or spheres or treated as standards or as more elaborate topiary. Obviously gardeners in the more moderate zones have a much easier time than those in harsher climates as a much wider choice of suitable evergreens is available.

Dwarf and semi-dwarf rhododendrons are ideal as they offer such interesting contrasts of leaf shapes, sizes and colours, ranging from clear greens to the very dark glossy greens and glaucous grey-blues as well as a rich bounty of flowers in whites, pinks, reds, yellows, blues and purples. It is true that in very cold weather the leaves curl up and hang as if dead, presenting a sad woe-begone appearance, but with the first thaw they return to normal. Actually the large-leaved hybrids and species are more obvious offenders as the effects of severe cold on dwarf rhododendrons with smaller lighter foliage are less noticeable.

Among the most popular evergreens are yews in various forms, the Russian olive (Elaeagnus), hollies in wide variety, boxwood, evergreen privets, mahonias, osmanthus, pieris and pyracanthas, loved for their foilage and brilliant persistent berries. Conifers are very popular too, particularly the prostrate frosty-blue junipers and spreading dwarf pines. Camellias, rhododendrons, kalmias and evergreen azaleas provide colour in spring, as well as fine autumn foliage in the case of azaleas, which have been hybridized so widely that there are literally hundreds of new varieties. Even in January I have seen striking clumps of their purple, red and crimson foliage. With such a wide range of evergreens to choose from, much can be accomplished, but a great deal will depend on the gardener's skill in grouping to make the most of the contrast of forms, textures and colours.

Ground-covers are generously used for striking, labour-saving effects. Banks, shady areas under trees, entire lawns in small, shaded, urban gardens, and verges along drives or shrubberies become carpets of ivy, periwinkle, and, most popular of all, the Japanese spurge (Pachysandra terminalis), with its bold evergreen leaves and white flowers. It likes shade and most soils, if not too acid, and it survives intense cold. Ground-covers are also used as underplanting for shrubberies and groups of flowering trees.

This simple planting, so prevalent throughout much of America, may sound dull and repetitive, but with the inclusion of a few trees such as flowering crab, silver birch, thorn, or the glorious dogwoods (Cornus florida and nuttallii) and with shrubs such as forsythias, flowering quince, magnolias (which do very well), mock oranges, lilacs and roses, the dark, perhaps sombre, evergreen setting is enlivened. Clumps of daffodils and tulips in spring, followed by a few irises, paeonies and lilies, are striking and often are more successful in small groups than when massed.

Our well-known love of specialization is markedly apparent in horticulture. Top favourites include camellias, azaleas, hemerocallis, and irises. As in all countries, roses, whether climbers, floribundas or hybrid teas, find their way in some form into most of our gardens. Annuals also do well in bright sun-lit conditions almost everywhere, and patches of their jewelled brilliance are useful to replace groups of hyacinths and tulips in the shrubberies and to provide colour in beds and borders. Annuals are also a useful source of cut flowers throughout the summer.

We return to the premise that it is the permanent base-planting that counts. If it is well carried out, the results can be surprisingly good, as it enhances the architecture and blends it into the landscape. True, there is a sacrifice of colour in summer, but this is offset by charm in winter, and although initial planting costs are high, there is a big saving on both maintenance and subsequent expenditures for plants.

Garden Records Pay

When the garden at my old home was started before the War, I wish that a record had been kept of the years in which trees and shrubs were planted, where they came from and even what they cost. Somehow there is a tendency to keep records of large gardens but not of small ones. What fascinating reading and reminiscing to look through old invoices and to recall the arrival and the planting of treasures, today in their maturity, or to recall some of the casualties, for all gardeners have them.

One of our resolutions for the New Year should be to keep more careful garden records. Past invoices will be filed away in a special garden folder and allowed to accumulate over the years. The other day a friend turned up an invoice for Japanese maples dated November, 1927, and thus we were able to determine the exact date of planting and by adding on a few years, the approximate age of his trees. Records of certain bulbs such as lilies may be sad to review, recalling the high rate of fatality through the years, but these same records are a tribute to the perseverance and the determination of the gardener on the one hand, and to the indispensability and dramatic beauty of lilies on the other. With few other flowers has the public been so persistent, and now with the advent of fine new hybrids each year, there is the possibility of a real breakthrough of past difficulties.

Records can be very simple. A notebook in which to write the name of the plant, source, date, price and possibly general notes will usually do. The entries can be made chronologically or alphabetically for an accumulative record, so that all roses, lilies or rhododendrons are grouped under their own headings. I have tried a card-index of new plants and find this satisfactory. One very methodical friend with a large garden enters the information listed above at the same time that lead Serpent labels are made. Collectors' numbers of special plants are also recorded, but that is definitely for the skilled gardener with rare plants from expeditions.

Another friend keeps a very different sort of record. He has tabulated, alphabetically, large collections of the old roses and clematises in his garden. There are weekly columns for the possible blooming season and

The erect racemes of yellow, lily of the valley-scented flowers and bold leaves make *Mahonia bealii* an outstanding winter-flowering shrub.

The Lenten Rose with its nodding flowers in shades of rose, cream and purple is a wonderful early-flowering herbaceous plant for shade.

at each week-end notes are made of plants in flower and of their quantity and quality. In this way he has an accumulative record of when each variety comes into flower, its duration of bloom and recurrent flowering. Over the years this record shows a remarkable consistency, for most varieties show far less variation than you would expect. Similar records could be kept for a number of other genera by those gardeners who have any spare time not occupied with weeding, spraying, dead-heading and other compelling tasks.

The artist has the great advantage of being able to record the beauties of his garden. In most cases he is more successful with individual flowers and plants than with general garden effects, which all too often elude the brush. Through the centuries the great botanical illustrators have largely clung to portraiture. Riotous borders are as great a challenge as sunsets or fall colour. Sketching has several advantages, for not only does it provide lasting portraits, but it offers the artist the opportunity to study, observe and memorize the beauty and subtle features of a plant. The camera gives an equally faithful record, but the photographer spends much more of his time looking at the meters, dials and controls than at the subject. Be that as it may, the superb records that are possible today with the colour-camera have opened up the possibility of useful documentation of flowers, which is both invaluable and a lasting source of pleasure. A showing of garden slides on winter evenings has become a popular and highly instructive pastime.

Another pleasant hobby is the collecting of catalogues of the outstanding nurseries and plant-specialists. Various horticultural libraries have collections of great interest dating back many decades. It has become necessary for a charge to be made for many of the better catalogues in view of the high cost of printing, but as some are in every sense garden books with illustrations which include good colour-reproduction and charming line-drawings, as well as a great deal of information about plants and their cultivation, pruning and general care, fifty cents or a dollar is relatively little to pay for them. For catalogues which are merely lists of plants with brief descriptions charges are considerably less, or they are supplied free. Most of the seed-houses still provide their beautiful catalogues *gratis* to customers.

Lessons of a Bad Winter

After a severe winter, the spring planting season is always fraught with difficulties. The public, the nurseries and garden contractors are all confronted with problems. Unprecedented weather of exceptional severity and duration obviously takes a toll in gardens, but we cannot know the length of the casualty-list for a long time. If plants are protected by snow, casualties from frost will be relatively light, but in areas where the bitter cold comes first with searing winds, the damage is bound to be heavier. We must be prepared to expect casualties, especially with half-hardy trees and shrubs, tender rhododendrons, camellias and fuchsias. Trees and shrubs are also easily broken by the weight of ice and snow. My advice is to be patient. Don't condemn plants until you are convinced that they will not recover. Trees and shrubs, apparently dead, may break into fresh growth in midsummer or even early autumn. Others may spring from the roots. Patience is a first requisite of the good gardener. After a bad winter I have seen vast numbers of plants scrapped, but many of these would, in all probability, have recovered if they had been kept.

In very bad winters stocks of cool greenhouse plants,

dahlia tubers, seed potatoes, and plants in tubs, including items such as agapanthus, daturas, geraniums and fuchsias may be frozen in protected sheds or orangeries which were previously frost-free. Other gardeners experience despair when heating in glass-houses fails because of power-cuts, shortage of fuel, inadequate heating systems, frozen oil-supplies or a number of other unforeseen catastrophes. This is both expensive and discouraging, but we should profit from the lesson of these calamities.

Nurseries have these same problems and many others. Stocks are destroyed, overhead costs for heating become astronomic, labour staffs are idle for weeks at a time when they usually are fully employed, goods may even be frozen in transit, while other goods which were packed at the beginning of the cold weather have had to be unpacked and planted in protected planting bays pending delivery. Worst of all, much stock in nurseries is killed or rendered unsalable for at least one season. It is a grim prospect, and when warm weather does finally come and the soil is frost-free and workable, the season for delivery before plants break into full growth may well be very brief.

What does all this mean to us as small gardeners? First, it is possible that some nurseries may not be able to execute orders or to accept new ones for certain plants. Secondly, we probably won't receive orders at the time we would like, and orders despatched in good faith may be frosted in transit. Contractors are probably unable to undertake new work and some will find it almost impossible to complete that to which they are already committed.

After a very severe winter, if good stocks of roses and shrubs are not available, temporary planting-schemes utilizing bedding-plants and annuals are practical and colourful stop-gaps. If shrubs have died or have had to be cut back, there will be large areas of bare earth which can be filled with drifts of hardy and half-hardy annuals. It is amazing what can be accomplished for a few dollars with annuals such as scented tobacco (Nicotiana), larkspur, zinnias, marigolds, asters, snapdragons and dozens of others. If you have glass, sow early to ensure a display in June; otherwise sow in open ground when the soil is warm and air temperature above 50°F (10°C).

After a bad winter the self-service nurseries and garden centres do record business. Endless correspondence is saved. You select and carry away the actual specimens, thus avoiding the bottleneck of packing and delivery. I tend to use self-service nurseries more and more; the plants do not suffer the checks and hazards of packing and delivery, and prices are lower because these two items are sizable factors in the cost of plants.

Container-grown Plants to the Rescue

In so many ways we have a far easier time in the garden than our forebears, although at the outset it must be admitted it was far easier for them to find a willing professional gardener and to pay him. Today the position is very changed. On the credit side, although we may be the sole gardener, plants are readily available over a very long season, if not for all twelve months. Much will depend of course on whether you garden in Maine, Michigan or Montana, with their icy winters with below zero temperatures and the ground frozen for many months of the year, or in California, Florida or Georgia, where there is no real winter and little frost.

Garden centres have completely changed the timing of planting. Gardeners in states where winter so suddenly becomes spring and summer follows on so quickly have a much longer period of grace as they can go to the nursery when the ground is right for planting and collect what they can deal with at that time. Plants lifted and packed and then sent by post, rail or road, may arrive with a freeze or a snowstorm. New plants are very much like babies. You have to take them on delivery and you can't send them back or tell them to wait. Planting around a newly constructed house can even be done in mid-summer if shrubs are kept well-watered and shaded if necessary.

Another advantage of container-grown plants is the fact that you can see what you are getting. If a plant has a good bushy habit and healthy foliage, you take it, leaving behind the rather anaemic, spindly specimen with yellowing leaves. The plants ordered from a nursery must be accepted unseen, and although most nurseries are reliable, there are disappointments.

Secondly, it is possible to take the plants and to set them out on the ground to see how many are required to fill a given area. How maddening it is suddenly to find that you need a couple more plants to create a suitable effect. Also if you need a pair of standard trees, bays or camellias for an important position, it is easy to match them. Lastly, I usually am inspired as I see new varieties or others I have forgotten. There is no doubt that actual contact with the plants is a very real incentive.

When planting container-grown plants, be sure that the root-ball is thoroughly soaked, well in advance. If it is dry when planted, almost no amount of surface watering will penetrate it. Prepare the planting pocket before removing the plant and make sure that the depth is correct. Most plants will probably be planted at the same depth as in the container, but this does not always follow. Tree paeonies, for example, should be planted so that the growth buds are four inches below the surface of the ground in cold climates. Don't crowd plants for the sake of immediate effect. Plants grow and spread, and there is always a tendency to take the short-term view.

It is fascinating to see landscaping with trees in full flower. In June I watched the planting of a municipal parking area in a suburb of New York. Mock oranges, three to four feet tall, flowering crabs, lilacs and elaeagnus were being planted in broad barriers, though temperatures were in the high seventies and even the eighties. The cans were slit open on the spot, as were the wire baskets for larger trees. Within a matter of minutes the trees were in their new homes and a hose was playing water gently on the root-areas to firm the soil and provide moisture at the root-tips. For success, water must be applied regularly until the tree is established. For this there is no short-cut. The stems were wrapped with hessian to prevent excessive evaporation. Staking is important in windy positions, so that the delicate hair-roots in full growth are not damaged by the rocking of the tree.

In New York and other large cities elaborate garden schemes are set out and changed with no regard to weather conditions. Large clipped yews can be followed by willows, rhododendrons or roses to achieve a highly original effect. The miracles of planting in Radio City or on roof-gardens and terraces of the tallest sky-scrapers show how highly developed the technique of container-grown plants has become. In a remarkable way, city gardens have come of age, and it is now possible to garden for immediate effect without reproducing conditions comparable to those in the country. A plant no longer has to be grown *in situ*. It can be put there in maturity at the peak of its prime. This opens up an exciting prospect. No longer is it necessary to select a tree or shrub on the basis of the catalogue's description. No longer is there doubt as to size or shape. We can go to a self-service nursery and select what we require. We know there and then how many plants we need to fill the allotted border. We see for ourselves whether we like the texture of the foliage or the shape and colour of the flowers.

Some plants lend themselves particularly to this treatment in containers, in which they must be grown long enough to be thoroughly established with a good root-ball, for it is not a matter of lifting plants and popping them into pots which are carried off a few hours or days later. The very opposite is true: herein lies one of the secrets of success. The plant must be potted-up in a good, loose, friable medium, usually high in peat and sand content, so that it has become thoroughly established with a mass of root-fibre.

If you buy canned plants at the nursery, the cans are cut open before your eyes and then tied up to hold them together until the moment comes for

planting, while plants in peat or composition pots can be planted in them. Whalehide or polythene must be removed but this is easy.

Spring Planting

After a long winter, prepare beds and borders as soon as possible for new planting and dig holes for trees, even if it means refilling them so that they do not fill with water. A covering of heavy polythene will warm up the soil. It is an enormous saving of time if all is in readiness when the bundles of plants arrive, and in a late spring it is always a gamble to get all the necessary work done. Give your plants an extra good start with plenty of humus, especially if your soil is light or shallow. Dig in liberal quantities of peat, hop-manure, spent hops, leaf-mould, rotted manure or good home-made compost. This treatment is also beneficial on chalky soils, and above all on heavy clays, though here peat, manure with lots of straw, and even coarse sand and cinders are particularly good.

I like to work peat, sieved compost or friable, relatively dry loam mixed with a little coarse bone-meal and hoof and horn through the roots of shrubs, trees and roses at planting time, especially if the soil tends to be cold and wet. On heavy soils this method of planting is extremely useful, as the large clods cannot be distributed through the roots and sizeable air-pockets are left. After a severe winter, the frost, however, should have broken down heavy soils, if the ground has been well dug in autumn. After applying several shovelfuls of friable mixture over the roots, shake the stem, lifting the roots gently to allow the particles to work through them.

Commercial fertilizers are also beneficial, particularly on ground that is poor or has had heavy cropping during the previous year or two. Remember that plants exhaust the soil and that nourishment must be put back for good results.

Let's resolve not to exceed the quantities prescribed, whether it is for fertilizers, either solid or liquid, insecticides or fungicides. Follow the manufacturer's instructions and do not succumb to the tempting theory that a little extra will be that much better. Actually, that little extra can be just enough to damage plants seriously or even kill them, and I often see plants suffering from too much kindness.

Winter or early spring is the time to check supplies and to order the necessary peat, fertilizers, composts, planting stakes and patented ties for trees. Overhaul watering equipment in case spring planting is accompanied by drought, as has become the pattern in some years. You can even write the plant-labels or strike them in plastic or lead.

Firm planting is a good resolution, but be careful

Giant Cow Parsley, evening primroses, bocconias, the evergreen fig-like leaves of *Fatsia japonica* and the spiky blades of yuccas make a tapestry of foliage outside the studio of an artist.

not to tread too heavily if the soil is wet. Stake trees as you plant. It is much easier to insert the stake firmly in the right position in relation to the roots and the stems before replacing the soil. Tie them securely, making sure that there is no possibility of chafing.

Plants grown in pots by the nurseries are a great boon, as they can be planted long after the season for lifting trees and shrubs in the open ground has ended. With pot-plants, lift out the root-ball carefully, breaking the pot if necessary. Remove the crock from the bottom and if the roots are matted and pot-bound, loosen the root-tips very gently with a stick or plant-label, so that they will grow out into the soil. If in peat or paper pots, plant the root-ball in its pot.

If plants are pot-bound they are not such a good proposition as a plant with vigorously growing active young roots, particularly if the tap-root has grown through the hole in the bottom and then been severed. Sometimes I have lifted a stunted plant after several years and found roots still curled round and round in a tight matted corkscrew, much as they were when removed from the pot.

Planting-depth is important. Plant at approximately the same depth as that at which the plant was grown in the nursery. Make sure that the soil does not settle subsequently and leave the top of the root-stock exposed.

ZONES OF HARDINESS In the following pages Zones of Hardiness are based on those used by the Arnold Arboretum. Nursery catalogues often indicate hardiness of plants, and maps indicating the various zones are reproduced in many horticultural books. Figures are in degrees Fahrenheit and indicate the average minimum temperatures for each zone;

Zone 1: Northern Canada
Zone 2: −50 to −30°
Zone 3: −35 to −20°
Zone 4: −20 to −10°
Zone 5: −10 to − 5°
Zone 6: −5 to +5°
Zone 7: 5 to 10°
Zone 8: 10 to 20°
Zone 9: 20 to 30°
Zone 10: 30 to 40°

Fertilizers for Feeding

The art of gardening involves a great deal more than ordering attractive plants and arranging them to be effective. Skilful cultivation is essential, whether we are dealing with trees, shrubs, herbaceous plants, annuals or pot-plants. Most gardeners recognize the value of organic fertilizers, but with the general shortage of manure and the difficulties of obtaining compost or leaf-mould, inorganic fertilizers play a tremendous role in our gardens.

In most cases we must strike a balance, providing humus in some form (particularly for light or highly alkaline soils), but it is even more important to provide certain essential elements that play a vital part in the life of a healthy plant. Do not underestimate the value of these elements, which include nitrogen, phosphorus, potash, calcium, magnesium and sulphur and a number of others. The first three are all-important, and inorganic balanced fertilizers are based on proportions of these three with perhaps other elements present as well.

BASIC COMPOSITION OF FERTILIZERS

Before considering different kinds of inorganic fertilizers we must understand in the simplest way the role that nitrogen, phosphorus and potash play in the life of a healthy plant, for without these three elements in proper balance the plant, whether herbaceous or woody, will suffer. By the same token, if there is an excess of a given element, the plant will again react differently from its natural habit. It is the overall combination of the different elements that makes balanced, healthy growth.

Nitrogen is paramount, as it acts as a regulator of growth, assuring vigour, rapid development and foliage of a good green colour. Obviously, leaf-vegetables need adequate nitrogen. Too much nitrogen, especially on herbaceous plants, will cause excessive growth and an over-abundance of foliage at the expense of flowers. I have seen hardy plants such as *Salvia superba* and dwarf Michaelmas daisies double their normal height, but with virtually no flowers, as the result of excessive nitrogen. It is also detrimental to strawberries, apples and raspberries, as it promotes a too rampant growth at the expense of the quality and quantity of fruits.

Sulphate of ammonia and nitrate of soda are the most widely used nitrogenous fertilizers, especially for vegetables and fruits such as black-currants and plums. For the border, finely-ground hoof and horn is excellent, though not cheap. Dried blood is another source of nitrogen, especially for feeding in summer.

Phosphorus, like nitrogen, also promotes rapid healthy growth, but it is particularly beneficial to vigorous root-action. Without it, root-development is slow and meagre. It is therefore important for root-vegetables and for the production of seed-crops. Principal sources of phosphorus include bone-meal and superphosphate. Phosphorus, although needed for fruit, is not as important as potash.

Potash (potassium) is important in combination with nitrogen, especially for fruit. If it is deficient, fruit trees will have very short growths, die-back will occur, foliage will be small, bluish in colour or even chlorotic or scorched, and fruits will be diminutive, sweet and lacking in flavour. Potatoes also need ample potash. Primary sources of it include sulphate of potash, muriate of potash and wood-ash, which is excellent and should be carefully saved. It is particularly good for roses, shrubs and fruit. As nitrate of potash combines both potash and nitrogen, it is excellent for sprouts, cabbages, cauliflowers and lettuces, as well as for spinach and celery.

These three elements, nitrogen, phosphorus and potash, often known as 'The Golden Tripod', are essential for healthy plants and form the basis of commercial compounds or complete garden fertilizers. There are a number of these under proprietary names and obviously many gardeners will prefer to use one of these rather than mix their own. For plants such as roses, dahlias, chrysanthemums and sweet peas, special fertilizers are sold.

Some fertilizers combine both organic and inorganic substances. For example, several are a combination of bone-meal and hoof and horn with the three basic elements of the 'Golden Tripod'. Fish-manures or fish guano are high in nitrogen, and contain phosphorus and potash as well. Soot often contains a high proportion of sulphate of ammonia and therefore of nitrogen. Inorganic fertilizers, especially proprietary brands, should be applied at the rate recommended by the manufacturer. Do not exceed this rate. Dosages are usually heavier for ground being prepared for planting than for feeding established borders, roses and shrubs. Application ten days to a week before planting is ideal and the fertilizer should be worked into the surface of the soil. If previous application is not feasible, fertilizers can be used at planting time. Three or four ounces per square yard is prescribed for unplanted seed-beds or borders and two ounces per square yard for established plants.

3 Trees and Shrubs

Windbreaks for Shelter

Not the least of the trials that beset the gardener is the provision of shelter, especially for gardens near the coast or in windy positions on islands, open plains, exposed hill tops or wide valleys. Some positions are so exposed that trees and shrubs are literally blown out of the ground in spite of staking and tying. Along the coast the stunted beach plums, bayberries, thorns and sycamores, shaped and shorn by gales, are nature's version of Japanese Bonsai. There is a very real connection, for it was in the stunted trees and shrubs of the wild that Bonsai derived its inspiration. On the windward side the trees have few leaves or branches, while on the sheltered side the branches grow more abundantly but are still bent by the wind. The rounded contours of these tough veterans with their leaning trunks and shortened growths often have a curious rugged charm in the otherwise barren landscape.

The gardener who lives under the lash of gales from the Atlantic or the Pacific knows full well the futility of planting until shelter-belts of some sort have been established. Some of the great gardens were created only because this necessity was realized at an early date and the necessary steps were taken, often so successfully that subsequently even the tenderest rhododendrons and camellias could grow secure from the whiplash of the winds. Pines are useful for windbreaks. The Austrian Pine (*Pinus nigra*) is one of the toughest (Zone 4) with a broadly pyramidal habit. The Monterey Pine (*P. radiata*) and the Italian Stone Pine (*P. pinea*), a picturesque tree with its curious flat head in maturity, are useful but less hardy (Zone 7). Arborvitae is a very useful evergreen as it is hardy and compact in habit, *Thuja occidentalis* being hardy even in Zone 2.

Fortunately there are trees and shrubs that will stand up to gales and salt-laden winds. For large gardens pines make effective windbreaks. Beech also forms a fine shelter, particularly on alkaline soils. Depth of

planting for shelter is essential, as a single row in exposed areas is vulnerable. There should be a front line backed up by secondary defences. Thorns are rugged trees which stand up well to tough conditions, if they are planted small and cared for until they are established.

Often screening is required for purposes other than shelter from wind. Privacy and the masking of unsightly buildings, such as factories and housing-estates, which bite deeper and deeper into the countryside, are ever-increasing problems. When selecting trees for this purpose, there are many factors to consider. Speed of growth has often been given too high a priority, for trees which grow rapidly, such as sycamores and poplars, may be highly undesirable later. I once saw a charming property where these two varieties had been planted at one end of a small garden to screen a newly-completed house. This indeed they will do in a very few years, but at the same time, the vegetables, fruits and flower-borders will be in heavy, dry shade and hungry roots will reach out further and further to rob them of their rightful food. How much more suitable a relatively narrow-growing evergreen screen would have been.

The Lawson Cypress (*Chamaecyparis lawsoniana*) with its various varietal forms is a faithful stand-by. It has many virtues. It is hardy, resistant to wind, adapted to sun and shade, and can be grown singly, in groups, staggered to make a shelter-belt of considerable depth, or in a straight line where a neat marginal 'wall' is required. For hedging, Lawsons should be planted at intervals of two feet and then clipped as a formal hedge. Some varieties such as 'Allumii' and 'Triomphe de Boskoop' have lovely glaucous blue foliage, while 'Fletcheri' is a grey-blue, slower-growing variety suited to a smaller hedge. For those with a penchant for warmer tones the varieties 'Stewartii' and 'Lutea' are welcome, with their cheerful golden yellow foliage throughout the year. A clear green variety with the appropriate name 'Green Hedger' is rated highly by several leading gardeners.

One of the most famous of all evergreens for coastal screening is the Monterey Cypress or Macrocarpa,

These topiary birds in yew are as dynamic as sculpture and have the merit of being effective both in winter and summer. Flowers are not needed in such a scheme.

Cupressus macrocarpa (Zone 7). It is a very rapid grower and has sheltered many a storm-swept garden from the ravages of wind. It has also obliterated many unsightly outlooks. Today its even more rapid-growing hybrid with *Chamaecyparis nootkatensis*, known as *Cupressocyparis leylandii*, has replaced it to some extent. Harold Hillier of Winchester, England, stated in his remarkable centenary *Catalogue of Trees and Shrubs* that it is the fastest-growing conifer in the British Isles. This catalogue is an essential reference book for the lover or collector of rare trees and shrubs and for serious plantsmen throughout the world.

I have planted Leylandiis in a number of garden schemes, ranging from windswept positions on highly alkaline soil on exposed coastlands to wet, acid, peaty soil in Eire and the light, thin soil of an urban housing development. It thrives under these varied conditions, giving a miraculous performance. When planted in informal groups its columnar habit and loose grey-green foliage soon become important landscape features, and, of course, it can be planted as a continuous screen or clipped as a vigorous and very quick-growing hedge. I have seen it used successfully to make a fifteen-foot screen between two medium-sized gardens. As it is such a vigorous grower, it should not be used for small restricted hedges, for it will become woody and coarse in habit by the heavy pruning that would be necessary to keep it within bounds in suburban gardens.

Another fine windbreak, because of its dense bushy habit, is the European Hedge or Field Maple *(Acer campestre)*, surely one of the loveliest and most useful of hedgerow trees, ranking with the Quick and Hawthorn. It is lovely, with delicate pink to maroon-red spring foliage and brilliant autumn colouring, ranging from clear golden-yellow to apricot and red, and forms a splendid cover for song-birds and game. It does not mind chalky soils and a shallow root run.

The flowers are pale green, but not spectacular like the yellow clusters of the Norway Maple. In time, it forms a rounded tree from twenty to thirty feet in height. Very old specimens have great character, as the boles are often hollow with fantastic knots and holes, rather like the lacework trunks of the very old olives in Corfu. It makes a dense hedge if planted at two-foot intervals or a broad screen if more widely spaced and left untrimmed.

For inland areas, our native crataeguses are ideal windbreaks as they are dense in habit. Their many merits include handsome foliage which colours well, clusters of flowers in early summer, gleaming scarlet haws from whence the name Hawthorn and hardiness (Zone 4). The Cockspur Thorn (*C. crus-galli*) is a hardy squat tree, native to New England, with attractive white flowers and unusually large deep red fruits, which persist until spring. It forms a useful windbreak if closely planted when small, as do *C. coccinea* and *mollis*, the Scarlet and Red Haws.

Handsome Helpful Hedges

As most gardeners have hedging problems, the selection of the right trees or shrubs is of great importance. Hedges serve many purposes, besides the primary ones of defining boundaries and providing privacy. In the United States and Canada, hedges are far less prevalent, as open planning prevails in many areas, the lawn and garden of one house merging with the adjoining one, giving a feeling of space with longer vistas. In Britain, however, this tendency, though developing with modern housing, is still relatively limited. Hedges not only make admirable windbreaks, they are also decorative and can be used internally in the garden either to provide mystery or to divide-off areas for special purposes. The plants suitable for hedging are legion, but must be selected with an eye both to suitability for the function they are to serve and to the scale of the garden.

Soil is, of course, an important factor. Beech and berberis will grow on alkaline soils; rhododendrons and azaleas will not. Yew, box and privet are reliable stand-bys, but yew is not suited to most industrial cities or other areas where there is a considerable amount of soot and air polution. Yew should never be planted where cattle or horses graze, as it is very poisonous. Privet grows almost anywhere.

The availability of moisture is important. It is difficult to establish hedges in very dry places, particularly under the heavy foliage of trees as little rain penetrates the thick canopy of a developed beech, sycamore, plane or chestnut. Sun and shade must also be considered. Rose, potentilla and berberis hedges require sun. Mock orange will grow in sun or semi-shade, while hemlock, box and yew are shade-tolerant.

No matter what the hedge, good drainage is essential, as is thorough preparation of the soil. Remember that a hedge is a long-term investment and be sure to make plenty of food available for future use. Careful planting at the right intervals will amply repay the effort.

One of the most important factors in selecting plants for hedging is the ultimate size. Flowering hedges are charming, but if certain shrubs are pruned hard, flower is sacrificed and the natural beauty and graceful habit of the plant are destroyed. Formal lilac or forsythia hedges clipped to geometrical symmetry are pointless. Plants such as these, along with many others, including potentillas, flowering currants, mock orange, deutzias, hydrangeas, *Berberis stenophylla*, (Zone 5) and roses, must be lightly shaped at the proper time to form loose, informal hedges, ideal for screening. Therefore these shrubs require more space and cannot be clipped to form narrow vertical walls like yew, privet, beech, *Berberis thunbergii* (Zone 5), *Cotoneaster simonsii* and hornbeam. In fact, we must distinguish between hedges and screens, as the two terms are so often confused. Obviously, careful selection is necessary, as a broad flowering hedge would encroach on the flower-border, vegetable-plot, or even the lawn. Where space is precious, very often a fence, either of close boarding, trellis or pickets with climbers or shrubs trained flat against it, is the ideal solution. A fence, painted white or a light colour, though adding to upkeep, often introduces a light gay note in an otherwise sombre setting and is a relief from brick.

The care of hedges is important. Obviously there is a right and wrong time to clip and prune. Many flowering hedges such as mock orange, forsythia and flowering currant, should be cut back immediately after flowering. Beech and hornbeam should be trimmed either in summer or winter, but I prefer the former. *Cotoneaster simonsii* and *Berberis thunbergii* and its varieties are pruned in winter, while the evergreen *stenophylla* and *darwinii* (Zone 7) should be dealt with after they have bloomed. Holly hedges are beautiful, especially of the smooth-leaved varieties such as *Ilex altaclarensis* 'Camelliaefolia'. They are best planted in early autumn or late spring. Pruning should be done in late spring or summer with secateurs and not with shears. Otherwise there will be damaged leaves, which are unsightly. This also applies to Portugal laurels, *Prunus lusitanica* (Zone 7), and *Laurus nobilis*, the Sweet Bay, (Zone 6–7) both of which should be pruned in April.

When planting hedges of holly, yew or Portugal laurel, it is essential to select plants well feathered or branched at the base. Avoid leggy specimens, as

A ten-foot beech hedge provides a windbreak for a deep herbaceous border in the flat windy countryside, as well as making the perfect background for bright colours.

usually they will not refurnish. I prefer to plant hedging material relatively small, as it results in a denser, more uniform hedge. Young beech, hornbeams and hollies two or three feet tall are definitely a much better risk than larger ones. They grow away quickly if properly planted and given adequate after-care. Watering is essential in dry weather until hedges are established.

Prudent Pruning Pays

It is remarkable how much can be achieved in a few hours with stout secateurs and a pruning-saw. As November follows on the dry golden days of October and trees at last shed their leaves, the time arrives for pruning trees and shrubs to prepare them for winter. It is just as important to know what not to prune as it is to know what to prune at this season; in a few hours or even minutes irreparable damage can be inflicted on trees by careless lopping. In fact, pruning-errors can destroy the shape of a tree for ever. Trees, after all, are the long-term plants of our gardens, providing the setting for our houses, flowers and lawns, so treat them with respect.

Certain precautions are essential. First of all, use good tools and make sure that they are sharp. Blunt clippers and a rusty saw can not only be inefficient but damaging – a cut should be clean and neat, not ragged or chewed. Sawing at an awkward angle, especially above one's head, is exhausting enough even with sharp tools, but murderous with poor ones. Also, be sure to have a tool of the right weight for the job in hand. Don't try to cut sturdy hard wood with light secateurs intended for cutting roses or sweet peas. Similarly, don't use secateurs for cutting-down sycamore saplings, a job easily done with long-handled loppers or a small saw. There is a wide choice of pruners of different weights with handles of varying lengths, just as there are long-arm tree-pruners and pruning-saws which reach up among the branches. Reliable makes such as Rolcut, Wilkinson, Snap-cut and Ratchet-cut offer splendid choice.

In autumn, depending on the zone, certain pruning jobs are essential. Cut back the long shoots of roses as the soft new wood will probably die back with winter frosts. These growths make the bushes top-heavy, so that they rock in the wind, either breaking the branches or destroying the hair-roots by the continual vibration. I do not advocate heavy pruning of roses in autumn, especially in cold districts or in industrial areas. If a severe winter should follow, there would be excessive die-back and bushes would be seriously weakened or even killed. Similarly long, lax new shoots of mock-orange, flowering currants and forsythias should be shortened by a third, so that the bushes are compact and tidy for winter. The main pruning of spring-flowering shrubs should be done immediately after blooming, as they flower next season on the new wood formed during the previous summer. However, remove all weak or spent growths. When the shrubs have shed their foliage, it is easy to be selective of these.

If the flower-heads of lavender have not been cut for drying, the bushes should be lightly trimmed in autumn to remove the old flower-stalks, but be sure not to cut into the hard wood. Severe pruning should be left until early spring, along with that of potentillas, blue rue, santolinas, *Senecio laxifolius* and the woody salvias. The wood of certain shrubs is brittle; hence it may be desirable with hybrids of *Buddleia davidii*, caryopteris, and deciduous ceanothuses, such as 'Gloire de Versailles', 'Topaz' and 'Henri Defosse', not only to remove the heavy flower-heads but to cut them back partially before the gales and snows of winter take their toll, the usual heavier pruning following in early spring.

Sometimes at the end of autumn I long for a sharp decisive frost to finish the flower-border, so that it can be cleared and put to bed for the winter. In any case, one must not over-do the tidying-up operations with knife and secateur, particularly in cold districts, on heavy soils or in areas of high rainfall. Don't cut back nepeta, French taragon and leggy border-pinks, or you may well lose them. Shorten the stalks of hollow-stemmed herbaceous plants such as delphiniums, anchusas and thalictrums, but not to ground-level, as the water will collect in the stems and rot the crowns. I like to leave at least several feet of stem.

Climbing roses should be pruned and the growths tied in to the wall. Wistaria should be spurred back to encourage a profusion of flower. A few long growths springing from below may be retained if it is necessary to refurnish bare areas. Use tarred string or plastic-covered wire for securing heavy stems.

For the winter pruning of trees, observe the following points. Remove branches as near to the trunk as possible, never leaving ragged snags. Make an incision on the under-side of the branch and then cut through to meet it so that the weight of the bough will not tear away a strip of bark or stem wood. Try to eliminate branches that are too crowded to let in light and to improve the habit of the tree itself. Remove branches that cross each other or that have grown against each other so that they chafe. Prune lower branches to allow vistas under the trees and to make mowing easier.

Remove the small lower lateral branches on trees with fine winter bark, such as *Acer griseum, Prunus serrula* and *Prunus maackii*, the beautiful birches with white or fawn-coloured bark such as *Betula albo-sinensis* and *B. jacquemontii*, and the snake-bark maples, including *Acer laxiflorum, hersii, forrestii* and *capillipes*. A clean stem is essential to get the best effect from the gleaming texture, rich colour and pattern of the bark. No garden should be without one or more of these attractive trees if there is room.

The Versatile Beech

Few trees contribute more to the winter landscape than the beech. It is a superb tree, growing into great specimens on a variety of soils, in many countries of the new and old worlds. It was a tree much in favour in the eighteenth century and we find old specimens, avenues and plantations in a number of parks and gardens. How familiar are the silvery-grey boles and branches, with the dry russet-brown leaves clinging on well into the spring. Lovelier still are the silky spring buds, swelling to unfold the silver-green new leaves, the very epitome of spring.

I like the beech because it has so many uses, not to mention the variations in habit and leaf-character of different varieties. Beech hedges are among the finest of all windbreaks and one of the most adaptable of hedges, especially on calcareous soils. They have a rugged quality that is suited to the rural landscape on the one hand, yet they can be used in formal schemes with telling results. In large gardens long alleys of beech are frequently used to create broad lofty walls of green, which in winter become walls of brown, in contrast to the green of the grass. Beech is excellent for a boundary hedge, but should not be used in confined spaces, as it must develop some breadth for satisfactory effect.

Beech hedges can be planted in autumn, early spring or, for the matter, throughout the winter, if the ground is open and free of frost. For hedges, plants of various heights, ranging from eighteen inches to three or four feet, are usually available from nurseries. For a good hedge, small beech will probably establish itself more easily and quickly than larger ones. I prefer staggered planting (a double row) at an interval of twelve to fifteen inches, depending on size. Staggered planting will make a broader hedge, and where a very wide one is required even three rows may be used. Where there is an awkward angle or a difficult patch of ground, it is often effective to plant a solid block of beech, remembering, however, that too wide an area will be very difficult to cut. Purple beech *(Fagus sylvatica purpurea)* can also be used for hedges, either on its own or combined with green beech for telling effect, the warm coppery-purple blending with the silvery-green, particularly in spring when the colours are fresh and subtle. There are two extraordinary variations on the usual beech tree, with its towering broad head of branches. Perhaps the most striking and useful is the fastigiate Dawyck Beech *(Fagus sylvatica fastigiata)*, which is columnar in shape and makes a splendid tree to be used either as a specimen or in pairs to flank a gate or drive or flight of steps. This remarkable variety appeared in a famous Scottish garden, from which it takes its name. It is extremely useful for a position where a tree with little spread is required. It is, however, a real tree and not a dwarf form, growing to a height of forty to fifty feet with a spread of not more than twelve to fifteen feet. The remarkable characteristic of this striking tree is its slender habit with branches to the ground combined with the ruggedness which is the essential character of beech. Like other beeches it colours well and retains its leaves through most of the winter. Equally arresting although often fantastic in shape, the weeping beech *(F. sylvatica pendula)* has branches which grow at curious angles to the trunk and then become pendulous, so that the tree has an irregular silhouette

with a curtain of foliage. These fascinating trees are seldom planted today. They require a lot of space, as they are not effective if crowded by other trees, and therefore are only suitable for large lawns and parks. Again, they are a true forest tree and not to be confused with weeping cherries and other dwarf weepers. There is as well a purple weeping form *(purpureo-pendula)*.

For beauty of foliage and grace of habit I am particularly fond of the Fern-leaf Beech *(F. sylvatica heterophylla* or *laciniata)*. The term Fern-leaf is apt, as the leaves are heavily cut, giving a delicate grace and texture to this fine tree. It should be planted for interest as well as for its great beauty. Again, it needs space for maturity.

Weeping Trees and Laburnums

I have recently been struck in various cities by the effective use of trees with a pendulous weeping habit in conjunction with modern architecture, their twisting curved branches making a remarkable contrast to the straight lines and simple geometric forms of contemporary buildings. Similarly, trees of unusual

Clipped beech hedges frame the three radiating grass avenues in the great landscape garden at St Paul's Walden Bury in Hertfordshire, the childhood home of Queen Elizabeth The Queen Mother.

form are used in conjunction with modern sculpture with equally satisfying results. Having been relegated to a minor role for some years, weeping trees are again in the ascendency. But there is sometimes a danger of using them in the wrong position, especially in small gardens where they take up a great deal of space unless they are chosen carefully. Many tend to have a broad head and hence block vistas across a lawn. Weeping trees are at their best where they grow freely in an uncluttered space or where the weeping pendulous habit has a background of contrasting colour. For example, weeping willows are lovely by a pool or lake where the graceful silhouette can be enjoyed as well as the reflection in the mirror of the water.

The silver-grey of *Pyrus salicifolia pendula*, the Willowleaf Pear, is most striking against a dark background of conifers or yew (Zone 4). Contrary to common belief, willows will also grow in such positions and do not require a great deal of moisture. They are wonderful value, with their colourful bark in winter and their shimmering haze of silvery-green in early spring.

An inmate of an old people's home told me recently that the thing she enjoyed most was a weeping willow on the lawn. This was a fine young specimen of the golden-barked *Salix alba tristis*, surely the most striking of all forest-size weeping trees, with a frame of strong spreading branches hung with golden-yellow branchlets (Zone 2). The warm colour stands out bright against the dull winter palette of browns and greys.

This colourful tree is listed variously in nursery-catalogues as *Salix chrysocoma*, *babylonica*, *ramulis aureis* and *vitellina pendula*. As it is sometimes prone to scab and canker, spray with Bordeaux Mixture to prevent or control this. For smaller gardens, *Salix purpurea pendula* is suitable, as it does not develop so broad a head and seldom exceeds twenty feet in height (Zone 4).

The beauty of willows should not be overlooked for parks, factory-sites, and the grounds of modern buildings, while dwarfer ones are suitable for smaller gardens. Weeping cherries are deservedly popular. *Prunus subhirtella pendula* is a joy in spring when its long slender twigs are a mass of delicately formed pale pink flowers. A variety known as *pendula rubra* (syn. *lanceolata*) is also very attractive, with its much deeper colour (Zone 5).

One of the loveliest of weeping cherries is the pendulous form of *Prunus yedoensis*, known generally as var. *pendula* but more correctly as *perpendens*. It has a broad habit with pendulous branches almost to the ground, smothered with pink buds opening to blush-white, large, lightly scented flowers. This cherry, also

The delicate tracery of the greenish-yellow trailing stems of weeping willow above a pond is a striking feature in the winter landscape.

called 'Shidare Yoshino', is a miracle of beauty in early spring (Zone 5).

A graceful weeping tree for smaller gardens is the birch with its slender habit of distinction. Birches are attractive planted singly or in groups of three or five. They are hungry and rob the soil through their masses of fibre-roots, but these can be cut back from time to time as necessary. A birch in first leaf is the very symbol of spring, and in autumn the leaves are a dull gold. They are ideal where light shade is required in conjunction with conifers, rhododendrons and camellias, and the effect is particularly pleasing as the white or pinkish-grey bark stands out boldly against the dark foliage. Birches are particularly attractive with heathers and they like similar conditions.

An exquisite weeping cherry, *Prunus subhirtella pendula*, with daffodils and camellias epitomizes spring. Note the old stone dovecote.

They are adaptable, growing happily in town or country, on light sandy soil or in moist woodland conditions. They are particularly useful as they can be moved at considerable size and are effective in large concrete tubs or in raised beds in modern buildings. They are an ideal city tree for roof-gardens, courtyards and urban sites.

The stems of some of the silver birches are quite dark when young, but in a few years the bark changes to pale honey or white. More than one nurseryman has been taken to task for sending what the purchaser considered the wrong tree. The common silver birch *Betula pendula (alba)*, known as 'Lady of the Woods' is a wonderful stand-by. The type form has slender pendulous branches and always retains a graceful narrow silhouette. In contrast, the form designated *youngii* is slower-growing with a broad, almost mushroom-shaped head, that could well grace a Japanese

garden. Because of its slow rate of growth and ultimate restricted size it is ideal for small gardens. By the side of a pool or stream it is charming and in limited areas it is more in scale than a weeping willow.

The weeping ash *(Fraxinus excelsior pendula)* is striking, as it is flat-topped and can be trained to form leafy arbours (Zone 3). A weeping beech *(Fagus sylvatica pendula)* is another very beautiful tree. Huge specimens over a hundred years old show their ultimate character, but young trees have grace and interest *(see p. 32).*

A tree that takes on a new meaning after seeing it in the wild is the laburnum, particularly *L. alpinum*, which in Scotland has a very special beauty. Often the trees have been so battered and pruned by the Atlantic gales that they are gnarled and contorted, like the best Bonsai in every respect except size. The wavering short racemes of yellow pea-like flowers

34

hang in sheets of shimmering gold, while the trees themselves are marvels of aged distortion. They are so right in the landscape, as right, in fact, as laburnums in other settings can look out of place. *Laburnum vossii* has far longer trusses and a delicate light scent, but it seldom has the character of shape and habit of the more humble *L. alpinum*. Plant laburnums as bushes if you want a thicket of shrubbery with golden racemes to the ground, or grow one as a half or full standard.

Laburnums lend themselves to training. In several famous gardens there are long tunnels with laburnums trained and clipped each year to form a continuous arched vault of shimmering golden racemes in May. Laburnums can also be used to form a simple arch by training two trees over a wooden or metal frame. I have even used an old dead one as a support for a climbing *Rosa filipes*, with its huge panicles of creamy-white, scented flowers. Small laburnums are also extremely decorative if grown in tubs or large pots in a cool-house for transfer to a spot where a large shrub or tree is necessary in a room. When they grow too large, these can later be planted in the open ground. Laburnums look splendid if trained flat against a high wall, like a wistaria or a flowering japonica. This means careful training when the trees are young, and the removal of some of the shoots. Laburnums grow equally well on acid, neutral or alkaline soils. Plant them in autumn, late winter or very early spring. They benefit by light shaping when small to make them compact.

There are few plants that I actively dislike, but among them is the weird *Laburnocytisus adamii*, a grafted cross between *Cytisus purpureus* and *Laburnum anagyroides (vulgare)*. The flowers are yellow, tinged with mauve and purple, and it has the extraordinary habit of also producing branches on which the flowers are entirely purple or entirely yellow. This curious tree, which originated in France in 1825, is more an object of interest than of beauty. It is the result of a graft rather than of cross-pollination. For those who like strange trees, this is a collector's item, but if you have room for only one laburnum, this is definitely not the specimen.

Laburnums are superb trees for small gardens, as they have a delightful habit and grow well under varied conditions. Though hardy in Zone 6, they grow best in areas with moist atmosphere, particularly in the Northwest and the milder parts of New England.

Beauty from Box

Sometimes when I suggest box-edged beds or borders as an essential part of a new garden, I am told firmly, 'No, not box'. It is curious that there should be such strong feeling about a shrub that has contributed to the charm of so many gardens and has played so important a role in their actual design. In this country, particularly in the South, and in France, Italy and Spain box-wood often dominates the schemes, and gives these gardens much of their special character, as the dark, gleaming, fine-textured foliage can be clipped into neat, tight hedges, geometrical shapes or amusing topiary of animals and birds. Box hedges are to paths and borders what frames are to pictures: they formalize and enhance by containing the exuberant colours and soft feathery shapes of the planting, focusing attention and defining the ground-patterns.

What, for example, is prettier than the contrast of the solid dark mass of box hedges around a mixed border of roses in shades of pink and mauve with regale lilies and silvery artemisias, or serried ranks of elegant lily-flowered tulips? In one garden that I designed I massed box-edged beds with a carpet of blue forget-me-nots, with here and there an informal scattering of the delicate red and white striped Lady Tulip *(Tulipa clusiana)*, and in others used deep purple violas with silver cotton lavender. For summer effect, there are the annual yellow and orange French marigolds, always lovingly referred to by a gardening friend as his 'oranges and lemons'. These have an added brilliance when planted near box. For blue and mauve, compact plantings of ageratum or the taller, looser-growing *Salvia patens* and heavily scented heliotrope are ideal.

Topiary has both elusive charm and character. The globes and tiered pyramids give height and form, as well as providing the perfect foil for the colour and texture of the foliage around them. Mellow brick paths add to the charm of such a garden. There is a fine example of box hedging in the reproduction of part of George Washington's famous garden at Mount Vernon in the grounds of The American Museum at Claverton Manor, near Bath (*see* p. 8). Here we find these same elements, and again the liberal use of box. A good example of topiary is in the lovely garden at Haseley Court in Oxfordshire, the home of an outstanding American gardener who has brought the traditions of Virginia with her (*see* p. 215).

The great advantage of box is its evergreen foliage, as beautiful in winter as in summer. This is why I like to plan formal box hedging near the house. If ground-planting in the beds is carried out with plants that also retain their foliage, so much the better. Lavenders, santolinas, blue rue, dwarf veronicas, rosemary and perwinkles can be used to advantage, as the great formal layouts of France and Italy demonstrate so well. Or consider the cloisters and patios of California and Florida, with their central fountain or well and

A French potager, designed by Russell Page, has box-edged beds of vegetables and flowers with interesting old fruit trees, trained like wine glasses, for height and interest.

box-edged beds of roses, violets, pinks and aromatic herbs, with possibly a tall cedar or lemons or pomegranates. Herbaceous plants with persistent leaves, such as irises, pinks, hellebores, *Stachys lanata* and winter-flowering pansies, are also invaluable.

As gardens are tending to become more and more limited in size, concentrated in design, and centred in urban areas, the introduction of box is very welcome, as it imparts a feeling of formality and tidiness. Here I should mention that hedges and topiary are not for dog-lovers, unless precautions are taken. I once had to replace large blocks of box flanking a garden gate, as they had been ruined by a black poodle. Box is also vulnerable to heavy snow, so make sure that the snow from paths or terraces is not shovelled on to nearby hedges. I have seen the pitiful results of this.

Box likes any reasonable soil. Everyone who has seen it growing wild on chalky slopes in England, or on broad slopes in Provence, knows that it likes lime and does not mind bright summer suns, shade or winter cold, unless this is extreme. Plant box deeply, as the stems root freely. Box has a mass of fibrous roots and this makes it possible to lift large specimens, if they are properly prepared in advance. In this country, people spend vast sums moving very large old specimens.

Box hedges are not always loved by professional gardeners, as they are supposed to harbour snails. This is true to some extent, but is not a problem in most gardens. Far more serious after the War was the presence of ground-elder, convolvulus and other invasive weeds. It is sad to think of the number of lovely old kitchen gardens that were despoiled of their fine hedges, still in good condition, in an attempt, often misguided, to save labour.

Box hedges are of two types: the vigorous *Buxus sempervirens*, generally used for hedges and topiary, including the pyramids and balls in tubs flanking doorways or gates, and *suffruticosa*, a smaller, slower-growing varietal form of it. Amusing golden or silver variegated forms are available, as well as several forms such as *latifolia*, with broad leaves, and the little-known *salicifolia elata* and *rosmarinifolia*. The delightful oriental *Buxus microphylla* is a compact, very small-leaved form seldom exceeding about three feet in height.

The gleaming gold and scarlet foliage of our native *Fothergilla monticola* and the lighter-textured crimson leaves of a Japanese maple make a striking harmony of autumn colour. Fothergillas are slow-growing, and suitable for smaller gardens on lime-free soils.

Autumn Glow from Trees and Shrubs

Autumn colour is one of the compensations for the shortening days and the approach of winter. The dazzling colour of certain varieties of trees and shrubs can usually be relied upon, while others may be extremely good one year and poor the next, often with little obvious reason. Some of the finest coloured foliage is to be found in the United States and Canada, where sugar maples, red oaks, sumachs, dogwoods and Sweet Gums are unbelievably brilliant in late September and October. The beauty of Indian summer, that delightful spell of weather when days are bright and golden and the nights crisp and frosty, is never to be forgotten, with its brilliant foliage, wild asters, golden rod and the smell of burning leaves and of ripened apples.

Many other trees are beautiful but perhaps less spectacular with yellows, golds, siennas and umbers. The burnished gold of beech trees, the clear yellows of birches, poplars and chestnuts or the russet-browns and deep reds of oaks, are a tonic when gardens have that untidy end-of-the-summer look. Comparatively little is known about the causes of autumn colour, except that waste materials and sugars gradually accumulate in the leaf as the production of chlorophyll ceases and the green colour fades. Yellow pigment (xanthophyll) becomes predominant, and this explains the brilliant clear yellow of some trees, as, for instance, ginkgoes, tulip trees and hornbeams. In other leaves a red pigment known as erythrophyll is manufactured in the presence of sunlight from waste products, including sugar and tannin. Factors contributing to autumn colour include soil, temperature, shortening periods of daylight, and rainfall. A sharp frost followed by sunny days often brings the best colour. Excessive rainfall is detrimental.

There are so many wonderful plants that it is hard to know which to recommend, and I shall name only a few trees and shrubs that are outstanding. One of the most spectacular is Sargent's cherry (*Prunus sargentii*), which develops into a large tree with a wealth of pink blossom in spring and unbelievably brilliant scarlet foliage in autumn (Zone 4). Liquidambers, or Sweet Gums as they are known, are a close second. *Liquidamber styraciflua*, a native of North America, has maple-shaped leaves, which turn brilliant shades of glistening red and scarlet. This tree has a relatively narrow pyramidal head, which under satisfactory conditions will reach a height of fifty or sixty feet. For brilliance of colour it has few equals. It likes rich, moist soil and is not satisfactory on chalky, shallow ground (Zone 4).

A little-used North American tree is the beautiful *Oxydendrum arboreum*, known as the Sorrel Tree or Sourwood, hardy in Zone 4. In July and August it bears racemes of small white flowers and in autumn the foliage turns to brilliant gleaming crimson. It dislikes lime and grows under conditions favourable to rhododendrons and camellias. Certainly it deserves to be better known.

A delightful tree for town and country alike is *Ginkgo biloba*, the Maidenhair tree (Zone 4). It is a curious plant, for it is coniferous, although the leaves are fan-shaped, not needle-like, as is usual with the tribe. It grows into interesting shapes and tends to be upright and pyramidal rather than spreading. In Washington, where it is widely used as a street tree, the delicate gold of the autumn foliage is like sunlight seen through mist. Although this tree will grow to considerable height, it is suited to small gardens and towns. There is a variety *fastigiata* with more erect, ascending branches. Trees are unisexual, the male being the more prevalent. Ginkgo trees need good deep soil and plenty of sun. As they are often very slow to establish themselves, do not be disappointed if for the first few years growth is meagre. Once established, they grow more rapidly. I have a great fondness for these trees and am always delighted when I see them used as a street tree in New York, Philadelphia and other American cities.

A smaller tree with an utterly different horizontal manner of growth is *Parrotia persica* (Zone 5). In its early years it is far more shrub than tree. It has great character as it matures, with its ascending arching habit, and its silhouette is an addition to our gardens in winter and summer alike. The foliage turns extraordinary shades of gold, orange and crimson in autumn and leaves often last for a considerable time. In March there are attractive but certainly not showy flowers distinguished by the clusters of dark red stamens. It helps to stake young trees to encourage the development of a leader, for otherwise they often sprawl on the ground. Judicious pruning also helps. In one garden that I know of, young specimens were planted on either side of a grass ride, and now in their maturity the branches meet to form a spectacular arch, while the famous planting at Westonbirt Arboretum in Gloucestershire of parrotias with tall slender evergreen *Libocedrus decurrens* is one of the most successful groupings of trees for contrast of habit, texture of foliage and colour that I know.

Among the smaller trees or large shrubs there is no doubt that first place must go to that striking, deep red Bloodleaf Japanese Maple, *Acer palmatum* (Zone 5). At various arboretums, fine established specimens fifteen to twenty feet tall and as much across, now three or four decades old, are so spectacular that they evoke the mixed emotions of adulation, awe and envy. The delightfully broad-spreading habit of this species and its other forms makes them ideal plants for specimen or group-plantings. They like a warm, sheltered position if possible, but have proved fairly hardy in Massachusetts and south along the Atlantic coast. They are delightfully easy, as they will tolerate most soils, whether acid or alkaline, and combine well in the garden or open woodland with a wide range of flowering shrubs including azaleas, rhododendrons and heathers.

Japanese Maples are slow-growing and need plenty of space to develop their full beauty. *Acer palmatum septemlobum*, like so many of the Japanese Maples, appreciates sun and protection from wind, and its variety 'Osakazuki' is no exception. The latter is green throughout the summer, but in the autumn takes on a dazzling fiery scarlet that makes it unique among the acers. This lovely form is relatively scarce, as it must be propagated vegetatively if it is to be true to its parent. Seedlings may or may not be good. Moreover, if you plunge for this beauty, you must be patient, for your rather large investment will take some years to fulfil its rich promise.

Acer japonicum and its variety *vitifolium*, with broad vine-like leaves, are of similar shape and size. These are widely planted because of their attractive habit and shape. The leaves are a delicate parsley-green tinged with salmony-bronze as they unfurl in spring and a riot of orange, yellow, scarlet and crimson in autumn. There is a beautiful cut-leaved variety known as *A. japonicum* var. *aconitifolium*.

Acer japonicum and its forms, except possibly the cut-leafed form, are more tolerant of sun and wind than *A. palmatum* and its varieties. This is very much a point in their favour for the average gardener. The closely related *A. circinatum*, the lovely northwestern Vine Maple, is possibly even more tolerant of diverse conditions than *A. japonicum*, (Zone 5). It will eventually grow into a small tree about twenty feet tall, ideal for a small garden. Another easy maple for small gardens is the bushy *A. ginnala*, whose drooping leaves, somewhat resembling elongated vine leaves, turn to brilliant crimson and claret-purple in autumn (Zone 2).

Last but not least there is Paper-bark Maple *Acer griseum*, perhaps the perfect lawn tree for a confined garden with not too dry a situation. It gives late autumn colour (even in November in some areas during a mild season) of a lovely orange-scarlet, while the peeling cinnamon-orange bark is attractive throughout the year (Zone 5).

Another delight is *Euonymus alata*, which makes a dense shrub with corky wings or fins to the branchlets. The colour of the foliage in autumn is a subtle blending of apricot, mauve and pink. I know of few shrubs that are better value. It is superb on chalk and I have seen it growing happily in varied soils and climates (Zone 3). Obviously, in such a position it helps if the soil is deeply dug and enriched to enable the shrub to send out its roots and become established. Another superb spindle is *Euonymus oxyphylla*. This forms a narrow-headed, wineglass-shaped shrub or, in time, even a small tree, effective as a specimen or in boldly planted groups. The foliage turns dusky red, a piquant combination with the orange fruits in their maroon calyces. *Euonymus yedoensis* is of similar shape and stature but has much larger leaves than either *E. alata* or *oxyphylla*. The foliage often turns yellow or red, but sometimes a subtle lemon-white stained with rose. It has most beautifully coloured fruits of an unusual waxy pale pink. A berrying shrub that always catches my eye is Sea Buckthorn *(Hippophae rhamnoides)*. This is a rather grand name for a very simple shrub, beloved for its silvery foliage, which consists of myriads of narrow strap-like leaves, and in winter for the quantities of orange berries on the female plants. Sea Buckthorn should always be planted in groups, so that cross-fertilization will be effected: as the plants are unisexual, several male plants must be included with the females. It will grow on almost any soil, especially by the sea. There are huge drifts on the northern coast of France and in many seaside places, as it holds the sands like beach plum and bayberry. It withstands wind and salty gales, so it is a shrub to be valued for exposed places. In time, it will form a small tree and because of its predilection for wind it assumes gnarled picturesque shapes. It is beautiful planted with *E. oxyphylla*.

Certain mountain ashes *(Sorbus)* give both berries and autumn colour, and many of them are of a shape and size to make them suitable for the small garden of today. One should in fairness add, however, that in nearly every case the birds don't waste much time in devouring the berries. It is interesting that they seem to care less for the pinks and whites than for the oranges and reds. The following are hardy in Zone 5.

Sorbus cashmeriana develops with age into a mushroom-headed tree, outstanding on account of its pure white berries the size of small marbles. These combine beautifully with the golden autumn foliage and in most seasons hang on the bare trees for some time. It has flowers of a subtle soft pink, unlike the creamy white of nearly all the others.

Sorbus hupehensis is an erect-growing pyramidal tree with lovely, waxy, greyish leaves in summer, which turn to dusty orange suffused with violet in autumn. It bears huge clusters of small white berries, often flushed with pink.

One other pink-fruited sorbus must be included, the lovely *S. vilmorinii*, a mushroom-headed small tree with exceptionally small, delicate leaflets, giving the tree an over-all ferny appearance. The fruits start by being maroon-red, gradually fading to deep rose (at which stage they are set-off by the dusky crimson foliage) and finally to pinky-white. They have a porcelain-like quality and in some seasons hang onto the leafless branches until February. *Sorbus* 'Joseph Rock' is erect and even columnar. The berries are the colour of no other ash, a delicate creamy-primrose, lovely in combination with the rich red autumn foliage.

Among the dozens of scarlet-fruited mountain ashes, *Sorbus sargentiana* is outstanding on account of its exceptionally large leaflets, sticky red-brown winter buds, like those of a horse chestnut, huge corymbs of scarlet fruits and orange-scarlet autumn colouring streaked with crimson.

The Holly and the Ivy

The holly and the ivy have for so long been associated with Christmas that we accept them as traditional. The former appears in a variety of roles, ranging from large boughs or trees to deck the halls of country houses, to little sprigs as a festive touch for gifts, button-holes or the flaming plum pudding. So, too, the ivy is used as decoration for a number of festive purposes. What concerns us far more, however, than these seasonal aspects, are the value of holly and ivy in the garden in winter.

The American holly *Ilex opaca* is of course native (Zone 5) while the decorative English holly *Ilex aquifolium* is more tender (Zones 6–7) English Ivy *(Hedera helix)* is luckily hardy even in Zone 4. There are also the dwarfer ilexes such as the Japanese *I. crenata* and its many forms, valuable for landscaping houses, and the handsome shrubby Chinese *I. cornuta*. English holly and ivy are tolerant of diverse soil conditions and withstand smog in cities and industrial areas. They will grow in sun or heavy shade and, when established, will withstand fierce gales. How many plants can claim so many virtues? Best of all, they are telling assets in the winter landscape.

Holly has still another merit. It will stand a great deal of clipping and thus is ideal for hedges and topiary. Drastic pruning does not daunt a holly tree if this is done carefully and at the right time. Hollies should be pruned in summer or late spring, when there is vigorous root-action. Strangely enough, this is also the right time to transplant them. They resent being disturbed and should be lifted with as large a ball of soil as possible to keep the root fibres intact, a process far easier on heavy soils than on light, sandy ones. The soil should be thoroughly dug and prepared in anticipation and the plants well firmed and thoroughly watered after planting. Syringeing the foliage also helps, particularly in dry weather. It is for this reason that September, when the air is less

dry, is a good time to transplant hollies, in addition to the fact that at this season the roots are active and there is plenty of time to develop new fibre-roots before heavy frost.

Hollies are usually unisexual. Therefore, female plants are needed for berries, but there must be a male plant as well to provide the pollen. Herein lies the answer to the failure of many hollies to fruit. The small white flowers, often with a pleasing sweet fragrance, are borne in dense clusters in the late spring. The berries are usually red, but there are orange and yellow varieties, though these are much less common.

The uses of hollies are legion. They make fine hedges, if you are patient and willing to wait for seedlings to develop. Plants of various sizes are also available from nurseries, larger ones, by necessity, being expensive because of the slow rate of growth. Hollies are superb as specimen trees on a lawn or in pairs to accentuate a flight of steps, to flank gateways or in tubs for courtyards or terraces. Standard hollies are both scarce and expensive. Hollies are also excellent for screening and as a windbreak. They are useful in shrubberies to give character and are particularly effective as a background for silver birches.

Hollies are lovely if underplanted with variegated ivies, the silver and golden variegated carpet lightening the dark of the foliage above. Good varieties of ivy are *Hedera colchica dentata variegata*, with green leaves and golden variegation; *Hedera canariensis variegata* ('Gloire de Marengo'), with leaves edged white with a dark centre and a silvery-grey middle zone; *Hedera helix aureo-variegata*, with leaves of suffused gold and a fine dense habit; 'Silver Queen', with moderate-sized leaves edged with silver; 'Sheen Silver', with small leaves similarly marked; and 'Glacier', also with small leaves washed with silver and strongly edged. These are a few happy choices for walls or carpeting dark, shady places. Ivies make a superb ground-cover and, if pegged down or if the runners are covered with soil, they root quickly.

Among the finest varieties of *Ilex altaclarensis*, a hybrid between the native English holly *(Ilex aquifolium)* and the Azorean holly *(I. perado)*, native to the Azores and the Canary Islands, are 'Camelliaefolia' with handsome large leaves almost devoid of spines (it bears only pistillate female flowers, so a pollen-bearing variety must be planted nearby), and *I. altaclarensis hodginsii*, with large glossy leaves and purple stems. *Ilex aquifolium pyramidalis* is a very free-fruiting variety with a neat pyramidal habit and clear green leaves.

There are a number of variegated hollies, both yellow and silver, which are lovely for specimens or for use in tapestry hedges. The grey bark and twisted contours of the stems of old hollies are another attraction.

4 Flowering Shrubs

Shrubs of Winter and Early Spring

The flowering shrubs of winter and early spring are precious not only for their cheerful wealth of bloom but for fragrance. To me, it is little short of a miracle that December and January should produce such seemingly fragile flowers as *Mahonia japonica* or the various species of *Sarcococca*, all with a delicate but quite strong scent. *Mahonia japonica* is as well known for its handsome evergreen pinnate leaves, which form boldly decorative whorls, as for its drooping racemes of pale-yellow, berberis-like flowers which appear, sometimes as early as mid-November, in a mild climate, and last throughout late winter and early spring. It is a very obliging plant, thriving both on acid and chalky soils, and in full sun, although it is best in half shade. It graces many an urban garden, standing up well to town conditions. An occasional syringeing helps to free the leathery leaves of soot, but in general they react to urban conditions far better than many other evergreens. Moreover, it grows quite rapidly and if allowed space, forms a massive shrub as high as six or seven feet and as much or more across, well clothed with side-shoots at the ground. This matter of lateral shoots is important, and if you can buy young plants already furnished with several, so much the better.

Judicious pruning of long growths invariably produces breaks below. With established specimens I like to remove a whole flower-head, with its ruff of foliage, for a winter vase. This is dual-purpose pruning, which provides a massive decoration, one stem of leaves and flowers often measuring several feet across, and improves the habit of the shrub at the same time. The individual flowers open a few at a time, working outwards, until the tip is reached. The scent is delightful and best described as being like lily of the valley, with that same fresh, sweet quality, although winter and early summer are far apart.

The closely related *Mahonia bealii* has erect, rather shorter panicles and is equally fragrant (Zone 7). Plants may be offered lifted from open ground or pot-grown. In the latter case the plants can be planted at any time. Make sure that they have been properly hardened off and give some protection, if winter planting is contemplated, as in windy exposed positions the foliage of young plants is easily scorched, but they are generally quite hardy and will recover.

The various species of *Sarcococca*, less spectacular in leaf and flower but no less fragrant, bloom at approximately the same time. The scent of the inconspicuous flowers is a mixture of vanilla and honey, a delightful shock on a grey winter afternoon. Would that the name, derived from the Greek for 'fleshy fruit', were more attractive and sounded less like an infectious disease, but I know of no endearing English vernacular name.

Sarcococcas are of easy cultivation, as they like cool positions in full or half shade and will grow in sun, if the soil is not too hot and dry. They like lime, but are equally happy on neutral or acid soils. All the species have lustrous evergreen leaves with small axillary flowers which open in late winter or spring, depending on the locality. *Sarcococca humilis* is slow-growing and spreading in habit, about two to three feet in height, while *S. confusa* eventually reaches four feet and *S. hookeriana didyma* grows a little taller. *Sarcococca ruscifolia* has smaller leaves and an attractive dense habit. All are hardy in Zone 7.

Where should they be planted? Under trees and tall flowering shrubs, around the base of climbers planted in pockets in paving, against a shaded wall, or even as a hedge, either free-grown or loosely trimmed. Try to plant near a gateway, path or door, so that the fragrance may be enjoyed. Sprays are useful for flower arrangements where graceful, small dark green foliage is required. Propagation from stock plants is easy, either from cuttings or rooted suckers.

Other sweetly scented winter-flowering shrubs include three deciduous bush honeysuckles, *Lonicera purpusii*, *fragrantissima* and *standishii*, the first being a hybrid of the other two. These may retain their foliage

Hardy, mauve and purple ponticum rhododendrons frame the boat-house on the banks and are reflected in the moat.

in milder areas. All grow to six or eight feet and are worthy of the name honeysuckle for the fragrance of the clusters of small flowers at the end of winter (Zone 6).

The winter-flowering Jasmine (*Jasminum nudiflorum*) is invaluable for flowering in dark places during the shortest days of winter. It was introduced by Robert Fortune from China in 1844. Like *Jasminum primulinum* it favours a mild climate (Zone 8). It flowers over a long period from October until March and has no whims, growing on acid or alkaline soils alike, in sun or shade, against walls or in the open. Prune it after flowering to encourage short flowering shoots for next season.

Viburnum fragrans was introduced by Reginald Farrer from Northern China in 1909 and immediately aroused very great interest. It has tight clusters of pink buds opening into fragrant white flowers that stud the large semi-deciduous bushes from late fall until early spring. Some forms retain a pink flush when open. There is also a pure white form, *V. fragrans* var. *album*. *Viburnum bodnantense*, a cross between it and *V. grandiflorum*, is another superb winter shrub.

Two more ordinary winter-flowering shrubs are often overlooked because of their ease of cultivation and their ubiquity in gardens, namely laurestinus (*Viburnum tinus*) and the Cornelian cherry (*Cornus mas*).

Laurestinus is so useful that it seems odd that it should ever be neglected, as flowering evergreens, suitable for screens up to nine to twelve feet and loosely pruned hedges, are all too rare, even in mild zones. Moreover, it produces its flat heads of white flowers from November until April, at a time when there are few other shrubs in flower and no others as showy. First, there are the pinkish flower-buds like tiny beads, then the conspicuous white flowers on reddish stems and in autumn blue berries which with age turn to black. Not least in importance perhaps are the bold, leathery, dark green leaves. In the wild on the Mediterranean hills it shows great variation in habit of growth, size and colour of both leaf and flower, and even in the degree of fragrance. So it is not surprising that we find listed *Viburnum tinus strictum* applied to a form with a narrower, more restricted habit, and 'Pink-budded Form' to one which is shorter, more compact and rather slower-growing than the type. It ultimately reaches a height of three to five feet with a spread almost twice as wide. This variety is good for small gardens.

Another fine form is *V. tinus*, 'Eve Price', which originated at Wakehurst Place in Sussex, the home of so many of the best forms of trees and shrubs. This variety, useful for tubs, because of its compact habit, is characterized by tight clusters of freely borne flower-buds tinged carmine. 'Clyne Castle' is another named clone which has gleaming dark leaves and bigger flowers than the type. There is even a variegated laurestinus with broad yellow markings. The rather tender variety *lucidum* is notable for its lax, open habit and large glossy leaves, often as much as four inches in length, and there is even a variety *purpureum* with very dark foliage tinged with bronze-purple when young.

Laurestinus is subject to winter-scorching and is not completely hardy (Zone 8). It is better planted in

Long, jade-green catkins in winter make *Garrya elliptica* a particularly attractive evergreen shrub, either in the open or against a wall.

The soft yellow flowers stained with purple of Winter Sweet *(Chimonanthus praecox)* fill the air with fragrance in the cold of winter.

at its base provide a perfect foil. It can also be effectively grown as a specimen and is suitable for tubs and large pots in sheltered positions. It is not particular as to soil and is ideal on chalk or limey soils or by the sea in gardens that are not too cold. It will grow in semi-shade, but flowers best in sun. In the South of France laurestinus is sometimes trainded as a half-standard. I like to plant grey lavenders or santolinas with it as the contrasting colours and textures of the foliage are pleasing.

Cuttings from half-ripened wood in summer strike easily in a light, sandy rooting medium and even more quickly if bottom heat is available. Pot-on the rooted cuttings and allow them to develop heavy root-growth before planting out.

Cornelian Cherry *(Cornus mas)* is one of the most subtle yellow-flowered shrubs of early spring (Zone 4). I say 'shrub', but actually it develops in due course into a broad-headed small tree up to twenty feet tall. It is less exotic than the Asiatic witch-hazel, but very charming, and it also flowers before the leaves. In the south of France I have seen huge groups of this lovely shrub gleaming yellow in the late afternoon sun. So spectacular were they and so heavily flowered that at a distance they formed great yellow clouds against the dark greens of *Pinus pinea* (Umbrella Pine) and *Quercus ilex* (Evergreen or Holm Oak). In autumn it has small bright red berries with a sharp rather pleasant flavour. Branches of the Cornelian Cherry, if cut and stood in water in a warm place, can be forced into bloom like forsythia or flowering quinces. There are several forms, with variegated foliage. *Cornus mas* var. *aurea* has leaves suffused with dull gold, and *elegantissima* combines yellow and pink variegations. My preference, however, is for the variety *variegata* with leaves margined with silvery-white, which makes a lovely mass of colour all through the summer.

Although unspectacular, *Garrya elliptica*, with its long grey catkins, is a favourite of mine; it has great character in its smooth, leathery, evergreen leaves and clusters of felted catkins. There are both male and female plants; the former has the longer catkins, running to five or six inches. It is a species native to California and Oregon. The genus *Garrya* was named after Nicholas Garry, a member of the Hudson Bay Company, who helped David Douglas with his plant-collecting in the early decades of the nineteenth century. *Garrya elliptica* is best in a protected position, preferably against a wall, but in mild climates it may be grown as a free-standing bush. The flowering season varies in different localities, but often starts in November and lasts until late spring. Plants are usually pot-grown as they dislike root-disturbance. Therefore garryas can be planted whenever available and ground conditions are favourable.

the spring in cold areas or windy sites as the young growth is often soft and scorches badly. It is also subject to yellowing as the result of soot and smog. If planted in the autumn, give it winter protection until it is established, except in mild areas. All the varieties mentioned may not yet be available but I hope several if not all, will be in time.

Laurestinus may be used as an evergreen flowering hedge, but remember that if it is severly pruned it loses its charm of habit and most of its flowers. Bushes can be shaped with judicious use of the secateurs, and will incidentally provide charming branches or short flower-heads for low bowls in the house. I know of a garden where a long alley is bordered with loose irregular masses which in winter are studded with white flowers. It is a joy all through the winter and in February the fringe of snowdrops

Pruning should be done when flowering has finished in early spring; and not in summer, as the flowers will be sacrificed the following winter.

Camellias for Flowers and Foliage

In recent years I have come to value camellias almost as much for their gleaming evergreen foliage as for the bounty of their flowers. Some are, moreover, proving far hardier than was at first realized, provided that certain essential requirements are satisfied. First and foremost, an acid or neutral soil is necessary. Camellias do not like an alkaline soil, in which yellowing of the leaves soon results. A proprietary chelating compound is a possible short-term remedy. The addition of peat or leaf-mould is beneficial when the ground is prepared at planting time and as an annual mulch, especially on neutral or slightly alkaline soils. Good drainage is vital: camellias do not like sodden conditions and vigorous root-growth is quickly impaired by excessive moisture. Over-watering of pot plants is often a cause of failure. By the same token, camellias should not be allowed to dry out, especially when forming buds and flowering. Bud-drop will often result from both these conditions. Camellia japonica hybrids are hardy in Zone 8 and a few such as the lovely pink semi-double 'Bernice Boddy' are hardy in Zone 7 and even in parts of Zone 6. Camellia sasanqua hybrids are hardier and are satisfactory in the latter zone.

Choose your site carefully. North and west aspects are to be preferred, as early-morning sun is disastrous to the buds after frost. Although camellias have long been considered shade-lovers, thriving as a secondary growth under trees in their native eastern-Asian homes, they enjoy quite a lot of sunshine, as is evident in California and the South as well as in Portugal, France, Italy, and Madeira. In many areas in Britain sunny aspects should not be ruled out, provided soil and moisture requirements are satisfactory.

Another important factor is feeding. As camellias flower so abundantly, they require ample nourishment. Humus is essential. In many gardens the dead flowers are allowed to form a natural mulch and, as I have said already, leaf-mould and peat are invaluable; so is garden compost, as long as you can be sure that it does not contain lime in any form. Well-rotted manure is good, but do not apply too much at once, and it should be well-broken down. Liquid manure in weak doses at regular intervals is excellent, especially on light dry soils and for pot-grown plants. Fish-meal or meat-and-bone-meal are also good. When feeding camellias, remember that young growth should not be encouraged late in the season as it will be soft and subject to die-back. Therefore withhold food after early summer.

Camellias should be planted individually for the true beauty of the bushes and massed for landscape effects. They are ideal for shaded town gardens, but beware of poor soil and the dry or dank conditions that may exist near walls.

Camellias are usually pot-grown, so they may be planted at any time. I can think of no nicer present for your own garden or for that of a friend. The amateur would do well to stick to the tried and true varieties, but there is an ever-widening range of new ones as well. Among the pinks C. japonica 'Lady Clare', 'Elegans', 'Preston Rose', 'High Hat', 'King's Ransom', 'Pink Perfection', 'Pink Pagoda' are very good. Reds include 'Adolphe Audusson', 'Arejishi', 'Fred Sander', 'C. M. Hovey', 'Glen 40', 'Flame', 'Blood of China', 'Tomorrow' and 'Donckelarii' (red marbled white). There are a number of good whites such as 'Alba Plena', 'Mathottiana Alba', 'Nobilissima', 'Finlandia', 'Snow White' and 'Sode-Gakushi', but these show frost-damage most easily.

I have also been very impressed by the beauty of new japonica hybrids such as 'Salutation', 'Donation', 'Inspiration' and 'Leonard Messel'; all are plants of great distinction in varying shades of pink. They are less hardy than the varieties of C. japonica listed above, but are admirably suited to woodland gardens, as may be verified by visiting some of the famous English gardens in Cornwall, such as Caerhays and Trewithen, or, in the home counties, the Savill Gardens in Windsor Great Park.

I am also very impressed with the C. williamsii hybrids, which are hardy and free-flowering, with lovely graceful habits that make them perfect for natural plantings, or they are also excellent against walls and fences in town or country. Good clones include 'Hiraethlyn', 'J. C. Williams', 'November Pink', 'St Ewe and 'Elizabeth Rothschild'.

Camellia 'Cornish Snow' stands rather apart. It is a hybrid between C. saluenensis and C. cuspidata. It is not fully hardy in the open, but again admirable for woodland treatment. The white, rather bell-shaped flowers seem to hover like butterflies over the graceful, pendulous branches. The leaves, too, are very distinct, being willowy in shape and suffused with a lovely coppery-chocolate shade in the young stages.

Today there are literally hundreds of fine American varieties and some are proving excellent in British gardens. These include 'Mrs Tingley', a double silvery-pink and salmon. 'Debutante', a large, paeony-flowered camellia, light pink on a vigorous-growing erect shrub; 'Guest of Honour', with shaggy paeony-type flowers of pink-shaded salmon and compact strong growth; 'Her Majesty Queen Elizabeth II', a rose-pink, paeony-flower with salmon glints, vigorous and upright in growth; 'Joseph Pfinsti', a large, semi-double, deep

Camellia 'J. C. Williams' was the first of the famous crosses between *C. saluenensis* and *C. japonica*, made at Caerhays in Cornwall, to become available for our gardens. It is remarkably hardy and quickly covers a wall.

Camellia 'Donation', with its soft pink, loosely semi-double blooms, is one of the great hybrids of this century. It is quick-growing, reasonably hardy, and extremely floriferous.

Camellia 'Contessa Lavinia Maggi', with stripes and flakes of carmine on a paler ground, recalls the splendour of Edwardian conservatories.

red; 'Mrs D. W. Davis', an enormous, blush-pink, semi-double, good for conservatories or for areas that are not too wet; and 'White Empress', a very large, paeony-flowered white with a strong upright habit. One of the finest japonicas from Portugal is the rosy-red, formal double with delicate purple veining and a white edge, known by the rather cumbersome name of 'Augusto L. Gouveia Pinto'. I have seen superb blooms in Portugal and it is proving very good elsewhere.

The sasanquas are remarkably decorative plants, either espaliered against walls or in the open. There have been marked advances in the colour range and in size and flower shape. They are particularly useful because of their autumn and winter-flowering season. In a warm spell between Christmas and New Years in Washington, D.C. I have seen them still blooming profusely, undaunted by severe frosts a few weeks before. Because of their charming graceful habit they can be trained against walls as espaliers. There are various colours, mostly shades of rose, pink and crimson. Some have a faint fragrance that is particularly rewarding. Singles include 'Blanchette', white

'Hana-Fuki' is a semi-double soft pink cultivar of *Camellia japonica* which flowers copiously in mid-season.

tinted pink; 'Hino de Gumo', white margined rose; 'Rubra Simplex' and 'Crimson King'. Among the many semi-doubles 'White Doves' of loose paeony form, the rose-pink 'Cleopatra', the large shell-pink 'Jean May', 'Sparkling Burgundy' and 'Pink Snow' are good choices.

Flowering Quinces for Walls

Few flowering shrubs are more decorative in early spring than the flowering quinces, varieties of *Chaenomeles japonica* and *C. speciosa*, whether used against walls or a shrub in the open, so that its great masses of brilliant flowers can be enjoyed from every angle with the sunlight filtered through the brilliant petals. The small, apple-shaped, stemless fruits, though bitter to taste when uncooked, have a good flavour for jelly and apple tarts, and although they do not give as bountiful a yield or fruits as large as the true quince, they are an excellent substitute. The idea that these fruits are poisonous is erroneous.

Another species little grown in England is *C. cathayensis*, a tall, rather lanky shrub with large pear-shaped fruits as much as five or six inches long, which are both decorative and of a delicious strong flavour. For keen shrub-growers with large gardens this is an excellent dual-purpose shrub. I remember my delight when I saw it in full fruit for the first time in early October at Dumbarton Oaks in Washington, D.C.

The numerous varieties of *C. japonica* and *speciosa* offer a wide choice of colours, ranging from white (*nivalis* and 'Snow') to pink and white ('Moerloesii' and 'Apple Blossom'), and from deep salmon-pink ('Umbilicata' and 'Pink Lady'), to shades of scarlet and crimson ('Cardinalis', 'Glowing Embers', 'Sanguinea' and 'Texas Scarlet', 'Firedance', 'Etna' and 'Crimson and Gold'). Most of these are single, but some are semi-double, such as the rather slow-growing, cream-flushed, salmon-pink 'Falconet Charlot' and the orange-scarlet 'Boule de Feu'. The last is superbly named, for the colour has a luminous flame-like intensity. *Chaenomeles japonica* itself has clear, pale orange-red flowers freely borne on a low sprawling bush with masses of long-lasting yellowish fruit like very small pumpkins. All are hardy in Zone 4.

Not only are there variations in the colours of the flowers, but also in the habit of the shrubs, making some ideal for training on walls and others more suited to act as free-standing shrubs. In cold districts they will of course flower much earlier on a sunny wall and all can be adapted to this method.

Flowering quinces do not require rich soil. In fact, poor soil as well as lime suits them and this should comfort the chalk gardeners: of course, thorough preparation of the ground is necessary. Another splen-

The quince-like Chaenomeles brighten many a dull wall in early spring with clusters of brilliant colour on the leafless branches.

did characteristic of these useful shrubs is the fact that they will grow in almost any aspect, as long as they are not in heavy shade or the drip of trees. Light shade suits them perfectly. Futhermore, they are very long-lived, so that old specimens can be cut back and allowed to refurnish themselves.

Proper pruning is important. As flowers are borne primarily on old wood, pruning should be done after the flowers are finished in May. Established shrubs should be thinned and the side-growths of wall-plants spurred back to three or four eyes. Later in the summer and in the autumn new growths should be tipped or cut well back to improve the shape of the bush and expose the flower-buds. Sometimes old bushes do not flower. In such cases drastic pruning is recommended, and feeding with bone-meal. Do not manure flowering quinces, as this encourages rank soft growth rather than hard established flowering wood. Young plants recently set out are best left unpruned until they have become well established. Now and then a bush will be found that does not flower even with treatment, and this should be rogued out.

The blooming season is a long one. For early flowering a warm wall is necessary and in such a situation buds may open in late January or February. In shady aspects and in the open, flowering will commence much later with the maximum bloom in April and early May.

In Japan, a great deal of hybridizing has been done, and there is a notable collection of quinces at the Villa Taranto on Lake Maggiore in Northern Italy. As this now belongs to the Italian Government, the gardens are accessible to the public. Similarly, in this country there is great interest in this highly adaptable shrub, which thrives in the hot summers, yet is able to survive the extreme cold of winter. Fine new varieties have been produced and I sincerely hope that all these will find their way to England in the future. One of the great collections is at Winterthur, near Wilmington in Delaware, where massed plantings in the open produce wonderful effects. This collection is also accessible to the public in spring when the gardens are open.

Branches force well if picked when the buds begin to swell and brought into the warmth. There is nothing more exquisite than the pale pink or coral-red buds, as they unfurl into delicate cup-shaped flowers with here and there a jade-green bud or tiny leaf. A sprig or two in a small vase on my desk gives me as much pleasure as a large arrangement.

The Beauty of Magnolias

Magnolias are wonderful plants for our gardens and obligingly come at different seasons. By late spring the majority have finished flowering, especially those that flower so spectacularly before the appearance of their leaves; these include *Magnolia stellata, soulangeana, denudata* and the tall Asiatic species, such as *M. salicifolia, kobus, dawsoniana, campbellii* and *sargentiana* var. *robusta*. The last three are suited to large gardens but only in milder areas. *Magnolia stellata* is highly adaptable for relatively small gardens; it is slow-growing, though ultimately becomes a large shrub. It is also lime-tolerant, as is the evergreen *M. grandiflora*. The former is hardy in Zone 4, while the latter is less so (Zone 7).

In late summer the huge, heavily scented flowers of *Magnolia grandiflora* show up superbly against the gleaming dark green foliage. Grow them against a large wall or in the open.

48

As is well known, *M. soulangeana*, after *M. stellata*, is perhaps the best for the average garden where only one or at most two or three magnolias can possibly be accommodated. What is less well known is that the finest forms of *M. soulangeana* are var. *brozzonii*, with lovely elongated tulip-like white flowers, and var. *lennei*, with enormous rose-purple flowers, much more globular in shape than the other forms and with superb leathery rich green leaves. Although *M. salicifolia* ultimately forms a tree of twenty to thirty feet in height, it could well be planted in smaller gardens (Zone 4). Like the related *M. stellata*, it flowers at a very young age and size. Moreover, the over-all tree-shape is slender, making it highly suitable for restricted areas. The bark when wounded gives off a very pleasant smell, recalling that of Lemon Verbena. *M. kobus* is one of the hardiest of tree magnolias (Zone 4) and very fine. Like *M. stellata* and *salicifolia*, it flowers before the leaves. There are superb specimens in the Arnold Arboretum and it was there that the form *borealis* was first introduced.

In summer there are other treasures in this exotic family. One of the most useful is the Japanese or Korean *M. sieboldii*, often still referred to by its old name of *M. parviflora*. It forms a broad shrub or small, rather open, lax tree from ten to fifteen feet in height, depending on the locality. The cup-shaped flowers are pure white with a central boss of deep crimson stamens around a central club-like column of green carpels. The petals have a delightfully smooth texture and the blooms exude a delicious fragrance which hangs heavy on the still night air. The flowers are tipped at a slight outward-facing angle, so that they look at you, in contrast to the pendulous flowers of the Chinese *M. sinensis* or *M. wilsonii*, which face the ground. This magnolia is fastidious, liking cool, rich, acid soil with leaf-mould (Zone 7). It is charming when grown as a specimen or on the outer edge of a shrubbery, especially on a slope. The flowers, have grace, refinement, fragrance and a long season, as the main burst of flowers comes in June and July but blooms appear on and off till as late as August, and in some seasons these later flowers are profuse. *Magnolia sieboldii* has attractive broadly elliptical leaves, dark green above and silvery below. Unfortunately it is frost-tender, and should not be planted in areas subject to late frosts, as it comes into leaf rather early.

In favourable localities, *M. sinensis* grows into a larger better-shaped tree as much as twenty-five feet in height. Its pendulous flowers are four to five inches across, broadly saucer-shaped and pearly-white with red stamens round a central green club of carpels. It is

Magnolia denudata flowers when young, but it will grow to thirty-five feet or more, with a considerable spread, so allow plenty of space.

delightful to walk under a large specimen and to look up into its fragrant flowers, framed by big obovate leaves; only then can the true beauty of these exquisite blooms be fully appreciated. *Magnolia wilsonii* is similar in flower and habit, but is characterized by narrower, more lanceolate leaves with a brownish furry velvet beneath. Both species have striking red fruits with bright crimson seeds. Their flowering periods are not as prolonged as *M. sieboldii*, usually being limited to May and June, although they may extend into July in cooler districts. They are best on the Northwest coast.

Magnolia sinensis grows well in various gardens with highly alkaline soils, so magnolia-lovers who think they are deprived because of gardening on lime should take heart. *Magnolia wilsonii* in a number of different localities is also lime-tolerant, but it grows superbly on acid soils in sheltered moist conditions. The famous hybrid *M. highdownensis*, believed to be a cross between these two Chinese species, is a superb plant which flourishes equally well on chalk, neutral or acid soils. It has large pendulous flowers, five to six inches across, profusely borne on a broad, shrubby tree.

Until they are established all these magnolias need to be cosseted by giving them shelter from early frost, plenty of leaf-mould and good drainage. They are obliging plants and lend themselves to shaping as they mature. Although they are shrubby in habit, I know of several gardens where they have been pruned very successfully to form standards. They can also be espaliered against a wall. For this, *M. sieboldii* is admirable, as the flowers look out from the wall more effectively than the completely pendulous *M. sinensis* or *M. wilsonii*. They are also effective when grown in groups or singly on a lawn.

Young plants of these three species are available from good nurseries and I find that in most areas autumn planting is more satisfactory than spring planting. As all three are deciduous, they shift better when dormant. Give them plenty of space, as they resent disturbance when established. Be sure to allow room for them to develop by removing nearby shrubs and trees as necessary.

A number of these magnolia species will come true from seeds sown in pots, but do not embark on rearing magnolias from seeds unless you are patient, as germination is slow and it takes some years for plants to flower.

I have always loved magnolias. Every spring I am overcome anew by each species in succession. I am especially fond of the lovely pure white Yulan Magnolia (*M. denudata*), with its large goblet-shaped blooms of heavy texture which open before the leaves appear.

This was formerly known as *M. conspicua*. Like *M. kobus*, it is very hardy (Zone 4) and flowers superbly in New England and over a large area of the country. The pure white, heavy-textured cup-shaped flowers appear before the leaves in early spring. In maturity trees grow to thirty feet and as much across. Hence it is not a permanent tree for a small garden.

If I could only have one, without a second's hesitation I would cast my vote for the evergreen *M. grandiflora*, native to the south-eastern United States, and this is no loyalty to the land of my birth. Devotion to flowers transcends even patriotism. It is a superb tree, growing to great heights in its native haunts or in the warm Mediterranean countries, such as Spain, Portugal, Southern France and Italy, where it is equally at home. I love everything about it – the large glistening, dark green leaves, often with rusty brown indumentum like rich brown suede on the under-sides, the fat oval buds which gradually expand into huge, creamy white, cup-shaped flowers as much as a foot across with a central boss of stamens; but above all I love the scent and its long flowering season.

It is a very effective tree for a broad avenue. It casts heavy pools of dark shade, welcome on hot summer days, and makes a wonderful foil for trees with light feathery foliage such as *Albizzia julibrissin* (Zone 6) or the Goldenrain Tree *(Kolreuteria paniculata)* with its huge panicles of golden yellow flowers in late summer (Zone 5). The wonderful specimens in the South, in cities like Charleston, Richmond, New Orleans, Savannah, Atlanta and Washington, where they form large trees as tall or taller than the houses, always fill me with envy, as do those in Southern Europe.

Magnolia grandiflora is hardy in Zone 7 and in Zone 6 in warm positions, if sheltered from icy winds. It makes a splendid wall plant if espaliered and is handsome in courtyards or the walls of an enclosure around a swimming pool. Young plants benefit by some form of protection in cold areas until established as the big evergreen leaves are subject to scorch. If this magnolia is to be treated as a wall cover, it must be carefully thinned and the branches tied in or it will become massive and heavy. Be sure to allow it plenty of wall space, preferably several storeys high and of generous breadth. It is as a tree that this magnolia is finest, reaching heights of sixty to eighty feet.

I have seen old trees that were still studded with velvety blooms in mid-October, strangely luminous in the twilight against the inky green of the foliage. Even if it had been deepest night, their presence would have been disclosed by the rich heavy fragrance, with its overtones of spice and lemon. Even after a wet, cold summer an unusual number of specimens can be seen blooming freely in various districts, though perhaps later in the year than usual. Few flowers tempt the painter more than magnolias. The dark gleaming leaves, the fat swollen buds, the strangely full flowers with their gentle curves, the rich creamy colour of the petals ageing to a rich parchment yellow, and the delightful colour and texture of the unfurling leaf-buds offer an exciting challange to the brush. Sir Winston Churchill loved them and there is a fine specimen on a wall at Chartwell, which supplied blooms for his pictures.

Magnolia grandiflora is not fastidious; it does well on both acid and alkaline soils, as long as drainage is good and the position warm and not too exposed. In cold areas try planting this magnolia against a sunny wall with a chimney, as the added warmth may make a real difference in a severe winter. A generous mulch of leaf-mould is beneficial after planting and yearly thereafter until plants are established. Be sure to keep newly planted trees well watered for the first year, remember that if planted against a wall, magnolias need extra attention as they may be shielded from rain.

There are a number of varietal forms of *Magnolia grandiflora* which have developed over the years, many of them of southern European origin. One of the most popular varieties is listed variously as 'Exmouth variety', *M. grandiflora lanceolata* and *exoniensis*. It is characterized by its earlier flowering habit and freedom of flowering. Another form known as 'Goliath' has broader leaves and slightly larger flowers, again produced on relatively young trees. In this country 'Majestic Beauty' is a spectacular variety with very broad leaves and a pyramidal habit. 'St Mary' has fine bronze-backed leaves and flowers earlier than the type.

The pearly-white, cup-shaped flowers of *Magnolia sieboldii* bloom for a long season, lasting from May until mid-summer.

The Bounty of Rhododendrons

Since the war no shrub has gained in popularity so quickly as the rhododendron. A delightful proof of its popularity is the size and brilliance of rhododendron shows in various sections of the country, particularly in the Northwest, where the widest range of species and hybrids is grown. Here conditions are similar to mild areas in Britain where the finest rhododendron gardens in the world are to be found. Many distinguished hybrids were developed by the owners of private gardens including Bodnant, Exbury and Leonardslee, names familiar to rhododendron enthusiasts the world over. The 'Bloody Reds' of Bodnant, Exbury hybrid azaleas and the famous fragrant Loderis need no formal introduction.

Rhododendrons are obliging plants; there is an extraordinary range in habit, size of bush and foliage, as well as in the shape and colour of the flowers. Not the least of their merits is the very long blooming season, with flowers in some mild districts from January to late July or August. As to size and habit, contrast the huge *Rhododendron macabeanum*, which can reach a height of thirty to forty feet in favoured woodland gardens, with the prostrate, slow-growing *R. forrestii (repens)*, which blankets rocks or banks in sheltered semi-shaded positions. Their flowers afford as great a contrast. The former has large, well-formed trusses of numerous, pale yellow, campanulate flowers with purple spotting at the base; the latter bears gleaming scarlet flowers singly or in pairs. A word of caution about the latter: *R. forrestii* is rather shy of flower at best, but the beauty and brilliance of the flowers on the finest forms make it a cherished possession for those who are patient.

Perhaps the greatest contrast is in the leaves. Those of *R. macabeanum* are about a foot long, dark green and leathery with greyish-white under-surfaces, while those of *R. forrestii* are obovate, heavily veined, not more than an inch or so in length and stained with purple on the under-sides. In spite of these contrasts they are both rhododendrons, flowering at about the same season.

Rhododendrons have certain fundamental requirements. They are lovers of acid soil, rich in leaf-mould or peat. They like moisture and semi-shade and as a family, they dislike lime. Where the soil is 'borderline', with a faint trace of lime, this can be corrected by feeding with peat and leaf-mould. If rhododendrons are suffering from chlorosis, the soil can be treated with Copperas and they will react quickly to the increased acidity induced in this way. Where there is a lack of soluble iron within the plant, there will be another form of chlorosis, as the manufacture of chlorophyll is impeded. This can be remedied by a foliar spray with chelated iron. All of this is highly technical but the subject is expertly treated in *Rhododendrons of the World*, by

The giant rounded trusses of creamy flowers and the huge silver-backed leaves explain the popularity of *Rhododendron macabeanum*.

David G. Leach (George Allen and Unwin, London, 1962). Mr Leach has vast knowledge of the cultivation of rhododendrons in his native country and in Britain as well. However, I advocate rhododendrons and ericaceous plants only for suitable soil.

The question of hardiness immediately comes to the fore. Obviously, rhododendrons which will grow in the moist, mild climates of Pacific Northwest coastal gardens are very different from those that thrive in exposed East Coast or inland gardens. Wind, rain, temperature, the amount of sunshine and the prevalence of late frosts are factors that must be taken into account. It is hard to predict with any certainty which borderline plants will grow in a given area, for there are constant surprises. So much depends on the severity

The compact floriferous hybrids of *Rhododendron yakusimanum* are proving to be ideal evergreen shrubs for small gardens. They are relatively slow-growing yet flower when young.

of the winters and on the nature of summers as well.

On the whole, the demand is for compact floriferous bushes, suited to restricted areas. There are a large number of rhododendron species for the rock garden, including *R. calostrotum* with its rosy-purple, widely flared, funnel-shaped flowers in clusters; *R. campylogynum*, a spreading dwarf shrub between twelve and thirty inches tall with delicately poised nodding flowers, ranging in colour from rose to purple; and for lovers of blue-purple there are the dwarf *R. impeditum*, the slightly taller *R. scintillans*, and the rich, deep purple *R. russatum*. The milky-white *R. leucaspis*, which flowers in March or even February on the neat bush seldom exceeding two feet in height, is rather more tender. *Rhododendron forrestii*, mentioned above, with gleaming, sealing-wax red, campanulate flowers of great beauty is another dwarf for the keen collector, as is the pale

yellow *R. hanceanum* var. *nanum*. The former is sometimes shy-flowering, but of great beauty. These few give some idea of the range of treasures for the rock garden or for sloping banks or the front of borders. All are hardy in Zone 6, save *R. leucaspis* (Zone 7).

Of even wider appeal are the small rhododendrons suited to shrubberies, where they can be planted singly or in groups of three or five, or in even larger masses. One of my favourites is the species *R. ciliatum*, rather tender but of exquisite beauty. The clusters of very fragrant white flowers tinged with pink and opening from deep rosy-red buds are profusely borne in late March or April. In a garden in Donegal I have seen in early April hundreds of plants in full flower on a steep rocky slope devoid of other colour save for the silvery boles of the trees and the carpet of brilliant green moss, in which they seed copiously. The scent was intoxicating. This species is excellent for the rhododendron-

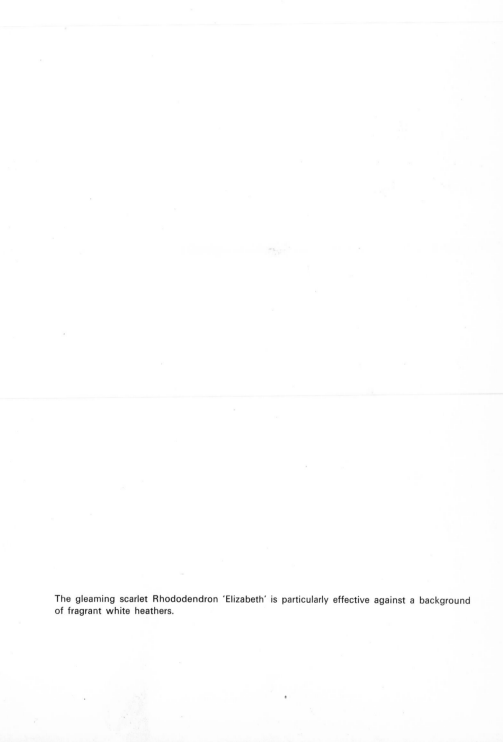

The gleaming scarlet Rhododendron 'Elizabeth' is particularly effective against a background of fragrant white heathers.

growing areas of the Pacific Northwest, where moist mild conditions are ideal and it is hardy in Zone 7.

Fortunately, R. ciliatum has proved an excellent parent, and by crossing it with hardier rhododendrons several first-class hybrids suitable for colder gardens have been produced. Particularly attractive is 'Racil', a cross with R. racemosum (itself a first-class pale-pink-flowered species), from which it derives hardiness and vigour. It has masses of compact trusses, pale pink flushed with deeper rose. 'Rosy Bell' is another delightful hybrid with a compact habit and slightly larger flowers. 'Cilpinense', an early Bodnant hybrid with tubular pinkish white flowers, is a gem for the rock garden. Its other parent is the January- and February-flowering R. moupinense, a charmer which forms a spreading shrub three to four feet high and even more across, which has small clusters of white-to-pink flowers with deep rosy-purple spotting which star the small gleaming leaves. It is hardy in Zone 7. It has been used as a parent for some lovely early hybrids, including 'Tessa' (deep lilac-pink and very early), 'Bric-a-Brac' (a dwarf white) and the soft cream, low-growing 'Bo-Peep'. The very early 'Praecox', is also a hybrid of R. ciliatum, as is 'Emasculum', which flowers later (March-April) and therefore is better suited to colder districts. Both have a profusion of lilac-pink flowers. Mature plants of the former grow to four or five feet, while plants of the latter are a little taller.

There are a number of fine blue hybrids, including the dwarf 'Bluebird', the taller, very fine 'Blue Diamond' (six to seven feet), 'Sapphire' and the sturdy, compact 'Blue Tit' (three to four feet), which is a rugged plant with neat trusses of deep violet blue flowers. All are hardy in Zone 7 and under favourable conditions in Zone 6.

One of the loveliest species is the April-flowering R. williamsianum. It forms a compact dome-shaped plant, seldom more than three to four feet in height, but rather more broad. The rounded heart-shaped leaves are of a delicate pale green, the new shoots and foliage being of a glorious purple-bronze. The pink bell-like flowers have particular refinement and grace. Plant it singly or in groups if you have a large rock garden, or at the front of a shrub border. There are delightful hybrids from it, and these are more floriferous than R. williamsianum, which in some gardens is a little shy of flower. Most of them are compact spreading bushes from four to six feet tall. These include 'Bow Bells' (rich crimson buds opening to bright pink flowers), 'Temple Belle' (rich rose flowers with fine foliage), and the delightfully named 'Humming Bird' (deep pink shaded crimson with dark foliage and a fine broadly mounded habit). All these are excellent plants for covering the ground. Like R. williamsianum, they are hardy in Zone 6 save 'Temple Belle' (Zone 7).

Yellow rhododendrons have a special charm, possibly because the yellows are cool and so often tinged with green. I am particularly fond of R. lutescens, which makes a large shrub up to ten feet tall with pale prim-rose flowers and gleaming bronze-coloured new foliage. Although it flowers as early as February and needs a sheltered position, it is hardy in Zone 7, with a long flowering season. A new early hardy hybrid of great interest is 'Chink', raised at Windsor by crossing R. keiskii and trichocladum. It is low-growing in habit with trusses of five flowers of pale clear yellow tinged with chartreuse green. Judging by its performance in the Savill Gardens at Windsor, where it flowers superbly

Rhododendron 'Rosy Bell', with its pale pink, pendulous flowers and glaucous foliage, is useful because of its spreading, mounded habit.

with early daffodils, it well deserved its Award of Merit in March 1961. I hope that it will be on the market in due course in this country.

There are many other yellows which include species like *R. caloxanthum, campylocarpum, litiense* and *wardii* and the giant *falconeri*, although the last fades to creamy white. There are also many hybrids, such as 'Fortune', 'Hawk', 'Dairy Maid', 'Damaris' (Logan form), 'Lady Bessborough', 'Letty Edwards', 'Mariloo' and the cream-coloured form of 'Penjerrick', surely one of the loveliest of all rhododendrons, but tender (Zone 9).

For the real enthusiast there are some excellent books. *The Rhododendron Handbook*, published by the Royal Horticultural Society in two parts, is invaluable as a reference for all serious gardeners. Part One (1967) is devoted to species with descriptions, awards, merit ratings, hardiness, etc.; Part Two (1969) deals with hybrids, giving parentage, as well as the material above. *Rhododendrons of the World*, by David Leach (Allen and Unwin, 1964), covers the field of rhododendrons in a very comprehensive way for both American and British gardeners. It is heavily illustrated and is a very useful book for amateurs and professionals alike, as there is a great deal of interesting material on cultivation, propagation, hybridization and other important subjects.

HARDY HYBRID RHODODENDRONS

No factor was to have a more electrifying effect on British gardens than the introduction of rhododendrons, including *Rhododendron maximum*, the Rose Bay of the Carolinas; the famous, and, to many gardeners, infamous *R. ponticum*, which took so kindly to conditions in the British Isles after its introduction from the Levant via Gibraltar in 1763 that today it seeds over vast areas; and finally the Himalayan *R. arboreum*, which flowered in England for the first time in 1825. Like *R. ponticum*, it has been a tremendous factor in rhododendron hybridization, as were *R. caucasicum, R. campanulatum* and *R. catawbiense*, which were three other early introductions. Using these as parents, the nurserymen of the nineteenth century produced a number of splendid hybrids which had stamina, beauty and a free-flowering habit. Many of them have survived the test of time and have found their way into our American gardens.

Today, hardy hybrids are very widely grown and in spite of the vast influx of new species from China and the Far East and the great range of exotic modern hybrids developed from them, there is still a demand for the old types of hybrids, which are good garden plants for the average garden.

Among the best of the old ironclad hardies suited to the extreme conditions of the Northeast are the following: red – 'Nova Zembla', 'America' and 'Charlie Dickens': pinks – 'Mrs C. S. Sargent', 'Roseum Elegans',

'Lady Armstrong', and 'Everestianum'; and whites – 'Catawbiense Album', 'Boule de Neige', and 'Album Elegans'. Slightly less hardy are the double soft mauve 'Fastuosum Plenum', the rose-pink 'Henrietta Sargent' and the striking 'Purple Splendour'. A number of the English hardy hybrids are excellent for the area which includes Philadelphia, New York and Long Island. 'Gomer Waterer', a white flushed pink; 'Azor', soft salmon; 'Blue Peter', more lavender than blue; 'Cynthia' warm rosy crimson; 'Mars' a rich dark red; 'Goldsworth Yellow', soft apricot; 'Bagshot Ruby', a fine crimson; 'Sappho', white with a dark blotch; 'Mrs P. D. Williams', ivory white with a brown spot; 'Mrs R. S. Holford', salmon-rose and many others.

Of unusual interest are the newer Dexter Hybrids which are proving remarkably hardy, raised by the late C. O. Dexter of Sandwich, Massachusetts, based on the fine collection of rhododendrons he amassed in his Cape Cod garden. Many of these compare favourably with the better British hybrids and are very widely planted in important collections open to the public. Gardeners near Washington, D.C., can see them at the National Arboretum along with a number of other of the finest introductions of both rhododendrons and azaleas. They can also see the many superb modern hybrids suited to semi-shaded positions in areas around Washington and the warmer parts of Maryland. These include some of the large-flowered very fragrant 'Loderi' clones, the pale yellow 'Lady Bessborough', the salmon-orange 'Fabia', the pink and cream 'Naomi' with its many clones, and the scarlet 'Britannia'.

ESSENTIALS FOR GOOD CULTIVATION It has long been established that rhododendrons need an acid soil with a pH of 5 or 5.5. Special attempts to grow rhododendrons on alkaline soils are sometimes successful for a few years, but unless they are grown on peat banks with no seepage from above, most varieties will 'go back' in time. What else do rhododendrons need for successful cultivation? Most of them prefer light shade, but the hardy hybrids flower best in sheltered fairly sunny positions but not full southern exposure, especially in warmer zones. Remember, however, that full sun in areas of high rainfall may suit a number of plants that prefer shade in drier, sunnier areas. Good drainage is essential. On heavy clay soils, or in areas of very high rainfall, it is sound practice to plant on low mounds and then to mulch the plants each year. When this is done, shrubs should be staked, as they are not as secure as when planted normally in the ground.

Wherever rhododendrons are sited, be sure to prepare the ground thoroughly and provide ample humus, either in the form of well-rotted leaf-mould, preferably from oak, beech or maple, but any deciduous trees are satisfactory, or peat. Avoid using the needles of

Evergreen skimmias, with their fragrant white flowers in spring and scarlet winter-berries, are underplanted with *Thlaspi cordifolia*, a little-used carpeter with clusters of white flowers.

coniferous trees. Peat is the ideal source of humus, and it should preferably be imported fibrous European peat rather than a fine granulated one. Peat is clean, easy to handle and relatively light. It is humus in an advanced state of decomposition and therefore more or less stable, not taking nitrogen from the soil as do partially decomposed mulches and manures. Peat should be thoroughly moistened before application or it acts rather like blotting paper, absorbing much-needed moisture from the rootball.

If peat or leaf-mould is not available, garden compost and old stable or farmyard manure are also satisfactory and of course these have nutritional value as well as providing humus. The hulls of buckwheat, beechnuts, peanuts and other organic roughage of this type will improve the texture of the soil and its moisture-retention properties, but they are second choices as they are not decomposed. The pros and cons of sawdust as a mulch have been weighed at length. Much depends on its age, texture, and the type of wood from which it comes. On the whole I do not favour the use of

it, even if old and well-weathered, for the private garden.

Peat is not a food and rhododendrons respond to feeding. Well-rotted manure is best, but coarse bone-meal, hoof and horn, dried blood after flowering, and the liquid-seaweed fertilizers are all useful where manure is not available. Recent extensive trials at the great rhododendron gardens and nurseries at Exbury in Hampshire conducted by the gardening staff in conjunction with scientific experts, have proved the desirability of the liberal use of peat at planting time and the importance of nutrition as well. This has been a valuable service with conclusive visual proof offered by the trials, showing the gratifying results in rate of growth and sturdy root-development, particularly with sphagnum peat.

SHALLOW PLANTING AND DEAD-HEADING Depth of planting is extremely important. Rhododendrons are shallow, surface-rooting shrubs. Never plant them more deeply than they were planted at the nursery. Water them well and do not allow them to dry out subsequently,

55

as the masses of fibrous hair-roots are so near the top of the ground. A mulch of leaf-mould, garden compost, or peat with well-rotted manure mixed with it will help to retain moisture. Bracken is excellent and is rich in potash. The depth of the mulch depends on its texture and the size of the plants.

Rhododendrons can be moved over a long period when not in active growth in late summer and autumn and planting can continue as long as the ground is open. Early spring is also an excellent time, particularly on the east coast and in inland districts where winters are severe. They will settle down and establish quickly, but they must be kept well watered through the summer and the roots must be moist when frost commences in the autumn. As rhododendrons are surface-rooting, the staking of large plants is essential in windy positions.

The dead-heading of spent flowers is essential, as the production of seeds saps the energy of the plant. In small gardens it should be routine practice, as it definitely increases flower production for the subsequent year and encourages uniform flowering.

Favourite Shrubs, Old and New

Each year sees the introduction of a number of new plants, and many gardeners are so busy looking for novelties that unusual plants of long standing are sometimes forgotten. A number of these new ones are always arresting and may in time prove to be all that they are claimed to be. Yet there are many old plants that are tried and true and merit attention, as they are of easy cultivation. I have a high regard for the old favourites as we know their needs and can count on their performance.

An excellent example is *Exochorda racemosa*, attractively referred to as the Pearl Bush because of its round white buds which resemble a spray of large graduated pearls. This shrub was introduced from Northern China by Robert Fortune in 1849. It forms a deciduous bush up to ten feet in height and of a rounded bushy nature, not unlike a mock orange which it resembles superficially. It blossoms in May, with a profusion of white flowers as much as one and a half inches across, borne in racemes of as many as ten. The result is a bush virtually white with bloom, but, alas, there is little, if any, fragrance. It is obligingly hardy (Zone 4).

Exochordas like rich loam or any good garden soil. They do not like shallow chalky soil, but may be grown on alkaline soil, if well fed and provided with plenty of humus. As sun is important, exochordas should be grown in a sunny border or, better still, on their own, either in a group of three or five or as single specimens, when they are particularly attractive, as the full effect of the flower-laden bush can be enjoyed.

There has been a tendency of late to plant shrubs in beds or continuous borders to avoid specimens in the lawn and to simplify mowing and edging. A splendid solution is to grow shrubs in rough grass through which a mown path winds. Exochordas should be carefully pruned after flowering by thinning out weak shoots to provide an abundance of short flower-bearing laterals, borne on the hard wood of the previous year, and by removing any spent old growths. There are several other species and the excellent hybrid E. × *macrantha*, raised by the great French hybridizer Victor Lemoine of Nancy, also famous for his paeonies, lilacs and ceanothus. In some catalogues *E. racemosa* is listed as *E. grandiflora*.

Another shrub with attractive white flowers is *Rhodotypos kerrioides*, erect in habit and seldom more than six feet in height. The four-petalled flowers, borne at the ends of short twiggy growths, are sometimes as much as two inches across and have a rather longer blooming period than those of exochordas. They start in May and flower through June and, spasmodically, in July. Black berries in small clusters follow. It is an easy shrub to propagate from half-ripened cuttings inserted in sand with bottom heat. It can also be raised from seed. Like *Kerria*, which it resembles, it is native to China and Japan and requires full sun and loamy soil. It is sometimes called Black Jetbead.

The Fringe Tree is another shrub or small tree, too little known. There are two species of the genus *Chionanthus*, not to be confused with *Chimonanthus*, the deliciously fragrant, yellow-flowered Winter Sweet. It is odd that with only two species, *Chionanthus virginica* should be an American native (Zone 4), while *C. retusa* comes from China. Both are beautiful when covered with a profusion of drooping panicles of white flowers with linear petals about an inch long, which produce a fringe effect. *Chionanthus virginica*, grown by Thomas Jefferson at Monticello, has rather longer panicles, sometimes as much as four to eight inches long, which are borne so freely in July that an established shrub or tree is a cloud of flower. There is only a slight fragrance, but then we cannot have everything. There are good specimens at Kew. It likes sun and hot weather, which possibly explains why it is so spectacular as a shrub in the United States and Southern Europe. As *C. virginica* is rather the better species of the two, it is the one usually listed by nurseries: *C. retusa* is seldom seen.

An even lovelier shrub and one well suited to our climate is *Staphylea*, commonly referred to as the Bladder Nut, a name suggested by the inflated membraneous seed-pods. All species require good soil, a fair amount of moisture in spring, and sunshine. The foliage is beautiful, attractively divided into three or five leaflets, and the new growths are often tinged with rose or

The creamy-white flower-heads of *Viburnum tomentosum* make a bold effect in May, and in the autumn the heavily ribbed leaves turn a rich red, tinged with bronze.

copper. *Staphylea colchica*, indigenous to the Southern Caucasus, makes a broad shrub about six to eight feet in height, with erect panicles of creamy white flowers at the end of the numerous young shoots which appear in May or early June. The flowers have a curiously sweet fragrance, reminiscent of that candy inextricably linked with childhood, coconut-ice. *Staphylea colchica* is therefore a plant of memories, for nothing is as nostalgic to me as the sudden scent of flowers, recalling faraway places and all the other associations, automatically set in motion by a single sniff (Zone 6).

Better known is *S. pinnata*, which, in time, grows into a small tree with drooping panicles which are rather smaller than *S. colchica*, but very freely produced with large inflated seed-pods (Zone 5). It is native to Europe. Loveliest of all is *S. holocarpa* var. *rosea*, which has pendulous, soft rose-pink flowers in graceful drooping corymbs. It was collected in Central China by E. H. Wilson, who, even at the time of its introduction in 1908, had very high hopes for it, and how right he was. It is definitely a plant for a warm sunny position in a mild area, where it will gradually form a small tree of character. It grows particularly well in a

garden on highly alkaline soil near the coast. Granted that the trees have been well cared for over the years and are sheltered from gales off the sea, but they flower in great profusion. Today the specimens are about eighteen feet tall, and this is interesting because, contrary to popular belief, they seem as happy on chalk as they do on lime-free soil. Incidentally, there is also a tree of *Chionanthus retusa* in the same garden now thirty feet high, so perhaps we can say the same for this plant. With all the various gardens that are open to visitors, we have a wonderful opportunity to observe for ourselves the growth of plants on special soils. Proof is surely the best guide to what to grow in our gardens.

Finally, to close this short list of uncommon white-flowered shrubs, there are two little-known species of the otherwise well-known *Deutzia* family, and unlike the preceding examples, these two deutzias, while tolerating sun, are happier in partial shade and even grow well under a tree canopy.

Firstly, there is *D. pulchra*, which can grow to as high as eight or ten feet in sheltered positions. It has exquisite waxy white flowers with orange stamens like

57

drooping spikes of lily of the valley in late June and July. It also has striking orange-brown peeling stems, which are attractive in winter, especially against a dark background. It is a native of Formosa. Secondly, there is the much dwarfer *Deutzia setchuenensis corymbiflora*, which has small, neat, greyish leaves and three-to-four-inch wide corymbs of tiny dazzling white stars. It begins to flower in July and lasts for six weeks or more in shade. It is a native of Szechuen and Hupeh in China. Both these deutzias should be planted where they are protected from early morning sun, as they are subject to injury by late spring frosts.

So much for a few plants introduced a long time ago, which I feel should now be better known. Let us now consider two or three plants of recent introduction. Near the top of any list comes the hybrids of *Rhododendron yakusimanum*, a compact shrub with pale rose flowers, which is proving a most excellent parent, as it imparts its dwarf, compact, free-flowering habit to its progeny. Its hybrids are ideally suited to the small garden, whether in town or country, and their relatively large showy trusses of flowers come in a wide range of colours, including pale pinks, rose and deeper reds. So far, only a few cultivars have been named, and the supply is limited, but in the next few years numerous named varieties should become available.

A shrubby potentilla in the orange range is certainly a new break. It is called 'Tangerine', and there is no doubt that it will be a success. A word of caution, however – it needs half-shade and a relatively moist position if it is to retain its full colour. Lovely as 'Tangerine' is, I still think that *Potentilla arbuscula*, *vilmoriniana* and 'Katherine Dykes' are the outstanding plants of the genus in our gardens today. They are free-flowering over a very long season and have both clarity of colour and an excellent habit. All are hardy (Zone 4).

One of the best shrubs of recent introduction is *Rubus* 'Tridel'. It is a cross between *R. deliciosus*, a hardy native of the Rocky Mountains, and *R. trilobus*, a relatively new, fairly hardy Mexican species. It has pure white single flowers as much as three inches in diameter with a gleaming golden boss of stamens and foliage similar to that of the latter species. After the profusion of flowers, borne in the leaf axils all along the arching stems in late May and June, have finished the bush should be pruned to encourage side-shoots which will bear flowers the following year. Sometimes young plants are so lax in growth that it helps to support the main branches with a stake or frame. With pruning, they soon form mounded spreading bushes as much as eight to nine feet across. Give this shrub good garden soil in full sun or light shade. It does not like a heavily alkaline soil, but is perfectly happy on moderate ones. It is a good shrub with which to cover large areas and it certainly deserves wider recognition.

Lilacs and Mock Orange for Fragrance

Lilacs are such wonderfully fragrant shrubs that we well understand Redouté's love for them in his paintings. It is often said that double lilacs are more fragrant than single ones. For this I cannot vouch, but with the mass of extra petals it seems possible.

One of my great favourites is 'Katherine Havemeyer', an old hybrid raised in France by that great hybridizer of lilacs, Louis Lemoine. It appeared about 1922, and to my mind is still one of the finest of all lilacs, as it has very large double pips carried in heavy, densely packed trusses with a very delicious scent. Best of all is its deep lavender colour flushed with purple, just as a lilac should be. Another lovely double raised by Lemoine and of even earlier introduction (1909) is 'Madame A. Buchner', a semi-double of a delicate rose with a mauve glow. The trusses are graceful and tapered and their fragrance is superb. It makes a tall bush with a rather open habit. Of the double whites, 'Madame

A heavily scented French lilac such as the double white 'Souvenir d'Alice Harding' should be planted in every garden where space permits.

Lemoine' is my favourite, and it well deserves its Award of Garden Merit as it makes a broad sturdy bush and produces an abundance of well-formed compact trusses with large pips.

Of the wide choice of single whites, certainly 'Maud Notcutt', introduced in 1956, is the finest, with its beautifully spaced flowers in very large trusses. It is vigorous, making a tall upright shrub. Other fine singles of recent introduction include 'Clarke's Giant', with huge trusses of large pips, pinkish in bud, opening to clear lavender; 'Esther Staley', a floriferous single pink of great beauty; and 'Blue Hyacinth', all raised in California.

For those who love huge flower-heads and very large single pips, the deep purplish red 'Massena' is out-standing, although to my mind the flowers are too large, as the trusses tend to droop in wet weather. There are, of course, many other fine hybrid lilacs from which to choose. All are hardy in Zone 3.

Too many of us concentrate on the French hybrid lilacs, forgetting the exquisite grace of *Syringa micro-*

'Virginale' is a fine, fragrant double Mock Orange which obligingly grows in sun or shade and on acid, neutral or alkaline soils.

The tapered trusses of the Canadian 'Preston Hybrids' are in striking contrast to the French. Good varieties include 'Bellicent' and 'Fountain'.

phylla superba, which produces two- to four-inch panicles of small, rosy-lilac flowers in late spring; in good years this exceptional lilac may well grace the garden with a partial second flush in late August or September. It is very sweet-scented, but with a fragrance quite different from the French hybrid lilacs. The leaves are less coarse, smaller in size and almost orbicular in shape. The bushes are broad and spreading and usually not more than five to six feet tall. It is charming for a small garden and can even be used to form a floriferous loose un-clipped hedge. Groups of it combine happily with early-flowering roses, such as *Rosa hugonis, cantabrigiensis, xanthina* and its lovely form, 'Canary Bird'.

Another charmer is the white Persian lilac, *Syringa persica alba*, which has a neat compact habit, forming a rounded bush about six feet high and seven to eight feet across. As the leaves are narrow and lance-shaped with a tapered tip, the foliage has a much lighter though denser appearance than other lilacs. The pure white flowers are carried on rounded panicles about three inches long and as much across. Persian lilacs are sweetly scented. The type form is the usual mauve colour, but variety *alba* is far more attractive.

These two species add immeasurably to the charm of a garden and blend perfectly into shrubberies. Lilacs with daffodils, fruit trees and possibly mock orange and shrub-roses are particularly useful for developing areas which are to be rough-mown. Trees or shrubs with a pendulous or weeping habit must, of course, stand alone and I like to see a huge bush of lilac standing on its own so that I can walk round it, enjoying its shape and natural habit. This is particularly true of various other shrubs, such as the varietal forms of *Viburnum tomentosum* ('Mariesii', 'Lanarth' or 'Rowallane'), Rose 'Nevada' and 'Celestial'. Even in borders it is possible to plan so that shrubs such as these are isolated with low ground-cover around them.

After lilacs have finished flowering, the flower-heads should be removed and if there are long extended growths it is advisable to shorten them by cutting back just above a pair of growth-buds. Weak or misshapen branches should also be eliminated. Drastic pruning is better done in winter when plants are dormant. Remember that by the pruning of terminal growths the number of flower-trusses will be decreased the following year, but with old bushes it is often necessary to reduce their size, and this will result in heavier bloom.

For fragrance lilacs have few rivals, but certainly philadelphus, the syringa or mock orange of gardens, is a runner-up, and its season mercifully follows that of the lilacs, so that their quite different perfumes can be enjoyed separately.

Here I have a definite preference for the singles, but this enthusiasm is not generally shared, as double varieties are perhaps more spectacular and possibly last a little longer in bloom. The most popular double philadelphus is 'Virginal', which has huge panicles of large, pure white, doulbe flowers on a six- to eight-foot shrub. Its abundance of blooms with their sweet scent has very rightly won it an Award of Garden Merit as a first-class flowering shrub for gardens (Zone 5).

A much smaller plant and therefore ideal for small gardens is 'Manteau d'Hermine', which has very fragrant double flowers borne in profusion on a compact bush seldom exceeding three to four feet. Other good doubles include 'Bouquet Blanc', 'Norma' and 'Enchantment', which is similar to 'Virginal' but claimed to be superior to it by one of the leading nurserymen. A double of American origin, with the amusing name 'Minnesota Snowflake', is a fine shrub for large shrubberies. All are hardy in Zone 5.

The singles are my real love. I am fascinated by the neat, four-petalled symmetry of the small cup-shaped flowers of species such as *P. coronarius* or its golden-leaved variety (var. *aureus*), which is so useful among the different greens, or the lovely *P. delavayi* 'Nymans', with its long racemes of cup-shaped flowers, each with a frosted blue-grey calyx. Although it develops into a very large shrub, it is well worth the room for its fine flowers and exquisite scent. Then there are a number of singles with a purple or rose-coloured blotch at the base of the petals. The old variety 'Belle Étoile', which grows to six to eight feet with a lovely arching habit, is still one of the best; its fragrance is superb and it flowers in great profusion. 'Beauclerk' has much larger white flowers, flushed with rosy pink at the base and very sweetly scented and is similar in size and habit to 'Belle Étoile'.

'Velleda', which has charming white flowers with crimped petals and a sweet scent, is a little less tall but broader in habit, while 'Silver Showers' is a rather erect shrub about three to four feet tall with cup-shaped scented flowers borne in profusion. 'Purpureo-maculatus' is about the same height, but of a dense well-branched habit with white petals stained purple at the base, as the name implies. The smallest treasure of all is *P. microphyllus*, which has a twiggy compact habit, tiny leaves, and small, intensely fragrant, perfectly formed flowers in great profusion. It is in my opinion the most fragrant of all, and though unspectacular it should have a place in gardens whether large or small. Yes, on balance, the singles have my vote.

Mock oranges should be pruned after flowering by thinning out old wood. Beware of blackfly on new growths which will appear in midsummer, as mock oranges are prone to play host, expecially on new growths. Spray at once with liquid DDT or reliable proprietary products.

The Mexican Orange Blossom

The delights of May crowd one upon another so closely that it is hard to comprehend them all and often familiar plants are neglected for the more exotic ones. It is the month in which *Choisya ternata*, the Mexican orange blossom, is in full flower against the south wall of my courtyard. Above it the first flowers of the wistaria are opening and soon there will be a curtain of shimmering racemes of pale lavender. Choisya is an excellent foil, with its gleaming evergreen foliage and large clusters of pure white, five-petalled flowers, each with a crown of white stamens tipped gold, surrounding a green eye. These are deliciously fragrant, particularly on a warm sunny day. The foliage itself is highly aromatic, and although some people find it unpleasant, I am fond of its astringent, slightly antiseptic smell. The terminal clusters are made up of five or six separate cymes, each bearing a similar number of flowers grouped round a central growth-bud. Usually,

Rose 'Scarlet Fire', which grows into a large spreading shrub covered with dazzling scarlet flowers touched with flame, should satisfy the lover of the brightest colours. The large pear-shaped heps last for many weeks.

Choisya ternata is useful evergreen shrub for sunny walls, with white, star-like flowers in early summer and glistening aromatic foliage.

as the flowers open, this bud develops into a central tuft of small glistening leaves, each with a prominent rib of very pale green. The mature leaves, made up of three leaflets, have great character. Choisyas are most satisfactory evergreen foliage plants, and I like to cut sprays of green throughout the year for the house.

This handsome shrub has a good habit, forming a rounded mass, branching at ground-level. In time it will reach a height of six to nine feet and will be even more across. As choisya is a native of Mexico, it is remarkable that it is hardy in Zone 7. Choisyas are a bit temperamental, withstanding severe frosts and yet being cut back badly in less severe weather. Its foliage is a pleasant contrast in shape to camellias and *Pittosporum tobira*, two of the best evergreen shrubs in milder zones. Choisyas are not particular as to soil, tolerating both lime and chalk, but they demand good drainage. I prefer to plant choisyas in the spring, and as plants are pot-grown they can be planted when available, even in summer. If planted in the autumn they should be given protection, until they are established, by stretching old sacking or polythene on a wooden frame over them during cold spells. The foliage is often burnt in a bad winter, but as soon as the new leaves break in spring the brown ones are shed and no harm is done, although there may be an untidy period. In several gardens I know, established plants are protected in winter with small sections of hurdle or interwoven fencing. This breaks the wind and gives much-needed shelter.

Choisyas should be pruned immediately after flowering to shape the bush and reduce excessive growth. In winter, if long branches are broken by snow, it may be necessary to cut them back in February. A few flower-clusters in a vase make a charming small arrangement and larger sprays are ideal with narcissus or tulips. The rather leafy branching habit makes short stems or branches particularly easy to arrange. Choisyas provide a delightful evergreen flowering hedge for a sunny protected position in a mild garden, while in warm areas it obligingly grows in shady positions as well.

Escallonias for Many Purposes

Evergreen flowering shrubs are always of interest to the gardener. Few have a wider variety of used than the various escallonias, though they are not as boldly spectacular at any given moment as rhododendrons or evergreen azaleas. For many years, this South American evergreen has been associated primarily with coastal areas and the milder climates; not without reason, as the large-leaved escallonias stand up to the salt-laden gales and have proved a superb hedge for a windbreak. They have also been used extensively in many parts of the country as wall-shrubs, as they lend themselves to training and clipping and, of course, enjoy the added shelter provided. The lustrous green leaves and masses of small flowers in high summer provide a good show, and with trimming and removal of the spent flower-heads their season can be prolonged into the late summer and autumn.

Chile is the principal home of escallonias, and therefore it seems strange that this family of shrubs should prove as hardy as it does, for in sunny positions it has proved hardy in Zones 7 and 8, and withstood heavy frost. In some gardens escallonias are killed back to the ground, but spring to life from the roots with renewed vigour and seem the better for nature's pruning.

One of the splendid things about escallonias is the fact that although they grow well on acid soils they are particularly good on alkaline ones. In cold areas they are best on light, well-drained soil, but in milder areas they thrive in shade or sun, often with a great deal of

61

moisture, as the prevalence of escallonias hedges in the west coast of Ireland, in Cornwall and parts of Scotland proves so abundantly. Escallonias resent root-disturbance, so many nurseries sell them in pots. In our own gardens, plants, if moved with care, will be none the worse. Established plants, however, need to be lifted with as large a root-ball as possible, or they may die back at the ends of the branches.

The individual flowers are small and not very exciting. Escallonias, in fact, belong to the saxifrage family, so we can hardly expect spectacular individual flowers. It is in their quantity that they become so effective. Also, the gleaming leaves make a wonderful foil for the white, rose or red flowers. The pleasant arching habit is another merit.

The name of the Slieve Donard Nursery Company in Northern Ireland at Newcastle in County Down, is synonymous with the history of escallonia hybrids, as in the 'twenties and 'thirties a series of excellent clones were developed from various species, including *E. rubra punctata* and the hardy but deciduous *E. virgata*, which provided stamina and hardiness to many crosses. Among the outstanding hybrids are 'Donard Seedling', which was one of the earliest introductions with apple-blossom pink flowers in abundance. It is vigorous, growing to eight or nine feet, and makes a fine hedge. 'Slieve Donard', very hardy with larger pink flowers but less tall (five to seven feet), is excellent for hedging. 'Apple Blossom' is one of the best known; it is free-flowering in June and July and has a vigorous, compact, bushy habit, making it suitable for small or medium-sized gardens. The new 'Peach Blossom' is similar except for colour. Of similar parentage and with the same compact habit are the deep pink 'Donard Radiance', the new and very large-flowered rose-pink 'Donard Star', and the clear, soft red 'Pride of Donard'. Escallonias lend themselves to pruning and therefore can be kept in check.

For a wall I am very fond of the old *E. × iveyi*, which originated at Caerhays in Cornwall as a chance seedling and is believed to be a hybrid between *E. exoniensis* and *E. montevidensis*. It is a little tender, so it needs a warm sunny wall. The panicles of white flowers from July to September and the extra large, dark green burnished leaves make a fine show. It is definitely not for exposed cold sites. *Escallonia montevidensis* is a lovely white-flowered species for mild localities. These are reliably hardy in Zone 9.

Escallonia hedges are excellent. The plants should not be closer than two feet apart and two and a half feet will be satisfactory for most varieties. Hedges of *E. macrantha* are particularly good by the sea. The flowers are bright red with large, tough foliage which makes a very good windbreak. The hybrid *E. × ingramii* also makes an excellent hedge for maritime districts,

as does 'C. F. Ball', another tall crimson hybrid, while 'Donard Seedling' makes a graceful arching hedge. Varieties such as 'Apple Blossom' and 'Pride of Donard' can be used for compact neat hedges. Pruning should generally be done after flowering, but 'Apple Blossom' and allied varieties can be pruned lightly in early spring. In cold districts spring planting is preferable, but if autumn planting is necessary the plants should have winter protection until they are established. A wind-break of hessian, polythene or bracken is suitable. Escallonias are easily propagated from short half-ripened growths, preferably with a heel, taken in August. These should be inserted in a light, sandy compost in a closed frame with a little heat or a glass-covered box.

Escallonias are not essentially long-lived plants. All too often we see leggy specimens in old neglected gardens. Like mock oranges, it may be worth cutting them back drastically in the hope that they will break from the bottom. I hope escallonias will receive the notice they deserve in this country, especially in the North-west where the climate is ideal for their cultivation.

Spiraeas Big and Little

Pink and red are always popular colours in the garden and when the shrubs flower in midsummer, as do some of the spiraeas, so much the better. Spiraeas are an attractive family with a long flowering season starting in March or April with the fragile beauty of *Spiraea thunbergii*, which bears such a profusion of tiny white flowers along the wiry stems that the bush becomes a dome of feathery white, followed a little later by *S. vanhouttei*, which bears a prodigous number of small, flat, white clusters. Both are hardy in Zone 4.

In high summer *S. japonica (bumalda)* is still in full bloom, the broad clusters of raspberry-red having first appeared towards the end of June. Its best form is 'Anthony Waterer', with brilliant carmine-red flowers. Here is a shrub ideally suited to town gardens, as it grows only to about four feet and is tolerant of some shade, although it flowers splendidly in full sun. It is not particular as to soil, but obviously the flowers last far longer on a slightly moist one. The foliage often shows variegation, but with no consistency, a branch here and there showing pink and creamy-white feathering while the rest of the foliage is green. I think it best to thin out a few of the old growths after flowering, leaving the strong younger ones and at the same time cutting off spent flower-heads. Then in March the shrub can be hard-pruned, if it is not compact or getting too large for its position in the garden. An abundance of flowers will result.

There are dwarf forms of *Spiraea japonica (bumalda)* listed by various nurseries. A form known as *alpina* is listed by a few nurseries. This is a treasure, with its low cushion habit three to four feet across and not more than two feet in height, studded with flowers of a warm rose-pink. It is a good shrub for the front of a border. With its lovely grey foliage it can be grouped with old shrub-roses or floribundas, particularly those in shades of red, purple, mauve and pink. As it flowers in June and July, sometimes lasting into August, it can be used with yellow *Potentilla arbuscula* or for an even stronger colour contrast with *Hypericum moserianum* or the taller *H.* 'Hidcote'. *Spiraea bullata*, a very slow-growing, compact Japanese species reaching only fifteen inches in height, is ideal for the rock garden. Its crimped leaves and crimson-rose flowers through June and July provide a striking patch of colour.

There is a group of tall-growing but extremely elegant spiraeas including *S. canescens* (syn. *flagelliformis*), *henryi*, *nipponica* (syn. *bracteata*), *trichocarpa* and *veitchii*, that flower in late June and early July. They are all very similar, so for the average small garden one does service for them all. The six- to eight-foot erect brown shoots of one season give rise during the next one to short horizontal laterals, each of which is crowned with dense corymbs of cream-coloured flowers. When the whole shrub is one arching mass of bloom, few subjects are more lovely in high summer. To appreciate their elegant shape to the fullest, these spiraeas are best planted as isolated specimens on lawns or in rough grass.

Several larger shrubs outstanding in midsummer are now listed as *Sorbaria* instead of *Spiraea*, as they once were, but not all catalogues accept this change. These have graceful pinnate foliage, rather like huge ash leaves, and a charming arching habit. They like moisture and are tolerant of shade, if it is not too dense. *Sorbaria aitchisonii* is my favourite, with immense panicles of white, like some fantastic feathery lilac. It grows to a height of nine feet and can be pruned to attractive arching shapes. As new growths are produced from the base, cut out old growths immediately after flowering or the shrub can become leggy. Some gardeners prefer to cut the stems back to the base in early March, but then, of course, a smaller shrub will result. The attractive reddish-brown stems add interest to the winter garden. Recently I saw a lovely group arching over the edge of a stream.

For large gardens *Sorbaria arborea* is magnificent and will reach a height of twelve to fourteen feet. The big panicles of white flowers are borne on three- to four-foot stems, and there is a curious rhythmic harmony in the foliage, the flowers and the habit of the shrub. Both these species are rapid growers and useful for an immediate effect the first year. They are rather like buddleia hybrids in this respect. *Holodiscus*

Sorbaria arborea, with its fern-like leaves and huge panicles of ivory-white flowers, growing by a path in a cottage garden.

discolor is another July-flowering shrub worth mentioning, as it bears resemblance to spiraeas and more particularly to sorbarias. It is tall (ten to twelve feet) with long drooping panicles of feathery creamy-white flowers at the tips of spreading arching branches. The big silver-backed leaves are striking when rustled by the wind.

Aruncus sylvester, though not a shrub, must be mentioned too, as it is akin. Goat's Beard, as it is so charmingly called, is a vigorous herbaceous plant with creamy-white plumes of flowers on branching five-foot stems in early summer. Clumps are lovely in a large herbaceous border, in a shrubbery, by the side of a stream or in a woodland garden.

Buddleias for Butterflies

After the wealth of flowering shrubs in spring and early summer, I often hear the complaint that there are too few for high summer and early autumn. This is hardly fair, when we consider the splendour of hydrangeas, perowskias, caryopteris, hibiscus, crape myrtles, hypericums, potentillas, vitexes and a number of others, including the showy and fragrant buddleias.

Buddleias are always associated in my mind with hot afternoons, when their honeyed scent earns them the name of Summer Lilac, and moths and butterflies hover around them. They are obliging shrubs, as they grow very quickly, making a good show in a border or shrubbery in their first season. Moreover, as they are raised in pots, they have a long planting season and can be purchased at the last moment if there are gaps or failures. One of my favourites is the very graceful, wide-spreading *Buddleia alternifolia*, with its delicate, long, arching stems, wreathed throughout the early summer with flat heads of sweetly-scented, mauve flowers. Plants often look spindly and unpromising when received from the nursery, but they will develop in time after a slow start. The secret is to allow them a great deal of room for full development. They are most striking if grown alone or in groups in the grass, either as bushes or as standards. Then their true grace can be appreciated far more than if grown in a border, crowded in among other shrubs or herbaceous plants (Zone 5). There are a number of named varieties of *B. davidii*, which flower continuously from mid-July until well into September. Colours vary and new introductions appear at frequent intervals. There are several good whites, including 'Peace', 'White Cloud' and 'White Profusion'; a clear pink called 'Fascination'; purples which includ 'Black Knight'; a fine new dark violet 'Ile de France', 'Purple Prince' and the popular reddish-purple 'Royal Red'. Then there are the lilac and bluish-mauves such as 'Empire Blue' and 'Fortune'. They are hardy in Zone 5.

Buddleia × weyeriana, a little-known hybrid of *globosa* and *davidii*, bears tight clusters of orange flowers shaded with mauve in August.

Varieties of *Buddleia davidii*, in colours ranging from white and mauve to deep red and violet, are most useful shrubs of summer.

Perhaps the finest hardy buddleia is *B. fallowiana* and its white form *alba*. I like the felted white leaves and stems which lend interest and contrast to any border. The long slender spikes are fragrant and the delicate mauve is perfect with the silvery foliage. Another fascinating species is the spring-flowering *B. caryopteridifolia*, which has the under-sides of the leaves, the young shoots and stems covered with white wool and the leaves are irregular and interesting in shape. Although this species is more tender than many, needing a warm climate or the protection of a sunny wall, its panicles of fragrant mauve flowers are freely borne in a number of gardens which are subject to ten or fifteen degrees of frost. Long hot sunny dry summers ripen growth, thereby enabling the plant to withstand winter-cold. Prune after flowering. *Buddleia crispa*, which is similar, is another tender treasure (Zone 8).

The largest flowers of all buddleias are to be found on *B. colvilei*, a Himalayan species with large drooping panicles of deep rose or reddish-maroon flowers. It grows to the size of a small tree, and although this magnificent shrub is not considered hardy, I am continually amazed at the gardens where it flourishes. The finest plant I have ever seen was in a well-known garden near Perth in Scotland, where in late July a broad spreading shrub of tree-like proportions, covered with a spectacular display of rich rose-red flowers, changed my evaluation of it. I was told that the secret is never to prune heavily and therefore it should not be grown against a wall, where it must be continually reduced in size to keep it under control, but in a sheltered position in the open, as it was at the top of a glen in light woodland at Glendoick. As there is considerable variation in the colour and size of the individual flowers of *B. colvilei*, it is worth while tracking down the best form. *Buddleia colvilei kewensis* has maroon-coloured flowers several shades darker than the type.

Anothet tender buddleia suitable only for the mildest areas or a cool greenhouse is the evergreen *B. auriculata*, native to South Africa. It has intensely sweetly-scented flowers in rounded panicles. These are creamy white with a golden throat. The shrubs, often as much as six to eight feet tall and the same across, have a pleasantly lax habit and are attractive if trained against a sunny wall or planted in a mass.

I have forgotten *Buddleia globosa* with its round balls of orange-yellow flowers borne on an open branching shrub, ten to twelve feet tall and as much across. This native of Chile and Peru, hardy in Zone 7, flowers in very late spring. Plant it with blue anchusas and blue bearded irises.

The summer-flowering buddleias, including *B. fallowiana* and varieties of *B. davidii*, should be pruned in February, as they flower on new wood. It pays to be drastic with them, cutting back the long flowering shoots to three or four buds from the base of the old wood. Buddleias which flower in late spring or early summer, such as *B. alternifolia, caryopteridifolia, farreri* and *crispa*, should be pruned as soon as they have flowered. *Buddleia davidii* and its varieties are propagated from hard wood cuttings taken in late autumn and winter. These can be inserted in the open ground in a sheltered position or in a frame. Other buddleias are best propagated from short, half-ripened side-shoots, taken in late summer.

The Fascination of Fuchsias

Fuchsias have a particular appeal for almost everyone. For some it is the wonderful colouring of reds, purples, pinks, mauves and whites or the delicate poise of the pendulous flowers. For others it is the nostalgia evoked for the fuchsias of old-fashioned gardens, conservatories opening off the drawing-room, or the charming winter gardens and display greenhouses which belonged to the Victorian and Edwardian eras. There are few lovers of flowers who do not experience a keen thrill of pleasure from the grace and airiness of the delicate pendulous flowers, quivering with each breath of wind. It is not surprising that they bear such names as 'Ballet Girl', 'Fascination', 'Flying Cloud', 'Swingtime', 'Melody' and 'Tennessee Waltz', for in their way they almost have the gaiety and quality of music, which more than compensates for their lack of fragrance, to me a black mark against any flower.

Since fuchsias enjoyed such enormous popularity in the past, it is a satisfaction that once again they are basking in grace and favour in gardens, large and small, public and private. For summer display they are rivalled only by geraniums. Fuchsias are delightful in beds in a paved garden, planted so that the graceful spreading branches and pendulous flowers are silhouetted against the grey stone. I like to fill lead vases with them as the purples, pinks and rich reds are effective against the dull grey surface. Add touches of silver foliage such as *Helichrysum petiolatum* with its graceful trailing habit. I do not like fuchsias and geraniums in combination. One spoils the other.

Fuchsias fall into two groups – the hardy and the tender. The former will flourish without protection in mild areas, but in winter need a four- to six-inch layer of cinders or mulch on the crowns in colder, less-favoured ones. It is remarkable how hardy they have proved in Britain and we should experiment with them in mild zones. On the West Coast of Scotland and in Ireland fuchsia hedges are a familiar sight, and it is not uncommon to see fuchsias growing to the eaves of a two-storey house. *Fuchsia magellanica* is a

The creamy-white and cerise 'Mrs Marshall' typifies the grace and elegance of single fuchsias, whether grown in pots or in open ground.

hardy graceful shrub with many varietal forms, the best of which is var. *riccartonii* with tube and sepals of gleaming red and a purple corolla. It will withstand rigorous pruning and propagates easily from cuttings. Less spectacular is *F. gracilis*, which makes up in quantity of bloom for the rather more diminutive size of the flowers, which are borne in groups of two or three at every joint of the stem. It grows to five or even seven feet in mild areas.

Other excellent hardy varieties include the familiar 'Mrs Popple', whose full-skirted bells are a rich contrast of violet and carmine; 'Madame Cornelissen', with large semi-double blooms consisting of white petals and reflexing rose-carmine sepals; 'Margaret', which is a delightful combination of carmine and Parma-violet; 'Lena', a free-flowering variety with flesh-pink sepals and a mauve skirt, in subtle harmony; and 'Graf Witte'. Among the best of the dwarf varieties are 'Alice Hofman', 'Dunrobin

Bedder' and 'Pumila', excellent for bedding or the rock garden. None of these exceed ten inches in height.

The choice of non-hardy varieties is bewildering, and they can be grown in a variety of forms. Needless to say, good standards and large pyramids are scarce; moreover, they are not easy plants to pack and deliver. However, they have a special charm in that the flowers are at eye-level, so that one sees their full beauty. This is the reason why hanging baskets of fuchsias are so effective. For this purpose use 'Cascade' (white and carmine), the self-red 'Marinka', 'Sensation', 'Trail Blazer', 'Glad Rags', and 'San Mateo'. Fuchsias are also effective in the front of window-boxes, in large pots or tubs, and as pot-plants in brackets against sheltered walls of roof gardens and terraces. Furthermore, they are superb as house-decoration, but should not be left indoors too long. Their uses, as we see, are legion.

Fuchsias need a rich potting compost, made from fibrous loam with leaf-mould or peat, and in order to flower freely they profit by an occasional feeding with liquid manure. They are good plants, as they grow in both sun or half-shade. The wintering of tender fuchsias is not difficult as long as the pots can be placed in a frost-free shed, garage, cellar or coldhouse. They need to be kept relatively dry until early spring, then pruned back hard and moved into a warm house, where they will soon burst into leaf. Just as they start to grow, they benefit from repotting with fresh soil. Cuttings root easily and relatively quickly. These can be taken at almost any season, but preferably in spring or late summer. Select strong flower-free shoots. Although fuchsias can be grown from seeds, named varieties can only be propagated from cuttings.

Fuchsias, particularly in pots or tubs, need ample water and food, as they are voracious and need constant sustenance to ensure the masses of flowers, which come in a series of flushes. How often pots will have to be watered will depend on the nature of the container, the compost used and, of course, the weather. Examine them each day, watering as necessary. Liquid fertilizers are excellent at fortnightly intervals. General-purpose fertilizer is also suitable for beds and borders of this lovely plant.

Of the varieties available, 'Flying Cloud' is white with a pale flush of pink at the base of the tube. 'Swingtime' is a full double with a white skirt, veined cerise to match the brilliant tube and sepals. 'Coachman' is a striking salmon and orange blend, while 'Bridesmaid' is very pale pink with a semi-double corolla of pale mauve. 'Marin Glow' is enchanting, with the tube and sepals of white and a blue corolla, flushed purple. There are endless other colour combinations for the enthusiast. It is interesting that other genera have flowers resembling fuchsias in appearance. My favourite is *Ribes speciosum*, a striking plant with ever-green leaves and clusters of brilliant red pendulous flowers, followed by small gooseberry-like fruits. How right is its vernacular name, the Fuchsia-flowered Gooseberry. Another is the charming *Begonia fuchsioides*, which is covered with a shower of gleaming red flowers over a long season in California and frost-free districts only.

Fuchsias can be trained as standards, half-standards, pyramids, fans, and even to form arches and arbours. Skilled pruning, stopping, tying-in, and above all, good cultivation with correct watering and feeding are needed for success. That patience is called for goes without saying. The results justify the efforts, and I can see why fuchsias become a hobby.

Shrubs of Summer

At the end of July few shrubs are more spectacular than the golden-yellow Spanish broom, *Spartium jun-* *ceum*, whose fragrant flowers will continue to brighten our gardens until September. It is best on light soils in full sun and thrives near the sea (hardy in Zone 7). In its natural habitat in Southern Europe there are great tracts of Spanish broom, growing with cistus, wild lavender, rosemary and other charming plants native to Spain and Portugal. This perhaps gives us hints as to other plants to associate with it. Its glowing yellow flowers are borne in terminal racemes on rush-like stems, almost devoid of leaves. It will grow to a height of ten or twelve feet, if it is left to its own devices, but this may result in a leggy specimen, often bare at the bottom.

Proper pruning is important. Clip the bushes in early spring, especially young ones, and numerous side-shoots will develop to make a solid specimen. As the flowers are borne on the current season's growth, a wealth of flowers is ensured. In late summer or early autumn shape the bush by lightly trimming. Spartium is usually sold in pots, as its roots hate disturbance.

The broadly flared corolla and the single pale rose sepals of Fuchsia 'Citation' make a particularly graceful flower, suitable for tubs and pots or the edge of a terrace.

Cytisus × *kewensis*, perfectly placed at the top of a dry stone wall, is so smothered in April or early May with creamy-white, pea-shaped flowers that little green is visible.

It can easily be grown from seeds as germination is generally good. This broom is effective on banks where a large yellow mass is required or in shrubberies, especially behind the grey-leaved *Elaeagnus angustifolia* or silvery sea-buckthorn *(Hippophae rhamnoides)*, another good seaside plant. It is a lovely contrast to shrubby veronicas *(Hebe)* and summer-flowering blue ceanothuses, such as the well-known powder-blue 'Gloire de Versailles' or the darker-toned 'Topaz' and 'Henri Defosse', or to hypericums, if even more yellow is wanted. Spartium is equally effective when grown as a single clump in an all-green setting.

For beauty of habit and wealth of summer flowers *Genista aetnensis* is one of the loveliest of all large shrubs, ultimately attaining tree-like proportions of fifteen to eighteen feet. It is akin to the Spanish broom, but is more refined and delicate in habit and in its smaller fragrant golden flowers. Its hardiness is surprising, for it comes from Sicily where it grows on the slopes of Mount Etna, whence its name, and also from Sardinia. It needs conditions similar to those favoured by Spanish broom, particularly full sun. It is wonderful at the back of a shrubbery or overtopping a wall. I know of a country garden where a pair has been used to frame a charming cottage. It is particularly suitable where only light shade is wanted, as the foliage is very sparse, yet the rush-like stems of clear green appear clothed. Nursery stock is usually pot-grown. Be sure to stake young trees, or they may either be broken or blown out of the ground. Prune for the first couple of years in early April to develop a bushy habit. The flowering season at the end of July, though not as long as that of the Spanish broom, is particularly useful.

One other golden summer-flowering broom deserves mention. *Cytisus nigricans* is a small, relatively compact shrub, seldom exceeding four or five feet, with attractive leaves. The erect tapered racemes of small, yellow, pea-like flowers are borne in great profusion on the shoots of the current year from late July until the end of August. A native of Central and South-east Europe, its cultural requirements are similar to those of Spanish broom. Its name is derived from the fact that the yellow flowers turn black when dried. This is a good plant for the front of the shrub border and for a bold group in a mixed one. These three lovely brooms have all had Awards of Garden Merit, from the Royal Horticultural Society.

To balance the predominance of yellow of this trio and the hypericums and shrubby potentillas, which are such generous plants with copious flowers over a long season, the hardy *Hibiscus syriacus* hybrids, with their hollyhock-shaped flowers, both single and double, are outstanding in a range of colours that includes white, pink, red and blue. They are also known as Althea and Rose of Sharon. It is surprising that so exotic a flower should be hardy in Zone 5. *Hibiscus syriacus* must not be confused with the spectacular but tender *Hibiscus rosa-sinensis* (Zone 10). They are beloved by the French and Italians, who use them lavishly in their parks and gardens, either in bush form or as standards. The French clip them severely, but in our gardens it is rather better to allow them to develop their natural upright bushy habit. If they grow too large, they may be severely pruned in April. Hibiscuses need rather better soil than the brooms. They can be used as standards for a formal effect, and although their flowering season is a late one, they are effective grown in tubs. A word of warning: be patient. They are late to break into growth, especially in the first summer after planting. In fact, plants sometimes do not leaf-out until the second season. Among the whites, 'William R. Smith' and 'Totus Albus' are excellent singles and 'Admiral Dewey' is a good double. 'Hamabo', a pale blush pink with a crimson blotch, and the double 'Elegantissima', of similar colouring, contrast pleasantly with the rosy-red 'Woodbridge' or the double deep red 'Duc de Brabant'. 'Mauve Queen', 'Coeleste' (deep blue) and the large-flowered 'Blue Bird' are all good varieties and there are various others, including 'Jean d'Arc' (double white), 'Ardens', (double violet) and 'Lucy' (double red). Standards of some varieties are sometimes available in very small quantities.

I cannot think of hibiscus without mentioning hollyhocks, which make such wonderful displays in summer gardens. They are a good midsummer stand-by for town gardens and country cottages as well. I like to let them seed at will and then to rogue-out the unwanted ones. I have a mass of different shades of pinks and reds, one very deep red, and a wonderful lemon-yellow. Personally I prefer the singles to the doubles, but that is a matter of individual taste. They

are easily grown from seeds, best sown in June or July, to flower next season. Seeds sown later probably will not flower until the second year.

Evergreen Ground-covers to Smother Weeds

There is great interest today in ground-cover plants, as they solve the practical problem of weeding in the garden and at the same time add much to its beauty, giving a well-furnished, luxuriant effect. I definitely belong to the anti-bare-earth school of gardening.

Because of its graceful pendulous habit, a spreading, free-blooming scarlet fuchsia is the ideal shrub for a large terracotta pot.

Vinca minor, with its gleaming, dark green foliage and flowers like blue pin-wheels, is an ideal ground-cover for shade on any soil.

The ideal ground-cover blankets the ground for twelve months a year, interest lying in the contrasting colours, shapes and textures of foliage and possibly in the flowers. A show of colour is certainly desirable but in my opinion far less important than the foliage. Good evergreen ground-cover includes such plants as prostrate cotoneasters, periwinkles (Vinca), dwarf rhododendrons, hypericums, heathers, ivies, Pachysandra terminalis, the low-growing berberis and mahonias, and even evergreen herbaceous plants such as Bergenia cordifolia, crassifolia and delavayi. There are also a number of charming plants which make good covers for the best part of the growing months from frost to frost such as polyanthus, pulmoniaria, lilies of the valley, the hardy cyclamen, hardy geraniums, epimediums, ferns, Blue-eyed Mary (Omphalodes verna) and a host of others. I first want to consider some outstanding plants in the former category.

One of the initial considerations is whether the ground-cover is to grow in full sun or shade. Next, is the soil lime-free or alkaline? These factors will immediately restrict your choice. In most cases groundcovers will probably be in half-shade, especially if they are used along the front of shrubberies, wood-land paths or as underplanting. Another important factor to be taken into account is whether the groundcover is invasive. Will it smother the surrounding plants?

One of the finest of all evergreen ground-covers is periwinkle, some with single flowers ranging in colour from blue to purple and white, and others with rarer double forms as well. Periwinkle has many virtues. It thrives on most soils whether alkaline or acid, and is equally at home on banks or level areas. It likes cool, moist soil yet it will survive drought for short periods. Its trailing growths root so easily that it quickly makes a thick carpet, and hence it is easy to build up a stock quickly. Lastly it is hardy (Zone 4).

There are two main species, Vinca minor, a smallerleaved, more graceful plant with many attractive varietal forms, and V. major, a useful plant but much less prostrate and hence suited to larger areas. Personally I don't like it as much. Both prefer semishade but will also thrive in heavy shade or sun if growing conditions are favourable. Vinca minor even grows under yew if there is plenty of air and the branches are not too low. For a quick ground-cover plant vincas at twelve- to fifteen-inch intervals; if heavy clumps are used this can be increased. One of the best is 'Bowles Variety', which makes neat compact clumps, studded from April to October with clear, light-blue flowers shaped like pin-wheels. Vinca minor alba is my favourite. Its white flowers, opening from neatly rolled buds, are in striking contrast to the gleaming, dark foliage. A single deep purple (var. atropurpurea) and a semi-double plum-purple (multiplex) are attractive. There is also a blue-flowered variety with leaves splashed yellow (aureo-variegata) and similarly a variety of V. major with creamy-white markings. These last two varieties are useful for lightening dark areas but they are not as attractive as the dark-leaved types.

Pachysandra terminalis is another valuable evergreen carpeter which increases so rapidly and forms such a dense ground cover that when it is established, weeding is virtually eliminated. As a boy I remember digging up the long, bleached, stoloniferous roots, to start a new colony. Pachysandra spreads so rapidly in dense shade or half-shade that today in many gardens in the United States it replaces lawn. It is excellent at the base of a wall, under trees where grass is difficult or in front of shrubbery. With a background of yews, junipers or other conifers its whorls of bold leaves are a striking contrast, as are the white flowers in late winter and early spring. Like periwinkle, pachysandra is available in pots or in established clumps. It is relatively inexpensive, and it can be propagated by layering or division. When planting, dig in leaf-mould or peat and two to four ounces per square yard of a mixture of bone-meal and hoof and horn to encourage underground roots to form new plants. Pachysandra, lifted from the open ground, can be planted in autumn or early spring; pot-grown stock, at any time, if watered. There is a variegated form but this is less vigorous as is so often true of variegated plants of all types.

Ivies are excellent as ground-covers, especially for heavy shade. The more vigorous varieties will grow under yew but they need encouragement at first. The ground should be thoroughly dug and fed as above. Remember that the soil under trees is usually exhausted. Pin down the long trailing stems to encourage rooting.

There is a wide variety of low-growing evergreen cotoneasters, obligingly tolerant of most soils and of sun or shade. Some colour well in autumn; all have decorative berries. One of the most attractive is *C. dammeri*, which grows flat on the ground with long trailing shoots which strike out vigorously, layering here and there as they go. Sealing-wax-red berries stud the stems in autumn. Another charming member of this obliging family is *C. buxifolius*, a slow-growing, spreading shrub with box-like leaves and an impressive yield of autumn berries. Others with a creeping habit include *C. congestus, C. adpressus*, which drapes or rather moulds itself over rocks, steps or low walls, and the various forms of the deciduous *horizontalis* and of *microphyllus*, which are particularly useful to cover large areas on banks. All are hardy in Zone 5.

Two conifers make splendid ground-covers. The first is the range of prostrate junipers with lovely feathery glaucous foliage. They are particularly suited to chalk or alkaline soils. One of the best is *Juniperus horizontalis (sabina procumbens)*, which will cover large areas with blue-green prostrate branches. Its cultivar 'Bar Harbour' is particularly attractive. There is also *F. sabina tamariscifolia*, which is perfect on banks or in the front of a deep shrubbery. In maturity it will cover an area as much as six to ten feet across. All these are very hardy.

As a contrast in colour the prostrate yew *(Taxus baccata repandens)* is useful, especially on difficult shady slopes or beside steps under other larger yew trees. It is a relatively slow-growing, charming plant which deserves to be more widely known. Conifers can be planted in spring or fall, but they must be properly watered, and in periods of drying winds syringeing daily or even twice-weekly will greatly help establishment.

One of the best deciduous ground-cover shrubs is *Potentilla fruticosa* 'Longacre Variety', which forms a low, spreading carpet, rarely more than twelve to eighteen inches tall with sulphur-yellow flowers in splendid profusion throughout the summer. It is even more prostrate than the variety *arbuscula*, which is still my favourite member of the genus and so very useful for sunny places. Potentillas grow happily on well-drained soils, even if alkaline and in light shade. The stems and dead flower-heads together form lovely mounds of warm russet-brown in winter, rather like the varieties of autumn-flowering heathers. In this sense they could be termed evergreens. Their warm brown colouring is lovely in conjunction with the rich bottle-green of the brooms or tree-heaths and the blue and yellow of conifers.

Shrubs for Small Gardens

Few plants are as useful to the gardener as small shrubs, particularly those with a long flowering season. They are a necessity in most small gardens and enjoy many positions in large ones, as they are ideal for narrow strips under walls, groups at the front of shrubberies and particularly for mixed borders where they give form and year-round pleasure to what was once devoted exclusively to herbaceous plants. Dwarf plants are also useful on the rock garden or scree. Let us consider a few of the best which have a long blooming season.

The term small shrub is difficult to define, but for our purpose let us say that it will not exceed three to four feet in height and can be maintained at that height by careful pruning without destroying its natural habit or floriferousness. Obviously, hypericums, hardy fuchsias, *Hydrangea paniculata* and a number of others could exceed their natural height in favourable localities if allowed to go ungroomed, but this might result in an ungainly shrub and a loss of flower.

Other plants, however, while they can obviously be kept within bounds, lose their grace and charm if heavily pruned. I noticed in the parks in Lausanne the very vigorous pruning of large shrubs such as lilacs, cotoneasters, mock orange and a number of others. They were so reduced in size that they became formal elements rather than the large graceful bushes to which we are accustomed. In the same way, the branches of weeping willows, false acacias and planes had been lopped so that the trees would not block the view of the lake, but as a result they had assumed rather unnatural habits of growth.

Most useful of all small shrubs are the many forms of *Potentilla fructicosa*, which flower from June until frost. They vary in size and habit, some tending to be erect, others broad and spreading. Of the low-growing ones, I single out *P. beesii*, a silvery mass about eighteen inches in height, studded with golden yellow flowers.

Potentilla arbuscula is my favourite. I am always grateful for its low (two feet) spreading habit and its bounty of large canary-yellow flowers. 'Elizabeth' and 'Gold Drop' are similar with large golden flowers and a fine habit. Newer low-growing varieties are 'Longacre' and 'Tangerine'. In the three- to four-foot range, 'Katherine Dykes', 'Moonlight', 'Primrose Beauty' and *P. veitchii* (white and erect in habit) are among the best. But perhaps the subtlest, if not the most immediately striking, is *P. vilmoriniana*, erect in growth up to three feet with creamy primrose flowers and silver-green foliage. Give potentillas sun or light shade, good drainage and any reasonable soil. Prune them in spring, hard if you like, and don't be frightened by their apparently dead appearance at the end of winter or upon receipt from the nursery.

Hypericums, also in the yellow colour-range, give a long period of bloom (July-October). They are hardy and free-flowering, particularly if planted in full sun. They grow in all soils, and, like potentillas, do well on chalk. The smallest and the most rampageous is, of course, *H. calycinum* (Zone 6) the St John's Wort, which is a superb ground-cover for slopes or difficult dry areas as it spreads rapidly and is evergreen in many areas. One of the finest hypericums, evergreen and low-growing (eighteen inches) is *H. moserianum*, with its profusion of large golden-yellow flowers. Rather taller are *Hypericum patulum henryi (forrestii)* and *H. patulum* 'Hidcote', the latter having the larger flowers. More beautiful perhaps than any, but definitely tender is *H.* 'Rowallane Hybrid'.

'Sungold' is a good cultivar with gleaming dark foliage and quantities of large golden flowers from late June until frost (Zone 6). The native *H. prolificum* is hardy and prolific but the flowers are small. *H. frondosum* a native of the South east, is the loveliest of the indigenous hypericums with its blue-green foliage and orange-yellow flowers about an inch and a half across on a four-foot shrub.

All the *Hydrangea macrophylla* hybrids can be kept to three or four feet. For the intimate private garden as distinct from the public show-garden, there can be little doubt that the more natural and delicate lacecaps are preferable to the large, coarse mopheads, suitable, as the late Victoria Sackville-West so rightly said, 'for the foyers of grand hotels and for race courses'. Perhaps the best *macrophylla* lacecaps are 'Blue Wave' and 'White Wave', occasionally flushed with a touch of blue.

The former was raised in France by Lemoine of Nancy. The huge flat plate-like flower heads consist of a number of small fertile flowers surrounded by a ring of showy four-petalled sterile flowers. Acid soil is necessary for good blue colouring. Although fairly hardy (Zone 7) it pays in cold areas to mound up soil

for six or eitht inches over the bottom of the stems or to mulch with hay, bracken or leaf-mould. There is also a silver variegated form of *H. mariesii. H. veitchii* is similar but has white sterile flowers surrounding turquoise-blue florets.

However, the varieties of *H. serrata* are much better suited than the above to the small garden, being naturally dwarf, rarely exceeding three feet. I recommend especially the varieties 'Blue Bird', of similar colouring to 'Blue Wave' but usually containing some pink, and 'Grayswood', whose ray florets change from rose to deep crimson in autumn.

I consider lavender, blue rue and santolina to be among the most useful of all shrubs as their colourful foliage and delightful texture are as useful as flowers in any planting scheme and they are attractive for twelve months of the year. Perhaps the best lavender for the small garden is *L. spica nana atropurpurea* ('Hidcote Purple'), which grows fifteen to eighteen inches high and has deep violet spikes. There is only one species of rue, *Ruta graveolens*, but the form known as 'Jackman's Blue' is supposed to be the bluest. As for santolina, the common *S. incana* is extremely serviceable but for milder gardens *S. neapolitana* is more attractive, having larger, slightly drooping, more finely cut leaves. There is also a species with vivid green leaves *S. virens (viridis)*.

Shrubs of Distinction

Hydrangea paniculata is a ubiquitous shrub in gardens. I can remember my annoyance over its lack of fragrance when I was little and I find it an impersonal shrub but certainly a useful one, especially because of its reliability in making a bold display when massed. The huge pyramid-shaped heads of creamy-white sterile flowers, ageing to rose, persist through the winter months and can be used for large indoor winter flower arrangements. It is hardy in Zone 4 and therefore finds its way into a surprising number of New England gardens. Prune heavily in early spring. This shrub can be grown as a bush or as a standard. I prefer *H. paniculata praecox*, which flowers earlier and has smaller, rather less symmetrical flower panicles with dentated ray florets.

If you travel to Ireland, visit Rowallane, that remarkable garden near Belfast which is the property of the National Trust for Northern Ireland, where *Hypericum* 'Rowallane Hybrid' originated along with *Chaenomeles* 'Rowallane Seedling', a flowering quince with a broad, spreading habit and large bright crimson flowers borne in profusion in spring, and *Viburnum tomentosum* 'Rowallane', ideal for the smaller garden. What a distinguished shrub it is, with its compact neat habit, its fine bronze foliage in autumn, and its

The Chinese tree paeony, *Paeonia suffruticosa*, is one of the handsomest May-flowering shrubs, with huge, pale-pink flowers.

Romneya coulteri is an ideal shrub for a sunny position, as it has fine foliage and a long flowering season. It is also lime-tolerant.

copious reddish berries which follow the splendid flat heads of snowy flowers. Here is a fine form of *Viburnum tomentosum* for those who have insufficient room for the more spreading 'Mariesii'.

Caryopteris, the Blue Spiraea or Bluebeard of our gardens, is a splendid late summer-flowering shrub, hardy in Zone 6 and with protection in Zone 5. It needs a sunny position, well-drained, good soil and hard pruning in early spring to make it compact. As the wood is brittle, the side-branches are easily damaged. Foliage is often attacked by flea-beetles and other chewing and sucking insects. These must be controlled with DDT, Derris or similar preparations in either liquid or powder form. Caryopteris has greyish foliage, so it combines well with the yellow of hypericums, potentillas or yellow floribunda roses, including 'Allgold', 'Golden Jewel' and 'Gold Maria'. There

are several species which are good garden plants. *Caryopteris mastacanthus (incana)* has lavender-blue flowers in late August and September. *C. clandonensis*, a hybrid of it crossed with *C. mongolica*, is a rather better plant. Good varieties include 'Blue Mist' and 'Heavenly Blue', a finer darker blue form that has been developed by the Wayside Nursery at Mentor, Ohio. 'Ferndown' is another outstanding blue of British origin. Butterflies are fond of caryopteris. I like to plant it in bold masses with grey foliage such as santolinas, artemisias, or helichrysums and a little soft yellow to enhance the blue.

Other useful blue-flowered shrubs of late summer and autumn are ceratostigmas. The flowers closely resemble those of plumbago but are a deeper richer blue. *C. willmottianum* is two to three feet tall and starts to flower in late summer continuing until cut by frost.

It is hardy in Zone 6, but it will probably be necessary to cut it to the ground in early spring and let it spring again from the base. Further south although top growth may survive, prune it hard to make it compact and floriferous. *Ceratostigma plumbaginoides* is an indispensable low-growing ground cover of a herbaceous nature, suited to sunny or shady positions. It spreads quickly and gives good value over a long period. Like *C. willmottianum* its foliage turns a glowing crimson and bronze in autumn, in striking contrast to the brilliant blue.

The Chaste Tree, *Vitex macrophylla*, is a useful shrub for summer and autumn flowering for sheltered sunny positions in Zone 6. This lovely southern European shrub takes its name Chaste Tree from the Greeks, as women decked their beds with it each year at the festival in honour of Ceres. The large star-shaped leaves are dark green above and grey beneath. The long, rather slender, often branched racemes of small lavender blue flowers are fragrant while the foliage and stems are aromatic. This shrub, correctly known as *Vitex agnus-castus*, is slow to break into leaf

The low-growing *Convolvulus cneorum* is a treasured shrub for mild areas because of its persistent silvery foliage and white flowers.

in spring. It can be effectively grown as a wall shrub in areas where it is doubtfully hardy. 'White Spire' is a white-flowered form of slightly less vigorous habit. The Chaste Tree can be grown from seed and half-ripened cuttings strike easily.

Lacecaps versus Mopheads

Hydrangeas are among the most controversial of all summer-flowering shrubs, as many people feel passionately about them, particularly the mopheaded Hortensias *(H. macrophylla hortensia)*. They are both loved and hated. They are associated with races, public functions and the great flower shows of Europe, but equally so with lovely woodland gardens, especially in moist climates or by the seaside, where they are superb. They are also extremely useful shrubs for more formal town gardens as they like some shade but grow well in full sun. They are not particular about soil and are relatively hardy, save in very low-lying positions where the frost settles. In other words, they have much to recommend them. I personally prefer the flat lacecaps, with the ray florets arranged around the central, very small, fertile flowers. This is also characteristic of the flower-heads of some of the species. Hortensias come in a wide range of colours but some of the most attractive are the pale pinks and mauves, recalling sugared almonds. They are hardy in Zone 7.

Another of their great merits is suitability to cultivation in tubs and vases. They establish quickly and yield excellent results as long as they are provided with reasonably rich soil and sufficient moisture. The matter of moisture can hardly be over-emphasized, as often during long spells of dry weather I have noticed the sad woebegone hydrangeas in dry city gardens, their leaves falling limp and the flowers collapsed and drained of their rich pink flushes. Several buckets of water on three plants in a neighbour's garden restored them by the next morning to some of their former splendour. In tubs there is a similar problem, and it is vital to soak the roots thoroughly at intervals and not to rely on a light watering, which in all probability will never penetrate the massive root-ball of established plants.

Colour is the next problem. In spite of catalogue descriptions, hydrangeas of the hortensia type need acid soil to produce the much-desired clear blue flowers. On the island of Madeira, where there is no lime content whatsoever in the organic soil, the blues of the hydrangeas which line many of the mountain roads in great banks, are of an intensity hard to believe. A variety listed in a catalogue as blue is bound to disappoint when grown on an alkaline soil. For this reason care should be taken in selection. It is far better to be contented with fine whites, pinks and reds

Hydrangeas are remarkably adaptable hardy shrubs for both town and country gardens in sun or light shade. Their colour is partly governed by the acidity or alkalinity of the soil.

on a strongly alkaline soil than washy pinks or the poor blues, perhaps achieved with extra feedings of aluminium sulphate or Blueing Powder, particularly on neutral soils.

If the foliage of hydrangeas shows serious chlorosis, characterized by lack of stamina and bleaching or yellowing of the leaves, an application of copperas or iron chelate as a foliar spray should correct it. There have been some good results.

It is claimed that the blues are best in semi-shade, while the reds show their greatest intensity in full sun. Certainly the vivid crimsons and carmines of hydrangeas growing in full sun in a hot dry summer in the small gardens where they are watered and cherished would confirm the latter, and the former is a well-established fact. The gardener who grows his hydrangeas in tubs holds the trump card, as he can control their colour by the compost used and, indeed, their future destinies by feeding and by using rainwater if his water-supply has a high lime content, thus ensuring that his blue hydrangeas grown in acid compost remain blue.

Hydrangeas are reasonably hardy. The dead heads protect the stems against frost and they should not be cut back in autumn. Hydrangeas dislike heavy pruning at any time, as much flowering wood is sacrificed. Weak shoots should be removed in early spring, and if plants are congested, cut out a few of the more vigorous ones as well to keep them open and well shaped. As hydrangeas break into leaf very early, they are subject to late frosts and may be cut back in areas where this is prevalent. By tipping growing shoots it is possible to increase the number of flower-heads but individual blooms will be smaller. This, to my way of thinking, is often desirable, as hydrangeas can be so over-sized as to look artificial.

Soils should be thoroughly prepared with a light dressing of manure, but do not overdo it. Bonemeal is as always, an excellent dressing. Young plants should be watered until established if the weather is dry, and a mulch of old manure, compost or peat over the root-area at the beginning of the season will help to conserve the moisture. Spring planting is preferable in severe climates, and

75

to be on the safe side, those planted in autumn should be given some protection until established. Sacking to form a tent can be used as covering in cold spells, but be sure it is securely anchored. Heavy polythene or plastic sacks that contained fertilizers, peat or compost, can also be used to provide shelter for tender plants.

A short list of good varieties in the white, pink and red range, suited to alkaline soil, includes 'Ami Pasquier' (compact, deep crimson), 'Hamburg' (deep pink for semi-shade), 'Westfalen' (crimson, medium growth), 'Mme E. Mouillière' (white), 'Vulcain' (dwarf, bright carmine for full sun) and 'Joseph Banks' (creamy pink, excellent for seaside gardens). Among those best suited for acid soils or, if you must, to 'blueing', on neutral soils are 'Générale Vicomtesse de Vibraye' (particularly adaptable to blueing), 'Goliath' (rather tall, deep blue), 'Blue Prince', 'French Blue', 'Kluis Superba' (dark blue, compact habit, for shade), while the dwarf 'Westfalen' and 'Vulcain' turn an in-

describable violet-blue, 'Parsival' is a compact low plant with deep blue flowers, but as for all blues, acid soil is essential. I warn readers that they will find variance in their catalogue descriptions, and, as pointed out, much depends on soil, subsequent treatment and whether in sun or shade.

I have already sung the praises of the lacecaps and several of the species, but after seeing *Hydrangea villosa* (Zone 7) again I want to remind readers who have gardens of sufficient scope to plant this superb species, although in infancy it is in no way impressive. It grows in the chalky soil at Highdown and Sir Frederick Stern paid it high tribute in his delightful and useful *A Chalk Garden* when he wrote: '*Hydrangea villosa*, one of E. H. Wilson's introductions, is the finest August-flowering shrub in this garden; it comes out in the middle of the month, covered all over with panicles of blue flowers and has grown into a large bush about ten feet high in the border facing north in the chalk pit. The flowers are a clear blue in the centre and the outer sterile ones a light lavender. It is perfectly hardy as the flowers are borne on the new shoots, which do not begin to grow till the frosts are over. Seedlings germinate all over the shady damp part of the rock garden where it faces north. They can be counted by the dozen, germinating in the damp *Arenaria balearica*, and in the moss covering the sandstone.' It should be ideal in the Northwest.

A much dwarfer treasure, but again a plant of distinction, is the double-flowered *H. involucrata* var. *hortensis*. This forms a low-growing shrub not exceeding eighteen inches in height and produces a number of charming and unusual flower-heads. It requires a protected shady position on the rock garden or in a small shrubbery.

Another species of considerable beauty and interest for a protected shady position such as a sheltered north wall is *Hydrangea quercifolia*, aptly named on account of its moss-green, large oak-like leaves, that turn rich crimson in autumn. It has cone-shaped panicles of subtle, greenish-cream flowers, resembling those of the better-known *H. paniculata*. It is hardy in Zone 5.

Finally, for woodland or for a really spacious sheltered shrub border, I would recommend the noble *Hydrangea sargentiana*, with its huge, dark green leaves, curious bristly stems and impressive lacecaps of lavender-blue and creamy-white. This shrub is quite winter-hardy in sheltered positions in Zone 7, but it must have shade and shelter from wind, the worst enemy of all large-leafed plants, from rhubarb to rhododendrons.

Hydrangea 'Ami Pasquier' is a deep red, long-lasting mophead of dwarf and compact habit, ideal for the many small gardens today.

Hydrangea 'Blue Wave' is one of the finest of the lacecaps, which are steadily gaining in popularity because of their grace.

Labour-saving Heathers

When the moors and downlands in many parts of Britain are mauve and purple with heathers, we realize what wonderful plants they are, standing up to winds and gales and the constant nibbling of sheep and grouse. There is a choice, including the common Ling Heather of Scotland and Yorkshire *(Calluna vulgaris)*, which covers vast tracts of countryside with its subtle purplish-pink and takes on new tones with the changing skies, rather like the colour of the sea; the Dorset Heath *(Erica ciliaris)*, rosy-red and dwarf; and the Cornish Heath *(E. vagans)*, which ranges in colour from white to rose and red. The Bell Heather *(E. cinerea)* is common on moorlands in many places. With this bounty of nature so near at hand offering a brilliant example of easy evergreen ground-cover, it is odd that more gardeners do not avail themselves of the wonderful varieties suited to our gardens, as well as the various European Heaths.

Heathers can easily assume a more major role in our modern labour-saving gardens, and not without good reason. If we list their merits it is an impressive array. First, they are evergreen, giving beds, shrubberies, rock gardens and peat walls permanent cover, an important factor aesthetically and practically. Second there are heathers for almost every month of the year. Third, some heathers are lime-tolerant, including the varieties of *Erica carnea*, which are winter-flowering, *E. mediterranea* and *E.* × *darleyensis* (the hybrid between these two). *Erica terminalis*, the Corsican Heath, is also lime-tolerant but, like *E. mediterranea*, rather more tender than the more northerly European heathers. Fourth, they are relatively easy to grow and to propagate. Fifth, they make ideal ground-cover, suppressing weeds and holding the soil on banks and difficult slopes. Last, and certainly not least, they associate happily with a wide number of ericaceous plants, including pieris, camellias, pernettyas, kalmias, enkianthus and a number of others, not to mention non-ericaceous genera such as potentillas, cistuses, brooms, berberis, rose species and fothergillas.

For winter flowering, varieties of *Erica carnea* are ideal. These include 'Springwood White', 'Springwood Pink', 'Cecelia M. Beale' (white), 'King George' (a real red), 'Queen Mary' (rich pink), 'Winter Beauty' (pink) and 'Ruby Glow'. For summer and autumn there are the varieties of *Erica vagans*, such as the pure white 'Lyonesse', the rose-pink 'St Keverne' and the stronger cerise-red 'Mrs D. F. Maxwell', as well as the varieties of *Erica cinerea*, *E. ciliaris* and *Calluna vulgaris*. Personally I treasure the winter-flowering heathers most, as they come at a time when there is far less in bloom. *Hamamelis mollis pallida*, or the early spring-flowering *H. japonica zuccariniana* (both lemon-yellow) underplanted with *Erica carnea* is one of the loveliest of plant associations, and there are many others using heathers.

All heathers require good, well-drained soil, richly laced with peat or leaf-mould. The lime-tolerant group listed above also benefit by the addition of humus to improve the soil as a rooting medium, particularly on poor, light, sandy soils, where heathers are invaluable. Work in liberal quantities of leaf and peat at planting time and use garden compost as well, or even on its own if peat is not available. On heavy clay soils dig deeply and work in peat and coarse sand. On the other hand, in solid peat, heathers may not be happy either. In such conditions, loam and sand should be added to make a loose, well-drained medium.

It helps to top-dress all soils with a generous mulch of humus in autumn or spring. It is easiest to do this after the heathers have finished flowering. Remove all spent flower-heads by a generous shearing of established plants to keep them compact and to encourage new growth from the base and side-shoots from the main stems. Dwarf varieties such as *E. carnea* will not require pruning every year but every second

A paved path leads through the sloping banks of a heather garden, densely planted with ericas, which are the perfect ground-covers.

more can be spaced out at intervals of two or two and a half feet. With vigorous varieties, which include *Erica carnea*, the lovely 'Springwood White', 'Springwood Pink' and 'Ruby Glow', this wider spacing is desirable, and, of course, the slightly tender tree heaths (*E. arborea*) should be spaced out at double the interval, as they will ultimately reach heights of up to six feet with a broad spread. The last species and the closely related, glowing rose-red Spanish Heath (*E. australis*) and its well-known white-flowered form 'Mr Robert' provide quantities of flowers from late spring through early summer.

Heathers, especially until established, need plenty of moisture. If they dry out they may well succumb, particularly in spring droughts. Heathers can be planted over a long season from early September into April, but do not plant when the ground is very cold or water-logged. Early planting in warm soil encourages immediate root action, and in a mild October plants will be well rooted by winter. Spring planting is satisfactory as long as plants are well watered. Ericas will tolerate violent winds but in exposed positions by the sea, where there are salt-laden gales, newly planted areas should be sheltered until they are well established. We all know how well heathers stand up to wind on exposed slopes in their native haunts.

Peat walls made with blocks of peat used rather like brick or stone with a distinct slope of a few degrees inwards towards the top are easy to construct and can take the place of rockeries. The peat blocks are light to handle and they stand up reasonably well over a number of years. If the top of the low wall is turfed or planted with a dense matting plant to protect the upper blocks from weather and frost damage, the life of the walls is increased. The area behind the walls should be filled with a light open compost, sedge-peat or leaf-mould mixed with loam and sand. This should be allowed to settle and should be well worked into the crevices between the blocks of peat.

Peat walls are an ideal home for all acid-loving plants. American gardeners who visit Britain should try to see the remarkable peat walls in the Royal Botanic Garden, Edinburgh, where peat walls were first used for rare blue meconopsis, dwarf rhododendrons and nomocharis, or in the Savill Gardens at Windsor, where there are remarkable collections of lilies, little-known Asiatic primulas and a number of rare North American wild flowers. The last include the pink Moccasin Flower and the Showy Lady Slippers (*Cypripedium acaule* and *reginae*), less common trilliums such as the Dwarf White, the Nodding and the Painted (*T. nivale cernuum* and *undulatum*), the enchanting, very fragrant Mayflower (*Epigaea repens*) a difficult plant at best in Britain, the Virginian Bluebell (*Mertensia virginica*) and the Shooting Star (*Dodecatheon media*). The fine Ameri-

or third. Plants left too long unclipped will grow leggy, tending to fall apart and to become bare at the centres. Incidentally, the clippings can be added to the mulch for other ericaceous plants as they rot down and put back into the soil their own goodness.

I am often asked how close to plant heathers. The answer depends on factors as varied as the extent of your purse, your impatience to see the brown earth solidly blanketed, and whether you are willing to wait a few years for well-grown fine plants. If you are impatient, plant about eighteen to twenty inches apart, so that they will form a complete carpet after two or three years. Obviously, in smaller gardens where groups are limited to five, seven or nine, close planting gives a better effect, while in large plantings on broad slopes or in massed plantings such as we find on estates and in parks, groups of fifteen to thirty or can lilies include *L. canadense*, the loveliest of all in my opinion, the bright golden, heavily scented *L. parryi* and *L. washingtonianum*, with white flowers fading to soft lilac-purple as they age. This charmer is a native of California and probably derives its name from the one used endearingly by the California miners, who called this lovely plant the Lady Washington Lily after Martha Washington. All these treasures and many more, familiar and unfamiliar, grow happily on the peat walls at Windsor.

Other plants that associate happily with general plantings of heathers include various brooms, genistas, rose species and shrub roses such as the golden yellow *Rosa hugonis*, the larger-flowered 'Canary Bird', the double yellow *R. harrisonii*, the equally brilliant but rather dwarfer *R. nitida* (18 ins) and *Rosa virginiana* with its brilliant autumn foliage and attractive red fruits, the magnificent *R. californica plona*, which is one of the loveliest of all shrub roses (give it plenty of room), and those with fine fruits such as *R. moyesii*, *multibracteata*, *rugosa* and a number of others. Shrubby potentillas, dwarf conifers of various types, particularly those with brilliant golden or glaucous blue foliage, and the small-leaved evergreen ilexes, pieris and leucothoes are also suitable. With a little imagination charming contrasts in shape, and in the colour and texture of foliage can be achieved, especially in winter. Plant generous drifts of small bulbs through the heathers, particularly colchicums and autumn crocuses, and dwarf daffodils in spring.

The Brilliance of Firethorns

As the days shorten and leaves begin to fall, autumn berries stand out in the landscape. Certainly one of the most spectacular and useful is the Firethorn *(Pyracantha)*. Here are shrubs or small trees which satisfy many requirements. First, they are evergreen, clothing walls and shrubberies throughout the winter. Second, the brilliant scarlet, orange and yellow berries are produced with such abundance in a good year that the effect is dazzling. Moreover, most years are good ones, as pyracanthas are particularly reliable in this respect, resembling their near cousins, the cotoneasters and thorns. The flat, white clusters of flowers in early summer are also a lovely feature of these valuable shrubs.

Pyracanthas have another virtue due to their hard, woody nature, which makes it possible to train them flat against walls in solid evergreen sheets to conceal unattractive architectual features or building materials. By careful clipping, buttresses of dense green can be formed against walls, and other shapes can be achieved such as arches over gates or the simple topiary forms of pyramids or umbrellas. The stiff sturdy main stems carry the heavy mass of foliage and berries with the minimum of support against a wall, making elaborate wiring unnecessary. I always admire pyracanthas cleverly trained as espaliers against a white wall so that they make a striking formal pattern of horizontal evergreen branches with tight clusters of brilliant fruits.

For freedom of flower and fruit pyracanthas are best grown as shrubs and only lightly pruned, if at all. They make broad masses against a wall or fence and in the open border will become large and spreading, reaching a height of ten to fifteen feet and very nearly as much across. Against walls pyracanthas will grow much taller. In small gardens they can be controlled by cutting out unwanted growth and a clipped very formal appearance can be avoided. In time they make small trees, and by removing the lower branches attractive standards are produced which have great character, rather in the Japanese tradition.

Often in October, I drive out of the city into the outlying suburbs. Seldom does one see such a brilliant display of berries. Each winter these same bushes are equally fine and the berries last well into the spring, unmolested by marauding sparrows, pigeons and bullfinches. Here, within a few miles, pyracanthas are used in a number of ways – trained flat against the walls of a factory to clothe the brick fabric with green; in bold mass-plantings against fences and in shrubberies; trained as an arbour over the door of a house; pruned as standards to flank a front-door; and even used in large concrete containers in a paved front-garden. Each treatment is successful in its own way, although for bounty of berries, lightly pruned shrubs are always the best.

I became fascinated by the prevalence of this plant, so I drove through some of the side-streets in this area. What immediately became apparent was that full use was made of this obliging shrub in positions where there was relatively little sun, for pyracanthas will grow in semi-shade and on a north wall, if a light one. I know of a number of houses where it has been used on a north aspect, but do remember, it will not thrive and fruit (it may exist) on a dark north aspect overhung with trees. Rich soil is not important as long as it is well drained and of reasonable quality. Pyracanthas grow equally well on acid or lime soils, and some of the finest fruiting trees I know are on chalk.

In cold windy positions pyracanthas sometimes suffer from scorch, and newly planted ones should have winter protection if planted in autumn in exposed positions. This can be done with polythene, hessian, boughs of evergreen, bracken or even with small sections of wattle fencing. Pyracanthas are pot-grown by nurseries, so they can be planted at any time, preferably in spring in colder areas. With container-grown plants now in good supply by an ever-increasing number of nurseries and garden centres in most areas, correct planting seasons are altered.

As to varieties to grow, there is a choice. Most of them are hardy in Zone 7 with some suited to Zones 5 and 6. One of the best-known is *P. atalantioides (gibbsii)*, a vigorous tall species with rather large dark gleaming leaves and crimson berries in profusion. Birds seem to leave this variety alone in many areas. The European *P. coccinea* and its variety *lalandii* are vigorous, very, floriferous and free-fruiting. They are erect in habit when young and therefore effective on walls, but old trees will develop a lovely graceful aching habit if left unpruned. *Pyracantha rogersiana* makes a broad, graceful shrub with clear green foliage and orange berries in profusion. Its yellow fruiting form var. *flava (fructuluteo)* is a delightful change from scarlet or orange, as is a new hybrid 'Buttercup', with an abundance of clear yellow fruits. *Pyracantha crenato-serrata* 'Rosedale' is a fine early-colouring variety and there are other various new introductions of merit.

Berberis for Flowers, Fruit and Foliage

The berberis family is a large one, containing vast numbers of both deciduous and evergreen species and hybrids. Mahonias were once included in the genus but today these are grouped into a distinct genus. There are two principal seasons for these lovely shrubs. The first is in spring when, for example, the glistening dark holly-like leaves of *Berberis darwinii* or the more graceful arching branches of *B. stenophylla* are wreathed with orange-yellow flowers (Zone 7). The second, which is my concern here, gives us wonderful autumn foliage and dazzling displays of berries. Massed plantings are unrivalled in their effectiveness.

I like berberis for other reasons. They make excellent decorative hedges, and there are different types and sizes to suit a number of situations, ranging from tall shrubs such as *B. darwinii*, *lologensis* and *stenophylla*, which grow to seven or eight feet or even taller, as in

The frosty-blue fruits of *Mahonia japonica* in summer are as decorative as the scented yellow flowers in winter. Few evergreen shrubs are as adaptable to conditions in shady town gardens.

the case of the last, to the delightful deciduous *B. thunbergii*, which grows to four or five feet and has the merit of colouring superbly in autumn and producing masses of brilliant red berries.

For small gardens there is a dwarf form, *B. thunbergii atropurpurea nana* ('Crimson Pygmy'). It is hardy in Zone 5. This little charmer is deep purple in autumn. It is slow-growing but will reach a height of two feet. I like to plant it in groups of three or five with grey foliage such as santolina, dwarf lavender or even masses of the woolly-leaved *Stachys lanata*. It is equally enchanting with a low yellow potentilla such as *P. arbuscula*, or the more spreading variety 'Longacre', or the pale pink single rugosa rose. 'Frau Dagmar Hastrup', with its yellow-tinted foliage in autumn and its large waxy-red heps. This dwarf berberis is one of the most useful of all shrubs, but it is expensive in that it takes three or four shrubs to do the work of one at roughly the same price. *Berberis thunbergii minor* is possibly even dwarfer, rarely exceeding eighteen inches, but is green like the type. There is a larger *Berberis thunbergii atropurpurea*, which wears its purple cloak throughout the summer and is superb wherever large groups of dark coloured foliage are wanted. It makes a rounded bush as much as six feet tall and four feet across.

A very useful shrub is the low, rather spreading *B. wilsonae*. Seldom exceeding three feet in height, it is covered with greyish-green leaves, which turn scarlet in autumn, and bunches of coral-red berries. 'Buccaneer' is striking with clusters of large bright-red fruits which last well into the winter. 'Barbarossa' is even more spectacular. I have seen bushes with arching branches so loaded with scarlet-red berries that they trailed the ground. Both these varieties grow to five or six feet. There are many other fine fruiting berberis, but *B. rubrostilla (wilsonae × aggregata)* is certainly worth singling out for its refinement and subtlety as it is an attractive shrub of medium size (four to five feet tall) with pale green, silvery-backed leaves. The fruits, borne in great profusion, are unusually large and translucent, and instead of being a solid colour show subtle gradations from silvery-white through coral to red. This fine berberis deserves a place in moderate-sized gardens where autumn colour is important. Every gardener has his favourite fruiting berberis, but these few show the possibilities.

Berberis have certain faults. Many gardeners hate the spiky thorns and dislike working in shrubberies where they are planted. To offset this, berberis make impenetrable hedges and can often be used to good advantage where people force access or take short-cuts. Very much on the credit side is the fact that some are such good ground-covers, forming dense masses which do not have to be weeded. Lastly, berberis like alka-line soils and chalk, colouring and fruiting particularly well on these soils. Certainly the credits are impressive.

Berberis can be planted in autumn or early spring. For hedging, the larger varieties such as *B. darwinii* and *stenophylla* should be planted at two-foot intervals. *B. thunbergii* and var. *atropurpurea* are widely used for this purpose. As it has a broad spreading habit, it lends itself to clipping and becomes a very dense hedge. The evergreen varieties used for hedging can also be clipped, but the graceful habit is, of course, sacrificed in part. There are several varieties of *B. stenophylla* (now known collectively as *B. × irwinii*) that are useful. One is

The translucent scarlet berries of the hybrid Berberis 'Cherry Ripe' are borne in great profusion and persist for many months.

B. corallina compacta, a low, spreading evergreen not more than three feet tall but much broader, with masses of orange flowers in May. Another excellent one in this group is 'Crawley Gem', which is a little taller with a very attractive habit and orange flowers opening from brilliant red buds.

At the other end of the scale there are one or two tall-growing species from six to ten feet in height, which have richly coloured autumn foliage and fruit, preceded by elegant pendulous racemes (at least three inches long) of pale yellow flowers. I think particularly of *B. jamesiana* and *B. vernae*. In addition, their height makes them very useful as screening and background material. This, however, applies even more to such tall evergreen species as *B. julianiae* (Zone 5) and *B. veitchii* (Zone 6). Both these have a sort of delayed-action 'autumn colour' in spring when the old leaves turn crimson and scarlet as the new ones develop.

Berries and Fruits to Brighten Autumn

With the approach of autumn we are increasingly aware both of beautiful autumn foliage and of fruits and berries. The majority of the latter are in shades of vivid red, orange and yellow as, for example, those of crataegus, cotoneasters, pyracanthas and many of the rose species, but others are less conspicuous in tone – dark blue, purple and black. Pinks, mauves, whites and magenta-purples are less common and therefore all the more striking. The fascination of this season in the great arboretums, estates and botanic gardens throughout the country is to a great extent due to the fact that trees and shrubs were selected with this objective of autumn display in mind, and many smaller gardens would be far more colourful if trees were chosen with

The clusters of scarlet fruits of *Sorbus aria* are another good reason for planting the vigorous silvery-leaved Whitebeams, which are sturdy trees for windswept positions and industrial areas.

an eye to berries and fruits in autumn and not merely to flowers in spring.

For those who live on acid soil, particularly a peaty one, pernettyas offer striking possibilities, with their profusion of berries in colours which include delicate pastels and subtle shades of magenta, purple and tawny reds. Pernettyas revel in moist acid soils, sending out a quantity of underground suckers so that groups of plants in time form a dense thicket from three to five feet tall in areas where little grows but heathers. In fact, in parts of Scotland, Ireland and the Pacific Northwest one often has the impression that they are indigenous rather than natives of the Straits of Magellan and the Falkland Islands, as they form dense ground-cover. The wiry stems clad in neat glossy evergreen leaves, often with a bronzy sheen, are the perfect foil for the colourful berries. In May and June there are small, white, heather-like flowers and by late August or mid-September a bounty of round, fleshy berries which persist well through the winter and often into the spring. They are hardy in Zones 6 and 7.

Pernettyas are particularly happy in association with heathers in the garden, but remember that the soil must be acid. Certain ericas, such as *E. carnea* and *E. mediterranea* and their varieties, are tolerant of lime. Pernettyas are definitely not. Ground should be well dug and prepared well in advance to enable autumn or early spring planting. Although they like moisture they do better where there is good drainage and the ground is not too sodden. They should always be planted in colonies to encourage free fruiting.

Pernettyas are listed by some nurseries in mixed colours only. These are attractive in mixture but I like to use them in large groups of a single colour for special positions. Other nurseries have selected forms by colour, but few as named clones. Considerable hybridization and selection was done to develop large-fruited forms of particularly fine colours and these strains bear the names of the two men concerned, Davies and Bell. Bold groups create autumn interest among rhododendrons and camellias, as there is not only the contrast of colour and texture of foliage but the brilliant fruits. However, remember that pernettyas need sun if they are to berry freely, although, of course, they grow happily in shade.

Whites are striking, but I particularly like the subtle mauves and pinks or the deeper raspberry-reds and purples. Sometimes pernettyas send up strong vigorous shoots which do not branch until well above the bulk of the plant. These can be cut back to encourage side-shoots lower down as well as active new growth from below ground. Propagation is easy either from layers, cuttings or by division. Pernettyas also can be grown from seed, but the selected colour forms will not usually come true. Among the best are 'Bell's Seedling' (a

The very large, quince-shaped fruits of *Chaenomeles cathayensis*, a tall, rather sparse shrub, with delicate white flowers flushed with rose.

large dark red) and 'Davies' Hybrids' (mixed or by colour).

Another useful shrub with berries of pastel colouring is the Snowberry *(Symphoricarpus)*. This plant conjures up pictures of straggling thickets with masses of leggy stems and a few little white berries. At its best it is a fine, hardy shrub for any soil, in sun or shade (Zone 5). It has attractive rounded leaves and the best varieties produce masses of decorative berries, usually white, although some are pink or red including the coral-berry *(S. orbiculatus* and *chenaultii)*. It spreads rapidly by underground suckers. *Symphoricarpus albus* and its variety *laevigatus*, which has larger berries, are both good. One nursery has a fine form known as 'Constance

Spry', which has arching sprays with an unusual number of white berries in long, tapered clusters. This shrub was loved by Constance Spry, as she found it invaluable for flower decorations. Snowberries are wonderful for game-coverts and for difficult corners where other shrubs will not grow happily. There are also good hybrids for hedges which are compact and grow to four or five feet. Perhaps the best of these are 'Erect', a strong compact grower with rose-lilac berries; 'Magic Berry', rather more spreading with pink fruits, profusely borne; and 'White Hedge', strong-growing, upright in habit and bearing a profusion of small white berries in erect trusses.

Symplocos paniculata is a remarkable small Chinese tree, somewhat resembling a hawthorn. It produces fragrant small white flowers in May, followed by clusters of brilliant blue berries, from whence the name Sapphire-berry. It is hardy in Zone 5 and does well in East Coast and New England gardens, preferably in light filtered shade. Plant it in pairs or groups to ensure cross-pollination. Another attractive berrying shrub is *Callicarpa*, which is spectacular in autumn with clusters of berries which persist well into winter, in shades of violet or lilac instead of the more usual autumnal reds, oranges and yellows. I remember five groups at Williamsburg.

Fine Foliage for Flower-arrangements

In every garden there is need for good foliage shrubs, which can be used, when established, for cutting to round-out flower-arrangements through the seasons. I never cease to marvel at what can be done with a few flowers if there is suitable greenery as a background. To ensure an adequate supply of this material it is desirable, when planting a garden, to get a balance

The golden, delicately cut foliage of *Sambucus racemosa plumosa aurea* is lovely in the garden and highly effective for arrangements. It prefers a dampish position but will grow on poor soils.

Potentillas are ideal shrubs for sunny borders, as they have a compact habit and a long flowering season from early summer until frost.

between evergreen and deciduous plants. A first essential is that the foliage must stand up to cutting, for a shrub that collapses in water in a day or two is no use. Even more important, the foliage must be decorative and useful as a background or ground-cover in the garden.

I am particularly partial to laurestinus. Its fine evergreen foliage with young growths tinged red and the copious quantity of flat, white flower-heads in late winter make it one of the most useful of all foliage plants but only in Zones 8 and above. Short stems or long sprays can be used as a base for bouquets. Plant it to make a hedge or it can be used for specimens or mass-planting. In catalogues look for *Viburnum tinus* and don't expect to buy large specimens, as stock is generally small, either bushy field-grown plants or small pot-plants. As it can be scorched by winter winds and frost, it should either be given protection in winter until established or planted in early spring. It grows splendidly on highly alkaline soils, so gardeners discouraged by chalk and lime should take heart (*see* p. 42 (*see* p. 42 for special forms). A wonderful evergreen shrub, but only for acid or neutral soil is *Leucothoe catesbaei*. I love everything about it, especially its arching graceful stems, which under favourable conditions will grow to six feet. It forms dense masses, the rather cumbent branches spreading rapidly. The burnished, tapered leaves take on unbelievably rich tones of copper and purple in winter and the stems of the young growths are a rich red. In April and May there are masses of short racemes of white lily-of-the-valley flowers. It keeps for a remarkably long time when cut, and because of the elegance of the leaves and the graceful habit it is easy to arrange, particularly with chrysanthemums and lilies. It is hardy even in Zone 4.

I have always been an enthusiast for golden privet (*Ligustrum ovalifolium aureo-variegatum*) with its bright golden foliage, which proves evergreen in many areas. It makes a wonderful mass of colour in dark shrubberies and is a splendid addition to large-scale borders. It is often used for clipped hedging and specimens, but I like it best when untrimmed or loosely shaped, although the more it is cut back, the brighter the colour. For smaller gardens *Ligustrum vicarii* is useful, with an attractive habit, not exceeding four to five feet. It is glowing warm yellow, particularly strong in spring. Both these varieties pick well, making a good foundation for large vases. Though privet is maligned because

of its misuse, I would not be without a clump or two.

A runner-up, though far less well known, is the lovely golden cut-leafed elder, with the cumbersome name of *Sambucus racemosa plumosa aurea*. It makes a shapely shrub six to eight feet in height, with delicately cut foliage of clear yellow, and produces in favourable seasons clusters of small, bright red berries. It is slower and less vigorous than its near-relative, the spectacular *S. canadensis aurea*, which, in spite of its brilliant foliage, is coarse by comparison.

Returning to evergreens, it is difficult to over-praise *Mahonia aquifolium*, the Oregon Holly-grape. The compound leathery leaves turn incredible shades of red and purple in winter and form a rich foil for the closely packed racemes of golden yellow flowers in February and March. Later, there are decorative blue-black berries. This accommodating plant makes a splendid three- to four-foot ground-cover, suitable for full sun or shady positions, even under trees on soils varying from chalk to peat. It cuts wonderfully, as it lasts a long time and is so decorative that it can be used on its own. There is a variety *undulata*, with brighter green, undulate foliage that tends to grow slightly taller, reaching six feet, and the variety *aldenhamensis* is again taller with distinguished foliage. Many gardens have the ideal position for *M. aquifolium*, such as dark corners and dry areas under trees. Remember that it spreads rapidly, forming broad masses. I know of a lovely patch as much as twelve feet across, all from a small rooted layer acquired from a nearby garden a few years ago. Mahonias, like *Leucothoe catesbaei*, make splendid cover for birds.

One other treasure, all too seldom grown, is *Danae (Ruscus) racemosa*, generally known as Alexandrian Laurel. The graceful stems of clear green tapered leaves have an airy charm. It forms broad evergreen clumps not more than three feet tall, in shade positions on good soil; if it is moist, so much the better. Few plants are more attractive for cutting, yet how rarely we see it, except in old gardens. There are small bunches of yellowish flowers followed by red fruits, but it is for its foliage that it is grown.

The foliage of *Camellia japonica* is one of the handsomest for vases, so much so that I like to use it on its own in the same way as I use sprays of eucalyptus. It is a dark gleaming green and because of its sturdy habit it arranges easily.

5 Climbers

Honeysuckles Round the Door

Many of us are confronted by difficult garden walls and slopes where relatively quick coverage is required, but conditions are far from ideal. Perhaps it is an east- or north-facing wall, or a draughty pergola; perhaps it is a rather steep bank where there is erosion due to heavy rains in winter, or even an old dead or dying apple tree in the orchard. In each case, the solution could well be a honeysuckle or, to be botanical, a *Lonicera*, which the French call *chevrefeuille*, or goat-leaf. The word honeysuckle immediately calls to mind fragrant bowers of woodbine, the common honey-suckle of hedgegrows, immortalized by Shakespeare and poets through the ages; quite rightly too, as the heady intoxicating fragrance has few equals. I have often heard friends say that they do not like the scent of jasmine or tuberoses or lilies, but never have I heard anyone express a dislike of honeysuckle.

There are both bush and climbing honeysuckles, but it is with the latter that we are concerned here. Best known are probably the Early and Late Dutch, both varietal forms of *Lonicera periclymenum* (Zone 4). This delightful species has a very wide distribution, covering Europe and extending south over North Africa and east to Asia Minor. Its fragrance lends enchantment to the dawns and the evening, when its scent is most pervasive. I like to plant them around the doors where their scent is constantly enjoyed. *Lonicera periclymenum* var. *belgica* is the Early Dutch Honeysuckle, producing quantities of clusters of red-tinged, creamy, fragrant flowers in June and early July. It is followed in August and September by the Late Dutch (var. *serotina*), with creamy flowers stained crimson, slightly larger in size. Where only two varieties can be planted, these will give a prolonged season. In town gardens they are often subject to attack by greenfly and blackfly, especially if grown in full sun. They thrive in any reasonable soil, acid, neutral or

The heavily-scented flowers of honeysuckle should grace every garden. They are suitable climbers to cover fences, walls, trees and banks.

alkaline, and in any exposure, as long as it is not too hot or dry. Cool moist root-runs are desirable. Both are deciduous, as is the hybrid *L.* × *americana*, believed to be a natural cross between the rather tender *L. etrusca*, native to the Mediterranean, and the hardier *L. capri-folium*. It produces a profusion of scented apricot and rose-purple flowers throughout June and early July and again is hardy enough even for a cold northern aspect. To confuse matters, it is sometimes listed as *L. italica* or *L. grata*. The last name I particularly like, for 'pleasing' it certainly is (Zone 4).

Another very useful honeysuckle is *L. japonica*, different in that it is an evergreen twiner native to Japan, Korea and China. It grows rapidly and will climb with no urging through hedgegrows and trees to a height of twenty-five to thirty feet. The heavily scented creamy-yellow flowers, suffused with purple, are borne in whorls both at the ends of the slender twining branches and in the leaf-axils, so that there are panicles of flowers intermittently over a long period from June until late September. It is hardy in Zone 4.

I always remember a well-house with a roof of grey cedar shingles from which an oaken bucket was suspended by a chain on an iron wheel. The well-house was so covered with this lovely climber that its low walls and four wooden uprights were concealed throughout the year. On summer evenings white and sulphury-yellow moths hovered above the scented honey-laden flowers and it was a thrill to be allowed to draw a bucket of cool water from the mysterious depths or to peep to see if the swallow's eggs in the nest under the eaves had hatched. Of all these memories, it is the scent of honeysuckle that lingers strongest.

A variety of *L. japonica* called *aureo-reticulata* has smallish leaves webbed with the gold of the mid-rib and the veins. It flowers reasonably well and is particularly useful where a lighter note in foliage is required. The fastest-growing variety of *L. japonica* is *halliana*, which is vigorous, sweet-smelling, and tough, with abundant clusters of creamy flowers from June until frost. This variety is invaluable on difficult slopes and has been widely used in America to clothe the steep banks along highways where deep cuts were necessary. Certainly, it is not so distinguished a plant as the varieties of *L. pericylmenum*, but it is extremely useful as an evergreen cover or screen. Moreover, it is resistant to aphides. Also evergreen is the Chines *L. henryi*, with distinctive, rather pointed dark leaves and flowers of purplish-red borne in pairs in June or July and followed by black berries, similar to those of *L. japonica*. Again, this climber is useful for fences, trellises, banks and pergolas.

Lonicera brownii, the Scarlet Trumpet Honeysuckle, is delightful. It is a hybrid of our native *L. sempervirens*. It has orange-scarlet, trumpet-shaped flowers, paler within, borne in whorls on elongated spikes. Equally striking are the pairs of glaucous leaves, some of which are joined, so that they surround the stem like a ruff. This hybrid has for me one great drawback – its lack of scent. But this is also characteristic of one of the most spectacular of all the family, *L. tragophylla*, with copious clusters of bright yellow flowers numbering as many as fifteen to twenty individual blooms, each of which is as much as two to four inches in length.

It requires moisture and grows best in shade. So spectacular a climber perhaps compensates for its lack of fragrance, and it is surprisingly hardy (Zone 5).

The bright yellow Giant Burmese Honeysuckle *(L. hildebrandiana)* has the largest flowers of all, but it is very tender, only suited to Zone 10 or to greenhouse cultivation.

The Goldflame Honeysuckle *(Lonicera heckrottii)*, another *L. sempervirens* cross, is very popular because of its coral-red and yellow, scented flowers borne in profusion throughout the summer and its hardiness (Zone 5). As it is not as rapid a grower as forms of *L. japonica*, it is ideal for smaller gardens.

Quick Coverage for Walls

A number of gardeners, particularly new homeowners, are confronted with the problem of covering walls, fences and trellises as quickly as possible with attractive climbers. This is a recurring problem in town gardens, where all too often three sides of the plot

'Heavenly Blue' is a perfect name for the loveliest of Morning Glories. No annual climber makes a gayer display in a hot, sunny position, whether in the open or in a cool or heated greenhouse.

have boundaries of this nature, and it is also a problem which may present itself in the country as well.

At the outset a fundamental decision must be made. Is the coverage to be permanent, temporary or a combination of both? The long-term view is usually the best, but often there are governing reasons why decorative vines, wall-shrubs, wistarias, roses, honey-suckles and jasmines will not provide the answer. Usually, the prime factor is our impatience, but there may be practical reasons, such as the prospect of a limited tenancy, the need to decrease the glare of white or pale-coloured walls in full sun, or proposed altera-tions to the house, that demand a short-term solution for garden problems. With a small garden there may be the desire to have variety from year to year. Under such restrictions there are excellent annual and her-baceous climbers which give rapid results.

Another consideration is paramount. Does the plant lend itself to the site? Most annuals need sun in order to make their spectacular growth, to flower and to seed in the few short months, if their life-cycle is to be completed. For a shady north wall annual climbers are not the easy answer. They need food, moisture and thorough soil-preparation. Use good compost and organic or chemical fertilizers as necessary after deep-digging to make an easy root-run and to improve the drainage, which is of supreme importance for annuals.

I place *Cobaea scandens* at the top of the list of desir-able climbers. Its rate of growth is phenomenal, often reaching the eaves of a two-storey house in a single season and covering a wide area if the growing shoots are fanned out and given proper support in the way of trellis, strings or wires. The vast number of tendrils make it easy to train, and it will even cling to old brick walls by its growing tips. The foliage is an attractive clear green with ovate leaves as much as four inches long. The large campanulate flowers, borne on six- to eight-inch pedicels, are particularly effective, as they stand well clear of the foliage. The broadly bell-shaped blooms open a pale jade-green, becoming tinged with lavender as they develop and deepening until the whole corolla is a rich violet with a greenish base. There is an even more lovely white form, which can be identified by the lighter green foliage.

The beauty of this plant does not end with the flowers. When these fall, attractive large green calyx cups remain, looking a little like green flowers. In a hot summer, pendulous plum-shaped fruits appear, at first bluish-green, but gradually turning to gold. As the weight of these is considerable, it is essential that the plant be given sufficient support to maintain

the wealth of flowers and fruits, the former starting in July and lasting until frosts. They are apt to become leggy and bare at the bottom. Strangely, they do not send out side-shoots readily if cut back. Therefore it is advisable to grow fresh stock each season, treating them in colder zones in the same way as Morning Glories, the Cardinal Creeper and the Cypress Vine *(Quamlocit)*.

The seeds should be sown in February, preferably in individual pots, and then potted on and given a warm position in the greenhouse. It is essential to keep each plant separate, or, when they start into active growth, they will intertwine and be difficult or even impossible to separate. Young plants require a small stick or cane as a support and should be carefully tied,

Cobaea scandens is a miraculous annual climber which grows twenty feet in a season with an abundance of campanula-like flowers.

89

as the stems are tender and break easily. It is important not to damage the growing tips, as cobaeas are slow to throw side-shoots and if damage occurs the growth of the plant is retarded. Some firms stock pot plants of this splendid climber in late May or June, so it is possible to buy pot-grown plants already eighteen inches or more in height. They should be planted in a sunny position and given normal growing conditions. They grow quite well in a large pot or tub (not less than twelve inches in diameter and preferably more) but must not be allowed to dry out. As a city dweller, it gives a very good account of itself. I know of one garden, newly planted in the spring, the walls of which were covered by late August, and a friend, who that same April had despaired of ever covering glaring white walls, telephoned in September with real concern as to whether she should provide extra support for the

stems which had reached the top of the high trellis and were billowing over in a curtain.

The Morning Glory (*Ipomoea rubro-caerulea*), one of the best-loved annual climbers, for some reason has proved temperamental in certain gardens in recent years, and at one time it was hounded by the authorities as a drug. As it is a sun-lover, it needs hot, baking conditions to give its best. It is admirable as a large pot-plant in a greenhouse, conservatory or orangery, where it can be grown against a wall or on circular or pyramidal forms. It is also useful for sunny fences, terraces, patios, window-boxes and, of course, roof gardens. Sow seeds in late January or February in small pots and grow them under glass or in a sunny window. As the seeds are very hard and hence slow to germinate, they should be soaked overnight in a saucer of water placed near a hot pipe or in an airing cupboard. Another useful trick is to nick the seed slightly with a nail-file, so as to fracture the outer shell. Fibre or peat pots are excellent, as Morning Glories resent root-disturbance. These pots are economical and tend to prevent the check that results when plants are moved into open ground. In areas with a long hot summer sow seeds directly in the ground.

To my mind, the loveliest of the Morning Glories is the accurately named 'Heavenly Blue'. This and other recent introductions including 'Scarlet O'Hara', which is really more crimson than scarlet; 'Pearly Gates', a large pure white; and a striking new white-striped sky-blue, with the topical name 'Flying Saucers'. The last is claimed to have flowers four inches in diameter. All these must be treated as tender half-hardy annuals, raised indoors and only planted out after all danger of frost has passed. Pot-grown plants of 'Heavenly Blue' are available at the proper season from many sources.

Similar to Morning Glories but nocturnal rather than matutinal, is the moon-flower *Calonyction aculeatum*, derived from two Greek words meaning 'beautiful night'. As a further attraction, like many night-blooming species, it is very fragrant. It requires treatment similar to that for Morning Glories and wants plenty of sunshine to hasten the production of its creamy-white flowers which catch the moonlight and become almost luminous. Nocturnal flowers like the evening primrose, the Four O'Clocks and the exotic Night-blooming Cereus have a great fascination.

A few other climbers deserve mention. The first is the Canary Creeper (*Tropaeolum peregrinum*), with attractive delicately cut leaves and sulphur- to lemon-yellow-fringed flowers. This, too, needs a sunny position and

The Passion Flower, *Passiflora caerulea*, is a quick-growing, hardy climber for warm sheltered positions. It clings by its corkscrew tendrils.

should be started under glass to ensure flowering. As it is native to Peru, it demands sun and warmth.

The ordinary climbing nasturtiums, which are wonderful in their profusion of brilliant red, orange, yellow and flame-coloured flowers, are also useful for walls and fences. They must be watched carefully, as they are very prone to aphides, particularly in town gardens. They grow rapidly if planted directly in their flowering position in April or early May and they need no cosseting. *Mina lobata*, another annual climber, has bulging tubular flowers, flaring at the mouth: they open orange-crimson and fade to yellow. This native of Mexico requires sun and feeding if it is to grow rapidly enough to give a worthy account of itself.

Wistarias and Early Clematis

Having driven more than once across France from Provence to Normandy, I am more convinced than ever that lilacs and wistarias are as much loved by the French as roses, for they are everywhere, in gardens of all sizes and descriptions, from the great châteaux of the Loire valley to the little houses and isolated farms in rural villages. Never have I seen such a profusion of flower on both the old common lilacs *(Syringa vulgaris)* and on the newer hybrids. Perhaps it is the hot sun of summer which ripens the wood. Perhaps it is the hard pruning after flowering, which is obviously practised, or perhaps it is that special love is lavished upon them. Whatever the answer, French lilacs and wistarias are a sight to be behold and they strengthen my resolve to grow more of them and to grow them better.

The grey stone or pale pink stucco of old walls make an enchanting background for a sprawling wistaria, dripping with purple racemes of fragrant flowers. In this country, wistarias growing through trees in the South and draping porches and pergolas in gardens everywhere, are a fragrant delight of spring. Most often it is *Wistaria sinensis*, with sturdy trusses of fragrant mauve to purple flowers, and now and then its white form, *alba*. Many show signs of hard pruning, as even very old trees are still compact and covered with bloom. The secret is to shorten the leafy growth of the current year back to about four buds in late July or August and to treat old plants in restricted wall-areas drastically in January and February to keep them in check. If they are allowed to sprawl without restriction, lack of flowers eventually results and the tangle will defy the bounds of law and order.

Wistarias can be grown in many fascinating ways. First, there is the high wall of a house or farm-building, where they may have ample scope. They need some form of strong support, as they are twining climbers, not self-clinging, and the weight of leaf and flower is considerable. They are particularly effective when

The shimmering racemes of wistarias frame the window of a country cottage, although wistarias grow equally well in cities and towns.

trained along a balustrade or an outside staircase, so that one walks beside the curtain of flowers with the light filtering through them. Trained over pergolas and arbours, either of wood or light metal, wistarias make long tunnels of bloom, and I have a particular weakness for them on metal frames in fanciful bird-cage designs, so that the long racemes are appreciated.

Give wistarias a warm sunny position, preferably south or west, and prepare suitable soil for them, with long-term feeding in the form of plenty of well-rotted manure dug well beneath the surface for the roots to tap at a later stage. Feed annually with bone-meal in the early spring and occasionally mulch in late autumn

91

A large-flowered clematis makes a striking curtain of colour against a wall. No climber is better suited to both sun and shade.

with longer flowers, var. *macrobotrys* having racemes up to three or four feet in length. If these are to be effective, they must be grown on a wall or pergola tall enough for the racemes to hang their full length. This particular form, long known as *multijuga*, is so listed in some catalogues. There are various forms including white *(alba)*, pink *(rosea)* and paler flesh pink *(carnea)*. Another very lovely species is *W. venusta*, which has broad white trusses of great character. Both the young shoots and foliage are covered with a silver down which enhances the bronze tints of the new leaves. It flowers a little later than *W. sinensis*, and in some localities the leaves tend to appear with the flowers. It is a superb plant, but generally not so easy to grow and certainly much scarcer in the trade.

Before the War, many unusual wistarias were imported from Japan. If you are ever in England in May, try to visit Pyrford Court, near Woking in Surrey, where there is a remarkable collection of species and varieties, including pinks, whites and purples, with double forms like Parma violets. Another notable collection is that at the famous botanic garden of the Villa Taranto at Pallanza on Lake Maggiore in Italy. Alas, some of these rarer forms are unobtainable today.

Standard wistarias take years to produce and plants of any size are not easy to find in the trade. However, standards have great charm and with patience can become a feature, as they are beautiful in habit, in flower and in leaf. They are effective in a rose garden, as in Sir Winston's and Lady Churchill's at Chartwell, their old home. This combination of mauve wistaria, grown either as a standard or as a climber, festooning a wall or fence with tulips in shades of pink, pale yellow, blue or mauve, backed by lilacs ranging in colour from palest pink to deep wine-red, opens up visions of loveliness for the May garden.

I am always inspired by the door-yard gardens of French villages, and combinations found there can be adapted to gardens of almost any size or type in this country, where lilacs, wistarias and tulips are equally at home. As in France, apple blossoms are a delightful and an inevitable adjunct.

Clematis also plays an important part in the spring theme, particularly the forms and varieties of the vigorous *C. montana* and *C. chrysocoma* and the smaller but delicate flowered *C. alpina* and *C. macropetala*. Another beauty is *C. armandii*, an early-flowering evergreen species for sunny warm positions in favoured localities.

For effect and rapid coverage *C. montana* is the gardener's dream. As it comes in a pot, it can be planted at any time, but preferably in autumn or winter. It grows rapidly, clinging tenaciously to any form of support and even clambering rapidly through the branches of old shrubs and trees. It is a wonderful plant for London gardens, as it will grow in any aspect, including north,

with well-rotted manure. Wistarias establish slowly the first year after planting and have a maddening habit of taking so long to break into leaf that one is tempted to condemn them. The secret is patience coupled with frequent watering and a syringeing each evening.

In addition to *Wistaria sinensis* there is *W. floribunda*

'Rose-Marie Viaud', with its clusters of rich lilac and parma-violet flowers in profusion, is an unusual, almost thornless, rambler to grow on poles, arbours and old fruit trees.

Clematis chrysocoma is similar to *C. montana* but is less rampant, and has a longer flowering season in May and June.

The yellow flowers of *Clematis orientalis,* with thick petals like lemon-peel, are borne in profusion in late summer and early autumn.

covering as much as three storeys in four or five years. It can also be pruned hard to give dense coverage of limited spaces, such as low walls and balustrades. A year after planting, be brave and cut the stems back to within two feet of the base in late winter to encourage the development of laterals and furnish the bottom of the wall. If properly trained, no clematis is more rewarding. After the frame of stems has been established, cut back the lateral branches along them to within a few inches to develop a wealth of flowers for the following year. *Clematis chrysocoma* requires similar treatment.

Clematises do well on alkaline soil. Good drainage is essential; if the soil is heavy, it must be lightened. Deep preparation and heavy feeding are also necessary. Plant the crown of the plant at least an inch or two below the level of the soil, firm thoroughly and protect the roots with flat stones. Clematis like their roots and lower stems in shade, so a slanting tile is useful, or alternatively plant a low shrub in front. Protect the stem with wire or canes. All too often the stem is snapped or cut in error.

There are various forms of *C. montana*, including *grandiflora*, a large white free-flowering form; *rubens*, which is rosy pink with purplish new foliage, and named cultivars of it, including 'Elizabeth', which is delicately scented, and 'Pink Perfection'. *Clematis chrysocoma* (pale mallow-pink) is similar to *C. montana* but has a much longer flowering period, blooming copiously in early June and then intermittently until October.

6 Annuals and Biennials

Success with Annuals

As the end of winter approaches it is time to prepare for the sowing of half-hardy annuals and vegetables. Some of these, such as stump-rooted carrots, parsley, parsnips, early peas and shallots, can be sown in the open ground when danger of frost is over in favourable areas and if the winter is an open one. Others, such as cauliflowers, summer or autumn-maturing cabbages and tomatoes, should be sown under glass.

The sowing of flower-seeds should be carefully considered, so that young, vigorously growing plants will be available at the right moment to fill the gaps when tulips, hyacinths, wallflowers and winter-flowering pansies are removed. It is essential to time the sowing of seeds correctly, so that there is no check in the development of young plants. For example, plants to replace Canterbury Bells and Sweet Williams, which finish flowering in late June or early July, should not be sown at the same time as annuals to replace early hyacinths and myosotis, unless, of course, plants can be potted and properly cared for.

Whether sowing vegetables or flowers, use a suitable proprietary brand of seed compost or make up the equivalent, consisting of two parts of sterilized sifted loam, one part granulated peat, one part of sharp clean sand and for each bushel of compost one and a half ounces of superphosphate of lime and three quarters of an ounce of ground chalk. Some gardeners prefer to use a richer potting compost for annuals, especially if they are to be sown and grown in composition pots. Small gardens often do not have facilities for two different composts. Potting compost consists of seven parts loam, three of peat and one of sand, with four ounces of specially mixed base-fertilizer and three quarters of an ounce of limestone or ground chalk per bushel. Be sure to mix compost thoroughly and have it properly moistened (it should be damp but loose and crumbly) when filling seed-boxes and pans. These should be crocked, using pieces of shard to cover the

The rich colours of nasturtiums give quick returns for little effort. Nasturtiums in sunny positions grow vigorously on poor, dry soils.

holes. Then put a layer of coarse leaf-mould or fibrous peat on top to ensure open drainage. In plastic seed-boxes, the broken crock may be omitted but use a generous layer of coarse fibrous roughage. Next, fill the containers with compost, shaking them to settle the soil, and pressing it firmly but not too solidly with a pressing-board or the bottom of a pot or glass jar.

Sow seeds thinly and evenly. Generally, very shallow planting is advisable, covering small seeds with a light dusting of sieved soil. Larger seeds, such as sweet peas, Morning Glories and nasturtiums, should be more deeply planted. Seeds sown in well-prepared open ground in the early spring should also be more deeply sown. Plant garden peas as much as two inches deep, and lima beans, French beans and runner beans two to three inches below the surface. Most other vegetables can be planted safely at a depth of about half an inch. Careful watering has as much to do with success or failure as using the correct seed-compost and planting at the right depth. If the compost is sufficiently moist when seeds are planted and if the boxes and pans are covered with glass and brown paper or newspaper until the seedlings germinate, further watering may not be necessary. If the compost begins to dry out, water at once with tepid water, using a can with a very fine rose. Pans and pots can be submerged up to the rim and left until the soil darkens with moisture. Be very careful not to float fine seeds or they will settle in slight depressions or around the rim. Be sure the soil doesn't cake or harden, as this can be injurious to tender seedlings. If there is condensation on the glass, wipe it clean each morning. As soon as seedlings germinate, remove the covering and make doubly sure that the boxes and pans never dry out.

When seedlings are large enough to handle, prick them out into boxes of potting compost at two-inch intervals, using a small dibber to make the hole and dropping the rooted seedling gently into it. Carefully firm the soil. Seedlings can also be planted in composition pots made of peat or wood-pulp such as Root-o-Pots or Jiffy Pots, which come singly in various sizes or in strips or blocks of six or twelve. Seeds such as Morning Glories, *Cobaea scandens* (one of the most lovely of rapid-growing annual climbers), nasturtiums and sweet peas can be sown two or three seeds to a pot and later thinned if necessary, leaving a single healthy plant. Young plants should be properly hardened off before planting out by placing them in open frames or cool sheds for a week or so, protecting them by night if there is danger of a late frost.

Half-hardy annuals and tender perennials that should be sown under glass include antirrhinums, *Phlox drummondii*, salpiglossis, ageratum, heliotrope, nicotiana and large-flowered penstemons, all of which are plants of distinction. Some annuals are improved if the growing tip is pinched out at an early stage to encourage side-branches. This is true of snapdragons, heliotropes, *Cineraria maritima* and a number of foliage plants, but with climbers such as the ravishing *Cobaea scandens*, *Ipomoea*, *Mina lobata*, and the clear yellow *Tropaeolum peregrinum* it is important not to disturb the growing tip. These plants should be given a cane at an early stage, so that each plant will have a support and not entangle with its neighbour. Cobaeas are particularly clinging and grow so rapidly that they become inextricably entwined, even in a few days. I have often tried to disentangle them, and this was bad for my temper and in several cases disastrous to the plants.

Annuals for Quick Returns

Each spring the seed-catalogues seem more enticing. Is it because I have forgotten the old ones or that the spring-like weather with the first of the dwarf crocuses and Roman hyacinths whets my appetite? Perhaps both are factors.

A mistake that occurs in some catalogues is to refer to *Salvia horminum* as Clary. This is wrong; Clary is the English name for *Salvia sclarea*, a much taller, fragrant herbaceous salvia, best treated as a biennial, except in mild districts, while *S. horminum* is a true hardy annual with spectacular coloured bracts borne in spikes on compact well-branched plants about eighteen inches high. These bracts are far more showy than the flowers themselves. Broad clumps provide wonderful blocks of colour in the border. I find 'Blue Beard' particularly useful, its velvety deep purple acting as a striking foil for grey foliage or pinks and mauves. There is a rose counterpart known as 'Pink Lady' and an even more vivid rosy-carmine dubbed 'Pink Sundae'. 'Purple-Topped', 'Oxford Blue' and 'White Swan' are all very useful. This useful annual will delight flower-arrangers, who are always looking for new adventures. It also harmonizes with herb gardens, where so many flowers, even though perfectly orthodox, look strangely out of keeping.

Another unusual annual, *Euphorbia marginata*, charmingly known as Snow-on-the-Mountain, is an attractive member of the large *Euphorbia* family, represented in California and Florida by poinsettias. The former has soft green upper leaves, broadly margined with white, and white bracts around the small clusters of flowers. It prefers a sunny, well-drained position in the border, where, if happy, it will seed itself from year to year. It is best sown *in situ* as soon as the ground is warm enough in April, but it can be raised under glass. Snow-on-the-Mountain will grow to two or at the most two and a half feet high, and plants should be spaced a foot apart. It is a useful floral decoration, but because of the flow of milky juice which pours from the stem, sear the cuts with a match or plunge the stems into boiling water as soon as possible to prevent flagging.

Bells of Ireland *(Molucella laevis)* is a first-rate annual for decorative purposes. It needs hot sun, and in cold districts is best sown under glass in spring. Light, well-drained soil is essential. The two-foot stems have whorls of dull, whitish flowers surrounded by large cup-shaped calyces of a lovely luminous apple-green with an intricate tracery of veining. If the leaves are stripped off the spikes of green will lend exceptional character to other flowers. Furthermore, if the plants are allowed to ripen, they age to a pale honey-colour and last through the winter perfectly in dried bouquets. Sow seeds in the open ground in late March or April and hope for a warm summer.

I have admired *Hibiscus trionum* in a number of gardens for a long time. It gives a particularly good account of itself in several well-known gardens where there is an abundance of sunshine and a light well-drained soil, slightly on the alkaline side. The flowers are hibiscus-shaped, pale yellow or creamy white, with a handsome chocolate-purple centre. After the flower falls, the calyx becomes swollen; hence the name Bladder Ketmia. Because of the relatively short life of the flower it is also referred to as Goodnight at Noon, a misnomer, as actually the flowers stay open until dusk. This plant seeds freely, perpetuating itself where conditions suit. It is sturdy and compact, reaching a height of two to three feet, but I have seen it taller in gardens in Mediterranean countries and Madeira, where obviously it revels in sun and warmth. The combination of the pale cup-shaped flowers with a deep purple eye and attractive lobed leaves makes this little-known but obliging annual deserving of wider recognition.

Love-in-the-mist *(Nigella damascena)* has always been a delight, with its whorl of foliage like a lace collar under the flowers and its delicate colours, such as that of the large bright blue 'Miss Jekyll', or 'Pure White' and 'Persian Rose', a charming, soft apple-blossom pink, deepening with age. There is also a mixture which I like called 'Persian Jewels', which includes soft mauve, lavender, rose and purple. A drift or two of this particularly subtle blend of colours would grace any border.

A formal scheme, laid out in an old walled vegetable garden, combines blocks of lavender and santolina with fragrant bedding plants, including sweet alyssum and heliotrope. In spring these are replaced by pink English daisies, blue forget-me-nots and tulips.

The inflated seed-pods with their horned carpels may be dried to dramatic purpose. Sow seeds in the open in March or April; better still, sow in September if early flowers are desired next spring. Nigella has no special requirements and transplants easily. Thin to about six inches, as the plants are spindly if crowded.

One of my favourite annuals is the graceful richly coloured *Salpiglossis sinuata*. The flaring trumpet-shaped corollas come in a wide range of colours, including velvety purple, gold, apricot and buff, with intricate veining in other fascinating shades. They are excellent grown under glass and are very effective for bedding or in clumps among herbaceous plants in the border. They are enchanting grown among irises, as they take up little root-space and thrive happily, lending butterfly colours above the spiky leaves. The foliage is so small that it in no way smothers or interferes with other plants, as would nicotianas or bolder subjects. Small plants should be transplanted, having been raised under glass. Do not sow them direct among the irises. Eschscholzias, the California annual poppy, are excellent for the same purpose but sow them *in situ*, as they transplant badly *(see p. 99)*.

Annuals come in an enormous colour-range, and I want to consider some of the most brilliantly coloured. These are of easy cultivation on most soils, as long as there is adequate sunshine. One of my special favourites is the nasturtium, which flourishes in so many countries with such brilliantly coloured flowers and such a delightful fragrance that it deserves reconsideration by the gardener who passes it by each year.

Nasturtiums have a particular fascination for me because of their beautiful rounded leaves, usually glaucous green but sometimes almost black. I particularly like to grow them under glass in winter, so that their cheerful colours can lighten the dark days. In January in New York I have seen a room where pots of brilliant orange and pale yellow nasturtiums trailed from the tops of bookcases and there were bunches of cut flowers as well on small tables. After the usual roses,

97

watched the sturdy plants suddenly collapse with the first frosts in October, so do not be too eager to sow them early.

There are several types from which to choose: they include tall climbers, both single and double, a compact dwarf strain known as 'Tom Thumb', and the semi-double Gleam varieties, which have a delicate, intriguing perfume. Colours range from scarlet, orange, gold and mahogany to salmon, pale yellow and apricot. Young stems and tiny flower-buds can be used in salads for their curious flavour. A useful novelty called 'Baby Salmon', makes compact bushy plants five to nine inches tall, smothered with brilliant salmon-pink flowers. 'Primrose Gem', a delightful double, growing only six inches high, is extremely useful for edgings or for low masses in the border or rockery. 'Empress of India' has single velvety crimson flowers, effective against dark foliage, while the double 'Black Beauty' has almost black leaves. Mixtures of nasturtiums are sometimes useful, as all the colours are warm and tawny and if any single one clashes it can be removed. Personally, I far prefer to grow a few selected ones. I must mention their tendency to attract blackfly, worse in town than in the country, but this plague can be controlled with a nicotine spray at its first appearance.

For bright colours calendulas are a splendid choice. They flower over a long season and last well into the autumn; unlike nasturtiums, they are very hardy. This favourite, known variously as English or Pot Marigold, brightened many an Elizabethan garden and was widely used for medicinal purposes by herbalists from the sixteenth to eighteenth centuries, and also as a flavouring for soups and stews, though I cannot, after giving it a trial, greet this idea with enthusiasm. Calendulas, like nasturtiums, are easy to grow as they have no idiosyncrasies as long as there is plenty of sunshine. Having started life as a small single flower of orange or deep yellow in southern Europe, the calendula has been hybridized to produce large double flowers, varying from pale primrose to deepest orange. Through the years there have been a number of developments, many from the Pacific Coast, which include shaggy, loosely double flowers on long, branching stems, ideal for cutting. I suggest sowing seeds in open ground in late March or April. If flowers are required earlier they can be grown under glass, where they germinate well, then pricked out in flats and eventually moved to their permanent homes. Calendulas are also lovely for the cool greenhouse or hot-house through the winter. If your soil is sandy, light or full

carnations and chrysanthemums they made an exciting change.

Few of us have the facilities to grow this gleaming beauty in winter, but we can all have them in summer, as they are among the easiest of hardy annuals. Sow the seeds about half an inch deep in mid-spring, selecting open, sunny ground, preferably not too rich or there will be an excess of foliage to hide the flowers. Nasturtiums are frost-tender, as all know who have of chalk, calendulas are ideal, as they will grow happily in such soil. An interesting development is 'Geisha Girl', with large intense orange flowers overlaid with glints of red. Unlike those of other calendulas, the petals are incurved, like a Japanese incurved chrysanthemum. 'Orange King', 'Lemon Queen' and 'Lemon Beauty' are particularly good for cutting, as they are well branched and produce an unending quantity of large double flowers. There are pastel colours as well — cream, apricot, buff and peach. An attractive mixture is sold under the name of 'Pacific Beauty'.

Another brilliant beauty is the Mexican Cosmos (*Cosmea*), which includes two distinct colour-groups, the first with a range of pinks, whites and reds developed from *C. bipinnatus*. The other has brilliant orange flowers developed from *C. sulphureus*. All are useful, but the latter has particular appeal to the lover of colour. The former are early-flowering and include the deep rose, shaded crimson 'Radiance' and the vermilion, semi-double 'Sunset'. The plants are slender and not quite as tall as other cosmos, seldom exceeding two to two and a half feet. 'Orange Ruffles' is a semi-double of glowing orange. 'Klondyke Orange Flare' has large vivid orange flowers, and 'Goldilocks', small golden-yellow flowers in graceful sprays.

For a riot of colour and quick returns few annuals can surpass the Californian poppy *(Eschscholzia)*. Again, requirements are easy – ordinary soil, good drainage, and sun. Poor soil is not a drawback. The foliage is delicate and feathery with a hint of silver and blue. Colours range from scarlet, vermilion, orange and carmine to tones of apricot, rose and cream, clear pale yellows and even a good double white. 'Miniature Primrose' is a useful dwarf, making compact six-inch plants with myriads of small flowers. It is enchanting for the rock garden, as an edging or in low drifts for underplanting. 'Mission Belle' is an unusual new dwarf strain with large, semi-double flowers that are particularly useful for display. I like to broadcast seeds through newly-planted iris, so that bright patches of gay colour appear through the green sword-like leaves and the feathery foliage does little harm. Shirley poppies are delightful if used in the same manner and do even less harm. There are mixtures of both singles and doubles. Sow the seeds of both these poppies in the open ground, as they do not transplant well. Plants should be thinned to about a foot apart.

One of the greatest delights of the garden in summer is the fragrance, as the shadows lengthen on summer evenings and the dew releases the subtle scents that the sun seems to destroy by day. Roses, phlox, summer jasmine, honeysuckle and lilies come to mind, but there are annuals and biennials as well which can give sweet rewards in record time with the minimum of expense and effort. Annuals are particularly obliging, as they can either be sown in February or early March under glass or a month or two later in the open ground when the soil has been warmed by the sun. Many, moreover, can be sown in early autumn to over-winter and to germinate at the earliest possible moment in spring.

Of scented annuals pride of place probably must go to the large white tobacco *Nicotiana affinis*. No garden should be without its delicious heady fragrance, which always calls up memories of far-away places, as it is definitely exotic and almost oriental. This plant is a vigorous grower, often over three feet tall, with large leaves that can easily smother smaller plants (particularly young slower-growing perennials and small shrubs that are just making their way in life). The deep red variety is also lovely but never seems to be quite as fragrant and has the disadvantage of not showing up against the green foliage at night. As this species is nocturnal, the flowers closing in the heat of the day, it

Nicotiana affinis is the most effective and fragrant of tobacco plants at dusk, but 'Daylight' and 'Lime Green' are more effective by day.

is not as decorative as the types known as 'Sensation' and 'Daylight', but to my mind its fragrance is indispensable. In areas with short summers seeds should be sown under glass and the seedlings pricked out as soon as they are big enough to handle, either in boxes or, better still, in small fibre pots, which will eliminate future disturbance.

Unlike tobacco, sweet alyssum gives out a wonderful fragrance in the heat of a summer day. I shall never forget the Trials in England a few years ago for long before I entered the trial-grounds through the lofty clipped hedge, I knew what plant I would find, even though I had forgotten, or more probably had never known, that sweet alyssum had been planted in broad blocks.

As I have always loved sweet alyssum, I have obviously sung its praises before. It is well named for its sweet honeyed fragrance. In old gardens it was largely used with blue lobelia as an edging, but there are endless possibilities. It makes a wonderful annual ground-cover in sunny positions for lilies, gladioli or standard roses; it can be used in broad drifts at the front of borders or even carried back through a bed to make a curving river of white or mauve or rosy purple. It is delightful as an edging in the vegetable-patch or when scattered broadcast on old gravel paths. I like to sow it among paving-stones so that there are spreading low mounds so covered with flowers that no green shows. In a garden near Dublin it has seeded itself for years and comes up everywhere in the formal beds, in the gravel paths and has even largely obliterated an old rockery. I like to mix the pinks, purples, whites and mauves. White varieties include 'Carpet of Snow', 'Little Dorrit' and 'Minimum'; and the coloured ones are 'Pink Heather', 'Lilac Queen', 'Rosie O'Day' and 'Violet Queen'.

Another old favourite is mignonette *(Reseda)*, which used to grace gardens, both large and small, wherever fragrance was considered important. I still love a few plants tucked in a half-shaded corner, so that there are sprays for cutting, but too often this old-fashioned flower has been pushed out by gaudy newcomers. It is still grown as a pot-plant in some greenhouses and is charming in a room. Alas, it does not do well as a house-plant, though admirable in a window-box or in pots on a ledge. If planted in a too hot, sunny position, it goes over very quickly. Sow it out of doors in April or May when the ground is warm, preferably in shallow drills or a well-firmed seed-bed and sprinkle with a light covering of soil. Thin the seedlings subsequently. If possible, choose rich moisture-retentive soil. If you live on dry sandy loam, don't bother to grow mignonette unless you are prepared to water it copiously through dry spells. If you love fragrance, as I do, a little trouble will be amply repaid, as the cut flowers keep well in water and add an old-world charm to bouquets. Flower-arrangers will find the greenish-browns and brownish-reds subtle foils for other colours. 'White Bedder' is a charmer, combining a neat compact habit, fragrance, and quantities of white star-like flowers.

The marigold, the Friendship Flower of America, will always be associated with the name of David Burpee, who, along with several others, has done so much to improve and popularize this very colourful native annual. It is indispensable as it produces flowers from seed much more quickly than most other annuals and over such a long season. There are many types including dwarf French, both single and double, and the fine dwarf Nugget strain, which are fully double and very floriferous. The giant F_1 Climax Hybrids including 'Primrose', 'Yellow', 'Golden' and the orange 'Toreador', with very double flowers as much as five inches across on bushy tow-foot plants, the Carnation-

A well-grown plant of Viola 'Blue Heaven' shows its neat floriferous habit. Dead-heading prolongs the blooming season until frost.

flowered strain of comparable size and specialities such as 'Orange Penny' and 'Red and Gold' are outstanding. The Bodger Seed Company are responsible for the excellent 'Golden Jubilee', 'Diamond Jubilee' and the 'Gold Coin' series. Mr Burpee hopes to produce a pure white one. Already the creamy ivory-white 'Hopeful' is nearing this end. What a useful flower it will be, especially for cutting, as marigolds, like zinnias, last very well.

Night-scented stocks (*Matthiola bicornis*) are as fragrant as they are unspectacular. The thin rather straggly stems, not more than about a foot tall, bear small lilac flowers. Scatter the seeds in drifts in sunny positions on any reasonable soil. As it is not showy, sow it through other plants so that although almost unseen, its fragrance will permeate the garden at night. I have even scattered pinches of seed through irises with excellent results.

I know of one garden where a narrow row had been planted on the inner side of a lavender-hedge along a terrace. Above all, plant a few near the garden door, under the sitting-room windows or near the garden-seat. If there is a white summer jasmine on the wall behind it, so much the better; the combined scents are delicious.

Closely related are the giant-flowered garden stocks, including the ten-week summer-flowering varieties, the spring-flowering (which must be grown as a biennial) and the various compact varieties so useful for bedding. All are fragrant and have a variety of uses. These must be treated as half-hardy annuals and sown under glass.

Petunias in Hot Sun

I always associate petunias with bright sunshine. This is not surprising as so many of our best loved annuals have their origins in South Africa, California, Mexico and the shores of the Mediterranean. Great advances in the hybridization of petunias have increased their colour range, the size and texture of the flowers and above all their stamina and floriferousness. There are various F_1 hybrids, classed as Grandifloras and Multifloras, both single and double. Fine hybrids are being developed not only in this country but in Japan where the hybridizers are also active. Now F_2 hybrids are also appearing.

Of all the work that has been done with F_1 hybrids, petunias have probably proved the most satisfactory, starting with early introductions including 'Comanche' and 'Red Satin' in the 1950's. One of the leaders in the hybridization of petunias in California is Mr Glenn Goldsmith, who is responsible for 'Candy Apple', a fine red grandiflora, 'Starfire', a red striped white multiflora, and the double multiflora 'Delight' series.

Petunia 'Pink Sensation' is typical of this free-flowering, sun-loving annual, which is ideal for bedding and window-boxes.

There are interesting F_2 hybrids which have even greater vigour. 'Confetti' comes in a wide range of colours including white, pink, rose, blue, peach and red. 'Colorama', a mixture introduced by Denholm, is equally fine, and 'Happy Talk' from Ferry-Morse has a bright future. California, the land of sunshine, is where most of the hybridization is done, but labour costs of hand-fertilization and other techniques that cannot be mechanized make the actual introduction of large quantities of seeds too expensive and therefore mass cultivation has been transferred to areas where growing conditions are satisfactory but labour is relatively cheap.

Let us consider for a moment the uses of petunias in various gardens.

Star turns in a paved office courtyard were broad, flaring containers, over three feet in diameter, filled with *Petunia* 'Snowcap', with large ruffled white flowers in great profusion. These were in bloom for many months and gave great pleasure, with their warm, sweet fragrance, another of the delights of this useful genus. What a variety there is and how decorative they are with their small compact flowers as well as the enormous velvety ones, both single and double. Petunias are ideal for sunny window-boxes. No matter how big or how small, there is a suitable variety. Some make neat little mounds for bedding; others trail and fall so that they spill over the edges of tubs, boxes and pots, draping the sides and concealing a beautiful urn and an ugly pot alike.

The choice of colours is exciting, and each year, as the result of extensive hybridization and selection on an enormous scale, new shades appear, as well as freer-blooming varieties with flowers of larger size and better substance. Today there are good yellows and creamy-whites which include 'Pale Face', 'Cream Perfection' and 'Yellow Gleam'. These fine soft tones are flattering with other colours, particularly the blues and mauves, such as 'Blue Bell', 'Blue Lace' and 'Blue Bonnet'. Pinks, reds and carmines are always in demand, and 'Pink Satin', 'Red Satin', and 'Coral Satin' have proved very popular. 'Fire Dance', 'Fire Chief' and 'Comanche' are all brilliant clear scarlets for those who like hot colours, and 'Bonfire' is scarlet-orange with a yellow centre.

'Sugar Plum' will have great appeal, as it is a fine large single with ruffled petals of orchid-lavender heavily veined with deep purple, while 'Plum Dandy' has fine fuschia-purple trumpets which are weather-resistant and should prove good in wet seasons as well as sunny ones. 'Apple Blossom', a large, light salmon-pink with a white throat, and 'Ballerina' with four-inch salmon-rose, softly fringed flowers have been All-American winners. The 'Cascade' varieties, which include pink, red and white, are strong, large-growing grandiflora types for bedding, pots and window-boxes. These have proved to be early and particularly free-flowering.

I don't like double petunias, but this is a personal whim. For those who do, the variegated rose 'Cherry Tart' with white markings, the salmon-pink 'Honey Bunch', the brilliant striped rose and white 'Presto', the pale salmon 'Mrs Dwight D. Eisenhower' and the colossal 'Shades of Rose' are other reliable choices.

The striped and starred varieties have a slightly bizarre quality that appeals to many. One of the most popular is 'Glitters', with medium-sized white flowers banded with five bold red stripes. 'Satellite' has caramine-rose flowers with a clear white star in the centre, and an unusual mixture knows as 'Stardust' includes a range of dazzling colours, all with star markings.

No-one can foresee the weather from year to year, but I am prepared to back the newer varieties of petunias for gardens where cheerful colours and freedom of flower are desired. For small gardens they are particularly satisfactory as they are easy to grow. Petunia-seeds are best sown in boxes during the late winter. They should be covered with glass until the seeds have germinated. Prick out the seedlings and grow on, being sure that the young plants are hardened-off properly before transplanting them to the open ground after the danger of frost has passed.

Sweet Peas for All Gardens

It is interesting how one's personal taste changes in the choice of flowers and even in the matter of colours. I used to like sweet peas in a rainbow mixture of colours. Now I prefer bold blocks of a few selected colours, so that there are enough of a given variety to make a vase. I also like to mix clashing pinks and reds or to combine the purples, mauves, blues and lavenders to get a wonderful harmony of colour. The choice of the large-flowered varieties is very broad, with every colour well represented.

Recently, there have been many fine innovations: Zvolanek's Early Multiflora Strain, for instance, produces five to seven flowers per stem, and the late Plenti-flora Strain flowers a little later but is otherwise similar. The best-known and probably the finest new strain is one grown under the group-name Galaxy, developed by W. Atlee Burpee, one of the great names in the development of modern sweet peas. These have proved superb on the show-bench and as garden flowers alike. Strong long stems bear as many as five to seven large flowers of fine form and texture.

Mixtures of this fine strain in a wide range of colours are available. Another strain is Cuthbertson Flori-bunda, like Galaxy, marking an advance in the size and number of flowers over old types. Named clones in the Galaxy Strain include 'Blue Sails', a soft pale blue; 'Gigi', light salmon-cerise; 'Purity', a large ruffled white; 'Jupiter', a vibrant carmine-rose; 'Milky Way', a soft creamy-white with a delicate flush; 'Fireglow', a vivid scarlet; 'Great Scot', a fine salmon-pink; and 'Great Britain', rose-pink on cream.

'Little Sweetheart', a compact, dwarf sweet pea, with masses of scented, frilly flowers, is ideally suited to small gardens and even to window-boxes and large tubs.

Great store in America is placed on awards from British authorities, as conditions in Britain are ideal for sweet peas. Good indications of popularity are the varieties which head the Audit of the National Sweet Pea Society's Annual Shows. Other useful yardsticks are awards made after trials by the Royal Horticultural Society and the Scottish National Sweet Pea Society. Outstanding varieties include 'Mrs Robert Bolton', almond-pink on white; 'Air Warden', scarlet; 'Carlotta', deep carmine; 'Margot', cream; 'Geranium Pink', cerise-pink suffused with glowing orange; 'Piccadilly', cerise-pink; 'Leamington', very sweetly scented lilac;

'Swan Lake', fine white; 'Pastel', very fragrant, ice-blue; and 'Sonata', warm salmon-pink, shaded cream at the base of the petals.

Scent plays a very large part in the fascination of sweet peas. A few outstanding ones in this respect include 'Lavender Lace', 'Vogue', 'Nocturne' and 'Evensong', all in the blue and lavender range; 'Rosy Frills' and 'Tell Tale', white with rose-picotee edge; 'Cream Gigantic', 'Mrs C. Kay', lavender, and the blush-lilac 'Silver Cascade'. The older types are, of course, often the most fragrant.

The development of dwarf sweet peas, suited to small

modern gardens, started with the Little Sweetheart and the Cuthbertson Cupid strains, which do not exceed a foot in height. The Zvolaneks, father and son, developed their Dwarf Pigmy strain and W. Atlee Burpee has now brought out the Dwarf Bijou, which is a semi-dwarf which promises a very rosy future. This is the ideal plant for small gardens. It grows about twelve inches tall and is ideal for tubs, deep flower-boxes, small beds on terraces and even roof-gardens. It is extraordinary that such relatively small plants should produce plants with sturdy stems as much as seven inches in length and bearing as many as four or five large well-formed blooms. In the Royal Horticultural Society's Sweet Pea Trials at Wisley this new strain has been impressive for its free flowering over a long period and its varied and pleasing colours. It has received eight First-Class Certificates in the Scottish National Sweet Pea Society's Trials. For several years only mixed seeds were available, but now a few selected varieties are offered by name; these include 'Catalina', amethyst on white; 'Pinkette', salmon-pink on cream; 'Rosette', deep rose; 'Sapphire', clear blue; 'Scarlette', bright scarlet-cerise; 'Mauvette', 'Rubyette' and 'White Pearl'.

For pots, small window-boxes or as an unusual edging the even dwarfer Little Sweetheart, which comes only in mixed colours, is charming. It flowers very successfully in various urban gardens, and in the country I have seen a cottage garden where a stone path was edged with loose, colourful hedges about eight to ten inches high. If you are growing this dwarf strain or the Bijou mentioned above, be sure that the plants don't dry out, particularly if they are in pots, tubs, or window-boxes. Sweet peas must have moisture and nourishment for success.

The Ferry-Morse 'Knee Hi' has been highly praised. When spring-sown *in situ*, it will grow more than a few feet in height and requires almost no support. If autumn-sown, it reaches four feet and makes a broad floriferous hedge. The stems are as long as those of the usual sweet peas and carry as many as five to eight flowers. Named clones of this excellent strain include 'San Juan', a scented white; 'San Francisco', salmon-rose on cream; 'Sacramento', rich scarlet; 'Santa Barbara', scented blush-rose; and 'Monterey', scented, rich blue. All of these received Awards of Merit from the British Royal Horticultural Society after trial in 1968. 'Knee Hi' makes a real advance over other dwarf sweet peas.

Quite obviously the dwarf sweet pea is here to stay,

The new Sweet Pea 'Knee Hi', supported here on wire, grows to about three feet tall, with long-stemmed, fragrant flowers of fine quality.

and seedsmen have been breeding new dwarf strains to meet the present trend towards plants for small gardens and those that are labour-saving.

An Autumn Sowing of Sweet Peas

Sweet peas are exceptionally good value in a cool, wet summer. Even if they have been damaged by heavy rain, a few days of warm sunshine soon encourages another flush of flowers. With consistent dead-heading there can be a continuous succession of blooms for several months. They are particularly satisfactory in the relatively cool moist conditions of the Northwest and New England.

Many gardeners who have suitable cold-frames or cold-houses prefer to sow their sweet-pea seeds in autumn and to winter them under glass. This provides sturdy, healthy plants for the next season and means an early start to it. Sow the seeds in October, making sure that they are good ones from a reliable source. Choose the strain and colours carefully. For autumn sowing I suggest only the large-flowered varieties or giant strains, which include the new Multiflora and Galaxy. The dwarf strains, such as Bijou and Knee-Hi, are probably better planted in spring. On light, warm soils sweet peas can be sown in the open ground in late September or early October. A shallow trench is beneficial, as it gives some protection against winter storms, and as the plants develop, the earth can be drawn from the sides to protect the stems.

If the seeds are sown in pots, sweet-pea tubes are admirable. These are made of black whalehide, two and a half inches in diameter and five inches deep. Regular pots (60's) can also be used, but the bottomless tubes, because of their extra depth, are ideal for the deep tap-roots characteristic of sweet peas. The tubes should be filled with seed-compost and then stood in seed-trays. Twenty-eight will fit nicely and make a compact, easily-handled unit. Allow a single seed or at the most two to each pot. Germination under good conditions will take place in two or three weeks, but with very hard-skinned varieties some experts advocate chipping the skin opposite the 'eye' to hasten growth, or soaking them overnight in tepid water. Hard-skinned varieties are often noted on the seed-packet.

The secret with sweet peas is to grow them cold. If the pots are placed in frames, leave the lights off so that the seedlings are exposed to the elements. Of course, in severe weather or during periods of heavy rain and snow, protection can be provided. When four leaves have formed, pinch out the growing tip to encourage vigorous side-shoots. The plants can be set out in early spring in their tubes in open ground, which

should have been thoroughly dug and enriched with manure either in the autumn or in the very early spring. I am a great believer in autumn preparation when possible, as the ground has time to settle and the action of frost is beneficial. Furthermore, it is a nice feeling to have the labour behind one, so that if spring is late, you are not backward with routine work.

Be sure to dead-head sweet peas constantly. Nothing will stop production of flower buds more quickly than allowing seed-pods to form. When cutting blooms, be thorough. Even if you do not want certain stems for the house because of their short length or imperfection of flower, cut them off. Dead-heading pansies is laborious, but there is no doubt that it pays an ample dividend in the prolonged flowering season.

The very large-flowered 'Elizabeth Taylor' is a fine variety that deserves its popularity. Seeds sown in autumn should give gratifying results.

7 Fruit and Vegetables

What Vegetables Shall I Grow?

For the lover of vegetables, few prospects are as pleasant as the first ones from his own garden in late spring and early summer. As the quantity and variety increase, there is a temptation to live more and more on their fresh bounty, so that none are wasted. The art is to grow exactly what you want and in the right quantity, so that there is not a glut of one variety or reason to lament that you did not plant half enough of it. This means careful planning. A few rules can be laid down, especially for those with small gardens.

First, grow what does well on your soil. For example, if you are on light, dry sandy soil, celery will be difficult, as it likes rich, moist soil. It is probably far better to buy what you require. If you have great trouble with slugs on celery, you must decide whether it is worth the battle. Second, grow what you cannot buy cheaply or easily.

New peas are one of the great treats of the year and today there is a choice of types ranging from giant climbing varieties to dwarf bush-peas, ideally suited for smaller areas. Choice will also depend on whether or not you want to bother with pea-sticks or netting. Obviously, if space is restricted, go for the early ones, which come as the greatest treat. Peas are heavy feeders, so be generous, and try to plant at intervals of about three weeks, starting in late February or early March, depending on the district and the season.

Leeks are one of the most delicious of all winter vegetables, with a variety of uses. As a vegetable with butter or cream sauce, with cheese, cold in salads or hors d'oeuvres and in a variety of soups, stews and sauces they figure prominently. Sow the seeds as early as is possible in a carefully prepared seed-bed which has been well dug, firmed and then raked to a fine tilth. The last item is important. Plant the seeds in shallow drills six to eight inches apart. Alternatively, the seeds can be planted in an open frame or a single drill in the garden, if only a small number are required. When the seedlings are about six inches high, they are ready for transplanting. Plant at intervals of eight to nine inches with the rows about sixteen inches apart. Drop the plants in the hole made with a dibber and then water the rows to settle the soil around the roots, which are brittle and fleshy. Alternatively, leeks can be planted in drills. In this case, draw the soil up round the bottom of the stems to blanch a little more of it. Leeks are so hardy that they can usually be left in the ground through the winter in mild areas and pulled as they are needed. It is often possible to buy leek seedlings locally if you cannot raise your own.

Succulent new carrots are delicious and successive sowings should be made from March until June at intervals of three to four weeks. Ground for carrots and beets should not be manured, but if it is poor, use a general-purpose fertilizer. The seeds should be sown in well-prepared soil at a depth of a generous half-inch. For beets and many other vegetables, careful thinning is essential. This should be done at regular intervals, so that ultimately there will be four to five inches between the carrots, depending on the size of the variety. (There are stump-rooted, intermediate and long.) It helps to water them after thinning, so as to settle the roots of the remaining plants, which may have been disturbed. The last thinning should yield delectable baby carrots that ought to be cooked whole. Beets for early use should be planted in April; for winter use, a later sowing at the end of May is recommended. There is a choice of round and long varieties. Select the former for early use.

A word about the usefulness of Jerusalem artichokes, with their delicious sweet nutty flavour. They make one of the best of all cream soups, and they are so easy to grow. Moreover, they are rather decorative and can be tucked in a corner of grown against a fence or shed as a tall screen. As they are vigorous, plant the tubers four to six inches deep and at least fourteen inches apart, with double that distance between the rows. The foliage and gay yellow flowers, like a large daisy on branching stalks often as much as six or seven feet tall, will be attractive through the summer. Cut

The decorative foliage and fine flavour of Artichoke 'Gros Vert de Laon' makes it a welcome addition to all gardens where there is space.

off the dead stalks in early winter and lift the knobbly potato-like tubers as required through the winter.

One of the best vegetables is the true French bean. Lots of beans enjoy this name on menus, but the ones in France are usually very different, for they tend to be round instead of flat, deep green in colour when lightly cooked, stringless and of superb flavour. Several firms offer what they claim to be the true dwarf French bean, so widely grown in France.

Many people have complained that they had difficulty in growing basil. If possible, sow it under glass and grow it as a pot-plant, but out of doors. Give it rich, well-drained soil and all the sun you can. Its wonderful fragrance is a delight and the flavour enhances any dish with tomatoes. Basil and tomatoes are as right as eggs and bacon or parsley and potatoes.

Kohlrabi is a little-grown vegetable with a purplish swollen stem rather like a turnip. The flavour is subtle, rather like a cross between cabbage and turnip. It should be picked young and not overcooked for the best results. Salsify, or Oyster Plant as it is sometimes called, is another subtle-flavoured winter vegetable, with a long narrow root a little like a white carrot. The roots can be lifted and stored or in mild areas left in the ground until they are needed.

Asparagus as an Investment

Asparagus is probably more highly esteemed by gourmets than any other vegetable and rightly; it has a delicious, distinctive flavour and appears in early spring when we are hungry for fresh vegetables. It has been a favourite of mine since I was six, not only because I like to eat it, but because I was fascinated by the way it poked its purple nose through the brown earth in spring.

Unfortunately, there is an idea that growing asparagus means a great deal of work. In reality, a well-made bed is a splendid long-term investment, certainly good for ten years and in all probability for twenty, if properly cared for. It should provide ample asparagus for your daily needs for eight weeks each spring, with possibly a surplus for the deep-freeze if the bed is large. In fact, asparagus is one of the better frozen vegetables, especially when processed at home, using tender, young, freshly picked shoots.

Today, many serious gardeners are finding that it is economic to limit the size of the kitchen garden and to grow only special favourites and items that are difficult to obtain locally. In other words, cabbages, sprouts, main-crop potatoes, carrots and runner beans are easy to obtain and relatively cheap. Asparagus, globe artichokes, new potatoes, true French beans, the finer lettuces, courgettes and herbs are expensive, scarce and therefore well worth growing. Everyone will have his or her special list, but on almost all of them asparagus will probably appear.

For success, choose a sunny position with well-drained soil, preferably a rich, light loam, though most good garden soils are suitable. If the soil is heavy and poorly drained, lighten it with coarse sand, coal ash, or burnt earth. Beds can also be raised eight to ten inches above the level of the soil to help drainage.

Obviously, the best possible stock should be planted. Prepare the site in the autumn or early winter, giving the soil time to settle before planting at the right time in early spring. Clean the ground thoroughly, so that there is no trace of perennial weeds or couch-grass. Double-dig and incorporate lots of well-rotted manure. Compost may be used if manure is not available. As asparagus is a heavy feeder and the bed is to last a long time, don't skimp. It used to be general practice to dig the manure into the lower spit, but it is better to have as much as possible in the top one, accessible to the wide-spreading roots. Asparagus does not like an acid soil, so apply lime if necessary.

Today, the single-row method is the generally preferred way of planting. Allow a minimum of four feet between the rows and fifteen to eighteen inches between the plants within each row. Asparagus can also be planted in beds four feet wide, with three rows of plants spaced so that there is fifteen inches between the rows and nine inches on the sides. Leave at least two feet between the beds. The interval between the plants should be fifteen to eighteen inches.

Asparagus may be raised from seeds sown in open ground in late March or early April. Sow in drills three quarters of an inch deep and at intervals of about two inches. Thin the seedlings to allow a six-inch interval. In dry weather, water and weed them carefully, both hoeing between the rows and hand-weeding as necessary. By the following April the seedlings will be ready to be planted in their permanent site.

One-, two- and three-year-old plants can be purchased from nurseries and specialists. One-year-old plants settle down quickly with the fewest casualties. Two-year-old stock is usually good, but three-year-old roots are often tricky and slow to establish themselves. Costs obviously increase with age. Therefore it is advisable to raise seedlings or to use one- or two-year-old plants. Insist on delivery in early spring when the ground has thawed, as the roots must not dry out.

Male plants are supposed to be preferable if obtainable, as the shoots are sturdier and more freely produced and myriads of seedlings cannot appear. The sex of plants may be determined by examination of the flowers (the male are staminate, the females pistilate) or by waiting to see if the plants set seed and discarding all that do. These theories are excellent, but in practice they do not work out and a great deal first class asparagus is unsexed. Fine asparagus may be of either sex and it is well-nigh impossible to buy all male plants, let alone to segregate them. So much for that myth.

Prepare the bed for planting by forking in February and again at planting time, when a balanced fertilizer should be applied at the rate of three ounces per yard.

To plant asparagus, open a trench fifteen inches wide and eight inches deep, with a ridge three to four inches high down the centre. Place the young plants on top of the ridge at the correct intervals and spread the roots. Work the soil through and over the roots to a depth of two inches above the crowns and subsequently fill the trench gradually as the stems grow.

It is essential that the plants should be kept well watered in dry weather and that the weed-population is always under control. As a boy, it was my task to weed the asparagus-bed two or three times every summer, and I remember only too well what a job it could be if I left it too long.

Do not cut shoots until the third year, but if three-year-old plants are used, cutting may start the second year after planting. This should not last for more than six weeks during the first year of cropping and subsequently for eight to nine weeks. Do not cut the fern-like foliage for decoration throughout the summer. When it turns a golden brown in autumn and before the seeds fall, cut the stem a few inches from the surface and mound-up the soil a few inches deep over the crowns. Mulch well with either rotted manure or compost each autumn, and rake off rough remains in early spring. Renewal of the ridges is important to keep the proper depth of soil above the crowns.

Agricultural salt at the rate of two ounces per yard in early spring was at one time widely used, but now this is not generally recommended, particularly for light, sandy soils. In Madeira and various areas in southern Europe seaweed is used as a mulch for asparagus with some success.

Good varieties of asparagus include 'Connover's Colossal', which is one of the best, 'Kidner's Pedigree', 'Purple Emperor', 'Purple Argenteuil', 'Martha Washington' and 'Viking'.

Lesser-known Vegetables

In spite of the fact that there are many delicious but seldom-grown vegetables, the majority of gardeners follow the same old pattern, growing the tried and true, year in year out – carrots, spinach, peas, cabbages, sprouts, snap beans and cauliflowers. And very good they are too, if picked young and eaten within a few hours, for that, after all, is the best reason for growing one's own vegetables.

To this list I want to add a few easy but neglected vegetables of real merit. First, there is a form of beet spinach known variously as Swiss Chard or Sea-kale Beet. I always think of it under the former name. It has handsome foliage with rich green leaves and broad fleshy-white mid-ribs. The green part can be used as spinach and the stems boiled separately and served rather like sea-kale, making two vegetables, each delicious but different in appearance, texture and flavour. The stems alone are excellent creamed, with a rich cheese sauce or with butter, lemon-juice and chopped parsley. Swiss Chard is easy to grow and lasts a long time, standing up well to cold weather. For this reason two crops are often planted. The first is sown as soon as the soil is workable in March or early April in drills an inch deep and a foot apart. Select a position on good rich soil that does not dry out quickly or that can be watered in dry seasons. Thin the seedlings to eight or nine inches. These will yield an abundant crop over a long season, if a few leaves are taken from a plant at a time, as more are constantly developing. A second sowing should be made in mild areas in August, preferably in a warm sheltered spot.

Although there are many lettuces on the market, adapted to varied conditions of climate and soil, other excellent salad greens deserve to be more widely grown to ring the changes. Lamb's lettuce or Corn Salad has rosettes of very tender leaves that make a delicate salad. It lends itself to cultivation in frames in autumn or early spring. Dandelions are a delicious spring salad. Cook the coarse outer leaves and serve with butter, freshly ground black pepper and lemon juice. The centre leaves can be tied together to blanch them, and then served as a delicious salad. The new white beet is very sweet and makes a delicious cool-looking salad or hors d'oeuvres. The merit of white radishes should not be over-looked, as they are mild, sweet and crisp. Curly endive is too little grown. Allow the centres to blanch to creamy white.

Shallots should be planted in spring after danger of frost is passed, and in favoured areas, even in late October. They are easy to grow, far easier, in fact, than onions, and as their flavouring is more subtle it is not surprising that French recipes often call for them. Also they combine well with herbs. Shallots are highly decorative for small gardens with their short, compact, dark green foliage in neat rows or blocks. They are an essential part of those little French back-gardens with parsley edgings, rows of carrots, lettuces, peas and, more likely than not, Madonna lilies, a lilac, a pear and an apple tree or two, neatly pruned.

Results with shallots are far better from bulbs than from seeds. The soil must be rich and open but not freshly manured. Press the bulbs into the soil to about half their depth. Allow four to six inches between bulbs, with a foot between the rows. Be sure to check the bulbs a few weeks after planting. Frost can heave them out of the ground; birds and mice are evil in their actions. Shallots will need little further attention, save weeding and loosening the soil. By late June or early July a cluster of smaller bulbs will have formed around the parent bulb and these will gradually swell to maturity. Meanwhile, the foliage turns yellowish and loses its firmness. Lift the bulbs when they are ripe at the end of July and spread them out to dry. Only then should they be separated and cleaned. If your children want a sure crop, shallots, like daffodils and hyacinths, are the obvious choice to accompany the inevitable radishes. Success is assured and as half of the bulb is exposed above ground, progress can be observed without frequent digging up and replanting.

For lovers of basil there is a variety called 'Dark Opal', described as having deep purple foliage and spikes of lavender flowers. Young leaves can be used for flavouring salads and other dishes. It sounds like a real addition to the herb border, where green foliage

is predominant, with grey a close second. It would be wise, though, to continue to grow sweet basil, as I cannot believe that the purple variety has as exquisite a flavour and scent. Both are annuals and should either be sown in open ground in late March or April or brought on under glass, potted or planted out.

'Caserta' is a delicious summer squash which has fruits about sixteen inches in length and four to five inches thick, but they should be eaten when half this size or even a little less. Then the pale yellowish flesh is tender with an excellent delicate flavour. These are yellowish green, mottled with a darker green. 'Blue Hubbard' is a fine winter type, which keeps well and has a good flavour. Fruits are large, weighing about fourteen pounds. The hard grey-blue rind is in striking contrast to the bright orange-yellow flesh. There is a smaller version, which I prefer, known as 'Baby Blue Hubbard'. For summer consumption use when the rind is still soft. In winter I am particularly fond of the small acorn squashes as they have rich sweet flesh that is light and dry when cooked. They are easy

Both the stem and the leaf of the decorative Sea Kale Beet, also known as Swiss Chard, provide delectable dishes for the lover of unusual vegetables.

The winged pods of the Asparagus Pea have a subtle flavour that explains the curious name of this exotic, easily-grown vegetable.

to grow and can be served in a number of ways. As they are so small half a squash makes an ideal portion.

Zucchini, a small, dark green, Italian vegetable-marrow, and courgette, a delicious French counterpart, are both finding increasing favour. Both are bush types and prolific croppers over a long period. The secret is to pick the fruits when small and tender with the seeds still unformed. At this stage they can be cooked unpeeled, either sliced or whole, in a variety of ways. Perhaps the best way is to fry them in butter or olive oil until they are tender and then sprinkle them with chopped parsley or grated Parmesan cheese, or boil them lightly and serve cold with French dressing.

Courgettes and zucchini are easy to grow, requiring the same treatment as summer squashes. In cold areas, sow the seeds in April in three-inch pots, preferably of peat or composition, in suitable seed compost. Grow one to a pot, but in case of uneven germination it is safer to sow several seeds to each pot and to thin them out as required. In late May or early June, when all danger of frost has passed, plant them out at two-foot intervals. Seeds may also be sown in open ground in late spring at a depth of about one and a half inches. There are three essentials: full sun, rich soil and plenty of moisture. Most members of the pumpkin and squash family have similar requirements. Well-dug soil with lots of manure is best. Courgettes and zucchini can also be grown on piles of turves, like melons and summer squashes, but this encourages drying out in warm weather. The more the young fruits are picked, the more the plants will bear and the longer the season. The marrows should not be allowed to exceed six inches to eight in length when picked and about three to four inches is a preferable size for some varieties.

Another delicious squash is a trailing variety of South African origin known as 'Little Gem', with rounded green fruits, similar in size to a Jaffa orange, and therefore excellent for individual servings. It is a trailing variety, so allow three feet between the plants. A great favourite of mine is the bush-type of Argentine marrow or Avocadella *(Zapallito de Tronco)*, which is

111

Custard squashes are not only beautiful in fruit, flower and leaf, but provide a welcome change from the usual green squashes.

about the same size as a small grapefruit and with an exceptional flavour. It is delicious as a vegetable served hot with butter, or as a main dish when stuffed with various fillings, including hard-boiled eggs or chicken and tomatoes in a white sauce with cheese, or cold filled with vegetables, shrimps or fish and dressed with French dressing, mayonnaise or a highly seasoned Russian dressing.

Instead of the usual large tomatoes, I suggest that you try some of the smaller-fruited ones. These are delicious and highly decorative, with their large trusses of gleaming small fruits. They are useful as salads and hors d'oeuvres and make attractive garnishes. They have become so popular that they are available in better shops and super-markets throughout the winter. 'Tiny Tim' has clusters of fruits about an inch in diameter, borne on a neat, compact bush. Other attractive varieties are 'Red Currant', with long decorative trusses of fruits; 'Red Cherry', which has larger fruits of good flavour about the size of the largest cherries; 'Yellow Cherry'; and 'Pear', another yellow with a delicate sweet flavour. All of these are charming if grown in pots, tubs or boxes for sunny positions on terraces or broad window-ledges, and they may be brought indoors when in fruit as house-plants.

They are particularly useful for sun-porches and conservatories.

The French are fond of *Mangetout* peas, also referred to as Sugar Peas, which are cooked whole, pod and all, when young and tender and have a very sweet unusual flavour. Several varieties are offered by seedgrowers, including 'Sweetpod', 'Sugar Pea', 'Sweetgreen', 'Dwarf Sugar' and 'Paramount Sugar'. These have great character, but, of course, do not replace the usual garden peas. Red Brussels sprouts are a delightful change and, like purple-sprouting broccoli, make a colourful addition to winter menus. 'Rubine' has handsome dark red sprouts of excellent flavour.

Most gardeners grow the usual curled parsley, but for flavour I far prefer the true French (uncurled) parsley. It is delicious in cooking, salads, and as a garnish. Its requirements are similar to other parsleys – a cool, rich root-run, a long period of germination, and the minimum of disturbance. It should be sown *in situ* and thinned.

For decoration only, few plants are as much fun as dwarf gourds. These come in a variety of shapes and colours, as typified by the names apple, pear, turban, egg, club, etc. Some are smooth, others are warted. Colours include green, yellow, orange, cream, white and striped. They require conditions similar to those for summer squashes – sun, moisture and rich soil. Grow them on trellises, mounds, old stumps or poles as important decorative features in the garden. The fruits keep for months when dried and provide amusing, colourful table-decorations throughout the winter. I repeat, they are not edible. They are usually listed in catalogues under Gourds (Decorative, mixed). After harvesting the gourds, dry them carefully in an airy place and varnish them to enhance their colours.

Finocchio or Florentine fennel, unlike sweet fennel, forms a thick, fleshy, bulbous stem just above ground-level. This is tender and very delicious as a vegetable when boiled and served with butter or cooked in cream with cheese. It is also excellent sliced or grated raw for salads or hors d'oeuvres.

Sow fennel in drills in well-drained open ground in a warm, sunny position in spring. Cover the seeds lightly and firm. Thin out the seedlings to about eight to ten inches apart. A friend of mine says that she had more pleasure from her crop than from any other vegetable, but she lives in a warm, sunny area. Fennel is very widely used in Italy and is now finding its way increasingly into better shops at certain seasons. Another remarkable attribute is the fact that pigeons and other birds seem to have no interest in it whatsoever, and this certainly is a boon.

Another splendid vegetable is celeriac, which forms a large, thick, underground root, often weighing a pound or two. It has a sweet nutty flavour similar to celery, but a harder, firmer texture. It is delicious grated or shredded raw and served as the French do, with a mayonnaise heavily flavoured with mustard. It also can be cooked and used for soups and stews. Cultivation is easy, as celeriac does not have to be banked with earth, like celery.

Dual-purpose Artichokes

Decorative value and delicious flavour are two compelling reasons to grow globe (French) artichokes. No vegetable has more handsome foliage. The long, silvery-grey, arching leaves, cut like an acanthus, vie with the bold globular flower-heads, borne on tall, branching stems. They are decorative in bud at the edible stage or when fully developed like an enormous blue thistle. Artichokes have one of the most subtle flavours of all vegetables, which explains why they are considered the supreme epicurean vegetable in Mediterranean countries such as Spain, Portugal, Italy and Greece, where vast quantities are consumed in season and the hearts are bottled, pickled or preserved in oil for winter use. They are widely grown in California and parts of the South where conditions are ideal. *Cynara scolymus*, the species, is native to parts of north Africa. They found their way to America via Britain. They were introduced into England by the Romans, and were so successfully grown and of such excellence in the sixteenth and early seventeenth centuries that stocks were exported to the Low Countries, France and Italy. Already in Elizabethan times they were being boiled and eaten with butter or oil and vinegar. Incidentally, the globe artichoke antedates the Jerusalem artichoke, which was introduced to France and thence to England about 1620 from eastern North America, where it was a favourite food of the Indians. Parkinson, one of the great eighteenth-century herbalists, dubbed them 'Potatoes of Canada', and the name stuck.

Artichokes are easy to grow if certain requirements are observed. They need space, as the plants will in time form massive clumps. They should not be closer than thirty to thirty-six inches. They are handsome along a path where the leaf-shape can be appreciated, and they should be included for decorative effect as widely in our vegetable gardens as in the French *potager*, or plant them in bold groups in herbaceous and mixed borders as cardoons are sometimes used. Choose a sunny, well-drained position, remembering that in the growing season they will require a good deal of moisture. They are happy on alkaline or light, sandy soils if properly enriched with well-rotted manure or humus to retain moisture. They even succeed on acid soils; I know of a fine bed in a Donegal garden where the soil has a peat base but has been enriched with farmyard manure over the years in the old

kitchen-garden tradition. They have been grown successfully on heavy soils which have been lightened with extra grit. Rich, light loam is obviously best. Good drainage is essential.

Many people labour under the impression that artichokes are frost-tender and cannot survive the winter cold because of their fleshy crowns and rootstocks. They were successfully grown in Williamsburg when it was the capital of Virginia and at Mount Vernon. They are generally hardy in Zone 7, and even in warm positions in Zone 6 on very well drained soil, if heavily mulched. In cold gardens they should be mounded-up with soil or covered with a mulch such as bracken, but in mild areas and gardens where drainage is very good, this is not necessary. Foliage should not be cut back until spring.

Plant new stocks at the end of April or early May in deeply dug rich soil. Nursery-plants will be rooted off-shoots or suckers, which should bear well the following year. Plant them immediately on delivery. They will often flag badly at first, but with watering and protection from hot sun they soon pull round. Once established, they require little care except weeding and an annual feeding. They do not need staking. Artichokes can also be grown easily from seed, but the plants will lack the uniform excellence of named clones. Sow seeds in the open in March (earlier under glass). Pot-up seedlings separately and plant out when the ground is warm.

Among the named varieties 'Gros Vert de Laon', the slightly more tender 'Camus de Bretagne', and 'English Globe' are good, the first two being best for flavour and texture. The last, however, is the hardiest and easiest to grow.

Artichokes can be served in a variety of ways, either hot with melted butter or hollandaise sauce or cold with sauce vinaigrette, French dressing or lemon-juice and chopped herbs. They are delicious in salads, or the hearts, stuffed with various fillings, are ideal as a garnish for chicken or meat.

The dried heads, either in bud or after they have developed into the flower stage, make wonderful subjects for large-scale winter arrangements. In fact, there are few more effective bold subjects around which to compose a vase.

Fragrant Kitchen Herbs

Every year in February I like to make a brief survey of the herb prospects for the summer, as herbs are vital for the pleasures of good food and for fragrance in the garden. Even small gardens should have a patch. I know of many a window-ledge or balcony in towns where pots or boxes of chives, parsley, tarragon, mint, basil, thyme and other indispensable herbs grow with a

Parsley, backed by a row of radishes, makes a charming edging for a garden path, as do chives, thyme, savory and alpine strawberries.

in sauces, soups, stews, poultry dressing and endless other recipes. *Thymus vulgaris* and the lemon-flavoured variety *T. citriodora* are best for seasoning. The former is easily grown from seeds. I am very fond of marjoram *(Origanum vulgare)*, which is much used in France and Italy for meat-dishes, especially with tomatoes in sauces and soups. So, too, is winter savory, another hardy perennial, and there are others. Once these perennial herbs are established in the garden it is easy to propagate them by divisions or layers and by cuttings of the woody ones like thyme and sage.

No garden should be without a sweet bay *(Laurus nobilis)*, which is just another laurel with delightfully aromatic leaves. Small trees are available, and if protected from extreme cold they develop fairly quickly and will in time grow to a height of twenty feet or more but will not survive in very cold climates without protection. They are hardy in Zone 7. Of course, they can be pruned heavily and controlled. Bays will need protection in cold areas. A leaf or two is a regular ingredient of endless dishes, be they Italian, French or Mexican.

Figs for Foliage and Fruit

I have always had a fondness for figs, not only as a fruit, bursting with honeyed sweetness and warm with sun, but as a decorative tree or wall-covering, with their lovely silvery-grey stems throughout the year and the handsome dark green foliage, so boldly decorative. A delicious subtle fragrance that always evokes Greek islands or the Mediterranean coast is exuded by fig trees on a hot sunny day. Obviously in cold climates you need to select as warm and sunny a position as possible. Lucky are the fig-lovers who live in California or warm southern districts where figs flourish unattended.

Sun and protection from cold winds are essential. Also necessary is a relatively meagre diet and root-restriction, for figs, left to their own devices in rich open ground, will send out enormous roots and bear little or no fruit. This probably explains why figs are so happy against the sunny back-wall of a greenhouse, often one devoted to vines and nectarines in the good old days. Here the walls and, in all probability, concrete paths check the roots, but if not, an artificial restraint is easily provided. Out of doors it is best to build a special bed or sunken trough for them, roughly three to four feet long, two to three feet wide, and at lest two and a half to three feet deep. This can be lined with concrete slabs, cement, bricks or asbestos sheeting. Stones, bricks, very coarse coal-ash or clinkers make a good bottom, permitting drainage. The bed should be filled with fibrous loam, but manure or very rich compost should be avoided. Bone-meal is an excellent

little coaxing. In country-gardens it is always assumed that there are parsley, chives, sage and mint, for these necessities are readily available. There are a variety of mints, but for cooking *Mentha viridis*, *M. rotundifolia* and *M. cordifolia* are all excellent. Mint 'walks' freely underground, so it should be planted where it can either be allowed to ramp or somewhere with containment, such as in a narrow-edged bed against a wall, or in a bucket with the bottom removed. Mint likes a cool, moist position, but any good garden-soil will do.

My favourite herb is French tarragon *(Artemisia dracunculus)*, but it is essential to obtain the right plant, as there is a lot of rank inferior tarragon masquerading as the true French variety. It likes a sunny position and well-drained soil. Tarragon is not completely hardy and suffers on heavy, cold soil or during very wet winters. Never cut tarragon to the ground in winter; leave the top-growth to protect the crowns. It is delicious with salads, fish, chicken, jellied eggs and many sauces.

Thyme is also invaluable to the cook, as it appears

114

long-term nutrient. Nitro-chalk or sulphate of ammonia at the rate of two ounces per plant is beneficial as a spring dressing. Mortar rubble improves drainage and provides the necessary lime.

Figs are always provided from pots and, although they are planted ideally in March, later planting is possible. Be sure to remove the broken crock and to disentangle the roots. The branches should be fanned out against the wall and carefully tied in as they grow. Pruning figs requires a realization that fruits are borne on the tips of the growths of the previous season. In all probability no pruning will be necessary the first year. The young growths of established trees should be stopped at about four buds in June. In warm districts and under glass, figs may produce as many as three crops in a year, but in northern zones only one is produced, usually in late August or September. In autumn, after leaf-fall, thin out old, spent wood and weak, spindly growths. Root-pruning is sometimes necessary if growth is too vigorous. In periods of drought in summer be sure that the plants have plenty of water, and a mild liquid manure helps to swell the fruits.

Two varieties are widely grown. The more reliable for annual fruiting is 'Brown Turkey'. It produces a copious quantity of large, brown, juicy fruits. Another relatively hardy variety is 'Brunswick', which has very large pear-shaped fruits with a greenish-yellow skin and rich yellowish flesh. Its leaves are more deeply divided than many varieties.

A fig trained fan-wise on a wall will require from twelve to fifteen feet and the wall should be fairly high. If the plants are too restricted, little fruit is obtained. Figs in tubs or large pots are very good for town gardens. The foliage is handsome, even though the fruit may not always develop. And as the roots like to be restricted, pot-culture is ideal. In cities and areas of high

A corner of the small paved herb garden presented to the American Museum in Britain by the Southampton Garden Club. Note the use of tender, scented-leaved geraniums among the permanent planting of rosemary, sage, hyssop, artemisias and tarragon.

pollution I find the embryonic fruits often drop in winters with bad fog or smog. Figs can be easily propagated from stocky cuttings about six to nine inches long, preferably with a heel (a small segment of the main stem). Pot them up in four- or five-inch pots and, if possible, provide bottom-heat to hasten rooting. If bottom-heat is available, late winter or early spring is a satisfactory time to make cuttings; otherwise strike them in the autumn when leaves are dropping.

Alpine Strawberries from Seed

I never can understand why more people don't grow the delicious Alpine strawberries, known variously as *fraise des bois* or *Quatre Saisons*, so-called both because of their parentage, stemming from the wild Continental *Fragaria vesca* and possibly the highly flavoured *F. moschata*, and their long bearing season. In general, the term Alpine is applied to the small-fruiting, perpetual-bearing varieties associated with summer luncheons in Paris or, for that matter, France in general. There is nothing so delicious if they are properly ripened and served in accordance with a few basic rules. Fortunately they are relatively easy to grow and so decorative that they can be used variously as an edging, as a dwarf hedge, as ground-cover, or even in small groups for the effect and beauty of the foliage and fruit.

Alpine strawberries fall into two classes, differentiated by whether or not they make runners. Runnerless varieties are usually propagated from seeds or by division of the crowns, but the latter is the less satisfactory of the two methods. Those with runners obviously increase very quickly by layering. Of the former group the most famous variety is 'Baron Solemacher', 'Charles V' and the Russian 'Catherine the Great' are also recommended. On the Continent other varieties are popular, but the tried and true 'Baron' does so well here that there is little point in undertaking the cultivation of others. Seeds of 'Baron Solemacher' are available and plants can also be ordered. 'Cresta' is an excellent runner-making variety.

Seeds mature quickly. In fact, if seeds are sown in the early autumn and the small plants pricked-out in boxes and placed in a frame or cool-house for the winter, they can be planted out in March or in cold areas in early April. They will bear fruit that same summer and in the early autumn. Seeds may also be sown in late February or March and the seedlings planted out in May. The seeds are very small indeed, so they should be covered with a very light dusting of compost pressed through a fine sieve and then gently firmed. It is worth preparing a special compost. with plenty of humus. Cover the seed-pans or boxes until

the seeds have germinated, and avoid watering if possible during this period.

Alpine strawberries have certain cultural requirements which must be fulfilled. They are heavy feeders, like all strawberries. Lots of compost and well-rotted manure is essential on light, sandy soils if the crop is to be prolonged and repeated. Moisture is also essential. They will stop fruiting if the ground is too dry. In our former garden we got very little fruit unless we watered and fed the plants during dry periods, and they failed to bear well in a border, robbed by the roots of a balsam poplar that had spread in an ever-increasing radius at the expense of other plants. They enjoy light shade and therefore can be used at the base of hedges, under fruit trees or flowering bushes. I particularly like to group them along the front of shrubberies, where they look enchanting and make an excellent ground-cover.

They are short-lived plants. The fruits are at their best in their first season. The second year the crop is larger, the berries smaller. For this reason it is well to renew plants every other year, if good fruits are desired. As viruses are not transmitted by seeds, a clean stock of young plants is assured. Moreover, as 'Baron Solemacher' and other name varieties come true from seed, it is possible to save one's own. For those who do not want the bother of raising plants from seeds, young plants are available for spring planting from various sources.

The picking of fruit is laborious but worth the effort. Berries should be very ripe if the full flavour is to be enjoyed and the exquisite perfume as well. Fruits should be sprinkled with sugar and allowed to stand for several hours to develop bouquet and flavour. They can be served with a liberal dash of white wine, port or even a sprinkling of orange-juice and Cointreau. To my mind cream is a mistake, as the flavour of the berries is too delicate.

The fruits are very light, and, if sold by weight, a pound of berries is a large quantity. They are expensive, but there are a few famous restaurants that sometimes have them. Several friends have raised them for this purpose. I particularly like the rich, very sticky jam that is made from these little fellows. As a great treat I once carried a jar in my suitcase to friends abroad but the porters on the dock treated it so roughly that the glass jar broke and the all-too-effective central heating of the hotel reduced the contents to a semi-liquid state before I had time to unpack. In spite of this calamity, I still like the flavour of this jam.

In selecting a position for wild strawberries in your garden, remember that they will commence flowering in late May. If your area is a cold one and subject to late frosts, choose as frost-free a position as possible. Set plants fifteen to eighteen inches apart and allow at least thirty inches between the rows. Although birds share my enthusiasm for Alpine strawberries, it is not always necessary to net the plants.

A Bumper Crop of Blueberries

A few years ago there was a superb exhibit of blueberries at a Royal Horticultural Society Show in London. These caused a sensation as the large cultivated hybrids are virtually unknown in Britain. Baskets of these superb cultivated blueberries, as much as half an inch in diameter, as well as sprays of berries and small plants were well shown. These monster berries, developed in the eastern United States, are the relatives of the highbush blueberry *(Vaccinium corymbosum)* of my youth in New England. How well I remember the sloping pastures, with their grey stone walls and masses of blueberries. We picked them into milk-pails, the first few making a dull thud on the empty metal bottom. They were sweet and flavoursome, whether eaten fresh with sugar and cream or cooked in muffins or blueberry pie. In autumn the foliage was a blaze of dark red.

Then came the cultivated hybrid berries, which we grew with care and love. But oh, the struggle to protect them from the birds!

Now, in an even more highly improved state, bushes are available. Their requirements are relatively easy. Acid soil is essential. If there is a trace of lime, forget blueberries. They like good drainage, but also ample moisture. There are fine plantations on Long Island, New Jersey and parts of Massachusetts, and in those districts, where they grow naturally. In areas of low rainfall, artificial watering may be necessary when the fruit is swelling and ripening, and they respond well to an annual mulch of old sawdust or leaf-mould and to feeding with sulphate of ammonia. Lime in any form is disastrous.

It is strongly recommended that at least two varieties are planted to ensure cross-fertilization and heavy crops of large berries. Two excellent ones are 'Ivanhoe' and 'Jersey'. Both bear copious clusters of fruit with an excellent flavour. The former is rather sharp, and the latter, rather sweeter, blander and a little smaller in size. It is, however, one of the best and easiest of croppers. Other excellent varieties include 'Blueray', 'Bluecrop' and 'Concord'. The bushes grow at least six feet tall, bloom in April or early May and fruit in mid-July, lasting well into September. Bushes bear lightly during the first season. Mature bushes produce as much as five pounds of fruit per bush.

Bushes should be planted in November or March, but the ground should be well prepared as far in advance as possible. No pruning is required at planting time, although after about three years thinning will be necessary. One of the most important factors is adequate protection from birds. If you can't provide this, don't attempt blueberries. The birds love them, and I know why.

A Bounty of Golden Quinces

Surely the loveliest of autumn fruits are the large, golden, pear-shaped quinces which are produced in such abundance. Even in November I have seen trees still loaded with them in a number of gardens. It is always a mystery why this highly decorative tree is not more widely grown today, not only for its fruits, which make such delicious jellies and preserves, but for the beauty of its flowers and fruits, and for the habit of the tree as well.

In Mediterranean countries it is more highly prized than here. In Portugal and Spain there are orchards of quinces, and a tree or two graces even the humblest gardens in areas where there is sufficient moisture for its successful cultivation. In early spring I have seen the branches studded with large, pale pink flowers, often as much as an inch and a half in diameter, against a bright blue sky. They have a beauty and perfection all their own, the clear blush-pink contrasting with the greyish tinge of the young leaves. In autumn the bountiful harvest in Portugal is converted largely into a delectable *marmalado*, the forerunner of orange marmalade, and in Spain into *membrillo*, a rich quince conserve or cheese, as it is called, that happily appears with great regularity in the Spanish diet. There is a counterfeit of it made from apples that is apt to be flavourless and insipid, but as this is golden-brown in colour rather than a warm rich pinky-red it can be detected at sight.

Quinces are undoubtedly of Eastern origin. *Cydonia oblonga (vulgaris)*, the quince of gardens, is widely grown in Europe, especially around the Mediterranean. The Greeks and Romans prized quinces of some kind, from which sweetmeats were made, and they were loved as well by the Persians, who realized that their decorative value was on a par with that of the much-loved pomegranate.

Quinces require moisture and rich soil. I know of several gardens where they grow on river-banks, but their roots are not in waterlogged soil. Bog conditions do not suit them. Sun is also essential if quinces are to ripen effectively. This fact undoubtedly has much to do with their success as a crop in this country as in Italy, Greece, Portugal and Spain. Quince trees do less well in cold windswept gardens or on light, sandy soils. The trees tend to be broad-headed and seldom grow more than twenty feet tall. Bushes are far more common than true standards or half-standards.

As quinces are self-fertile, they do not require a

pollinator and hence a single tree can grace even a small garden. I favour them for their decorative value, which was understood by the Elizabethans and the Carolingians alike, who planted them with medlars, mulberries and magnolias. I know of one garden where quinces have been used to make a hedge, accented at the corners with standards. True, the hedge is decorative rather than utilitarian, but it has undeniable charm. In another garden standards flank a flight of steps, and in another a standard overhangs a garden wall covered with blossoms like wild rose in early May and later with the quince's beautifully formed fruits.

The fragrance of ripened quinces is permeating. I am partial to it and like to have a single, downy, yellow fruit on my desk, as it scents the whole room, rather like a pomander, but some people do not share my enthusiasm. Curiously, the flesh of the raw fruit is yellow, hard and unpleasant to taste, but with cooking it becomes deep pink and flavoursome. The core and seeds are extremely rich in pectin, so quinces can be made into jelly with the minimum of trouble. A few slices of quince improve apple pie and make the world of difference to apple jelly.

Quinces should be planted at any time from the autumn until early spring, and require handling in very much the same way as apples or pears. Little pruning is necessary save for shaping, if required, or the removal of dead wood. I know of old specimens that have grown for years with virtually no care whatsoever. One of these is in a chicken-run where it gets a little natural mulching. Another grew in an unpromising back-garden, but survived all the trials of the fog and soot of a big city.

There are only a few varieties available. One of the best known is 'Portugal', which has large pear-shaped fruits copiously borne on a vigorous upright tree. 'Vranja' is a delicious variety with large fruits and 'Bereczki' is very similar. 'Champion' has more rounded fruits of rather milder flavour. It is a good grower and crops heavily when established. Another variety, known as 'Pear-shaped', has fruits of moderate size and crops well. All these quinces ripen in October or early November and are not harmed by a touch of frost. The fruits should be spread out on trays and stored in a cool fruit-store or airy cupboard. Here they should last for several months, but obviously before that time has elapsed they will be converted into jam, preserves or 'Quince Cheese'.

The Fascination of Medlar Trees

There are so many charming fruit trees that the medlar has of late been thrust into the background, but it deserves a better fate. *Mespilus germanica* is, in fact, a most attractive tree for decorative effect. Moreover, it is suited to smaller gardens and is happy in town as well as country. Like the quince, the medlar has a long history, for it is native to southern Europe and Asia Minor. Possibly it is indigenous to England, but about this there is some doubt, although it was present in medieval and Elizabethan gardens. It found its way to Virginia and the Carolinas in the 18th century.

Both the type and the garden varieties usually grown are singularly attractive, because of the rather twisted gnarled habit of old specimens. It is indeed a tree of great character and will add interest to the garden which boasts only rather neat symmetrical trees of a conventional nature. Often medlar trees are flat-topped and spreading, with pendulous branches so that they are clothed nearly to the ground. Medlars live to a great age, though they are not as long-lived as mulberries, with which they so often shared a place in old gardens. Mature trees may reach twenty to twenty-five feet and cover broad areas. The leaves are elliptical and of heavy texture. The flowers in late May or June are charming, rather like those of a quince, with five large white petals, sometimes tinged with pale pink, around a central boss of stamens with deep red anthers. One of the distinguishing features is the calyx, which consists of long, woolly sepals which extend beyond the outer rim of the blossom and persist on the fruits themselves.

The medlars of our gardens are borne in profusion on the tips of the branches and side-shoots. They are apple-shaped and several inches in diameter and are easily identified by the wide-open eye surrounded by the calyx. The eye is open, so that the carpels or seed capsules are exposed. The fruits when picked in late October or November are hard, bitter, dark greenish-brown, and definitely not ready for use. They must be harvested on a dry day and spread out on a shelf in a cool airy place, so that they do not touch each other. After three or four weeks they will turn a rich russet-brown. This process of ripening or, in fact, of bringing them to the point that they are mushy and on the verge of decay is known as 'bletting'. Chaucer mentions the bletting of medlars and it is a common term in old literature. The fruit is now ready for the table and not before. It may be eaten with sugar and was once used as a dessert or to clean the palate between wines. The peculiar flavour is not liked by everyone. The fruits can be used for jelly, either on their own or to give character to apples. This jelly is excellent with game or meats and resembles guava in flavour.

Medlar trees have yet another charm. Their foliage colours superbly in autumn, turning a rich golden-yellow and then a warm golden-brown and persists for a long time. A huge tree studded with brownish fruits is such a memorable sight that each time I see

Medlars are beautifully-shaped trees, attractive in flower and fruit, although the latter is definitely an acquired taste. Medlars may be used for jelly, to eat with game or meat.

one I resolve firmly to plant more medlars, and, as you may guess, quinces and mulberries also.

Their cultivation is relatively easy. They like rich, well-drained loam, but will succeed on most soils if reasonably good. Cold, wet soils with insufficient drainage are not suitable. As in the case of quinces, moisture is an asset, and very dry, sandy soils will need fortifying with humus to retain moisture. Planting should be done in autumn, early spring or, in fact, at any time when the groung is workable. Medlars are best grown as half standards or as full standards. I prefer the former. Fewer nurseries stock them than in earlier days. Alas, with current problems nursery-lists tend to shrink each year. However, a few nurseries offer them, either as a good but unnamed fruiting variety or under varietal names such as 'Nottingham', 'Royal' or 'Dutch'.

Medlars are grafted on to various understocks, including pear, quince and crataegus. The wild *Mespilus germanica* is a species and hence is grown on its own roots. It has spiky thorns nearly an inch in length, but the cultivated varieties are spineless. Little pruning is required except the removal of dead wood or weak shoots, but medlars repay a little shaping. I know of one charming old flat-topped tree which has been thinned at the middle and now under its canopy of light shade boasts a carpet of cyclamen, hellebores and other shade-lovers. In another garden, children have a secret hideaway under the drooping branches where they play for hours.

8 Roses

Shrub-roses, Early and Late

In a late season the few early shrub-roses always seem lovelier than usual. Among these are several of *Rosa rugosa* parentage. What superb roses these are, on every count. In gardens where shrubs to cover the ground are required they are outstanding, as many of them make large spreading bushes, flowering from ground-level. The rich green, heavy-textured foliage is clean and disease-resistant and turns a clear golden-yellow in the autumn. The flowers, borne over a very long period from May until October, are often followed by large brilliant red heps. Scent, powerful and often reminiscent of crushed cloves, is another attraction.

Rugosas are excellent when used as specimens. I know of one garden where large spreading shrubs of the rich crimson-purple 'Rosarie de l'Hay' flank steps leading to a terrace, so that the beauty of the pointed buds and the semi-double flowers can be enjoyed at close range. They are useful when grouped in shrub-beries or planted as hedges, either trimmed or un-trimmed. If lightly trimmed, they are more floriferous and, of course, more compact. 'Rosarie de l'Hay' is lovely when associated with the delicate, clear pink, single-flowered 'Frau Dagmar Hastrup', which is a little less tall (three feet), or with the semi-double pure white blooms of the old, much-loved 'Blanc Double de Coubert'. As this rose is taller and slightly open in habit, it needs a little pruning to keep it as compact as the others.

Rugosas do well on light, sandy soils or, for that matter, on most soils, although they are poor starters on chalky ones unless the ground is thoroughly pre-pared, deeply dug and enriched. They are better than many other roses by the sea, as the heavy foliage stands up to both the gales and the salt carried by them. Rugosas are the ideal shrub-rose for mixed borders, forming, as they do, spreading mounds of foliage,

The climber 'Pink Perpétue' is welcome for its profusion of pink, double flowers and its perpetual-flowering habit lasting from June until frost.

flowering for a very long period, particularly in late summer and autumn. Rugosa roses are also to be treasured for their large decorative heps, although the two semi-double varieties form relatively few, if any. 'Frau Dagmar Hastrup' sets a large quantity, the crimson fruits and the clear pink flowers in late summer being particularly attractive. The type *R. rugosa rubra* and *alba*, although less exciting in flower, make up in quantity of flowers and the glory of their brilliant heps. The variety 'Scabrosa' has strong, clean foliage, big magenta-pink flowers as much as four to five inches across, and the largest heps of all, but it is rather looser-growing in habit and forms a large bush.

There are very good hybrids of *Rosa rugosa*, my favourite being the warm mallow-pink 'Sarah van Fleet', which is one of the first to flower and is equally bountiful in autumn. Its habit is erect and vigorous, with handsome foliage, making it a good subject for the middle of large borders or for the back of small ones, and it makes a good tall hedge or screen. I have occasionally seen this rose used for roadside planting of late, and it always gives me pleasure. Rather similar is 'Conrad F. Meyer'. a silvery-pink, well-formed rose of distinction, though unfortunately it tends to be a little leggy and tall. Both these varieties have deliciously scented flowers which are charming when cut, though rather short-lived in water.

Rose 'Hunter' is a new *rugosa* hybrid of note, raised in England. I hope it will soon become available here. It is a wonderful clear red with no trace of blue, double and free-flowering over a long period with excellent autumn blooms. The foliage is clean and characteristic of its ancestor. The habit is bushy, making it good for hedging or for specimen or group-planting. There is one sadness – it does not have the delicious scent of other rugosas.

Other shrub-roses are largely in the creamy-white and yellow range. The single, butter-yellow *Rosa hugonis* is a fleeting beauty, now usually replaced in gardens by the hybrid *R. cantabrigiensis*, which has rather larger flowers, delightful foliage, a good habit and scent. The large, creamy-white, single-flowered *R. altaica* (a form of *R. spinosissima*), the double yellow

The Scots or Burnett Briars *(Rosa spinosissima)* are treasured for their globular shape and spicy fragrance. As some varieties sucker freely, they form broad masses, as in this country garden.

R. zanthina and its variety *spontanea*, which has very large, rich yellow flowers which have earned for it the charming name 'Canary Bird', and two modern shrub-roses of unusual distinction and merit, 'Nevada' and 'Frühlingsgold', offer a difficult choice for early summer-flowering in a normal year. They are exciting possibilities in combination with lilacs, irises, tree paeonies, early ceanothuses and a host of other shrubs and herbaceous plants.

A delightful, yellow, early-flowering climber is the vigorous 'Lawrence Johnston', a hybrid of *Rosa foetida*. It was raised in France by the late Major Lawrence Johnston. His ancestry was American, and he became one of the great gardening figures in England and the Riviera. This rose is grown to perfection in England at his old garden, Hidcote Manor, in Gloucestershire. Although of the same parentage as 'Le Rêve', it is of a

more brilliant yellow, with the merits of vigour, scent and good foliage, and in my humble opinion the better rose of the two. It needs plenty of room and a warm sunny position and unfortunately has a rather short season. I have seen it flowering against a grey stone wall in combination with an early blue ceanothus and a mauve *Solanum crispum*, to make a picture I shall not soon forget.

Shrub-roses are at their best in early July. I am particularly taken with *Rosa moyesii superba*, a large shrub with fine foliage and semi-double, rich crimson flowers, poised on the stem like those of the single *moyesii*. For those who like a show of bright colour, 'Scarlet Fire' is a winner, although its season is short. It is well named, for its large, sensational, velvety scarlet, single flowers, borne in profusion in mid-summer, are of an unusually luminous intensity. This rose can be grown as a bush or used on a pillar, wall or fence. Place it carefully, as it will overpower most colour-schemes and clash with a lot of colours.

Two large-growing roses, but only for gardens where there is room, are *Rosa webbiana* and *R. dupontii*, the latter a hybrid between *R. gallica* and *R. moschata*. The former has delicate fern-like foliage of a soft grey-green and myriads of pale pink, single blooms followed by small, tapered, glowing crimson heps. All in all, it is very good value for foliage, flowers and fruit. *Rosa dupontii* makes a large bush seven to eight feet tall and as much across, with handsome greyish-green foliage and large single flowers, creamy-white flushed with pink at the margins. The fragrance is pervasive, a strange blend of banana and musk. Both these roses are ideal for the wild garden or for the mixed border, though they are lovely if grown so that their shape can be appreciated and not crowded in with other shrubs and roses. This is true of so many of the rose species. I particularly like to plant them in grass, so that I can walk round them and see the light through the flowers from different angles.

A comparatively new shrub-rose by which I have been struck is the beautiful one appropriately named after the late Constance Spry, who did so much to further the appreciation and cultivation of old roses, as well as for flower-arrangement. Rose 'Constance Spry' is a huge globular flower of exquisite colouring in shades of pink, salmon and peach, with incurved petals which give a lovely form to even fully open blooms. The scent is curious and reminiscent of myrrh. It was raised by Arnold Austin by crossing the pale salmon-pink Gallica 'Belle Isis' with the pink floribunda 'Dainty Maid'. The blooms are attractively borne on a large, rather lax bush, which will grow six to seven feet across and possibly more. Its habit is perhaps its one fault, but if given a little support, which is needed by many shrub-roses, it will prove a welcome addition to the gardens of old-rose enthusiasts. The large globular flowers cut well.

For the lover of old roses with a small garden there are a few to add to my list of 'musts', in which I would include 'Celestial', 'Fantin Latour', 'Madame Isaac Pereire', and 'Königen von Dänemarck'. 'Belle de Crécy' has neat, perfectly formed, scented flowers that are a blend of strong cerise-pink with purple undertones which fade to Parma violet. It makes a lax bush not more than four feet tall and as it is not spreading in habit, perhaps space can be found for it. I also like

'Belle Isis' for its fully double flowers of a very subtle shade of pink with a glint of salmon not common to old roses. 'De Meaux' is a treasure with flat, little, round, very double flowers of clear pink, freely produced on an erect small bush.

I love the Scots Briars, as the *Rosa spinossissima* group are called. There is enormous variation, but all are fragrant and the old 'Double White' is perhaps the most fragrant of all. As these are on their own roots, they will sucker and run about in the border. I love 'Williams' Double Yellow', the soft, clear pink 'Falkland' and the dwarf, deep crimson and plum 'William III', which is a real treasure. Although the flowering

'Nevada' is one of the most popular of all modern shrub-roses, as it flowers with great freedom in June and again in autumn.

season of the Scots Briars is short, do include one or two for their scent and charm. Among those I would recommend are the Spinossissima Hybrids 'Frülingsgold', 'Frühlingsmorgen' and 'Frühlingsduft', which are all fine, early-flowering, shrub-roses, but do give them lots of space.

Autumn roses do well, particularly in cottage gardens, where even a few bushes will put forth an exceptional display. Vigorous hybrid teas and floribundas top many a stone wall with a mass of bloom, and some of the old shrub-roses have a second burst of bloom. Exceptionally good are two of the Bourbons, 'Souvenir de la Malmaison', with its large, flat, flesh-pink flowers, quartered and sweetly scented, and 'Madame Isaac Pereire', a wonderful vigorous rose that produces a liberal crop of very large, cup-shaped flowers, light crimson and richly scented. Both of these are to my mind better in autumn than in summer, as the blooms are larger, more perfectly formed and of richer colour. A third which is outstanding is the hybrid perpetual 'Gloire du Ducher', with large sumptuous flowers of rich crimson-purple, emitting a fragrance as rich and delicious as the colouring. These three

'Grandpa Dickson', a fine, new hybrid tea with clean, gleaming foliage and full lemon-yellow flowers, has received the highest honours.

should be included in gardens where autumn roses are treasured and where there is room for these large bushes. Although they can be grown as pillar- or wall-roses, I prefer them as free-growing shrubs. All three are in my opinion the better for judicious pruning and should not be allowed to go untouched for too long, as many growers of old roses advocate. They should be pruned after the first flush of flowers to encourage side-shoots that will bear flowers later.

Hybrid Teas for Pleasure

Of the many modern hybrid teas, some are varieties to acquire and others are worth watching to see how they will behave in the open ground and react to brilliant sun or rainy weather. I have always been very much influenced by the fragrance of flowers and now that hybridizers are deliberately working with fragrance as a primary aim, the results are gratifying. In fact, the old story that roses have lost their scent has been pretty well put to bed. Lots of old roses are fragrant, but so are many of the new ones.

On the whole brilliant orange, salmon and vermilion varieties are increasingly popular, witness the universal acclaim of 'Tropicana'. There seem to be fewer bicolors. In fact, self-colours with shadings in the same colour range tend to predominate. The public never tires of pinks, and as I have a preference for these, I am indeed happy with this trend.

'Pink Peace' is a tall-growing, vigorous rose raised by Meilland. The large, strong pink, scented blooms are delicately ruffled. 'Swarthmore' is a richly coloured rose of character as it combines velvety rosy red with clear deep pink. Good foliage enhances its beauty. The flowers are enormous and have a delicate fragrance. 'Chicago Peace' is a splendid sport of 'Peace' with the same size and vigour. The flowers are a blend of pink and yellow with copper tones. It is more fragrant than 'Peace' and has the same lustrous green foliage. 'Prima Ballerina' is already in some of our gardens. I like its deep, rich pink buds shaded with red, which open into large, very fragrant, full blooms with subtle shadows and highlights in shades of pink. For scent this rose is a 'must', and as it has a fine sturdy habit and does not grow too tall, it is an exceptionally good bedding variety. 'Pink Favourite' is another strong self-pink which has given an excellent performance. Its vigour, freedom of flower and dark, glossy, disease-resistant foliage make it a good all-weather rose.

'Silver Lining' is well named because of its delicate silvery sheen; it, too, is fragrant and more will certainly be heard of it. One of my favourite old pinks and still a fine fragrant variety is 'The Doctor', worth a place in all our gardens, as is 'Lady Sylvia', with its exquisitely pointed buds and delicious scent. It isn't large by modern standards, but it has certainly stood the test of time since its introduction in 1936. It is still extremely popular as an indoor variety and also does well outside in the garden, along with the other old hybrid teas of similar character, 'Madam Butterfly' and 'Ophelia'.

'Fragrant Cloud' is an enchanting name for an enchanting rose. The colour is rich deep vermilion with a strong undertone of red. It is wonderful as a cut flower and its fragrance is delicious. As it is free-flowering, I put it high on my list. It is an easier colour to use than 'Tropicana', which has so many good qualities, not the least of which is the long-lasting habit of its flowers when cut. After a week in the house, it still holds its petals and remains a good colour. Its fragrance permeates the room or the garden in the evening. 'Tropicana' is a great rose.

Red roses are symbolic and have a lot to live up to, including a special fragrance, different from roses of other hues. But, alas, many reds suffer from certain faults. Some tend to turn bluish with age; others are subject to mildew, or hang their splendid heads in wet weather; and some are not as free-flowering as we would like. 'Papa Meilland' is a splendid flower as we see it on the show-bench, but it is not proving free-flowering in some gardens, doing far better in certain areas than others. 'Champs Elysees' is a glowing crimson, and the much-heralded 'Christian Dior' is another fine crimson, again with little scent.

'Mister Lincoln' has large glowing dark red blooms borne on long sturdy stems. It is extremely fragrant as a red rose should be. In colder areas it may be a little shy of flower. 'John S. Armstrong' (Swim), is a brilliant currant-red with overtones of cardinal. The flowers, three to four inches in diameter, are borne in abundance. Alas, its fragrance is slight. 'Red Devil' (Dickson) is a fine very full double of a light glowing red with a vigorous disease-resistant habit and powerful fragrance. 'Ernest H. Morse' (Kordes) is a winner, and 'Scarlet Knight' promises well as a grandiflora.

I hope that these new roses will fill a gap in some beds, but 'Etoile de Hollands', 'Josephine Bruce', 'Ena Harkness', 'Grimson Glory', and the rather smaller but distinguished 'Mme Louis Laperrière' are still reliable, tried and true favourites.

White hybrid teas are relatively few in number and perhaps less satisfactory than other colours. 'Memoriam' is an outstanding fragrant off-white with a pinkish glow, 'John F. Kennedy' is a huge white flower with long petals with a creamy base. 'Pascali' is a vigorous white bred from 'Queen Elizabeth'. It is proving highly satisfactory and seems to withstand wet weather. Of older varieties 'Virgo' and 'Message' are good but not outstanding. In many ways I prefer

'Fragrant Cloud', which is a darker vermilion than 'Tropicana', has a delightful strong fragrance and is a fine cut flower.

the white floribundas which are so much more prolific, including 'Saratoga', 'Ice White' and 'Iceberg'. The old favourite 'Frau Karl Druschki' is still excellent, though scentless.

Of the yellows, 'Dr A. J. Verhage' is impressive on the show-bench. I like its refined shape and rich colour and scent. 'Gold Crown', raised by Kordes in Germany, is a tall, glowing, deep yellow. It is a descendent of 'Peace' and 'Spek's Yellow', with good qualities from both. 'Summer Sunshine' and 'King's Ransom' are both successful yellows. The latter is of moderate size, ideal for cutting, and a fine clear colour. Other good ones are 'Belle Blonde', 'Beaute', 'Buccaneer' and 'Grandpa Dickson'.

The bright turkey-red 'Ernest H. Morse', raised by Kordes, is one of the outstanding red roses to date. It is richly fragrant, vigorous and tall-growing.

Standard Roses in the Garden

When I was young I was always intrigued with standard roses and flowering shrubs. Perhaps it was because I associated them with formal gardens, while most of the gardens which I knew intimately were informal. Perhaps it was because standards were difficult to obtain and expensive. In any case, I still find that they have a definite fascination and it is fun to search out unusual ones. Standards have a number of uses, but, like garden ornaments, it is as important to forego them if they are inappropriate as it is to use them well where they are suitable.

Their uses are numerous. We all know the standard bays, privets and box bushes planted in tubs and decorative pots to flank doors, gateways and paths in so many towns and suburban gardens. Then there are the familiar standard fuchsias and geraniums,

which can be similarly used, or can serve as accents in formal bedding-schemes, just as standard hybrid tea roses can punctuate the corners of beds or define paths. On the other hand, they are charming in conservatories or in informal schemes outdoors, lending height and interest to borders even in humble cottage gardens.

Charming floribunda roses are being produced in ever-increasing numbers, and we find bold groups of these backed with standards or half-standards of the same variety to form tall masses of colour at eye-level throughout the summer. Some of the most successful mixed borders contain floribundas, or even hybrid teas, used in this delightful way.

Winters take their toll of standard roses. Many of us have found that rose bushes covered with a deep layer of dry snow are warm and safe, while standards exposed to searing cold winds may succumb. After a bad winter I have heard of casualties to bush roses such as _R. moyesii_ 'Geranium', 'Canary Bird' and even to weeping standards of varieties as tough as 'The New Dawn', 'Albertine', 'Alberic Barbier' and 'Danse du Feu'. Casualties are inexplicable, as they may occur in one garden, while the same variety survives untouched nearby.

Weeping standard roses have a grace all their own. These are usually grown on five-and-a-half-foot stems, while hybrid teas are grown as half-standards on three- to three-and-a-half-foot stems. The reason for this is a matter of proportion, the broad head of a weeping rose, with its graceful long streamers bearing a multitude of blooms, obviously requiring greater height to be effective. Weeping standards are lovely where important features are required to accentuate gateways, to make repeats along a broad-walk, or to give added height at intervals in rose hedges. The training of weeping standards is enormously assisted by the use of wire frames to which the new shoots can be tied.

Increasing numbers of roses, both hybrid teas and floribundas, are available as standards. Among the latter are 'Allgold', clear golden yellow; 'Masquerade', yellow, ageing to flame-red; 'Frensham', deep red and very floriferous; 'Iceberg', white with touches of flesh-pink; 'Fashion', light salmon; 'Red Favourite', deep blood-red in large trusses; 'Rosemary Rose', gleaming currant-red with very full flat flowers, rather like an old shrub-rose, and dark red foliage; 'Queen Elizabeth', clear pink, very vigorous and semi-double; 'Camelot', deep coral-pink and 'Apricot Nectar'.

New Shrub-roses

There is a need in many gardens for bush-roses that will continue to flower after the great burst in June and July, yet of a character that will be in harmony with the old shrub-roses and the species in their lovely

'Nymphenburg' is a vigorous modern shrub-rose of Hybrid Musk ancestry with soft salmon-pink flowers tinged with gold, which are borne throughout the season.

shades of pink, purple, deep red, mauve, clear yellow and white. Many of the newer shrub-roses and flori-bundas have brilliant hot colours, lovely for cutting, but not, alas, easy to use in the same part of the garden with others. Some are so brilliant that they have a man-made look rather than a God-made one.

Here are a few shrub-roses which have proved out-standing and will be appropriate in gardens where old roses are grown. 'Lavender Lassie', of hybrid musk parentage, has clusters of double, pinkish-lavender flowers, particularly sweet-scented. It forms a free-flowering bush up to five feet in height and needs plenty of space.

'Nymphenburg', like 'Fritz Nobis', is a Kordes intro-duction. It makes a large, lax bush about six to seven feet across with glossy deep green foliage studded with a succession of attractive apricot buds, which unfold into loosely double, deliciously fragrant flowers, shaded with warm glowing orange-pink and clear yellow at the base of the petals. 'Golden Wings', a single of rather erect habit, produces a series of large, scented, canary-yellow blooms. The long and elegantly pointed buds are borne singly and in trusses. 'Lilac Charm', of medium height is a single, scented floribunda, well named for its dusky lilac colouring, so popular with flower-arrangers. As it grows to about two feet, it is very effective when grouped in front of taller pinks and yellows.

Of the shrub roses, hybrid musks are still not suf-ficiently appreciated in this country. These have been developed from the very fragrant musk rose *Rosa moschata*, many of them by a clergyman, the Reverend Pemberton in Essex, England, back in the seventies. They have the great advantage of two blooming seasons, the first in June and July, and the second in late summer and autumn, when they are often at their best. Secondly, most of them are strongly scented and come in a pleasing range of colours.

I consider 'Penelope' among the best. The pinkish buds in clusters open into semi-double, very fragrant, creamy-white flowers tinged with pink. It forms a sturdy bush six feet high and as much across. Of similar size or slightly smaller, 'Buff Beauty' is a vigorous grower with amber-yellow buds and fully double creamy flowers which tend to deepen to warm apricot-yellow in autumn. These are borne in large clusters above the foliage, which is tinged with bronze. The fragrance is strong and very sweet. 'Buff Beauty' is lovely with drifts of blue *Geranium grandiflorum*, *Anchusa italica* and silver artemisias or *Stachys lanata*.

127

In the pink range there is a choice of the richly scented double 'Cornelia', salmon-pink in bud, soft shell-pink in bloom, with a broad spreading habit; 'Felicia' with rather larger fuller flowers, similar in colour; and 'Pink Prosperity' with light pink double flowers in large clusters. All of these are excellent for hedges. 'Pax' has large semi-double white flowers with a lemon-yellow centre, while 'Vanity' has a big deep pink single flower, borne over long periods, on a rather taller less dense bush, which may be as much as nine or ten feet tall. Don't use 'Vanity' or the tall, double, white 'Prosperity' for hedges.

For the lovers of roses *Shrub Roses of Today*, by Graham S. Thomas (Phoenix House, 1962) is authoritative, practical and charmingly illustrated with sensitive drawings and water-colours by the author, who is the leading collector of old shrub-roses in the world today. Another very useful book on this delightful subject is *Old Roses for Modern Gardens*, by R. Thomson (Van Nostrand, New York, 1959).

In a number of gardens I have seen numerous suckers growing up among the hybrid teas, floribundas and even the shrub-roses, such as the rugosas. Suckers are growths from the understock on which the variety of budded and can be identified as a rule by the thorns on the stems, usually larger and more numerous. With rugosa stock for standard roses the leaves are heavier textured, larger and a darker green. Suckers should be removed as soon as they appear, as they are far more vigorous than the rose, and as they spring from the stem and root below the true bush, they will take the nourishment before it reaches the top growth. Having located the sucker, resist the temptation to cut it off at ground level as this will mean even more trouble, as there are other buds waiting to be forced into growth. Instead, remove the soil and uncover the junction of the sucker on the underground root or stem. This will have relatively smooth bark in contrast to the woody rather knotted stem of the rose itself. Then tear out the sucker with a strong sharp pull, inward and upward. It will come away, taking the guard-eyes with it. If these were left, new growths would soon form, but by tearing out the sucker the trouble is cured. It is advisable to hold the plant firm with one foot to make sure that it is not lifted from the ground. If in doubt about whether a shoot is a sucker on bush roses, it is advisable to wait until it flowers.

I find Hybrid musks very effective if used with groups of harmonizing floribundas in the foreground. Use a clear yellow such as 'Sunspot', 'Gold Marie' and 'Buccaneer' with 'Buff Beauty' or 'Pax', and pinks such as 'Fashionette', 'Pink Parfait' and 'Camelot' with 'Felicia', 'Pink Prosperity' and 'Cornelia'. Hybrid musks are lovely in a shrub border with the amethyst foliage of *Rosa rubrifolia*, the dark purple Smoke Tree (*Rhus cotinus atropurpurea*) or the handsome rich foliage of *Berberis thunbergii atropurpurea*.

Rose 'Magenta' has pinkish-lilac, fragrant flowers approaching the quality of a fine floribunda, borne in large clusters on rather lax stems. It is lovely with pinks or yellows and of course with deep vinous purples. Silver foliage is the perfect foil. Try combining it with a lower planting of the enchanting perpetual-flowering Rose 'The Fairy', which has big clusters of small double pink flowers, heliotropes, purple violas and silvery stachys.

In the red range there is 'Wilhelm' with huge quantities of velvety scarlet-crimson flowers and 'Will Scarlet' a sport from it, both of which are excellent for a hedge on in combination with red floribundas. Stay clear of orange and orange-scarlets as they will clash. 'Frensham', 'Europeana', 'Sarabande' and 'Lili Marlene' are good choices.

Roses as Ground-cover

We are all interested in ground-covers and for those of us with large areas, particularly on slopes or banks, few shrubs are as suitable as some of the trailing and lax bush roses. In a few years they form large sprawling masses of colourful and intensely fragrant flowers. Almost no pruning is required, and when bushes are established, weeds are more or less blanketed, though for the first couple of years the area around and under them must be weeded. As with all plants that are to remain in one place for a long time, be sure to prepare the ground thoroughly and to feed heavily at planting time, preferably with well-rotted manure or with liberal dressings of good garden compost.

As suggested before, one of the very vigorous shrub or climbing roses can be planted at the top of a quarry, bank or gulley to cascade as it grows. In Scotland I have seen a fine plant of *R. moschata* which had been cleverly planted near a stone bridge at the head of a deep ravine. The masses of yellow buds opened into great panicles of heavily scented flowers that were wonderful near at hand and made a superb picture at a distance, framing the waterfall below. *Rosa filipes* 'Kiftsgate' or the hybrid 'Wedding Day' can be used in similar fashion.

For smaller areas, which are a more frequent problem, there are a number of solutions. Ramblers, particularly those derived from *R. wichuraiana*, are ideal, with their glossy foliage, fragrant flowers over a long period and close-growing, matted habit. 'Albéric Barbier', 'La Perle', 'Sanders White' and even our old but fleeting favourite 'Albertine' are suitable. In the United States rambler roses are sometimes used to cover cuts along highways and underpasses, where they make a dense weed-free covering, floriferous, colourful and fragrant. Another plant used for this purpose is *Lonicera japonica*, or the evergreen *L. henryana*. In the evening the scent is caught by the banks, and one drives through the rose- and honeysuckle-scented darkness.

There are a few other roses which are ideal for carpeting. One of the finest is *R. paulii*, which makes a dense spreading thicket of gracefully arching stems. In June and early July there is a profusion of large, single, white flowers with golden centres. A single plant will cover as much as twelve feet in a few years and seldom exceeds three feet in height. There is a pink form *R. paulii* var. *rosea* which is very lovely indeed and has the same rich scent, reminiscent of cloves. In many ways this sprawling hybrid of *R. rugosa* is more satisfactory than the *R. wichuriana* ramblers, as its growth is thicker and weeds are more completely discouraged. However, there can be no doubt that roses used as ground-covers must be weeded or the grass scythed around them until they have had a few years to mature. This, of course, is true of other ground-covers, such as periwinkle, pachysandra, or even the variegated nettle *(Lamium galeobdolon variegatum)*, none of which are labour-saving until they have become densely matted.

I know a garden where *R. paulii*, planted over rocks on the face of a steep hill, has gradually created a summer glacier of white roses. In another garden it tumbles over a bank above a rushing stream, sharing honours in spring with poeticus narcissi, which thrust their way through some of the outer stems. Another fine ground-cover is 'Max Graf', a hybrid of *R. rugosa* crossed with *R. wichuriana*. Small wonder that it has attractive dense foliage, a sprawling habit and clusters of clear, vivid pink flowers, heavily scented with apple.

There is a group of roses derived from *R. macrantha*. These tend to be taller but spreading, making broad mounds as much as eight to nine feet across and four to five feet tall, depending on the varietal form. *Rosa macrantha* is of French origin and is a cross between *R. gallica* and *R. canina*. With this ancestry it is an ideal rose for the wild garden, hedgerows or the front of shrubberies. Like the others, it is charming if allowed to sprawl over a low wall. It has large, single, fragrant, pink flowers copiously borne in midsummer. One of the best-known forms is 'Lady Curzon', which has an unusually dense habit and quantities of pink flowers. 'Daisy Hill' is similar, with extra petals, making a more showy garden shrub, although the individual blooms are less perfect in shape. A recent hybrid is the charming 'Raubritter', a most lovely semi-double with clear pink flowers in clusters. The rounded shape of the flowers is particularly attractive and they last well. Its habit is low and trailing, making it ideal for

banks, terrace-walls and large stone tanks. Alas, it is a rose prone to mildew in some localities and therefore I cannot recommend it as wholeheartedly as I should like. In some areas where it is free from mildew, it is certainly one of the most lovely and useful of the *R. macrantha* hybrids and has the delicacy, shape and refinement of the best of the old Bourbon roses.

Climbing Roses for Walls and Pillars

Few plants are as treasured as climbing roses, which drape our walls and fences with fragrant colour from early summer until frost. Each year sees the introduction of a few new varieties, but progress with climbers is relatively slow. For this there is a good reason. While the average gardener may have room for a dozen, fifty, or even a hundred hybrid teas and floribundas, there is only relatively little space for climbers and ramblers. As a result, growers in most countries, for obvious economic reasons, concentrate on the former types. Germany is a possible exception; large numbers of climbers are widely used there in public parks to achieve spectacular effects.

Climbing roses should be used with care. During the long months when they are leafless they are boring and contribute nothing to the winter landscape. They should be combined with evergreen climbers and wall-shrubs, such as camellias, *Viburnum* 'Park Farm Hybrid' and *Cotoneaster microphyllus*. Roses must be carefully pruned and tied in against walls and fences. Be sure to prune newly planted ramblers and climbers fairly drastically the first year, especially if they have been planted in spring. It is important to encourage vigorous young shoots low down so that there will be flowers at the bottom as well as at eye-level and higher up. Train the branches so that they fan out on the walls, and don't select rampant growers for confined areas. Be sure that climbing roses have enough moisture, as conditions tend to be very dry at the base of walls.

Of Banksian roses the double yellow *R. banksiae* is the hardiest, but it should be given a warm, sunny wall with lots of room to grow. It is lovely sprawling through old trees in warm southern or west coast gardens where the new growths are so covered in late spring with clusters of tightly packed, butter-yellow, violet-scented flowers, that the glossy evergreen leaves are hardly visible. There are other forms of Banksian roses, including the single yellow (var. *lutea*) and the double white *(albo-plena)*, both very heavily scented.

One of the excellent modern pillar-roses is the coral-pink 'Dream Girl', which has large very double, heavily scented flowers, recalling the old shrub-roses

'Mme Grégoire Staechelin', a tall-growing climbing rose with large, ruffled, pink flowers, is only suitable for big wall-areas.

'Royal Gold', 'Leverkusen', 'Golden Showers', climbing 'Allgold' and 'Goldilocks'.

For understandable reasons there is a considerable demand for climbing red roses, perhaps because they are so striking against grey stone, pink-washed stucco, or the white weather boarding of the country cottage or the town house. Or is it because so many of the reds have such a warm rich perfume? Or because we feel a need for an attractive foil for the lighter clearer colours? Certain old varieties come at once to mind, including the climbing form of the much-loved 'Étoile de Hollande' and 'Crimson Glory', both dark rich reds and heavily scented. Then there is the ravishing 'Souvenir de Claudius Denoyel', which covers itself with an abundance of velvety rich crimson, heavily scented flowers, or 'Guinée', so dark that the depths of the flower are nearly black. It tends to be rather extended in habit, but careful pruning helps to correct this tendency. All of these are suitable for walls, poles or fences. The single bright scarlet and maroon 'Soldier Boy' is a perpetual bloomer with intermittent flowers after the main season. 'Blaze' is semi-double, with a repeat blooming season, a good habit and dark autumnal foliage. Both are particularly effective if grown as pole-roses.

'Red Empress' with very large, deep red, loosely-cupped flowers is recurrent and therefore useful. A fine perpetual-flowering climber which has a real future is 'Casino', a large, double, soft yellow with silvery margins to the petals. It has had an extraordinary success in England. 'Blossomtime' is a reliable, ever-blooming, double-flowered beauty in two tones of pink. 'Clair Matin' has long pointed semi-double pink flowers and delicate sweet-briar fragrance. The climbing form of 'Tropicana' will be a good companion to 'Danse du Feu' for lovers of spectacular colour.

Roses in High Places

When I let my thoughts wander to the perfect garden, roses are the first flower that always come to mind. How I love them, not only in my own garden, but in all the gardens of friends and strangers, including the cottage gardens of country lanes, where climbers and bushes grow over the sheds and walls, through the trees and even in the hedgerows. Then there are the roses in housing developments, municipal parks, factory-sites and even as roadside planting. In fact, there are roses wherever we go in ever greater profusion.

in its tendency to quartering. It flowers rather later than many and the blooms are recurrent. This American rose was a seedling of 'Dr Van Fleet'. I have planted in many gardens 'Coral Dawn', 'Dr. Nicholas', 'Aloha' and 'Parade', which are other pinks that bloom over a long period. Many so-called climbers are really lax bushes that lend themselves to training against walls and pillars, but can be used as big bushes if pruned and given a little support.

For the lovers of hot colours there is 'Cocktail', a brilliant red suffused with crimson with a golden eye that blushes pink with age. There is also the loosely double 'Danse du Feu', gleaming scarlet-red with overtones of orange and dark lustrous foliage; and 'Hamburger Phoenix', one of Mr Kordes's fine efforts, with semi-double dark crimson flowers. These last three all bloom more or less continually and make excellent pillar-roses at the back of borders or in a rose-garden where height is needed. They are also useful on metal pyramids. Good yellows include

In spite of severe winters, rain and weather, roses flower copiously. Most species are particularly free-flowering and I am repeatedly struck by their usefulness for clothing buildings, walls, old fences and even banks and difficult slopes. The vogue for planting climbers to cascade over old trees has come to stay, and rightly so; there is no more lovely sight than a great bower of roses tumbling in profusion, scenting the air and showering the grass with a coloured carpet. For this purpose, use fine vigorous species such as *R. helenae*, *gentiliana*, *filipes* and *moschata*. All are single and creamy-white, with masses of flowers in clusters. Their scents vary – that of *R. helenae* and *gentiliana* is of orange, while *moschata* has a delicious musky fragrance. *Rosa brunonii* is another heavily scented treasure for a hot wall or a sheltered woodland position, but, like *R. moschata*, it is less hardy than the others. Have you ever had the pleasure of seeing the Cherokee Rose *(Rosa laevigata)* in bloom in southern gardens in spring? Actually it is the State flower of Georgia. The creamy white single flowers with golden stamens spread a curtain of fragrant bloom over trees and roofs as it is a very vigorous climber.

Rose of this type should be planted at the base of the tree and trained so that the leading shoots find their way into the branches, where they will grow to the light. Trees with dense foliage are not suitable, but old apple trees or conifers that are beginning to die back are ideal. Old thorn trees are also good, as they are sturdy and twiggy and give lots of support. In the courtyard of our old house, *R. filipes* clambered over a dead laburnum and in the garden the same rose completely covered a curved stone balustrade and climbed into a pollarded willow. For three weeks every year in late June and early July the display was superb. These vigorous roses require room and are not satisfactory for small trees or confined areas in small gardens.

Flowering a little later than these, *R. longicuspis* has myriad clusters of banana-scented flowers in the second half of July. 'Wedding Day', a lovely hybrid of *R. sino-wilsonii*, raised by the late Sir Frederick Stern, one of the great amateur gardeners of England with many friends in this country, is a fine vigorous climber with glossy dark leaves and clusters of tapered yellowish buds, which open to clear white flowers. These become spotted with pink as they age. 'Silver Moon' is another distinguished hybrid, with single to semi-double, creamy-white flowers opening from long, tapered, yellow buds. It is a fine rose for a sunny wall, trellis or an open tree.

A charming old rose known as 'Seven Sisters' is suitable for trees and pillars. The clusters of small flowers combine shades of pink, mauve, lilac and purple. Other very useful ramblers for trees or walls or to sprawl over roofs are the hybrids of *R. wichuriana*. 'Albéric Barbier', with its pale yellow, double flowers

The old ivory-yellow climber 'Paul's Lemon Pillar', growing in a raised bed, is beautifully trained against the wall above the door.

ageing to creamy-white, borne in profusion over a long summer season, and its handsome, gleaming, dark foliage is a constant joy. I consider it one of the most useful of all ramblers and it will grow to twenty-five or thirty feet. Related to it is 'François Juranville', pale pink with shadings of salmon and apricot. Both have a light, pleasing apple scent. 'Kew Rambler' is a charmer with single, clear pink flowers, white-eyed and borne in clusters above the grey-green foliage. Similar to 'Albéric Barbier' is 'La Perle', a creamy-white rose of surprising vigour with flowers densely packed with petals and showing distinct quartering. These hybrids of *R. wichuriana* make excellent ground-cover for slopes if they can be given space. Until

131

established, they must be kept free from weed and the grass must be cut short around them.

For smaller trees, poles, dead tree-trunks, walls and fences, a large number of other climbers and ramblers are suitable. One of the most charming is 'Félicité et Perpétue', a fragrant old hardy rambler of French origin, with neat reddish buds that open into dense pompoms of creamy-white. Its counterpart, 'Little White Pet', a low-growing bush for small gardens, is one of my fondest treasures. Among the most satisfactory of all climbers is 'New Dawn', which has the virtues of fine foliage, a perpetual blooming habit and fully double, delicate pink flowers of good form. It is certainly one of the most perpetual climbing roses in our garden and is particularly fine in autumn. There is 'Coral Dawn' as well, which is of a deeper colour, as the name implies; 'Parade', a free-blooming rich reddish-pink of large size, 'Aloha', a vigorous ever-blooming climber with large, double, coral-pink flowers; and 'Leverkeusen', one of the Kordesii perpetual climbers with good foliage and large flowers of creamy-white, deepening to gold and apricot at the centre. There are, of course, a number of others, but I have mentioned the last five because of their perpetual flowering habit. Many of the new climbers are rather stiff and less rampant in habit than the older climbing roses. Hence, they can be grown as pole-roses or on wooden supports to form massive tall shrubs.

Good perpetual climbers have been too much neglected until recently but there are some good debutantes, including a seedling of great promise called 'Pink Perpétue'. It forms a thick curtain of gleaming dark foliage studded with clusters of well-formed, rich pink flowers flushed with red. This has proved to be an important and long overdue addition to perpetual climbing roses. It is descended from the peerless flesh-pink 'New Dawn', still one of the most beautiful and reliable of climbing roses. It dies gracefully, like its parent, an important feature for a climber, as house-maiding roses is not feasible for most of us. Lovely as is 'Parade', with its large rose-red flowers lasting for many months, it does not shed its petals as I would like. 'White Dawn' is a lovely repeat-flowering double white climber. As there are so few whites of this type, its rather shy-flowering habit can be forgiven. Watch for 'Swan Lake', which promises to be a fine new double white climber, bred from 'Memoriam'.

Second Thoughts on New Roses

Autumn Rose Shows are events that gardeners anticipate with keen interest, as there is the opportunity to consider for the second time the novelties which made their debut in June. Second thoughts are important and many of us have now had the opportunity to see the varieties growing under trial or in the nurseries. The more we see of roses in other gardens, whether private or professional, the better our estimate of their true worth. Moreover, a visit to a famous rose-garden at the height of the season will no doubt provide very useful suggestions – in fact, my notebook is usually too full – but it is in the light of the midsummer doldrums or during bad weather that we should be making just as copious notes.

The constitution of roses varies enormously, but they are fickle. It is hard to understand why a beauty such as 'Rosemary Rose', which is prone to have a film of white mildew on its handsome reddish foliage in so many gardens, should be completely free from this plague in others, where roses are never sprayed or where the climate is unfavourable, such as a humid, damp one. 'Frensham', that splendid old stalwart red, which recently seems to be losing much of its vigour, reacts similarly. The heavily petalled, flat blooms of 'Europeana' are welcome in gardens where a glowing, rich, scarlet-red floribunda is required. Here is a rose

'Sea Pearl' is a well-named new floribunda in shades of silver, pink and ivory. The blooms are full and beautifully formed.

'Marguerite Hilling', a sister seedling of 'Nevada', with the same habit
and a repeat flowering season in autumn, deserves to be better known.

The beautiful shape of the old Bourbon roses is typified by 'Louise Odier',
which should find her way into many more gardens.

with the same red foliage that stands up better to weather conditions.

Rust on roses has recently reared its ugly head. Last year it appeared in a relatively new garden where all the bushes were planted in the last five years. It appeared first on the *rugosa* hybrid 'Sarah van Fleet'. This shocked me, as rugosas are generally resistant to diseases and relatively trouble-free. Spraying was of little avail, so the bush, contrary to advice (the bonfire pile was suggested), was moved last autumn out of the garden to splendid isolation among a few thorns and hazels and pruned hard. Recent examination shows that this summer the foliage and wood are clean. No care or preparation was given the soil, although it is a strong clay on which trees and shrubs thrive. It raises the question whether the deeply dug, heavily manured borders encouraged too lush a growth.

Rust is a serious malady. Until recently it has not been prevalent and, in fact, was non-existent in most gardens. One well-known rose-grower told me that he had no first-hand experience with it. Would that all gardeners could say the same! In August and September I saw roses badly infected. In one rose-garden a large bed of 'Mischief' suffered so badly that it was largely defoliated, while other varieties including 'Tropicana', 'Peace', 'Étoile de Hollande' and a number of others were not troubled.

Controls for rust include Liquid Copper Fungicide, Dithane and Orthocide, but, alas, they are drastic and not always satisfactory. Good cultivation and feeding can help to prevent it – which is easier than curing it. I would certainly burn all infected foliage, and any badly infected plants should be isolated or destroyed before the rust spreads to the rest of the garden. A winter wash of tar-oil is said to have proved effective in one garden I know.

Now for a few varieties to look for at rose-shows. Obviously many of the old shrub-roses will be missing in autumn shows, as these exquisite beauties are one-time flowerers, though the Bourbons and the hybrid perpetuals are generous with autumn blooms. So, too, are the hybrid musks, which are among the most satisfactory of all shrub-roses. 'Marguerite Hilling', the big little sister of 'Nevada', is a charming pink sport with loosely semi-double pink flowers, five to six inches across. It has been flowering freely for the last few weeks, and I have been very taken with its grace and beauty.

The first 'Blue' roses caused a sensation that does not die. The delicate almost ethereal beauty of the single 'Lilac Charm' is enhanced if it is planted with pale yellow or pink. I have successfully massed it with the taller 'Golden Wings', another distinguished single, and edged the border with the frosted silver *Artemisia pedmontana* and *Stachys lanata* 'Olympic'. 'Sterling Silver'

'Pink Parfait' has proved one of the most floriferous floribundas and is being used extensively in rose breeding. The flowers of Hybrid Tea quality last particularly well when cut.

is a subtle lilac hybrid tea, scented and fairly free-flowering, which all devotees of flower-arrangement have seen repeatedly, if they have not taken the plunge. 'Blue Moon' is another even bluer rose which has a career with the same enthusiasts and also as a garden rose, as it is vigorous and richly scented. The art is to place these rather subtle colours so that their dull shading is heightened by contrast.

The arresting lilac and purple 'Lavender Girl' is a beautiful compact floribunda with a sturdy, compact habit, unlike the rather floppy but very attractive 'Magenta'. It is a deep rich colour with well-shaped ruby-red buds, and it has far more character than some of the other mauve roses. There is a light pleasing scent as well. 'Silver Lining' on the other hand is very fragrant indeed. This well-shaped hybrid tea is a cool silver-lavender with a few of the outer petals tinged purple on the outside. It is a boon for the flower-arranger and attractive in the garden, where it will be striking with a good pink rose such as 'Royal Highness', 'Garden State' or 'Pink Favourite'. I particularly like 'Lavandula', with full flowers of a deep lilac with a reddish-purple glow. It will be happy with old shrub or modern roses alike. In the same colour-range the old purple moss-rose 'Lanei' is outstanding. It is a richer colour than 'William Lobb' and lovely in the border.

'Escapade' is a new British floribunda to watch for, as it is going to be extremely useful because of its subtle

colouring, a soft magenta-lilac with a white centre, and its generous graceful habit of growth, making it suitable to combine with old shrub roses, for bedding and even for an informal floriferous hedge. The very fragrant semi-double flowers are produced in profusion throughout the summer. I shall have fun using this to good effect; I almost feel as if it were made to my order.

'Sea Foam' is a white shrub rose, worthy of so descriptive a name as it flowers abundantly throughout the summer and has a graceful spreading habit, growing to three feet or a little more. Plant it where it can spread over a path or terrace. 'The Fairy' is an indispensable shrub-rose producing large clusters of small clear pink flowers on bushy spreading stems perpetually from early summer until frost. It cuts well and is ideal as a filler-in with taller more upright roses. Cut out old growths when pruning as it produces a large number each season from the base. It will reach three feet when established.

I liked the floribunda 'Apricot Nectar'. Here is a charming apricot floribunda which is lovely in the garden and for cutting. The floribunda 'Goldgleam' should prove to be a worthy successor to 'Allgold'. It has rather larger, brighter yellow, fragrant flowers, borne in profusion on a sturdy bush of moderate height. In the trial-ground its neat habit and gleaming healthy foliage assure its place as an outstanding bedding-variety. 'Sunspot' has butter-yellow buds that open to large creamy-ivory flowers. The flowers are very full with almost the appearance of the better hybrid teas. This floribunda is just the soft yellow rose I have so long wanted to make the perfect colour transition for blues, pinks, mauves and strong yellows in the garden. 'Arthur Bell', a clear yellow, promises well from its high quality both on the show-bench and in the trial-ground. Although the buds are tinged with red, the large full flowers are a pure clear yellow. 'Golden Fleece' appeals to me as it is a particularly attractive soft yellow with a lot of character, both in the shape of flower and in the colour harmony of flower and foliage.

One of the loveliest of the newer roses is the yellow climber 'Casino', with sumptuous double blooms of rich clear yellow paling to silver at the outer edges. A free-flowering perpetual climber with blooms of hybrid tea quality is certainly a boon to gardeners.

Many of the floribundas seem to be coming from Britain and the Continent rather than from this country. These include an interesting group of five new seedling roses with romantic names, based on King Arthur's

The Rugosa Hybrid 'Sarah Van Fleet' is a strong shrub-rose covered in early summer and again in autumn with fragrant, soft pink flowers.

Court and worthy of their fragrant beauty. There were four floribundas, three of which have 'Pink Parfait' as a parent. The heritage is obvious, as all are fully double and elegant in shape. 'Pink Parfait' is itself a fine bedding-rose, prolific over a long period, healthy and strong. In fact, one gardener complained that it flowered too freely.

I particularly like 'King Arthur', a rich deep salmon flushed with red. The flowers have a perfection of form, substance and glowing colour not usually associated with a floribunda. 'Sir Galahad' is similar but a glowing wine-red, shown off to advantage by the gleaming dark foliage. 'Merlin', a strange blend of red, pink and yellow, will appeal to those who like multi-coloured roses. Frankly, these are not for me. I am enamoured of the glowing apricot 'Sir Lancelot'. Here is a floriferous floribunda in a striking new colour with the fragrance of an old tea rose. Its subtle colour will be lovely in the garden.

In this group there is one hybrid tea, a clear rose-pink of fine form called 'Guinevere'. Its parentage, surprisingly enough, is 'Red Dandy' crossed 'Peace'. It is strange that a bright red floribunda crossed with a yellow hybrid tea should produce a clear pink of such distinction, but such are the chances of hybridization. As 'Guinevere' has proved a sturdy, weather-resistant rose, it should have a bright future.

'Molly McGredy' is a fine floribunda of hybrid tea type, raised by S. McGredy IV, a member of that well-known Irish family of rose growers who have introduced so many fine varieties over the years. The McGredys and the Dicksons, also in Northern Ireland, prove that the land of shamrocks produces not only internationally famous horses but also roses. Incidentally, as all daffodil enthusiasts probably know, the two greatest breeders of narcissi lived in Ireland, the late Guy Wilson and J. Lionel Richardson, who were responsible for raising the finest whites and pinks. But let's return to 'Molly McGredy', which was awarded both the President's International Trophy for the best new seedling rose of 1968 and a Gold Medal by the Royal National Rose Society. It is to be distributed in this country soon. It has well-shaped, full, cherry-red blooms with silver reverses to the petals and an upright bushy habit with dark green, glossy, disease-resistant foliage.

Another rose which is bound to have a remarkable career in this country is 'Duke of Windsor', raised by M. Tantau in Germany. It was judged the most fragrant rose in trial irrespective of country of origin at the British Rose Trials for 1968. I find its fragrance particularly pleasing as it is strong yet subtle. The attractively shaped buds open to light orange-vermilion flowers, that last well in water. 'Duke of Windsor' should be a very good garden rose for those who like

The single yellow flowers over a very long period and the lustrous dark foliage of 'Mermaid' explain the popularity of this great climber.

strong colours, and it will be a success on the show bench. Another rose to watch for is 'Baronne E. de Rothschild', raised by Louisette Meilland in France. This fine hybrid tea won Gold Medals in the 1968 Trials at Rome and Lyon and a Silver at Geneva.

American successes in foreign trials include two floribundas, 'Zorina' (Jackson and Perkins), which was awarded a First Certificate at Orléans, and 'Roman Festival' (J. B. Williams), which received a Silver Medal at Bagatelle and a Certificate in Rome.

The All American Rose Selections for 1968 were the hybrid teas 'Angel Face' (H. C. Swim) and 'Pascali' (Louis Lena, Belgium), and two floribundas, 'Comanche' (Swim and Weeks) and 'Gene Boerner', raised by the late Eugene S. Boerner. These have been so much publicized that further description is not necessary, but it is interesting to note that three of these four prize roses were bred in this country.

9 Herbaceous Plants and Borders

Perennials from Seeds

Many gardeners are finding the cost of herbaceous plants such as delphiniums, lupins and paeonies high in relation to roses and flowering shrubs. Obviously, this is largely because of the cost of labour and handling. After good varieties of hardy plants have been established, they generally multiply rapidly, and large stocks of plants such as Michaelmas daisies, *Chrysanthemum maximum*, campanulas, pyrethrums, phloxes and a number of others can be developed quickly. Too few of us, however, resort to the raising of herbaceous plants from seeds. Where species are concerned, this is an excellent method, as the plants will come true, and it is possible with a little care to raise astrantias, hellebores, valerians, *Campanula persicifolia*, *Alchemilla mollis*, *Lysimachia ephemerum* and a host of others.

I must make it clear at the outset that named clones of flowers such as lupins, delphiniums, and phloxes must be propagated vegetatively to ensure perpetuity, as the characteristics of hybrids are not fixed and therefore are not consistantly transmitted by seeds. Hence, if you want *Phlox* 'Dodo Hanbury Forbes', *Lupin* 'Wheatsheaf', or *Dianthus* 'Doris' you must have an actual piece of the original clone, either from a division, a cutting or, in the case of some plants, a layer. Therefore, we must be selective in the flowers we choose to grow from seeds. Many plants, such as delphiniums, particularly the Pacific-Coast strains, long-spurred columbines, *Campanula lactiflora*, laced pinks, *Alstroemeria* 'Ligtu Hybrids' and others are attractive in their variations and subtle shadings, which produce striking effects when massed in the garden.

Seeds of most perennials should be sown from March until early June. Biennials are best sown in late spring or early summer. A few perennials, such as alstroemerias and meconopsis, germinate more readily if seeds are sown when fresh, but early May is ideal for good germination and rapid growth of seedlings. Best results with very fine seeds or expensive ones are obtained by sowing in pots or seed-boxes, either wood or plastic, using a commercial seed compost or a home-made one consisting of two parts medium loam, one part peat

and one part coarse sand, by loose bulk. Add three-quarters of an ounce of ground chalk or limestone and one and a half ounces of superphosphate to each bushel of compost and mix thoroughly. Sterilized soil is a great help with seedlings. Coarser seeds, such as hollyhocks, baptisias, astrantias and some biennials, can be sown directly in a well-prepared seed-bed. Soilless cultivation in a rooting medium also gives satisfactory results.

The secret of success with seeds depends on a number of factors. The following hints may be helpful. A fine tilth is essential, especially if planting in a cold-frame or in the open ground. The surface should be even and the compost firm. Sow seeds thinly and uniformly and cover them with a fine layer of sieved soil, usually just a little thicker than the size of the seeds. Water very carefully. Fine seeds, if sown in a pot, can be watered after sowing by submerging the pot up to its rim in water and leaving it until the top becomes a darker colour.

Cover the pot or box with a sheet of glass and with brown paper to protect it from direct sunlight. As soon as the seedlings appear, remove the covers to give them air. Water the seedlings very carefully with tepid water, using a can with a very fine rose, so as not to dislodge the tiny hair-roots. Be careful not to over-water, but make sure that the seedlings never become dry or they will suffer real harm.

When seedlings are large enough to handle, prick them out in boxes or frames and later, when well established, line them out in the open ground so that sturdy plants will be ready for permanent homes in the autumn or spring. Periods of germination differ greatly, as does the rate of growth. Alstroemerias, for example, are very slow, as are paeony species. Fibre or peat pots are excellent for herbaceous plants as the seedlings establish and no root-disturbance will be necessary. I have grown aquilegias and hardy penstemons very successfully in this manner.

The light-blue *Brunnera macrophylla (Anchusa myosotidiflora)* and the vivid dark-blue *Cynoglossum nervosum* are useful perennials for a shrubbery, spring garden or woodland, and they come easily from seed. I am fond

Box-edged beds and topiary are a wonderful foil for the soft colours and silvery foliage of herbaceous plants in the restoration of an eighteenth-century garden in Williamsburg, Virginia.

of two perennial foxgloves which are fairly hardy: *Digitalis mertonensis* is a charming sturdy plant with two-and-a-half-foot spikes of crushed strawberry-pink flowers in July and August. The other is *D. ambigua*, which has creamy yellow flowers, freely borne on two- to three-foot stems above velvety dark green leaves. Both these plants like rich soil and a semi-shaded cool position. *Acanthus mollis* and *A. spinosissimus* can also be grown satisfactorily from seeds. Both are decorative plants with superb foliage, as well as flower-spikes suited to drying for winter flower-arrangements.

Double Flowers or Single?

Taste in flowers is unpredictable. Some gardeners have a predilection for rhododendrons: others, only for the rose. Some limit their fondness to flowering shrubs while others feel the attraction of the glorious flowers of herbaceous plants, or perhaps only for those with fine foliage, such as hostas, epimediums, bergenias and rodgersias. This makes for variety and interest in gardens. When it comes to the merits of single flowers versus double ones, opinion is again strongly divided.

137

On the one hand double flowers, such as tulips, heavily fragrant narcissus (*N. albus plenus odoratus*), huge shaggy dahlias, asters, roses and lilacs, to name just a few at random, have a rich opulence that delights many gardeners. On the other hand, single flowers have a simplicity and perfection of form that appeals to many, particularly to the artist, who thinks in terms of shape and form. It is easy to defend both points of view, though I must admit I have a preference for the singles.

A great deal depends on use. Obviously, double flowers tend to be more spectacular than singles and, as a rule, more lasting. Single flowers are generally complete with reproductive organs, while in a fully double flower, such as some camellias or tuberoses, the stamens and ovaries are suppressed in favour of petals. In the complete flower the coloured petals and fragrance usually cease to serve a useful function as soon as the flower is fertilized, and therefore, quite logically, single flowers are shorter-lived. This evanescent quality adds to their fascination. Witness the fleeting exquisite

charm of the single pink dog rose or the golden chalice, with its boss of darker stamens, of *Paeonia mlokosewitschii*, the loveliest of paeonies, in spite of its cumbersome name.

The merits of single and double flowers can well lead to argument, and it is easy to defend both points of view. As there is no right or wrong involved, we fall back on personal preferences. Certainly, for spectacular efforts doubles have advantages, particularly for flower-arrangements.

Let us pursue the question of paeonies a little further. Singles are gaining in popularity, particularly those with anemone centres where the stamens have become petaloid. Among the loveliest of single whites are 'White Wings' and 'Whitleyi Major'; 'Lord Kitchener' is a deep maroon, and 'Lady Wolseley' a vivid deep rose. Of the June-flowering petaloid type the bright pink 'Bowl of Beauty', 'Globe of Light', pure rose with a golden centre, and 'Kelway's White Lady' are outstanding. However, it is the huge, double, heavily

Huge, fully double, herbaceous paeonies are among the finest of hardy plants for beds and mixed borders. The heavily-scented flowers last well when cut and even the tight buds open.

scented pinks and whites such as 'Duchesse de Ne-
mours', 'Festiva Maxima', 'Sarah Bernhardt', 'Marie
Crousse' and 'Kelway's Glorious' that are sensational
in gardens in June and, of course, invaluable for
cutting. Every bud opens in water, if picked just as the
outer greenish sepals are spread apart by the expanding
ball of tightly packed, coloured petals. In a country
garden there should be room for both doubles and
singles, but remember that paeonies are slow to settle
down. Patience for several years is well rewarded, as
each year thereafter there will be an increasing dividend
of sumptuous bloom with the minimum of effort
except feeding with an autumn mulch of well-rotted
manure, or, barring that luxury, of compost or leaf-
mould with bone-meal.

Stocks are a delightful flower, loved for their spicy
fragrance and subtle, chalky colours, ranging from
whites through pale yellows, pinks and mauves to rich
purples and crimsons. Here doubles triumph, as single
stocks are dull at best, and almost weedy in character.
So true is this that gardeners are rather annoyed when
single flowers crop up among the double Bromptons or
Ten-Week strains. Stocks are useful for pots as well as
for the garden.

Sweet Rocket *(Hesperis matronalis)* is a lovely plant
for naturalizing. It is perennial, sweet-scented and
readily seeds itself. Its branching stems of four-petalled,
mauve or white, single, stock-like flowers brighten
many a wild garden and informal border after the
daffodils and bluebells. Once established, it will per-
petuate itself, seeding freely and coming up everywhere
on any soil. There is a double form of Sweet Rocket,
which is a scarce plant. Lucky is the gardener who can
obtain plants of this shy beauty, with its neat rosettes of
flowers, though it used to grow freely in old cottage
gardens. It does not set seed, and divisions and cuttings
are often difficult. I know of no nursery that lists it.

Another charmer is the old-fashioned double wall-
flower 'Harpur Crewe'. What a treasure it is, with its
shrubby habit forming a compact solid plant several
feet across with a quantity of branching spikes of neat
golden-yellow flowers opening from dark bronzed
buds. In addition to its fragrance it has the great virtue
of flowering over a long season, far more protracted
than its more numerous, single-flowered, biennial
relatives. It can be propagated from cuttings of half-
ripened short laterals, preferably with a heel. Well-
rooted plants are available from a number of nurseries.

One of the most intriguing plants I know of is a
superb double form of *Trillium grandiflorum* which I
have seen in several botanic gardens and those of a
few connoisseurs. Its large double flowers with neatly
arranged imbricated petals are outstanding. Unfortunately it is still very scarce indeed, and, to my
knowledge, very few are obtainable commercially.

Single paeonies with their feathery petaloid centres are even more
beautiful than the doubles, although a little more fleeting in flower.

For those who like unusual herbaceous plants for
the border, several should be singled out. One is the
double Crane's Bill *(Geranium pratense purpureum plenum)*
which has neat, double, deep violet-blue flowers
copiously borne in early summer on branching stems,
two and a half to three feet tall. There is a paler blue
(coeruleum plenum) with more loosely arranged petals,
and *album plenum*, the rare double white. I have a
great fondness for these plants, as they are less fleeting
in bloom than many of the Crane's Bills. Another delight
is the double-flowered peach-leaf campanula *(C. persicifolia alba flora pleno)*, which is certainly one of the best
cut flowers in late June and early July. Other particularly
fine forms include 'Fleur de Neige', 'Wedgwood' (semi-
double blue) and 'Wirral Belle' (double deep blue).

Some doubles are actually unattractive to my way
of thinking. There is a double day-lily, *Hemerocallis
fulva flore pleno*, which has none of the form or beauty of
the single varieties, nor do I like the huge ruffled
Japanese irises *(I. kaempferi)*, although they are spectacular and enjoy a considerable vogue.

The King of Hardy Plants

There are a large number of plant-nurseries but those of Blooms Nurseries Ltd, at Bressingham near Diss in Norfolk, England, are exceptionally interesting for the lover of hardy perennials and alpine plants. The nurseries, forming part of a four-hundred-and-forty-acre farm, are essentially wholesale, and the six-acre display gardens at Bressingham Hall are entirely the creation of Alan Bloom, who purchased the property when it was derelict in 1946. Today it is the largest herbaceous nursery in the world. Well over two thousand different varieties are grown, and between three and four million plants are raised annually in the fields, not to mention about six hundred thousand that are raised in pots and plunged in sand. An operation on this scale requires imagination, co-ordination, the right equipment, reliable staff and, above all, courage and hard work.

Many gardeners do not realize the enormous wealth of hardy herbaceous plants available from all parts of the world. It is fascinating to see the number of America species of wild flowers that are either grown for their own merit, including Butterfly Weed (*Asclepias tuberosa*), the wild blue Sweet William (*Phlox divaricata*), the Virginian Cowslip (*Mertensia virginica*), the wild bergamot (*Monarda fistulosa*), Blazing Star (*Liatris spicata*), *Lobelia cardinalis*, asters in wide variety, Goldenrods, Sweet Joe Pye Weed (*Eupatorium purpureum*), the highly esteemed False Solomon's Seal (*Smilacena racemosa*) with its fragrant feathery flower spikes and dozens of others. These have been propagated and in a few cases hybridized by Mr Bloom. British and European gardens would be very different places without all these North American natives.

It is interesting how each individual country has developed different genera. Although *Phlox paniculata* is native to the Northeast, it is in England that most of the important early garden varieties were produced. The fine Russell lupins were eventually also developed there, but using the Californian tree lupin (*L. arboreus*) and the colourful Northwestern *L. polyphyllus* as parents. The long tapered spikes of bicoloured flowers – pink and yellow, blue and cream, or rose and purple like racing colours – were the ultimates of this cross.

The United States leads the world in the development of bearded irises, day-lilies and paeonies, the last at one time the speciality of the French. Now our Pacific Coast delphiniums and polyanthus have received international recognition. Annuals are another great American speciality and in this field there are no peers. The Spencer sweet pea, one of the great high spots in new breaks, occurred in England as did their early development but now the United States is the leader in the development of fine strains including the dwarf Knee-Hi. The Dutch and Germans have done a lot with perennials, particularly with astilbes, sedums, goldenrods and heleniums.

Where do Mr Bloom's new plants come from? Some, as we have seen, are imported from overseas sources and tested at Bressingham to ensure their desirability and reliability. Others are grown from seeds of species collected abroad. Still others are the result of painstaking selection and hybridization, a great deal of which is done at Bressingham. In every case, the merits of a plant are considered very carefully before stocks are built up and it is eventually released to the trade. Still others are unusual forms acquired from outstanding plantsmen.

Let us consider a few of the notable plants developed by Alan Bloom and his able staff, particularly Percy Piper. The sturdy blue monkshood *Aconitum* 'Bressingham Spire' is a useful plant for smaller gardens because of its compact pyramidal habit. Its spikes of closely set, violet-blue flowers seldom exceed three feet. Erigerons are one of Alan Bloom's great achievements. What useful plants they are, with their blue, mauve, pink and purple, rayed, daisy-like flowers copiously borne on robust stems from June to October. 'Charity' is a tall light pink; 'Festivity', a subtle lilac; 'Prosperity', a nearly double blue, shaded mauve; and 'Unity' and 'Vanity' are good pinks. It is no small wonder that many of these plants have received awards and have found their way into better gardens in many parts of the world.

Another triumph of hybridization at Diss is the outstanding strain of heucheras. These are highly floriferous with brilliant colours; they include scarlet 'Red Spangles', the outstanding 'Coral Cloud', the intense carmine-pink 'Carmen', and many others. The two pink varieties of *Veronica spicata* 'Bacarolle' and 'Minuet' have enjoyed equal success. Other triumphs include *Aubretia* 'Bressingham Pink', *Phlox* 'Mother of Pearl', *Achillea* 'Moonshine' and the bigeneric cross *Heucherella* 'Bridget Bloom', with its foam of tiny white flowers tinged with pink. All of these are well known today and are generally available from reliable nurseries.

Another interesting facet of Alan Bloom's personality is his interest in motors and engines. This has stood him in good stead, as so much of the battle with the land and the elements was won by the ingenious use of mechanical equipment. This ultimately led to the formation of his collection of steam-engines and the building of a model railway. Fourteen steam-engines dating from 1890 to 1931 are on display, and on a nine-and-a-half-inch-gauge railway track, which was laid in 1964 on one side of the garden, is a model train which is the delight of children.

Gardeners owe a real debt to Alan Bloom, for he has enriched their gardens, providing new plants and vast

The felted grey leaves and candelabras of yellow flowers of *Verbascum broussa* are a striking feature in a border including irises, anchusas and columbines against a background of shrubs.

This Hartstongue fern *(Phyllitis scolopendrium crispa)* is beautiful, with its bold wax leaves that catch the light.

stocks of standard varieties for the trade, both at home and abroad. He has, moreover, opened his fine gardens as an inspiration to plant-lovers. Lastly, he donates the very generous proceeds from the gate to worthy charities.

Bright Future for Ferns

Few plants have been more neglected than ferns, but now, due to a marked revival of interest in foliage plants and the changing pattern of gardening, I foresee a bright future. I base this optimism on the fact that so many ferns are easy adaptable plants, suited to specialized positions such as dry shady banks, boggy areas near water, sunny verges, vertical crevices in walls and pockets on the rock garden. The truth of the matter is that ferns take kindly to a lot of positions that other plants dislike, but ferns will not be carefree from the start. It is essential to give them proper soil, rich in leaf-mould or peat, good drainage and regular care until they are established. Secondly, ferns are a splendid foil for other plants, and delightful associations, one of the secrets of successful planting, can be easily planned with a little thought.

For example, large clumps of the Royal Fern *(Osmunda regalis)* make a splendid contrast to the sword-like leaves of water irises including the Japanese *(I. kaempferi)*, and the Siberian irises with their more grass-like foliage. In autumn the foliage turns a rich russet-brown with striking spore-bearing fronds like tapered clusters of flowers, decorative throughout the winter and especially lovely when rimed with frosty silver. Royal ferns grow to a height of three or four feet but in favourable positions may double this. We associate them with water but they grow happily in cool shady borders and open woodland.

Ferns are lovely with woodland plants such as trilliums, Virginian Cowslips, erythroniums, lilies, violets and all manner of primulas. They are particularly useful to cover the bare patches left by early-flowering bulbs including snowdrops, aconites, scillas, chionodoxas and wood anemones, which largely disappear before ferns develop. I often scatter small groups of ferns among bluebells, daffodils, camassias, and the silver and green *Ornithogalum nutans*. They are in perfect harmony, enjoy similar conditions and eventually in late spring mask the yellowed withering leaves. For this purpose choose some of the many Lady Ferns *(Athyrium)*, the easily grown Male or Buckler Ferns *(Dryopteris)*, the Shield Ferns *(Polystichum)*, and the Hartstongues *(Phyllitis)*.

Ferns associate happily with hostas, their delicate tracery with the simple, broad, heart-shaped leaves making the perfect contrast in shape, texture and colour. Bergenias, euphorbias, hellebores, epimediums, Solomon's seals, smilacenas, veratrums and rheums are equally striking in juxtaposition. When it comes to planting, remember that the beauty of ferns will be lost if crowded with other plants. Many are seen to best advantage when planted in single clumps. This problem of spacing is one of the most difficult ones in gardening, as most amateurs tend to overplant, either because they cannot visualize the ultimate development of the plants or because they are impatient for immediate effect. This we may get for a year or two by crowded planting, but ultimately the beauty of the groupings is destroyed, and it will be necessary to do a lot of transplanting and rearranging. Ferns don't like disturbance, so space them out when planting. The fascinating fern garden in the National Arboretum in Washington, D.C., is well worth a visit to see how they should be grouped.

141

Polyanthus Parade

A great deal of the charm of the spring garden is derived from bulbs, but second place must go to primulas and especially polyanthus, the result of that most happy marriage between the oxlip and a red primrose, probably a red form of the sub-species of *Primula vulgaris* called *sibthorpii*. This parentage over the years, achieved by patient crossing and selection, has developed the great polyanthus strains associated with the names of Veterlee and Reinelt of California, and the British firms, Blackmore and Langdon of Bath and Sutton and Sons of Reading. There are other strains, of course, many of them excellent, and in the long run, selection from these is a matter of personal taste, according to the size and type of flower and the purpose for which it is required. The colour-range is tremendous, and the central golden eye, varying in size and shape, makes an even greater variation within a colour, adding sparkle and brilliance.

Polyanthus are at their peak in spring and in a cool season last for a long time. We see them everywhere, in broad drifts at the front of shrubberies or herbaceous borders, in clumps at the foot of grey stone walls in cottage gardens, as underplanting for fruit trees, and for bedding-schemes in town and country. There may be hundreds of them, or only five or six, or even one. The polyanthus is a plant for every garden. It will grow on any reasonable soil, but prefers a moisture-retentive, rich, fibrous loam or leafy soil. Although they are better in half-shade if they are to be grown as permanent planting, they flower superbly in full sun, although they may flag in hot weather. They are the answer to prayer for bedding- and border-schemes.

Seeds are often sown in February or March under glass so that the plants will flower the following spring, but many growers prefer to plant the fresh seeds in July or August (the earlier the better in the North and in cold areas) so that young plants are ready for planting out before the frost or, better still, for wintering in a frame. Seedlings sown one summer will make superb healthy plants, but will not flower freely until a year from the following spring. Seeds of polyanthus may also be sown in April or early May, preferably in pots or boxes, or in an open frame or even in a drill in a carefully prepared seed-bed. These will provide a mass of seedlings that can be pricked out when they are large enough to handle. They should be planted about four inches apart and kept weeded and well watered. By early autumn they should be large enough to be planted in their permanent homes. Mature plants can be ordered for delivery at the proper time in early autumn. Young seedlings of very good strains, ready for lining-out, are available in spring for those who do not want to sow the seeds. In any case, anticipate your needs, preferably while you can still assess these lovely flowers.

It is interesting to see how taste varies in the use of this delightful favourite. I have one friend who likes them only in masses of mixed colours. Another prefers only rose and pink shades; they are lovely in her garden, with the blue-grey foliage of pinks, lavender and the strong spikes of iris as a foil in foliage shapes. In another garden all the warm orange, russet and red shades are used with the deep red plumes of uncurling paeony-leaves, which glisten in the sun, giving almost as much pleasure as their huge scented flowers that follow in June. Then there are the blues, which evoke cries of ecstasy from endless admirers. Beautiful as they are, they seem to me slightly unnatural, but perhaps this is heretical.

A bed of mixed polyanthus nestles happily in a corner against a cottage wall. In a mild winter they commence flowering very early.

I like polyanthus planted on their own in a setting of pale yellow, such as the delicate pendulous flowers of large bushes of corylopsis, surely one of the loveliest of the flowering shrubs in April, or of forsythia, which in spite of its prevalence in gardens, still makes my heart leap anew with gladness each spring. My own favourites in polyanthus are the clear golden-yellows and creamy-whites, which are so beautiful with daffodils and all the blue-flowered bulbs, such as chionodoxas, scillas, muscari and blue forms of *Anemone blanda*. Of course, I love them all, but these golden and lemon-yellow beauties are to me the essence of spring.

I notice a tendency to plant groups of polyanthus only along the front of borders and shrubberies, though a much better effect can usually be achieved by carrying them in drifts through the middle and even to the back. For example, if there are lilacs or large shrub-roses towards the back, a generous planting of primroses or primulas can be left there undisturbed in the shadows of the summer foliage. Planting such as this draws the eye and gives a better balance, making a wide border far more interesting.

No-one should ever underestimate the usefulness of polyanthus for cutting. Blocks of them in the kitchen garden or in cutting borders are a source of great pleasure, as flowers are often produced from autumn and spasmodically throughout the winter if it is mild, with a big crop in spring, providing little posies or big bowls of them as the season advances. They arrange easily, and mixed colours will provide the right tones for any arrangement.

Polyanthuses need well-prepared rich soil for good long-term results. It is better to lift the plants after flowering in hot dry positions to a cooler position at the base of a wall, under shrubs or fruit trees. Here they can be allowed to grow and be re-planted in the early autumn to positions for spring. Frequent watering in dry weather is helpful. It is advisable to rogue-out any colours which you do not like. After flowering, divide any specially good varieties to increase the stock. In this way you can be selective with your own plants. I saw a garden recently where by systematic grouping over a few years broad plantings of yellow and cream shades and others of reds and oranges had been used to underplant shrub-roses very effectively. One of the finest polyanthus I know of is of a fine, velvety, dark red with almost no eye at all. The stems and foliage have a bronze tint, and the plants are in every way exceptional. This fine form appeared in seeds from the original Pacific Strain raised by Vetterle and Reinelt, of California. By dividing the few plants of this fine red form, a good stock was built up in a year or two. A coral shade from seeds raised in this country also was outstanding.

Division of plants is necessary, probably every two or three years, depending on the soil and the position. This is best done after flowering in late June or July, but it can be done in early autumn with success in areas not subject to early frost. In fact, in comparatively frost-free and forward areas, division even in winter can be successful. Relatively young plants divide easily if the crowns are gently pulled apart. Larger clumps, especially if they are woody in the centres, will best be prised apart with two forks, held back to back, and then the woody centres can be discarded and the individual crowns gently disentangled so as not to damage the roots. Every rooted bit is a potential plant, so here again is another honour for this obliging perennial.

City gardeners will find them very useful because they like shade, one of the requirements so easily catered for in walled gardens in towns, and because they flower over a long season. Food and moisture assure good results. Mulching with damp peat will help to keep them from drying out in summer. Polyanthus grow better in deep boxes or tubs where they have depth of soil for their roots than in pots and shallow window-boxes. In many town gardens they will probably be discarded after flowering to make way for the summer show of geraniums and annuals.

Rock-plants for Spring

One of the great joys of spring is the bounty of rock-garden and alpine plants which provide such a dazzling show, lasting well into the summer, with others like the autumn cyclamen and gentians stretching out through the year. In fact, the rock-gardens can have flowers in every month. The range of plants is enormous, including those that are easy for the novice as well as some that are a real challenge even to the most experienced. Such a plant is *Corydalis cashmeriana*, with its intense bright blue flowers borne in small umbels on short stems.

One of the nice things about most of the so-called rock-plants and alpines is that they are broadminded and don't insist on a rockery. The most satisfactory rock-gardens are those that exist where there are natural outcroppings of rock. Others can be constructed with care and provided with a setting so that they merge into the landscape. In smaller gardens, rockeries, often built on banks or difficult slopes, are apt to be less convincing. What should be avoided are the little heaps of stones in odd corners that have no relation to the garden and look as if it had been too much trouble to cart away the surplus stones and rubble. In small gardens a substitute for a rockery can be provided by building walls to create a raised bed or by a series of shallow terraces, often flanking steps or a walk. Then there are beds rather like billiard-tables, surrounded by dry walls, which can be built to any

The cheery citron-yellow flowers of *Ranunculus gramineus*, borne on nine-inch grassy stems, are a delightful feature in a rock garden.

Dryas octopetala makes a dense mat with shining dark leaves and charming, white, golden-centred flowers followed by fuzzy seed-heads.

height required. These are easy to look after as they involve the minimum of stooping, and little treasures are much nearer the eye than if planted at ground-level. In my own garden, small flowers such as the South African rhodohypoxis, with their small pink or white stars, were more effective on raised beds than at ground-level. Actually, of course, the sloping construction of most rock-gardens accomplishes this same purpose.

In raised beds or in pockets on rock-gardens, soil can be provided to meet the specialized requirements of any given plant, and a position can usually be found so that a plant can have full sun, shade or a combination of both, so that its roots are in shade and its growth in sun. It is amazing what cool shade and shelter from wind a pocket on a rock-garden provides. It must always be remembered that on chalky soils, pockets of neutral or acid soil for special plants will, ·with continuous watering, become alkaline unless the water is free of lime. This goes for pots of camellias and other plants as well. Rain-water collected from the roofs in water-butts is an excellent solution, although

in prolonged droughts supplies are soon exhausted. I am always amazed at the number of gardeners who make no attempt to catch the wonderful, soft rain-water.

Where colour is the primary aim there is apt to be a preponderance of mauve, purple and blue aubretias, bright yellow *Alyssum saxatile* and sheets of *Phlox sub-ulata*. These can present some very trying colour combinations if not carefully placed. When a bold display of colour is desired, group the different shades carefully and in broad masses. Do not make a series of spots of isolated colour. Also remember that there is a lovely, soft, lemon-yellow variety of alyssum known as *citrinum*, which is a lot easier to blend with other colours than the brighter golden-yellows. As grey foliage is the perfect foil for all these plants, use hardy pinks in groups or low-growing artemisias, such as *A. stelleriana* or *schmidtii nana*, or even *Stachys lanata* to soften the bright colours.

There are many treasures for the alpine enthusiast. The range of enchanting primulas and auriculas alone is bewildering; then there are the delightful dwarf

144

irises, including the miniature flag irises *(Iris chamaeiris)* and species such as the very small *I. cristata*, which in May produces soft blue, fringed flowers marked with rich gold; and the charming *I. graminea*, with its bright lilac-purple flowers scented like ripe apricots, and *I. tectorum* and its variety *album*, natives of Japan, which are particularly attractive in late May or June if grown in a warm sheltered spot. My favourite is *Iris innominata*, native to Oregon and Northern California, which in spring produces quantities of handsome flowers on six-inch stems in subtle shades of apricot, buff, mauve and orange with delicate pencilling. This little iris does not like lime but otherwise is not difficult.

Then there are fascinating saxifrages, sempervivums, cyclamen, gentians, pinks and a host of other plants. In fact, so wide is the choice of hardy rock-plants alone that selection for a small garden is not easy. And there are also the dwarf shrubs, which include rhododendrons, daphnes, brooms and salixes, as well as evergreen trees.

One of the best ways to acquire rock-plants is to go to the various nurseries that specialize in them and make a selection on the spot. As most of the plants are pot-grown, it is easy to carry them away. When selecting alpines and hardy plants, don't be seduced by those in full flower. These should be merely treated as samples. Choose well-furnished sturdy specimens with plenty of flower bud, perhaps very backward, which will develop and flower over a longish period. Even if there is no bloom, you will be rewarded next year, by pretending for this season that flowers are a minor consideration. And they are. What is important is to establish healthy clumps with a future. After all, you aren't buying cut tulips or carnations at the florist.

Pansies and Violas

Few flowers are a greater asset to the gardener than pansies and violas. They flower over a very long season and range in size from small ones, like the reddish-brown and yellow Jackanapes, which has such character, or the neat tufted mounds of *Viola gracilis*, with its exquisitely formed flowers of velvety violet-blue, to the giant modern pansies, descendents of *Viola tricolor maxima*, with fragrant ruffled flowers as much as three or four inches in diameter on long stems. The varieties are numerous and include clear self-colours, subtle shadings with central zones or eyes, and the famous faces, always associated in the mind's eye with this garden favourite. Few flowers have such a complete range of deep rich tones of crimson, violet, burgundy, ruby-red, midnight-blue, chestnut-browns and even velvety blacks. These deep colours are very useful in the garden, as colours too often tend either towards pastel shades or fiery hot ones. Pansies and violas are

hardy perennials, although in many gardens the former are better if treated as biennials.

Their uses are many. We all know the delightful bedding-schemes that can be created by using pansies, either as sheets of colour on their own, or as a rich carpet for May-flowering tulips. The pansies, of course, outlast the tulips for they start far earlier and continue to bloom long after the petals of the tulips have fallen. In fact, they are still blooming when uprooted to make way for the summer scheme. Pansies and violas make fascinating borders and edgings, whether used as a straight edge or in irregular sheets of colour running back through the groupings of shrubs.

Violas and violettas, descendents of *Viola cornuta* or *V. gracilis*, are often used as underplanting for old shrub-roses, hybrid teas or floribundas, and I know of gardens where they form luxuriant mats. Attractive as they are, some gardeners will complain that such a dense carpet makes the upkeep of the roses difficult, as winter-mulches are impossible. On rich, cool soils violas, especially vigorous-growing varieties, may have a smothering effect, climbing up the rose-stems and blanketing everything. I love this luxuriant tangle, and the blues, mauves and purples are wonderful with the soft pinks, clear yellows, rich reds and mauves of the roses. Pansies and violas are effective in flower-boxes, especially in cool semi-shaded windows where they can be watered and cherished. No plant responds more kindly to dead-heading, rewarding our efforts with successive flushes of blooms. They are equally attractive in bays on the rock-garden, especially the smaller compact varieties, or in clumps or as borders for paths in cottage gardens in country lanes and villages.

Pansies come in a number of giant strains in mixed colours and are listed by different firms. They include Giant Fancy, Floradale Giant Hybrids, Perfection, Exhibition, Trimardeau Steele's Jumbo, Read's New Century Scented and Ruffled Butterfly Hybrids. A popular new early-flowering strain is known as Clear Crystals, with bright self-colours of orange, blue, yellow and apricot with no markings. Then there are a number of extremely popular named varieties, such as the sweetly-scented 'Coronation Gold', the Wedgwood-blue 'Ullswater' with its dark central blotch, the pure gleaming white 'Mount Everest', 'Violet Queen', 'Crimson Queen' and 'Black Prince'. These average six to nine inches in height. Then there are colour-selections, such as Sutton's Giant Wine Shades, Bunyard's Rose Shades, or Dobies' Violet-Blue Shades, which give delightful variations within a given colour, so that there is a lovely shimmering effect.

One of the finest strains of pansies is that developed by the Rogli Brothers in Switzerland and offered by W. Atlee Burpee and other seed houses. This superb large-flowered strain includes the snow-white 'Jung-frau', garnet-red 'Alpengluhn', gentian-blue 'Thuner-see' and the pinky-mauve 'Blumlisalp'.

Summer-flowering varieties should be sown in March under glass, pricked-out into flats or small fibre-pots when large enough to handle and planted out in May or early June. Alternatively, if grown as biennials (which is probably the most satisfactory way) and for winter-flowering varieties, sow the seed in boxes or a cold-frame from late May until July, prick-out when a suitable size and plant in September and October. Outdoor sowings can also be made when the soil is warm, but seed-beds must be carefully prepared.

Violas are raised in similar fashion, and if seeds are sown in February or early March, flowers may be obtained during the first summer. They flower over a very long season and are truly perennial in cool, moist soil, with a little shade. Good bedding-varieties include 'Arkwright Ruby', 'Chantreyland' (rich apricot), 'Jersey Gem' (violet) and a number listed by colour (white, yellow, mauve, etc). Plants are offered by a few nurseries, especially old favourites such as 'Maggie Mott', 'Pickering Blue', 'Miss Brookes', 'Jersey Gem' and 'Moonlight'. 'Martin', a deep rich purple, is exceptionally floriferous over a long season, and 'Blue Perfection' smothers itself with flowers. All of these can be readily propagated from cuttings and divisions.

Let's plan for masses of these useful fragrant colour-ful flowers, as there is a place for them in every garden. They are excellent for picking and this induces an even greater profusion of bloom.

Dwarf Bearded Irises

Dwarf bearded irises are always a delight, whether used on the rock-garden, in groups along the front of borders, in raised beds, in pockets in paving, or in sinks or troughs. Their charming, perfectly formed flowers resemble the more familiar flag irises. These are the forms of *Iris pumila* and of *I. chamaeiris* and now an increasing number of hybrids of great refinement and delicacy. A great deal is being done with this group, particularly in this country, and very soon an increasing number should become available in the trade. As a result, a new system of categories has been worked out on a basis of height. Both these species and their progeny are sun-lovers and lime-lovers. Gardeners on chalk take note. Irises require shallow planting, so that the tops of the rhizomes are exposed to the sun, and they are best divided or moved after flowering. There is considerable confusion between the species, and many plants listed as forms of *I. pumila* are really forms of *I. chamaeiris*.

The former is a native of Eastern Europe, while the latter is indigenous to the southern Mediterranean countries. Travellers in spring in southern France, Spain and Portugal are familiar with them by the road-sides in certain localities. In our gardens these irises flower in April or early May and sometimes even in late March in mild localities. *Iris chamaeiris campbellii*, with large deep blue flowers on four- to five-inch stems, is a charmer, and the form *italica* is also noteworthy.

Attractive as these species and the old French hybrids derived from them may be, the real excitements are the new hybrid dwarf bearded irises which have these two species as parents, coupled with *I. flavescens* and *I. flavissima*, the last being much used in the United States. There will be an increasing number of these fine hybrids.

There are good clear self-colours and many have subtle shading and blending. Often the beards are contrasting. They range in height from about six to twelve inches and some of the newer ones are a little taller. Their great merit is their useful blooming sea-son; they herald the tall bearded irises at the end of May and June and most of the species, but follow the much earlier bulbous types like *I. reticulata, histrioides* and *danfordiae*, which appear in late winter or early spring. The flowers have great refinement and have been developed so that the falls of many are flaring rather than tucked under, as in *I. chamaeiris*.

In this country there has been a great deal of hybrid-ization of dwarf irises as their value as good garden plants is recognized for massing at the front of borders, for clumps on the rock garden and for raised beds in town gardens or for old people, who like to see their treasures near them and incidentally do not have to bend. Dwarf irises can be planted at any season.

Interesting varieties include 'Sambo', dark violet; 'Tampa', a floriferous warm soft red; 'Excelsa', pale lemon-yellow; 'Bright White', white standard with pale lemon falls; and 'Lilliput' with light blue standards, darker falls and a white beard on twelve-inch stems. 'Green Spot' has exquisite form and colouring, a gleaming pure white with large green spots on each fall. It has been widely used in breeding.

Pinks and Silver

In recent years the value of silver and grey foliage plants, both shrubby and herbaceous, has been in-creasingly recognized, not only because of their beauty, but also because of their usefulness as a foil for flowers. There is nothing new about their use; they were dearly loved by Miss Gertrude Jekyll (1843–1932), that great gardener, who had such a profound and lasting in-fluence on decorative gardening. Mediterranean gar-deners have long made the most of these sun-lovers, so many of which are native to the Southwest and the various Mediterranean countries. This is not surprising, as grey-foliage plants, many of which are covered with silken hairs, withstand the searing sun and the salt-laden sea winds.

If such is the native habitat of artemisias, lavenders, santolinas, rock-roses, helichrysums and thymes, it follows that they need good drainage, sunny positions and alkaline soil, although the last is not essential. They do not tolerate wet, dark, poorly-drained soils or sooty areas, as the dirt clings to the felted surfaces and clogs the pores. Thus, after a very wet winter, that old stand-by *Stachys lanata*, which I would not be without, fares badly in town gardens and on wet, heavy soil. Even *Senecio greyi*, a shrub that will stand a good deal of heavy frost, may suffer in similar positions, largely because the new growth is unlikely to ripen if there is a lack of sun.

When soil is heavy, it can be lightened with coarse sand, mortar-rubble, crushed brick, gravel, rough ash or burnt clay to improve the drainage. If it is acid, lime in some form will be beneficial. I find that grey-foliage plants, such as lavender, santolina, *Convolvulus cneorum* and *Senecio maritima*, grow extremely well where they overhang paving, brick edgings and gravel paths

or terraces. The successful cultivation of silver-foliaged plants on screes or sunny pockets in a rock-garden is readily understandable.

Let us consider some of the silver and grey herbaceous plants. Artemisias are particularly useful to screen blank patches left by anchusas, alstroemerias, delphiniums, clumps of tulips and similar early summer-flowering herbaceous and bulbous plants. Most of the artemisias are sold from pots and so are a number of other greys and silvers. 'Silver King' is particularly satisfactory if used in this way, as are *versicolor*, *ludoviciana* and *palmeri*. These grow to about two feet in height, though the first two will grow to about three. *Artemisia arborescens* is at least three feet tall and very useful in the middle ground of borders and pretty against a red brick wall. Dwarfer artemisias include *A. pedmontana splendens*, which is very feathery and lovely with heliotrope, and the exquisite low-growing 'Silver Mound' which will form a silvery cushion at the front of a border. All of these are hardy and withstand cold positions in gardens where there is sun and reasonable drainage in Zones 7 and 8.

Anaphalis yedoensis and *A. triplinervis* are similar in

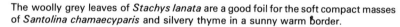

The woolly grey leaves of *Stachys lanata* are a good foil for the soft compact masses of *Santolina chamaecyparis* and silvery thyme in a sunny warm border.

147

that they both have greyish foliage and clusters of white everlasting flowers. I much prefer the former; it is dwarfer in habit (one to one and a half feet) and is an excellent ground-cover, as it spreads rapidly to make a dense clump. These are two easy plants for almost any soil. Similarly, several of the achilleas are easy plants for the herbaceous or mixed border. *Achillea taygetea* has silvery green foliage and flat heads of yellow flowers which last well and are wonderful for cutting and for drying (one and a half feet). 'Moonshine' (two feet) has even greyer finely-cut foliage and clear yellow flower-heads from late May until July. Both these plants are lovely when combined with seahollies, such as the steely-blue *Eryngium tripartitum*, 'Blue Dwarf', and *amethystinum* or the darker blue *Salvia superba* and its dwarfer forms 'Lubeca' (two feet) and 'East Friesland' (one and a half feet). I find all these herbaceous plants extremely satisfactory, as they have a long flowering season, are short enough not to require complicated staking, and combine so effectively. All of them are splendid for cutting.

I cannot think of silver foliage plants without associating them with pinks. Somehow they are as natural an association as ham and eggs. Grey foliage is flatter-ing to all flowers and is as telling in a border as pink tulips or blue lupins. I like to use it along paths and terraces with drifts of blue catmint and fragrant pinks. Try the soft, feathery grey of *Artemisia* 'Silver Mound' with the spiky blue-green blades of irises. The blue foliage of pinks looks even bluer next to silver. With the taller greys such as *Artemisia discolor* and 'Silver King', pinch out the growing tips at regular intervals to make them bushy and to keep them from flowering so they won't flop and require staking.

A Plethora of Pinks

When we think of cottage gardens, pictures are evoked of masses of roses and pinks, their scents mixing to form an intoxicating fragrance. Pinks are a mainstay of the summer garden, and even in winter their glaucous green mats of foliage lend interest to many a dull border or to the vertical surface of a bare stone wall.

As they like good drainage and a sunny warm position, pockets in paving or crannies in brick walls offer ideal homes. Large areas of paving in terraces or paths can be softened with a few pinks, the off-whites, pinks and mauves contrasting pleasantly with the blue-grey foliage and the grey stone. Dwarf blue companulas and clumps of fragrant thyme make charming contrasts in colours and textures.

Pinks associate happily with roses. In winter they relieve the bare thorny stems, and in summer their flowers are completely harmonious in shape and colour. They are charming in borders along paths, spilling over gravel, bricks or paving in natural abandon, and, unlike nepeta or violas, the foliage persists in winter. Pinks are charming if used in broad groups at the front of herbaceous borders, but take care that more invasive plants do not swamp them before they are established. They are particularly effective in mixed borders, providing just the right interest in colour and texture of foliage with lavender, rosemary, blue rue, potentillas, shrub-roses and cistuses.

The rock-garden is their natural home, and for this purpose the choice is very wide. There are charming dwarf varieties, floriferous and compact in habit, such as the double clear rose-pink 'Little Jock' and the dark red 'Mars', or the sprawling and spreading variety, like the dainty Maiden Pink *Dianthus deltoides*, suitable for the tops of dry walls or where they can spill over the stone surfaces. It smothers itself with a shower of rosy stars or in the case of *deltoides albus*, white ones, or deep red, as with 'Huntsman' or 'Wisley Var'.

Double garden pinks are superb plants on well-drained soils, preferably alkaline. When cut, they arrange easily and keep extremely well.

Flesh-pink 'New Dawn' is perhaps the most satisfactory of all climbing roses because of its abundance of bloom throughout the summer, quick vigorous growth and clean foliage.

The striped Gallica rose 'York and Lancaster', with pink floribundas and taller hybrid musks in a mixed border made by the author.

D. deltoides alpinus, with large pink flowers on three-inch stems, and *D. arvernensis* with silvery-grey mats of leaves and small clear pink flowers, are excellent for the rockery. *Deltoides alpinus*, 'Little Jock', 'Mars' and the dwarf pink, sweetly scented 'La Bourbille' are useful for troughs. In fact, pinks are very versatile plants.

They like lime, so are a natural gift to chalk gardens. They are ideally suited to city and town gardens as long as they have relatively sunny positions and good drainage. Well-broken-down garden compost or even a little rotted manure well worked into the soil, is beneficial, particularly to perpetual flowering Show Pinks or Border Carnations. Avoid peat and use leaf-mould sparingly, except on limy soils. On neutral or slightly acid ones limestone chippings are excellent as a source of lime.

The old-fashioned single or semi-double Cottage or Village Pinks can be grown from seed or bought as plants, and of course, like all pinks, they come easily from cuttings. There is a profusion of colours with enormous variations in the size and form of the flowers, which can be fringed, notched or smooth-edged. Some are self-coloured; others have delicate striping or zones of different colours. There is an excellent strain known as 'Highland Hybrids', single, free-flowering and heavily scented. 'Elizabethan Pinks' are another good strain with a neat upright habit. Single *D. allwoodii* are hardy, perpetual-flowering and scented. All are easy from seed.

An old favourite, particularly for borders, is 'Mrs Sinkins', which flowers freely, though for all too short a season. The flowers are white, full and spicy-sweet, but the calyx cups tend to split and the flowers are ragged; on balance they are not the best of old favourites. 'White Ladies' is supposedly a better plant, but really there isn't a great difference. One of the loveliest of the older varieties is 'Musgrave's Variety', which is white with a cool green eye. This eighteenth-century pink is one of my great favourites, along with the laced pink charmingly named 'Dad's Favourite', a semi-double white, laced ruby-red with zones of chocolate-purple.

The peer among garden pinks is the race known as *Dianthus allwoodii*, the result of crossing *D. plumarius* with perpetual-flowering border carnations. Show Pinks are similar but even more perfect in form. This race is hardy, of good constitution, free-flowering, perpetual and scented. Of course, some varieties are better than others. My favourite is 'Swanlake', a double pure white of perfect form, heavily scented and long-lasting. 'Iceberg' and 'Blanche' are other good ones, excellent for cutting. 'Doris' is an outstanding shrimp-pink with a red eye, prolific, fragrant, long-lasting in water and with a long blooming season.

Other good pinks include 'Pink Bouquet', 'Joan', 'Helen', 'Dawn' and 'Enchantress'. The charmingly named 'Cherry Red', the bright free-flowering crimsons, 'Barbara' and 'Ian', and the rich, glowing scarlet 'Roger' and 'Robin' are also attractive. They are wonderful flowers for cutting. A few in a small vase on a desk or dressing-table or masses in big bowls on a dining-table are equally effective. They are charming mixed with Garnette roses, either red or pink, as they are of about the same scale and similar in shape. Pinks are to my mind the perfect buttonhole.

Pinks are best planted in August or September or in the late spring on cold soils, but can be planted at almost any season in favourable districts. Be sure that the plants have good root-development and are properly hardened-off. If in doubt, it is worth potting-up new plants from nurseries in inclement weather and placing them in a frame or sheltered place until weather conditions are good or the plants are more established.

Seed sown in late winter or early spring under glass should provide flowering plants for the following year. Sow in pans or flats and prick-out in a frame or boxes. Spring- or early summer-sowings in the open ground will flower the second year. Rogue-out any seedlings which do not have flowers of good size or habit. In this way future seedlings can be improved. It is well worth saving your own seed of the best plants and making sowings every year or two for replacements, as old plants gradually grow leggy and may die back at the centre. Only some varieties will set seeds.

The Charm of Crane's Bills

If I were asked to name the herbaceous plant which I find most useful in gardens it would probably be one of that attractive group of hardy geraniums, more commonly known as Crane's Bills. They are indispensable on many counts. First and foremost, they are so easy and adaptable, thriving on any soil, in many cases either in sun or semi-shade, and providing handsome foliage for at least eight or nine months of the year. Already in the first week of April in herbaceous borders and shrubberies the delicately-cut leaves of hardy geraniums are a telling feature, and in autumn some varieties take on magnificent colouring. Then there is the profusion of flowers, often over a long flowering season, and the fact that most species come readily from seed. I hardly need continue this paean of praise, though there are other desirable features, such as the fact that most species are easily propagated by division, for usually even the most unlikely tuft will root and establish.

The uses of hardy geraniums are legion. As border-plants they are superb. The rich purples, violet-blues,

The violent crimson-magenta, black-eyed flowers of *Geranium psilostemon (armenum)* are startling but effective with mauves, greys and pinks

In autumn the foliage takes on bright tinges of claret and crimson. In a mild winter this plant proves very nearly evergreen, especially in mild, favoured gardens. There is as well a white-flowered form and a deeper reddish-pink one. With this species I always couple the Caucasian *G. renardii*, which again has a neat, domed habit and scented leaves with remarkably decorative sage-green, slightly felted surfaces, attractive patterning and intricate reticulated veining. It, too, makes dense ground-cover. *Geranium renardii* grows best in sun. The flowers are white, delicately picked out with violet veining at the bases of the petals. Although the flowering season is short, it matters little with foliage as rewarding as this.

There are a number of Crane's Bills in the blue-violet range. One of the loveliest, but certainly not the easiest, is *G. wallichianum* 'Buxton's Blue'. This is a heavenly plant, with hints of violet, accentuated by the milky-white zonal ring round the dark stamens. The flowering season is a long one, but it is a plant which needs good, cool soil in sun or half-shade. It has a grace and elegance all its own and is superb in autumn. Then there is the showy *G. grandiflorum*, and its variety *alpinum*. About a foot tall and of enormous vigour, this fine plant produces clouds of strikingly veined, violet-blue flowers, their round symmetrical outline a foil to the crisply-cut foliage. It, too, has a few weeks of added glory in autumn, when the leaves turn gleaming copper-red. *Geranium ibericum platypetalum* has foliage and flowers of similar distinction.

For brilliance of colour, *G. pilostemon (G. armenum)* has no equal. The dazzling magenta-crimson flowers seem even more vivid because of their black centres. This striking combination is further enhanced by bold decorative foliage, for this is a vigorous large variety, often exceeding two and a half to three feet. It is lovely with silvery-grey artemisias, *Senecio maritima*, *Stachys lanata*, and a number of others, and is particularly French in colour-scheme if combined with pink or mauve old shrub-roses, such as 'Celestial' or the purple Moss 'William Lobb'. Their flowering seasons coincide with enchanting results.

My list could grow, for there is still the Widow's Geranium, *G. phaeum*, with its neat, small flowers approaching very near to black, the aptly-named Bloody Crane's Bill, *G. sanguineum* with its variety *lancastriense*, palest pink with fine reddish-pink veining, and the white variety *album*, as well as a number of others (for doubles, see p. 139).

Geraniums are best planted in early autumn or spring. As they increase rapidly, stock can soon be built up by division of established clumps. Species can also be grown from seeds sown in spring or early summer.

clear pinks, whites, maroon-black and magenta-crimson provide a feast for the lover of bright colours. Next to be praised is their usefulness as ground-covers for shrubberies, beds of old roses, banks and a number of other spots which are not easy to conceal. Hardy geraniums are excellent for town gardens, as many of them are relatively shade-tolerant and patient under difficult conditions. Lastly, they establish quickly and are completely hardy.

For me, *Geranium endressii* 'Wargrave' is a peer among plants. It has a charming spreading habit, growing twelve to fifteen inches tall and covering an area of several feet when established. The small, brilliant salmon-pink flowers are borne in rapid succession from June until frost. It is useful as a loose, flowing edging against gravel or grey stone paving and for striking groups in a mixed or herbaceous border. It is an ideal ground-cover under lilacs, big rose species or other large shrubs, as it is tolerant of half-shade.

For areas where shade is more intense there are two superb answers in this genus. *Geranium macrorrhizum* is a charmer, with delightfully aromatic, sticky, roundish leaves of a clear light apple-green. The soft pink flowers are profusely borne in June and although they are short-lived the attractive reddish calyx cups linger on.

Sweet Columbines of June

One of the most charming flowers in late May and June is the long-spurred columbine *(Aquilegia)*, which is one of the most fragile and exquisite of all hardy herbaceous plants, not only for the flowers, but for the refined, slightly glaucous, trifoliate leaves, which are lovely in themselves and rather resemble thalictrums. In fact, columbines are as much an asset in the spring border for their foliage as many plants grown exclusively for that purpose.

The flowers, beautifully poised at the tips of thin branching stems, are composed of five slender, curving, spurred petals, hollow like elongated cornucopias, alternating with five flat, rather pointed, petaloid sepals round a high boss of golden-tipped stamens with protruding pale green stigmas. It is a complex flower of exceptional grace.

The colours are particularly subtle, the flat sepals being usually the same colour as the tube of the spur, while the upper flaring cup-shaped part which forms the centre of the flower is often of a much lighter or a contrasting shade. Thus we find combinations of purple and pale mauve, rose and shell-pink, apricot and buff, deep gold and canary-yellow, pale blue and white, strawberry-red and creamy-yellow, and white and blue selfs. They are lovely when restricted to groups of a separate colour, but even more enchanting when the mixed varieties form a delicate rainbow. It is strange that the colours of certain flowers never clash. In the case of columbines, is it because the individual flowers are so fragile? Or is it because the colours are so delicate, even when clear and strong?

Columbines are obliging, as they grow readily from seeds, which can be sown under glass in March or April and then pricked-out and later transplanted to their permanent home, where they will flower abundantly the following spring. Alternatively, the seeds may be sown in June in open ground or in a frame and moved to their flowering-site in early September or the following spring. A light loam with ample leaf-mould is an ideal compost. If the sun is very hot, it may be well to shade the germinating seeds and later the young seedlings with muslin or frames. As birds are very apt to disturb seed-beds, the finely prepared tilth serving as a tempting dust-plunge, protection may be needed.

Columbines have a vigorous, long tap-root. For this reason it is advisable to move plants when young and manageable, preferably as seedlings when several inches high. Sowing seeds *in situ* is effective, but the soil must be kept moist until they germinate. Strew the seeds very thinly and thin out the seedlings, transplanting the crowded ones as necessary.

There are many charming ways to grow columbines. I like them in drifts in borders, where they associate happily with bearded irises, pink or blue hardy geraniums, violas, pyrethrums and sometimes, in unusually late seasons, with the last of the tulips. In borders, a few plants or even single ones, tucked in here and there, make charming incidents of colour, yet they will not leave large gaps when they have finished blooming. They are a wonderful foil for the bold foliage of herbaceous plants such as acanthus, *Senecio clivorum*, bergenias and the half-grown spikes of bocconias and hollyhocks. As all these plants develop rapidly, they will fill in the gaps left by the columbines after flowering. They are charming if planted in the paving of paths, steps or terraces, or, better still, if allowed to seed there naturally. They belong to that useful group of plants which are so necessary for jointing and for odd corners that need softening.

Aquilegias are particularly attractive if grown in half-shade, which particularly suits them, as they do not like excessively dry positions. I know of several gardens where they grow under fruit trees, luxuriating in the cool shadows and perpetuating themselves by seeding. They are charming with irises or in rose-borders. I love the casual stray plants in informal gardens because they never look out of place.

On light soils columbines need watering in periods of drought, and they benefit by an occasional soaking in all gardens during the summer months. When the foliage starts to turn yellow and wither early in the season, reach for the watering-can or the hose. Old-established clumps can be moved or divided, but with some difficulty because of the tap-root, and they often take a year to settle down and flower freely. It is far better to grow a new batch from seed. Young plants are also readily available from good nurseries.

In most of our gardens there are probably plants of the old-fashioned common blue or white columbines, which cross readily with the long-spurred varieties. The progeny is apt to be predominantly short-spurred and disappointing. For this reason it is wise to buy seed from the specialist seed-houses rather than save your own, which may not come true.

In May or June we should sow biennials, preferably in the open, including foxgloves *(Digitalis)*, Canterbury Bells *(Campanula medium)*, wallflowers and forget-me-nots. If you want a few of the giant silver thistles as a feature in the border or shrubbery, buy a packet of *Onopordon acanthium*. If germination is good, you will have enough for several gardens, as only a few are needed to give an effect. Again, they have a tap-root, so plant them *in situ* or transplant the young seedlings into their permanent positions in the late summer or early autumn. Once established, onopordons will seed themselves freely. Globe artichokes have equally handsome silvery foliage and are true perennials in reasonable climates, especially on well-drained soils.

Hardy Plants for Alkaline Gardens

Many people express despair at the thought of gardening on alkaline soil. Although it restricts the scope of plants that can be raised successfully, by ruling out ericaceous shrubs such as rhododendrons, camellias, enkianthus and a host of others, it very often makes for a garden which is gayer in character and more ingenious in the variety of flowering shrubs, perennials and bulbs than many of those gardens where plants are limited almost exclusively to rhododendrons. They produce a mass of dark, heavy foliage with a concentration of colour in spring.

It is possible to alter alkaline soil by the use of iron chelates, so that ericaceous plants can be grown, but this is an artificial process and not one which I would advocate for the general gardener. The important thing in a successful garden is to grow what is happy and thrives. I take no pleasure in moderate specimens, even though their cultivation against odds may be a triumph. The important thing to achieve in every garden is a luxuriant, attractive setting into which choice plants or special features can be introduced. For the gardener on chalk there is a wide range of trees, shrubs and herbaceous plants that will thrive. One has only to look at the wealth of British flora on the South Downs since the advent of myxamatosis and the almost complete eradication of the rabbit population. The variety and beauty of this flora should certainly hearten the sceptic.

If still in doubt, think of the shores of the Mediterranean which support one of the richest of all floras. Dwarf cyclamen, crocuses, scillas, tulip species and enchanting dwarf daffodils, particularly in Spain and Portugal, thrive on highly alkaline soil. Portugal in March or April is unbelievable with wild paeonies, orchises, asphodels, dwarf irises, wild calendulas, and scores of others, making the slopes above the sea and the inland country a veritable *primavera*.

There are as well wild cistuses, lavenders, rosemaries and helichrysums, making a thick aromatic scrub among the rocks. Yellow brooms, Judas trees, fragrant honeysuckles and wild roses enrich this floral carpet. Based on this flora, which I love so well, I feel disinclined to shed tears for the gardener on an alkaline soil if he is imaginative.

Furthermore, with lilacs, mock orange, cotoneasters, rose species and exotics like the bright blue South African Nile Lily *(Agapanthus)*, only moderately hardy, but ideal for tubs, and the graceful *Galtonia (Hyacinthus) candicans*, with tall spikes of white snowdrop-shaped flowers in mid-summer, all of which are lime-tolerant, I am afraid I am not sympathetic in spite of my next remarks.

Turning to plants of a herbaceous nature for chalky soils, there are many conventional border-plants that are not very satisfactory and may prove short-term tenants. Lupins are out; delphiniums are only moderate. Phloxes on chalk are difficult and not outstanding. All of these need deeply-dug, heavily-enriched soil, so shallow chalky soil certainly does not satisfy their requirements.

On the other hand, there are a lot of naturals. Anchusas, flowering from May until June and in some gardens into July, are superb on chalk as their blue seems even more vivid. There are many splendid varieties of *Anchusa italica*, but outstanding is 'Loddon Royalist', which only grows to about three feet and requires little, if any, staking. Its large, intensely blue flowers are superb. 'Opal', a clear sky-blue, 'Morning Glory', which needs no description, and 'Pride of Dover', a strong medium blue, grow to five feet and are beloved by bees. I have found it useful to pinch-out the growing tips when the plants are several feet tall to make them throw out side-shoots at a lower level. Certainly this improves the habit and the quantity of flower, though the blooming season may be a little delayed. 'Royal Blue' is another cultivar of recent introduction which seldom exceeds three feet.

I find anchusas a tremendous stand-by, particularly in new borders, as they make a grand show the first summer after planting and will fill in gaps while other herbaceous plants, slower to establish, or to break into growth, are maturing. When anchusas have flowered, they can be cut back to make room for others, and often in a favourable summer many clumps make a second growth and flower again but, of course, in a less spectacular way. As the roots of anchusas are long and fleshy, be sure to plant them in a large enough hole. I have seen a group in a garden with the crowns six inches above the ground instead of just below it.

Anchusas are very apt to be short-term plants, as the long fleshy roots rot very easily. In cold gardens on heavy soil it may be necessary to replant them every year and to treat them as a biennial. They are stocked by good nurseries which deal in herbaceous plants, although supplies sometimes run low, particularly after a bad winter. Anchusas are propagated from root-cuttings taken after flowering, or quite reasonable plants can be grown from seeds, but not the named cultivars listed above. Anchusas are good on various soils, but on heavy clay be sure to provide good drainage. Coarse sand or coal-ash is useful for this purpose.

I like to grow blue flax *(Linum narbonense* or *L. perenne)* for its bounty of clear blue flowers and lovely silvery-green leaves. I find its graceful arching habit particularly attractive with other plants, and with sun and good drainage it grows happily on lime soils. It is lovely with silver foliage and pale yellow or pink flowers, such as rock-roses, *Geranium endressii* and

The exquisite steely-blue flower-heads of *Eryngium alpinum* last for months in the border, combining beautifully with the flat, yellow heads of achilleas, silvery-grey artemisias and santolinas.

garden pinks. It can be raised from seed or bought as plants, usually from pots.

Other valuable plants for herbaceous or mixed borders on chalk are the hardy geraniums, which include *G. grandiflorum, G. ibericum* 'Johnson's Blue', *G. pratense*, all strong growers which flower copiously in July, with spasmodic later flowering for the latter two. The delightful pink *G. endressii*, preferably 'Wargrave Var.', blooms throughout the summer and never exceeds more than about twelve inches. These are very different from the geraniums of window-boxes *(Pelargonium)* and are not suited for bedding-out. For underplanting shrubs, the front of a border or in drifts in half-shade in informal plantings they are invaluable.

Other excellent plants on chalk are the showy tall verbascums or mulleins, garden pinks in all forms, *Gypsophila*, day-lilies *(Hemerocallis)*, which obligingly grow on any reasonable soil, either in sun or half-shade, and penstemons. Madonna lilies *(Lilium candidum)*, *L. regale, L. × testaceum* and *L. henryi* and its various hybrids are the most satisfactory of the more readily-available lilies. So the list grows, and there are many other plants that should be noted, including hellebores, bergenias and epimediums, the last of which are very useful in half-shade in spring *(see* pp. 156, 172–3).

Blue flowers are always popular, both in the garden and for indoor decoration. Among the most useful are the various varieties of scabious which have many merits, not the least being that they grow best on calcareous soils and are even happy on chalk, as long as there is good drainage, yet sufficient moisture. The perennial varieties are derived from *Scabiosa caucasica*, a native of the Caucasus, hence their predilection for lime. I am always fascinated by the large number of blue flowers that are lime-tolerant; they include anchusas, blue salvias, lavender, anagalis, cornflowers, echiums and pulmonarias.

For success with scabious certain rules must be followed. Soils should be light loam and alkaline, or slightly so. There should be adequate moisture, so that the plants never dry out in summer. Transplanting should be done in spring or early summer and top-growth should be left for the winter and cut down in spring. Don't move them in the autumn, as they will not settle down before the frost. Scabious benefit from dividing at regular intervals, as vigorous young clumps flower more profusely and over a longer period than old ones. Discard the woody, poorly rooted sections of the old plants, retaining the good vigorous outer growths. Division should be made in April, if possible. Constant cutting of flowers encourages the formation of new flower-heads. Planting at the correct level is important, as scabious like deeper planting than many herbaceous plants and the crown should be well under the surface of the soil.

153

There are a number of varieties, both old and new. By far the best known is 'Clive Greaves', which has been claimed to be the largest-selling of any variety of herbaceous plant in Britain. This sweeping statement seems incredible, but if one considers the piles of boxes and great bunches of these charming blue flowers at Covent Garden, in florists, and even on barrows, it may well be true, for it is a fine cutting variety, with its long stems and flat, deep blue flowers. Scabious are equally popular in gardens for these reasons, as well as for their long flowering season. Other good ones include the vigorous medium blue 'Floral Beauty', the paler wistaria-blue 'Floral Queen', the large-flowered deep 'Moorheim Blue', and the dark 'Penhill Blue'. These last two are good, rather newer varieties.

White scabious are not as popular as blue, but are very useful. The best-known is the creamy-white 'Miss Willmott', which is not as tall as most varieties, not exceeding two feet, and the outstanding 'Loddon White', a taller plant with very large flowers borne on sturdy strong stems, excellent for cutting. Plants are available from good nurseries stocking herbaceous plants, and several varieties, including 'Clive Greaves', can be grown from seed.

There are annual varieties of scabious which are developed from *Scabiosa atropurpurea*; these come in a wide range of colours, including pink, white, purple, red and blue. Autumn-sowing has proved successful, though scabious can be treated as half-hardy annuals. They are excellent as cut flowers or as decorative border-plants. Because of their sturdy branching habit, no staking is required.

Other blue herbaceous flowers, suited to alkaline soils or chalk, are the Sea Hollies *(Eryngium)*, Globe Thistles *(Echinops)*, various campanulas, particularly *C. persicifolia*, Sea Lavenders *(Limonium)*, veronicas, and the many blue and purple salvias.

Herbaceous Ground-covers

In Chapter 4 I dealt with ground-covers of an evergreen and shrubby nature, and now I propose to discuss a few good herbaceous plants for the same purpose. This is an extremely interesting subject, for

Lamium galeobdolon variegatum, with its patterned leaves, is one of the most successful ground-covers for shady places. Its trailing stems root as they grow, making a dense mat of silvery-green.

most of us have ground-cover problems in our gardens, whether they be large country ones or small town cat-runs. I personally dislike bare earth. It detracts on the whole from the aesthetic effect and it entails constant hoeing, forking and weeding. The front of shrubberies, the base of a wall with climbers, those difficult sloping banks which are hard to mow and need a dense cover to hold the soil in heavy rains, and the bare patches left by the daffodils or bluebells — all these and many more must be dealt with and most of us are eager for the easiest way.

Two groups of herbaceous plants are required, shade-lovers and those for full sun. Some that I recommend are for small areas, others are suitable for covering larger ones. In principle though, the larger areas are best planted with shrubs which cover the ground, including heathers, the low-spreading coton-easters, *Hypericum calycinum*, cistuses and helianthe-mums. Following the theory that grey foliage is as good value as colour in the garden, I place Lamb's Tongue *(Stachys lanata)* high on the list of cover for sunny positions. Its grey felted leaves, covered with dense

white wool, form thick spreading mats over large areas in borders or along gravel paths or paving where it can spill out and 'walk'. In fact, on some soils it is too rampant and must be cut back if it is not to swamp its neighbours. It is easy to build up a quantity from a few roots. The spikes of purplish flowers are attractive, but in some positions it is preferable to remove the spikes as they form, so as to encourage a more luxuriant compact mass of silver. *Stachys lanata* is not a good plant in industrial areas or in very damp localities. In city gardens it is usually partially defoliated by the end of winter and looks so untidy that I prefer to start with fresh stock.

There are many ground-covers with blue flowers. I have previously mentioned Blue-eyed Mary *(Ompha-lodes verna)*, an excellent April- or May-flowering cover for half-shade or even fairly dense shade. The larger *O. cappadocica* is equally good. Their brilliant blue flowers make a carpet and both are tolerant of chalk, even thriving in gardens on the Downs. Lungwort is another blue ground-cover for spring. There are several species, but the most attractive foliage is that

Bold-leaved hostas are the ideal plants for this shady bank, with its informal path and stone steps. Hostas require ample moisture, soil rich in humus, and protection from slugs.

of *Pulmonaria saccharata*, the basal leaves of which are prominently blotched with white, and the foliage is persistent throughout the summer. The flowers, rose-pink at first, turn blue with age. This plant requires a cool, not too dry position in any ordinary soil. *Pulmonaria angustifolia* and special forms including *azurea*, 'Munstead Blue' and 'Mawson's Blue' are all similar, with vivid blue flowers and lovely green foliage throughout a wet summer. An under-carpet of blue, perhaps with primroses, polyanthus, scillas or chionodoxas, is delightful under forsythias or some of the early rhododendrons. *Pulmonaria rubra* has coral-red flowers and blooms early, sometimes even in February.

A special favourite of mine is *Brunnera macrophylla (Anchusa myosotidiflora)*, with panicles of forget-me-not flowers borne in such profusion in late April, May and June that there are clouds of blue about eighteen inches high. The leaves, bold and heart-shaped, are persistent throughout the summer, if a not too dry, shady position is provided. *Lithospermum doerfleri* is hardly blue, but a violet-purple; nevertheless, it can be included in this group. It grows in semi-shade or sun, producing clusters of drooping flowers on stems about a foot tall, well clothed with dark green leaves. It thrives on chalky soils and spreads by underground stems, but not rapidly.

A charming carpeter is *Tiarella cordifolia*, a rampant herbaceous ground-cover, delightfully named Foam Flower, for its myriads of feathery white flowers on nine-inch spikes above a dense carpet of heart-shaped leaves. This is the ideal plant for shady shrubberies, under trees or for difficult north borders. It requires lime-free soil, preferably moist, and with a little leaf-mould it romps along at a great rate. Its near relative, also native to eastern America, *T. wherryi*, is similar but more compact, and not stoloniferous in its habit, like *cordifolia*. Similar is the charming bigeneric cross *Heucherella tiarelloides* and its cultivar 'Bridge Bloom'. Both are very desirable, having *Tiarella* as one parent and *Heuchera* as the other. 'Bridget Bloom', like the type, flowers in May and June, and again in autumn, producing spikes of small, clear, pink flowers on eighteen-inch stems above handsome foliage. Good soil and light shade or sun are the requirements.

Epimediums, outstanding as foliage plants, obviously make a lovely cover for either shade or sun, but not for hot, dry positions. The heart-shaped leaves are very delicate and colour well in autumn. The dainty little flowers, beautifully poised on wiry, branching stems, appear in early spring and range in colour from white, yellow and rose to crimson and orange. As the flowers are often damaged by spring frosts, it is wise to leave the old leaves as protection. Very tidy gardeners, take note. In the yellow range, *E. pinnatum, versicolor, sulphureum* and *perralderianum* are excellent and not too expensive. *Epimedium rubrum* is an attractive crimson with foliage that colours well in autumn.

A semi-evergreen herbaceous ground-cover deserves mention, a variegated nettle with the difficult name, *Lamium galeobdolon*. This obviously sounds a curious suggestion to those who are battling with stinging-nettles in other parts of their gardens, but it is a lovely and obliging plant. The leaves are heavily patterned with silvery white. It grows with rapidity, rooting at the leaf-nodes and producing small, creamy-yellow flowers in early summer. In mild climates the foliage is persistent throughout the winter, surprisingly so in view of their fragile, delicate appearance, which lends a gay note in contrast to the dark green of rhododendrons and laurels. *Lamium galeobdolon variegatum* is best in shady, moderately moist positions, but it will withstand drought. It grows on acid or alkaline soils alike and is a useful quick plant for difficult positions in town gardens.

Lamium maculatum (garganicum) is a closely-related species with purple, rather showy flowers and very similar foliage. It is, however, far less rampant, which makes it the better plant of the two for the average garden. There are white and pink forms also.

One more semi-evergreen herbaceous ground-cover plant for sun or semi-shade must be included. *Prunella* produces masses of flower-heads in June. There is the soft 'Pink Loveliness', 'Blue Loveliness' and a white one, *alba*, which I like best of all. It spreads rapidly and is not particular as to soil or position. Its appearance is greatly improved by dead-heading, but this is not essential.

Vigorous Invaders

So often it is the ordinary plants in our gardens that provide the most attractive effects. In June in gardens throughout this country, ranging from those of large country-houses to the small confines of cottages or city dwellings, humble plants like the silvery-leaved *Cerastium tomentosum*, charmingly named Snow-in-Summer, with its masses of neat white flowers, are the most appealing. Anyone who has grown it knows that it has invasive underground roots which are apt to spread through other plants, sometimes creating delightful informal effects, but possibly with injurious results ultimately. I remember a bank planted with vivid blue *Lithospermum diffusum* 'Grace Ward', one of the most brilliant blue of all spring flowers. Its dark green leaves were set off to advantage by the silvery foliage of cerastium and the white sheets of flower were a foil to the blue. This seems a curious pair of bed-fellows, as lithospermum, unlike cerastium, is not an easy plant, requiring lime-free soil and good drainage. It grows by whim, while the other is a romper. In this

This combination of shrub-roses with irises and the graceful spikes of foxgloves is so easy yet completely satisfying in the harmony of colours and the contrast of shapes.

Alstroemeria aurantiaca is so invasive that it can become a pest, but these lovely apricot and pink 'Ligtu Hybrids' are easily controlled. Alstroemerias are some of the best of all cut flowers.

case the usually shy and diffident partner seemed to be getting the better of the tougher one, but undoubtedly the gardener in charge had a controlling hand.

Cerastium is wonderful for a sunny bank, and if it can be kept free of weed until established, it makes a dense grey mat. It is often an excellent answer to old rockeries, as it drapes itself over stones and curtains walls with relative ease and speed. It is beautiful in great sheets against the green of a lawn or of a dark hedge, such as yew or holly. Some enthusiasts combine it happily with mauve and purple aubretias. The flowers overlap for a bit and the two foliages are complimentary. Cerastium is a useful edging along paths or paved terraces and can be used with great success to drape flower-pots and vases in sunny positions. Early spring bulbs will nose their way through the silvery leaves and bloom before much new growth appears.

In cities cerastium is not reliable in winter, as it suffers from fog and atmospheric pollution. In my old garden cerastium did not die completely, but I often wished that it would, because it looked so untidy at the end of winter and was slow to break into leaf. It is easily replaced, as plants are readily available from nurseries and it may be grown from seeds. These should be sown in late spring or early summer to flower the following year.

Another grey foliage plant that I would never be without is the ubiquitous Lamb's Tongue (*Stachys lanata*), with its heavily-felted leaves and woolly spikes of mauve flowers. The latter are no great enhancement and I prefer to pinch-out the flower-spikes as they appear, so that the full beauty of the low masses of grey foliage can be appreciated, but flower-arrangers value the flower-stalks as they are everlasting. The plant is a splendid grower, spreading along the surface of the ground and rooting wherever the stems touch the earth, and hence its dense, matted habit. In time, the central portion of the clump may become sparse, while the outer ends remain healthy and flourishing. This is the signal to lift and divide, operations to be carried out in the autumn or throughout the spring. From a clump or two it is possible to make a number of plants. On cold, wet soils and in areas of smog, stachys is best planted in spring.

On good soil, it is vigorous and rampant. It is often

necessary to be ruthless or it will smother its smaller, less sturdy neighbours. It combines effectively with a variety of plants. I like to use stachys near the spiky foliage of montbretias and irises, and it is the perfect foil for the bold, smooth-textured leaves of bergenias. It is charming in a border with the Peruvian lily (*Alstroemeria*), the silvery foliage making a splendid contrast to the tender glaucous green. Later, the silver-grey is a wonderful background for the orange tones of the flowers of *Alstroemeria aurantiaca* and its varieties, such as 'Moorheim Orange', or the wonderful vibrant tones of pink, salmon and orange of the finer, but rather tender, 'Ligtu Hybrids' (Zone 7).

Returning to easy old favourites (alstroemerias are not in that category), I again sing the praises of London Pride (*Saxifraga umbrosa*). It is a wonderful ground-cover, thriving in sun or deep shade. Its foam of pink flowers carried on twelve- to fifteen-inch stems makes clouds of lacy pink. I know a shady path with borders of it interspersed with clumps of deep purple violas, a few glaucous hostas and ferns: this effect is enchanting and very easy to achieve. London Pride is excellent in town gardens, liking any type of soil, including chalk. It doesn't like drought and on light soils is best in shade. Use it with Crane's Bill, such as *Geranium endressii* 'Wargrave', or the delightful aromatic *G. macrorrhizum*. It spreads rapidly and is easily divided at almost any season.

London Pride is a true shade-lover. We are grateful for plants such as this. Hostas are a natural and enjoy ever-increasing favour. Columbines with their fragile beauty and delicate colouring are happy in semi-shade. Solomon's Seals and lily of the valley, so often planted together as the former is said to make the latter flower, are both shade-lovers. The Japanese anemones, both pink and white, are among the best perennials for light shade, flowering in August and September. Dicentras are enchanting and the new hybrids such as the ivory-white 'Silversmith', the flush pink 'Debutante' and the fuchsia-red 'Bountiful' flower intermittently in summer and again copiously in autumn.

Delphiniums of Many Hues

June and early July are wonderful months in the border, as delphiniums, shrub-roses and lilies flower in exuberant profusion. The tall spikes of delphiniums in a wide range of blues are striking against the pinks, clear yellows and reds of the roses. There are, as well, delphiniums in subtle mauves, silvery-lavenders and rich purples, alone or in combination, and, perhaps loveliest of all, the whites. Delphiniums are, in fact, very often the mainstay of early summer herbaceous borders.

In the last fifteen years there have been great ad-

Modern delphiniums include whites, pinks and lilacs, as well as subtle blends, with expressive names like 'Sea Mist' and 'Silver Moon'.

vances, not only in the range of colours, but in the size of both the spikes and of the individual flowers, as well as in their general vigour, constitution and habit. The advent of Frank Reinelt's 'Pacific Strain' from California has been a very important factor. These are best raised from seeds, clones, of course, being perpetuated by divisions or cuttings. Many nurseries now offer plants of this fine strain in mixed colours. There is a notable group of whites known as 'Giant Pacific Galahad'. Generally, the whites are a little less vigorous than other colours and do not grow as tall. The 'Black Knight' series is limited to velvety dark purples as much as three inches in diameter with a dramatic black bee. The 'Blue Bird' group, clear delphinium-blue with white bees, are superb in very way. 'Summer Skies' are lighter blues of great uniformity, even from seed. 'Astolat' includes subtle lavender-pinks with black or gold bees. The 'Connecticut Yankee', developed by the great photographer, Edward Steichen, is a dwarf bushy strain, seldom more than twenty-four to thirty inches tall in mixed delphinium blues.

Seeds of all delphiniums germinate best when sown as soon as possible after ripening. If this is done, fresh seeds will be available in late summer, and sowing can take place in late August or September, but only if a greenhouse, or at least a cold-frame, is available. Seeds sown in January or February under glass grow without check until frost and should begin to flower in late summer and make a show the following June. In other gardens seeds can be sown in outdoor seed-beds in April or even later, and by autumn will make good plants which can be moved into their permanent positions in the border. After germination in pans or seed-boxes, seedlings should be pricked out in three-and-a-half-inch pots or in flats. They will need protection from strong sunlight for a few days until they are established.

Named clones, many with enchantingly romantic names such as 'Ringdove', 'Silver Moon', 'Bridesmaid' and 'South Seas', and others commemorating great names in delphinium lore, such as 'Charles F. Langdon', 'George Bishop' and 'Guy Langdon', can be easily propagated from division or cuttings taken from February to early April. The shoots should be two to five inches in length with a bit of hard wood as a heel. Cuttings, firm and solid at the base, should be inserted in a suitable rooting medium and kept moist in not too dry an atmosphere until they have rooted.

At various British delphinium shows I have been particularly struck by named cultivars shown by Ronald Parrett. The first was 'White Nylon', with large (two and a half inches in diameter), well-spaced, white florets with a creamy-yellow eye. An unusual feature is a light vanilla scent. It has a good habit growing to five feet, a reasonable height for moderate-sized gardens. 'White Nylon' propagates easily and a sizeable group can soon be propagated from a stock plant or two.

Flower-arrangers will be enthusiastic about Mr Parrett's 'Theodora Parrett', the seed of which came from Frank Reinelt and is therefore one of the Pacific Strain. It is a very delicate pale mauve-pink with large florets, well spaced on relatively short stems, three and a half feet being a fairly uniform height, according to the raiser. Its long-lasting qualities in water are another attractive feature. A very good white is the early 'Swanlake', with its five- to six-foot spikes of well-formed florets with a striking black eye. 'Silver Moon', one of the loveliest of all delphiniums, has had a remarkable success and justly so, having had a series of awards at shows and, even more important, in delphinium trials, which are a severe test. The double, very large florets in a delightful combination of silvery-mauve and sky-blue are carried on broad well-formed spikes. It is a truly outstanding delphinium.

For smaller gardens, the Belladonna Hybrids are useful, their large number of branching spikes in a loose open habit making them light and airy. As they are of smaller stature (three to four feet) than other hybrids, they are very desirable plants for small gardens. They come in a range of lovely clear blues. Good cultivars include 'Blue Bees', 'Orion', 'Wendy' and 'Bonita'. There are also dwarf delphiniums of the larger-flowered types, and these are the same height. They include 'Blue Tit', 'Blue Jade', 'Cinderella' and 'Pageboy', all of which are excellent for small gardens or for windy ones where tall delphiniums are vulnerable.

The Seventeenth-century Trinity Flower

Tradescantias, known generally as Spiderwort or Trinity Flower, take their Latin name from John Tradescant, gardener to Charles I, who died in 1638. These lovely obliging perennials of our gardens are either forms of *Tradescantia virginiana*, native to the eastern United States, or hybrids of it with closely related species. They are extremely useful, either in borders or natural plantings in wild gardens and shrubberies, as they have a long flowering season owing to the large number of flower-buds on each stem, and come in a wide range of colours, some with subtle flushes of other shades.

Their requirements are simple. They will grow on any soil, provided that it is reasonably good, in positions that are not too dry in full sun or partial shade. They like moist conditions, but are in no sense bog-plants. As they increase rapidly, it is possible to build up a large stock by dividing established clumps, either in the early autumn or early spring. Their growth is vigorous and upright, not exceeding eighteen to twenty inches, so no staking is required. I like to use them in clumps at the edge of a path or border, so that their long narrow sword-like foliage and leafy bracts are not crowded in among other plants. If tradescantias are planted in groups in the middle of a border, be sure to leave a little extra space round them.

The name Trinity Flower arises from the three petals, three sepals and six stamens, while the less attractive term Spiderwort comes from the very hairy filaments of the stamens, which, to someone less fond of this flower than I am, may resemble a spider. Some lovely garden varieties of tradescantias have tufted plumes. Such a one is 'Osprey', which is white with a feathery blue centre, or 'Iris Pritchard', another white, shaded with pale violet and with a violet-bearded centre.

Tradescantias are useful in town gardens as well as country ones. The flowering season is very long; plants that flower in late June are often still in flower in early September. The individual flowers last only for a single day, but the number of buds and the development of

Tradescantia virginiana and its many varieties are good, hardy plants of easy cultivation on any soil and with a very long blooming season.

Kent, and were Royal Gardeners to Charles I and Charles II. Their contributions to botany and to horticulture through the introduction of many of the finest plants from America in the seventeenth century, as well as numerous varieties of fruits and flowers from the Continent and even further afield, are impressive. To them we owe the first lilac, the first robinia, and the occidental plane. They were responsible for a remarkable collection of rarities of all kinds – biological, geological, anthropological, artistic, as well as botanical, which were to form the Museum Tradescantianum at the Ark in Lambeth.

In her book Mrs Allen paints a brilliant historical picture of the seventeenth century, with portraits of the great figures with whom the Tradescants lived and worked and the touching human fabric of their lives. The narrative unfolds with voyages to Europe and the New World and pictures of life at the time and of the Great Fire of London. Later, to a background of intrugue as exciting as any modern thriller, she tells how the Ashmolean Museum came into being. How different history might have been if justice had prevailed in the light of evidence which she has assembled.

In an Appendix is given the astounding garden list of 1634 of John Tradescant the Elder, which shows what rarities he assembled from all over the world, and, having perused it, we shall look at many of our native American plants with a new awareness.

New World Day-lilies

I have always had a weakness for day-lilies, or *Hemerocallis*, to give them their botanical name. This in itself is highly descriptive, as *hemera* means a day and *kallos*, beauty. A flower that lasts for only a day, or possibly two, may sound useless for garden display, but there are such a large number of flowers on each scape and such a number of these on established clumps, that there is a wealth of flowers for several weeks or even months. When I was a boy there were great banks of day-lilies by the stream in the next-door garden, and I always marvelled at their emerald-green leaves, which appeared in February, defying frost and even snow. In early summer there were hundreds of tawny-orange flowers, for these were the common *H. fulva*. In my own garden there were clumps of *H. citrina*, which were my delight, with their cool lemon trumpets, opening in the later afternoon and mingling their fragrance with white phlox and Four O'Clocks in the evening.

What a long way this splendid flower has come as the result of hybridization, a great deal of which started in this country and some in Britain as well. For some time now day-lilies have been tremendously popular in the United States and each year sees new hybrids bearing little resemblance to their humble forbears.

new growths ensures a succession of blooms. There are a number of good varieties: *T. virginiana rubra* is a crimson-red with a little purple in it. I like this colour, but it may not be to everyone's taste. One of my favourites is 'J. C. Weguelin', a delicate violet-blue, which makes a nice contrast to the large-flowered violet 'Purple Dome'. 'Isis' is another large-flowered variety, with clear Oxford-blue petals and fluffy centres. There is also a form 'Flore Pleno', which is a semi-double blue shaded with mauve. 'Leonora' and 'Pauline' are other good blues.

Of the books that have come to me in recent years, I have found *The Tradescants* by Mea Allen (Clifford Russell, 1964) one of the most rewarding, for it is a remarkable biography of the John Tradescants, father and son, who played such a prominent role in the making of great gardens, including Hatfield in Hertfordshire, Cranborne in Dorset and Cobham Hall in

160

In fact, the colour-range has widened to include not only yellows, oranges and reds of every description, but also pinks, apricots, buffs and lavenders, as well as blends and bicolors. In size and substance the flower has changed; so have its stamina and freedom of flowering.

Hemerocallis are obliging plants with the merits of hardiness, easy cultivation and a long blooming season. They will grow in most soils but prefer a rich moisture-retentive loam. They are tolerant of lime, so are suitable for gardens generally. If the soil is sandy and light, add manure or humus in the form of garden compost, peat, leaf-mould, spent mushroom compost or hop-manure. Day-lilies are tolerant of shade, but flower best in full sun. They are lovely in dappled shade and flower well if they have direct sun part of the day. Claims are often made that they grow well in full shade. Grow they will, but flowering is a little sparse. I have had several clumps in full shade which seldom flowered, while others of the same variety flowered well in light shade with sun in the mornings.

Ground should be well dug. How often I stress this. A certain amount of work, such as thorough preparation of the ground, cannot be eliminated even for labour-saving plants such as day-lilies. Once planted, they look after themselves and hence are ideal for borders, the wild garden and for groups in shrubberies. Planting can be done either in the autumn or early spring. It helps to work in bone-meal as a long-term food when planting. Some varieties are more vigorous than others, but as a general rule put them about two feet apart. They will take a year to establish and then can be left alone until they require dividing, probably in four or five years' time. Plants set out in the autumn usually flower the next summer season. As hemerocallis are moisture-loving, plants benefit by being watered during dry spells, but they do not require bog conditions as some people may think.

I once saw a lovely picture where three varieties had been planted in light shade at the edge of a lake, so that the flowers were silhouetted against the water. In another country garden there is a splendid group which has a corner to itself, so that the shape and colour of the flowers stand out against a tapestry of dark clipped yew and box. They follow the splendour of the paeonies and the old roses, prolonging the colour into late summer. A clump or two can bring to life a dark shrubbery or make an exciting border in bold groups with hardy agapanthuses, the clear lemon- and greenish-yellows being particularly effective with the blue.

Prices vary a great deal. Inevitably, the newer colour-breaks and the still very scarce tetraploids are expensive, just as new irises or daffodils command what seem to be exorbitant sums. But time usually solves this as soon as scarcity is overcome. Remember, too, that just because a flower is exciting and new on the show-bench it is no guarantee that it is a good garden-plant. If possible, choose varieties that have had awards, have been on trial or have stood the test in gardens.

I have a weakness for the clear pale yellows. If they have a hint of cool green in the throat or the outer side of the trumpet, so much the better. These clear tones are wonderful in the garden and show up superbly against green foliage. Moreover, they are at their best in the early evening, when they have an almost luminous quality. One enchanting flower bears the name 'Golden Chimes', which aptly describes the small golden blooms, not more than two inches across, borne in profusion on graceful stems, Another favourite of mine is 'Lark Song', with wide-petalled, pale canary-yellow flowers. Drifts of it in a wooded glade in a friend's garden always give me special pleasure. 'Nancy Treadwell', 'Lime-Painted Lady', 'Diamond Dust' and 'Giant Moon', are clear pale yellows of good form. I very much like 'Nancy Treadwell' with very large

The advances in the development of day-lilies are well illustrated by the large, heavy-textured blooms of Hemerocallis 'Jake Russell'.

greenish flowers, which have heavy-textured crepy petals, and the well-named 'Burning Daylight', with huge, bright orange flowers. In the same moderate price range is the splendid golden-yellow 'Cartwheels', with very heavy-petalled buds which open into huge, rather flat flowers, and the superb light yellow 'Blythe Spirit', with its greenish throat. 'Marion Vaughn', a tall (forty-two inches), waxy, pale lemon flower with suffused green in the throat and a distinctive prominent silvery mid-rib, has had a number of awards and is a fine garden plant of moderate price.

'Crimson Glory' is a very floriferous, early, glowing, rose-red. 'Buzz Bomb' is a low-growing (twenty inches), velvety red of great intensity, and 'Holiday Mood' is a little paler but with ruffled petals and attractive veining of a darker red. 'Jet Scarlet', a spectacular fiery red, is very fine but still expensive. 'Royal Command' is a velvety red with an almost black halo and a green throat.

For those who favour pinks there is 'Frances Fay', a large-flowered, clear melon-pink; 'Colonial Dame', an inexpensive apricot with shadings of buff and rose and a whitish throat; 'Pink Frills', a clear dawn-pink self; and the vigorous well-known 'Pink Damask' with a hint of salmon. 'Paradise Pink' is rather expensive but a subtle harmony of soft pink with a golden throat, and 'Evelyn Claar' is orchid-pink with a silken sheen. 'Drama Girl' is a fine variety with large flamingo-pink flowers. 'First Formal' is a light clear satiny pink, which stands up to weather conditions and blooms abundantly. 'Crestwood Ann' is a superb pink tetraploid and 'Crestwood Lucy' a salmon-pink with a red throat. 'Fashion Model' and the well-named 'Chantilly Lace' are other charmers.

The indications are that there may be some very fine doubles in the not too distant future, as in this country several leading hybridizers are experimenting, evidently with considerable success. I cannot think that these will be an improvement on the grace and beauty of the singles, but we shall have to wait with an open mind until we can judge for ourselves. In all probability, they may be longer-lasting than the singles, as are so many double flowers.

Perennials for Island Beds

There is today a mild prejudice against herbaceous borders, and the drift since the War has been towards shrub-borders and mixed borders combining herbaceous plants, shrubs and roses. Now by careful selection and close planting a large number of hardy plants can be grown without staking. Obviously the taller delphiniums, hollyhocks, heleniums and Michaelmas daisies are to be avoided. Secondly, do not overfeed or lots of herbaceous plants become vulnerable to wind and rain. If plants are closely planted they tend to support themselves but they must be vigorous and healthy as well. Good choices in this respect are phloxes, *Sedum spectabile*, kniphofias, Japanese anemones, and dwarfer varieties of *Salvia superba*, anchusas, monkshood and hardy asters. Relying upon these, island beds of herbaceous plants have become popular. It is pleasant to be able to walk around curving beds, viewing them from all sides rather than from just the front as is the case of borders planted against hedges and walls. Strangely enough, walls, which should shelter plants from wind, sometimes have the reverse effect and the wind can ricochet off them, battering the plants. In

Bold architectural plants such as the giant silvery-grey *Onopordon arabicum* play an increasingly important part in modern garden design.

Groups of herbaceous plants including bergenias, *Stachys lanata* and *Alchemilla mollis*, planted with lavender, yellow potentillas and pale pink rugosa roses, make a delightful foreground for this river view.

the same way courtyards and patios can suffer from whirlwinds rather than being the sheltered havens we expect.

Flowers for cutting can be grown on the same principle rather than in the usual blocks or rows. Where possible it is an enormous advantage to have a separate cutting area.

In many summer herbaceous schemes the yellows and the blues particularly catch the eye. *Heliopsis* 'Golden Plume' has large, double, rich gold flowers of fine form on four-foot stems. It stands erect in spite of the weight of the large double flowers. *Achillea* 'Moonshine' is a favourite of mine; I love its flat heads of unfading soft yellow, borne above silvery, finely cut foliage. It likes a dry position but is not particular as to soil. It flowers from mid-June until August. The daisy-flowering *Anthemis sancti-johannis*, with deep yellow flowers shaded orange, likes similar treatment. On heavy, cold soils anthemis may be short-lived, and they are best planted in spring, as are pyrethrums and scabious. Goldenrods are so common in American country lanes and meadows in August and September that it often comes as a shock to gardeners visiting Britain that it has such an impressive name as *Solidago*, that it is so much used in herbaceous borders and that it is an extremely useful cut-flower. There is the soft primrose 'Lemore', which grows to about two feet; 'Golden Mosa', slightly taller and brighter gold in mimosa-like plumes; 'Golden Shower', with deep yellow arching sprays; and a recent one called 'Crown of Rays'. *Coreopsis verticillata* is a splendid, neat, front-row beauty with feathery, finely divided leaves and rich yellow flowers of unmistakable coreopsis shape, copiously borne throughout August and September.

163

I much prefer it to the large-flowered varieties. None of these, incidentally, require staking.

Now for a few blue flowers, which are so attractive with the yellows. In fact, any blue border is improved by a touch of yellow, preferably primrose or sulphur. *Salvia superba* is a delightful stand-by, as is the form 'Lubeca' with multiple spikes of dark reddish-purple buds and sepals with more vivid blue-purple flowers. The former make a good show even after the flowers fall. It grows to about three feet and the cultivar 'Lubeca' is similar, but rather shorter and more compact. It is a splendid plant and the colour is lovely with yellows and pinks. Other good blues are the various veronicas, eryngiums, platycodons, campanulas, blue linums and the extremely useful erigerons, which have a long flowering season.

The intense lilac and crimson-purple of the various species of *Liatris* make an effective grouping. A new variety called 'Kobold', with compact spikes about two feet long, is another excellent front-row plant. Liatris has the peculiar habit of opening its flowers, from the top of the spike rather than from the bottom.

Sidalceas are charming, too, with mallow-shaped flowers in a range of pinks, from the clear rose of 'Rose Queen', the warm pink of 'Sussex Beauty' and 'Elsie Heugh' to the soft rosy-crimson of 'Crimson Beauty' and 'Monarch'. An attractive new one in a new colour-range is the glowing salmon-pink 'William Smith'.

Bright Border Phloxes

We all have ideas of the dream garden and often this is coloured by memories of gardens that we enjoyed at a much earlier period of our lives, for nostalgia is a very potent force in creative gardening. Few flowers arouse remembrance of things past more vividly than the

Border phlox planted behind a feathery mass of silvery artemisias makes a desirable association of colours, and textures. Good artemisias include 'Lambrook Silver', 'Silver Queen' and *A. ludoviciana*.

hardy herbaceous phloxes *(Phlox paniculata)*. First, there is the vision of masses of colour – mellow and pastel, brilliant and glowing like coloured lights, deep and rich like the base notes of an organ. Or perhaps I should have put first the delicious scent of phlox on a summer's evening when the air is heavy with fragrance and moths hover about the honeyed panicles. Of course, the practical gardener thinks of those broad masses of colour which need no staking and will last for weeks on end.

For me, summer and phlox and heavy fragrance are all one. Perhaps it is because I love the garden best in early morning or evening light when colours show up to best advantage and when scents, whether honeysuckle, rose or phlox, hang heavy on the air. I only wish that more people grew this glorious border-plant in greater profusion. The answer, of course, is in the fact that it flourishes in some localities, languishes in others. It is a natural in one garden and sulks next door. Here, then, is the challenge.

What are the supposed requirements for success with phloxes? At the head of the list I would place adequate moisture. They succeed best in moisture-retentive soil where there is adequate rainfall or where the soil is sufficiently heavy or so liberally laced with leaf-mould, compost or peat that it does not dry out quickly. Sandy soils and shallow poor ones do not grow phloxes of which we are proud. Next, the ground must be rich and well fed with garden compost or manure, well rotted and thoroughly dug into the planting area. A natural rich soil which by its very nature produces vigorous clumps is a great asset. Phloxes do best in cool, light shade, but thrive in full sun if the above requirements are fulfilled and it is not too hot.

The planting season is a long one, as phloxes can be divided after flowering and established in the autumn or in early spring. Clean stock is essential as this plant is subject to eel-worms. Phloxes establish slowly and if they dry out or are exposed in spring to cold winds and draughts, the lower leaves may well be shrivelled and brown. Plenty of water is essential, especially in a dry season. Be forebearing and do not judge, let alone condemn, phloxes in their first season because they definitely take time to settle down. Feed with a liquid fertilizer or work in a little dried blood or bone meal to ensure vigorous growth.

It is often said, at times not without a slight hint of boasting, that the phloxes are best in New England or the Northwest. In this there may be some truth, as the climate may be damper and the sun a little less strong and persistent, so that there is less bleaching and the temperatures are lower and therefore less demanding. Be that as it may, I have seen superb phloxes in the Middle Atlantic States, particularly during cool, moist summers.

The colour-range is wide, running the gamut from whites (perhaps the loveliest of all) through pale pastel pinks and mauves to flaming oranges, deep rich violets and wine-reds. Then there are varieties flushed with a deeper colour or with a distinct ring or eye, such as 'B. Symous-Jeune', a pink with a large red eye, and 'Sandringham', a cyclamen pink with a deeper eye, or, as in the case of 'Duchess of York', a clear pink with a white eye. Of the white, 'Mia Ruys' is an early dwarf variety, usually about two feet tall with large individual pips. 'White Admiral' is a taller, later white, reaching as much as three feet, and 'Snowball', 'Iceberg', 'World Peace' and 'Rembrandt' are other tall-growing ones for the back of the border. Of the very popular bright colours the orange-red 'Brigadier' is certainly one of the finest phloxes, strong, free-flowering and tall, and 'Leo Schlageter' is a big scarlet-red of considerable distinction. Clear pinks include 'Pink Gown', 'Dodo Hanbury Forbes', the very pale 'Dresden China', 'Elizabeth Arden' and a number of others. Deep-hued phloxes are particularly useful as, like violas (*see* p. 146), they provide the same rich notes of dramatic quality. Favourites include 'Border Gem', a good violet-blue: 'Queen of Tonga', a vibrant purple; 'San Antonio', a fine purple-red; 'Vintage Wine', a rich colour well named and 'Russian Violet'. I have seen several newer varieties to which I am very partial. One is the subtle 'Mother of Pearl', a superb weatherproof white suffused with pinkish lilac; 'Silver Salmon', a soft shell-pink suffused with an orange glow; and 'Almond Blossom', a delicate slightly bluish pink like a sugared almond. There is a fine, new, weather-proof white, 'Mount Fujiyama', the very dwarf 'Pinafore Pink', said rarely to grow more than six inches tall yet with large trusses and 'Starfire', an early, brilliant red. This should be useful for the front of the border. Watch out for all of these.

Phloxes are lovely in clumps in the border. They can be combined to harmonize or to make vibrant clashes. Seldom does a gardener have a more tempting palette at his command. If you are in doubt about growing them, look at your neighbours' gardens, and if still in doubt, why not take a deep breath and experiment, remembering that you cannot judge results the first year?

Late Summer Perennials

In one of the loveliest gardens in Kent there are several of my favourite perennials which flower in late August. They include *Artemisia lactiflora*, a spectacular herbaceous plant of the late summer border, which I grew against a smooth background of clipped yew when I had a garden in the United States. The loose panicles of creamy-white flowers on four- to five-foot stems have

an elegance and usefulness that makes this hardy perennial indispensable for all gardens where there is room and conditions are ideal. To me it is the almost perfect plant for the large herbaceous or mixed shrub-border. It stands up to almost every test – the boldly dissected, dark green foliage has a handsome pattern, the tall straight stems are self-supporting, and a clump occupies the space it grows in and does not sprawl, as many artemisias are wont to do.

Artemisia lactiflora is an enchanting flower when cut. I like it mixed with phloxes in tones of mauve, purple and claret. The looseness of the creamy-white trusses are the natural leaven for a large vase of grace and charm. It requires good soil and a moist position, or rather one that does not suffer from excessive drought

in dry seasons and hence preferably a position in semi-shade. It spreads rapidly to form a generous clump, so do not plant too close – twelve to eighteen inches would be suitable. By a miracle it does not need staking. It is excellent in a group in front of delphiniums, anchusas or lupins, all of which die back after flowering.

Another charmer is Bergamot (*Monarda*). I love it for so many reasons – its delicious, aromatic, lemon-scented foliage, which places it among herbs, its gay colours, its freedom of flower, its long flowering season, and its usefulness as a cut flower. Here is another plant that is happy on moist, heavy soil or a well-enriched border. Its ancestors are North-American wild flowers, as is the charming, pale pinky-purple *Eupatorium purpureum*, with the endearing name of Joe Pye Weed, which grows in ditches, roadsides and moist meadows throughout New England, or our North-American Golden Rod (*Solidago*), of which there are a number of delightful species from which modern hybrids have been derived. These prefer drier positions.

Monarda is represented by two principal species – the bright scarlet *M. didyma*, from which so many garden hybrids are derived, and *M. fistulosa*, a variable plant in the wild with a wide range of colour. There are many garden hybrid monardas. Among my favourites are 'Croftway Pink', a rose-pink of depth and clarity, which blooms freely from late June until early September, though like all monardas is at its best in August; 'Adam', a superb ruby-red, which if used with care can bring a border to life; 'Melissa', a subtle soft pink; 'Cambridge Scarlet', the most vivid red of all; 'Dark Ponticum', a deep lilac-purple with foliage tinged with bronze; 'Mrs Perry', dark reddish-crimson; and *M. fistulosa violacea superba*, a deep violet-purple, which is said to grow on drier soil than the varieties above. For this I cannot vouch, but for gardeners on dry soil it is worth the experiment.

Monardas grow from two to three feet in height, but on very vigorous soil can well reach four feet. As they are surface-rooting, a clump will soon become a mass of matted stoloniferous roots, overlaying each other. These should be separated regularly at intervals of two or three years in early spring, or clumps will die back at the centre. On the whole, monardas do not need staking. Even after hot dry summers, the displays in nurseries are phenomenal and in gardens big clumps of this American native have made me sit up and take notice, the massed colours being every bit as effective as phloxes. They can be grown with very little of the trouble. In waterside gardens they come into their own, as do day-lilies, astilbes and candelabra primulas.

Varieties of *Anemone japonica* are among the loveliest of summer perennials, and have the virtue of colonizing in full sun or shade.

The American Indians used the dried leaves of *M. didyma* for tea, hence the name Oswego Tea and the even more endearing name Bee Balm, with which I grew up. This refers to the monarda's attraction for honey-bees and explains why they are often planted in bee-gardens.

Kniphofias, better known by the appropriate name of Red-Hot Poker or Torch Lily, provide a wonderful autumn display. I know an unusual country garden where a broad mass of rich coral and flame-coloured spikes, rising behind a broad clump of silver *Senecio laxifolius*, makes a striking picture in October against the yellow stone of an old tithe barn. This combination is a particularly happy one as the rich bright colours bring out the warm tones of the local stone. By the same token, kniphofias can clash with the colour of walls if the bricks are harsh in colour.

In another garden that I like, clumps of the graceful and very delicate orange and saffron *Kniphofia galpinii* are at the peak of perfection in October, following closely upon a similar but earlier small-growing species, *K. macowanii*, with orange-red flowers carried well above the grassy leaves. Both these species have great refinement and do not grow more than two feet high. Kniphofias like good sharp drainage and will withstand long dry periods. There are summer-flowering varieties as well, including the charmingly-named 'Maid of Orleans' with its three- to four-foot spikes of ivory-white flowers throughout July and August. This is a delightful newcomer of real merit and it combines effectively with a wide variety of colours. I have seen clumps grouped with the bright clear blue of *Salvia patens* with the violet-blue *Aster amellus* 'King George' massed in front of it. Kniphofias should be planted in autumn or early spring in deeply dug, well-prepared soil. They often take a year to settle down, but old-established clumps offer rich rewards. As they are native to Africa and Madagascar, they are not hardy in colder zones.

Salvia ambigens is a very fine tall perennial, but, as it flowers in September and October it should not be planted in cold gardens where the growing season is short. Even more important, it is rather tender. It is hardy in several sunny coastal gardens where drainage is good, and in gardens in milder zones it should offer no difficulty. It is best planted or moved in spring. The flowers of a rich azure blue are fairly large and borne in racemes consisting of five to seven whorls. *Salvia uliginosa* is another very late, bright blue perennial, but again it is best in warm gardens as otherwise it will not flower in time. In a mild season it will continue to bloom well into the fall. Divide or plant it in spring.

Physostegia is a reliable border-plant for late summer and early autumn. It is known as Obedient Plant, as the flowers, which are borne in tiers on a spike, can be moved horizontally from side to side at will. It likes good soil, preferably not dry, and spreads rapidly in either sun or semi-shade. A few nurseries list it as *Dracocephalum*. There are various varieties, all forms of *Physostegia virginiana*, which, as we see from the name, is one of our native wild flowers, which is often found by the edge of streams. Its rosy-lilac flowers, borne on branching stems, appear in profusion in July and August. In rich soil it will grow to nearly four feet. There is a white variety, *alba*, which is not quite so tall; 'Summer Snow', a lovely new introduction, is an improvement on it. The spikes of flowers are densely

167

The long, trailing stems of *Oenothera missouriensis* bear huge, scented, pale yellow flowers from early summer until fall.

packed and it has a neat compact habit, growing to one and a half to two feet tall. 'Vivid' is of similar height with brilliant rose-pink flowers from August until the frost comes. 'Bouquet Rose' is deep pink, but rather taller and earlier to flower. I find all these plants extremely useful as they have a long flowering season, great vigour and a good colour-range, and because so many summer and early autumn herbaceous plants are in the yellow and orange range. Moreover, physostegias are excellent as cut flowers.

Sedums are Good Rent-payers

The last days of September are so beautiful that we all spend as much time as possible in our gardens. There are fine displays of Michaelmas daisies, dahlias and wonderful roses, but I think I get almost as much pleasure out of a few clumps of *Sedum spectabile*, or Ice Plant as it is commonly called, as from all the others. The flat heads of mauve-pink are a perfect complement to the blue-green leaves, and the dazzling butterflies that hover to sip the nectar make even gayer spots of colour to gladden our hearts and dispel the sad thoughts

of summer's end. Ice Plant is one of the most useful of all herbaceous plants; in fact, it is nearly faultless. Its foliage is a delight throughout the growing season from the first unfolding rosettes, rather like tiny Brussels sprouts of jade, in early spring until frost turns the heavy-textured, glaucous leaves to pale gold. It has an ideal habit, growing stiffly without support even when bearing its large flower heads on fifteen-inch stems, a splendid characteristic common to other delightful and even more colourful members of the genus described below. It has a long flowering season throughout late summer and fall. Sedums are virtually disease-free, develop quickly to form heavy clumps, are suited to most soils, withstand droughts and cut well for bouquets. Moreover, the fleshy roots are easily divided in early spring or in the autumn after flowering, with a spade or trowel, and cuttings in early spring root easily. This really is an impressive dossier.

There are various varietal forms, which are similar in habit. 'Brilliant' is well named as it is a true rose-pink, more telling where a brighter pink is required than the mauve-pink of *S. spectabile*. 'Carmen' is a deeper richer pink verging on red, and 'Meteor' is the deepest of all, probably best described as carmine-red.

Sedum telephium is similar in habit but rather more branching. I have used the following varieties a lot for different effects. 'Autumn Joy' with large heads of bright salmon-rose, tinged as they age with bronze, is of German origin and believed to be a cross between *S. spectabile* and *S. telphium*. It grows a little taller than the former. The flowers dry on the plant and last even longer than others. 'Ruby Glow' is shorter and different in that the leaves are purplish-grey and the flowers are a real red, a lovely harmony of rich colour and very effective with grey foliage.

Two other sedums demand attention. *Sedum maximum atropurpureum* is an unusual plant with deep purple foliage with a hint of bronze and in late summer flat, dull rose flower-heads. Although a little less dense and laxer than *S. spectabile*, it usually does not need support. It is lovely in a border next to silvery-grey artemisias, santolinas or the small, steely-blue flowers of *Eryngium planum* or *E. tripartitum*. It is also very effective with clear pinks and yellows. Here is the ideal plant to provide the dark patch of colour so often needed in a border, where there is an excess of greens and even greys. It is lovely with *Potentilla arbuscula*, one of the finest of all dwarf shrubs, which even in autumn, after flowering most of the summer, is covered with large, clear yellow flowers. This sedum's heavy-textured fleshy leaves have great character which, not surprisingly, are beloved by flower-arrangers. It is not quite as vigorous as the other sedums which I have described, as its root-stocks develop more slowly, but it is a reliable plant when established.

Another species, little known and well worth growing, is *S. populifolium*, a charming spreading plant with an almost shrubby habit from twelve to fifteen inches tall. It has glaucous leaves, very much the shape of a diminutive poplar-leaf with dentated margins, and masses of white, hawthorn-scented flowers flushed with pink on branching stems from July to September. This delightful plant can be used in mixed borders, on the rockery where a large clump is required, or at the front of an herbaceous border.

Michaelmas Daisies for Autumn Splendour

Mid-September is a spectacular time in the garden as Michaelmas daisies, dahlias and the last of the annuals flower with exuberant abundance and autumn roses often surpass June ones in colour and fragrance.

I love Michaelmas daisies in great profusion. They have their drawbacks and more than one nurseryman has said that a rainy summer and autumn always cuts the demand for them the following year. Be that as it may, there are few flowers that give such a colourful display for four to six weeks. A well-planned border, preferably with the plants propagated afresh each year and moved in to follow spring seasonal bedding, makes a splendid show which more than justifies the effort. Similarly, groups in a mixed border and clumps of compact dwarf Michaelmas daisies in the front of shrubberies or rock-gardens can bring to life an otherwise dull area.

There is no doubt that Michaelmas daisies are dull plants when not in flower; it seems a long wait through the late spring and summer before we reap rewards. That is why they are best grown in seasonal gardens or

A paved terrace of pink brick and grey stone in the shade of an old pear tree makes a cool, flowery retreat with its borders of fragrant shrubs, roses and tubs of multi-coloured geraniums.

combined with other herbaceous plants to take over in September. In recent years there have been enormous advances not only in size of flower and the range of colours, but in resistance to mildew, which is a problem in certain areas. Gradually, disease-resisting varieties are being introduced. Already there is the lovely 'Royal Velvet', which has gleaming violet, nearly double flowers on two-foot stems with foliage that is claimed to be mildew-resistant, as is that of the double, pale lilac-pink 'Tapestry'.

Good new varieties to watch for include 'Autumn Glory', a rich, vinous, claret-red with large semi-double flowers often as much as three inches in diameter on three- to four-foot stems; 'Fellowship', a splendid pink of about the same height, which has received a well-deserved First Class Certificate; and 'Freda Ballard', a new rich red, semi-double and not more than three feet tall, which keeps well when picked. Another good cutting-variety is the new, double, deep-pink 'Mabel Reeves', on sturdy three- to three-and-a-half-foot stems. In the deep-mauve range 'Sarah Ballard', also fairly new, is rather shorter, with large, well-formed flowers borne on strong stems that need no staking. This variety is again described as mildew-resistant. There are endless older varieties, too familiar to list, but excellent and readily available from good nurseries.

Having said a lot about newer varieties, I would like to make the point that there is no merit in a plant just because it is new. This applies to bulbs, annuals, trees, shrubs and herbaceous plants alike. I urge every gardener to see plants growing under different conditions and to view new plants and old ones with an open mind. Awards after trial are often a useful indication. Many old varieties have never been superseded. A good example is the lovely old *Aster novae-angliae* (New England aster to me) 'Harrington's Pink'. It has clear rose-pink flowers, on strong, four-foot stems. It still enjoys a prominent place in many gardens, and deservedly so.

Dwarf Michaelmas daisies are particularly useful as they need no staking. They range from eight or nine inches to eighteen or twenty, and make neat pouffes, humps or mats. They are charming as low hedges or edgings for paths, as in a small urban garden where in September there are ribbon-borders of mauve, blue and pink dwarf varieties, superbly grown and a solid mass of flower. One of my old favourites is 'Audrey', a large-flowered blue, suffused with mauve. It is vigorous and grows to about fifteen inches. The colour of 'Margaret Rose', 'Pink Lace' and 'Rose Bonnet' you can well guess. 'Snowsprite' is a good dwarf white about twelve inches tall.

Much as I like the Michaelmas daisies that I have mentioned, what particularly appeals to me are the small-flowered spray types with delicate star-like flowers in great profusion on graceful stems. *Aster cordifolius*, like so many species of this very varied genus, is native to North America. There are several varieties of it, including 'Silver Spray', charmingly and aptly named, as it bears a myriad of small silvery-white flowers on arching three- to four-foot stems in September and October. A clump of it in a border or shrubbery is a wonderful subtle foil for bolder masses of colour or large, rather stiff flowers such as dahlias. 'Sweet Lavender' is similar in habit, but the flowers are pale lilac. It blooms a little earlier, as do 'Photograph' and 'Ideal', both delicate mauve.

Another North-American species from which a number of varieties is derived is *A. ericoides*. These again are very small-flowered with branching stems that provide broad panicles of bloom. They include 'Ringdove' (rosy-mauve, October), 'Perfection' and 'Chastity' (white, two to three feet, October), 'Esther' (pink) and 'Blue Star' (two and a half feet). These should be freely used in combination with the larger flowered Michaelmas daisies, and they are lovely grouped in front of pink or white Japanese anemones.

One of the most striking tall plants in the garden in autumn is *Chrysanthemum (Pyrethrum) uliginosum*, the Moon Daisy. It is sometimes grown instead of tall white Michaelmas daisies. The large, single, white flowers, with a greenish eye which turns dull gold as the flowers develop, measure as much as two inches across and sometimes more. They are borne at the tips of much-branched stems. The central stem is erect and often five feet in height. Groups of this giant daisy are lovely at the back of the border where height is needed, and the flowers can be relied upon from September to the end of October or until frost. Few plants give such good value and it cuts beautifully. The Moon Daisy is easy to grow as it is not particular as to soil and divides and establishes easily. Many nurseries do not list it and several describe it under *Pyrethrum*, a genus which usually should only be divided and moved in spring, but *C. uliginosum* is not particular.

Chrysanthemum rubellum is another charmer, with single-daisy flowers on stems seldom exceeding two to three feet. Hence it is obviously more manageable in smaller gardens. It begins flowering in August, and continues until the October frosts. It is, in fact, an outstanding plant for gardens of all sizes. 'Clara Curtis', probably the best known, was the first named clone. The clear rose-pink flowers are refined in form and profusely borne. Again, it is ideal for cutting.

Foliage Interest in Winter Borders

The dreary bareness of herbaceous borders in winter counts heavily against them, particularly in the smaller

The bold, rounded, evergreen leaves of bergenias are effective in winter in borders or mixed plantings. Here a clump masks the top of a stone wall and contrasts pleasantly with epimediums.

garden, where borders are in close proximity to the house. The fact that they are labour-consuming is a practical consideration, and, though not our concern here, I would like to emphasize that this point has been over-laboured.

There is beauty in a border in late autumn when the foliage of heleniums, Michaelmas daisies and artemisias turn a rich golden-brown, made even more entrancing by the silvered prismatic crystals of frost, dazzling in the morning sun or starkly white in the mist of late afternoon. But the moment comes to cut down the border, leaving only a few varieties like nepeta, romneyas and a foot or two of hollow-stemmed plants such as delphiniums, thalictrums and lupins to help keep the moisture from penetrating to the crown. Your border is now virtually bare.

One solution is the mixed border, with groups of lavender, rue, rosemary, potentillas, santolinas, vero-

nicas, *Senecio greyi* and shrub-roses, particularly the rugosas, with their more persistent foliage and fine red heps. Another solution is the inclusion of herbaceous plants with persistent foliage more or less resistant to ice and frost.

Two that generally vie for first place are dianthus and bergenias. The first is, of course, our old friend the Garden Pink, varying greatly in size and habit from the neat little silvery tufts of the dwarf varieties suitable for rock-gardens or small borders to large sprawling mats of glaucous grey, particularly effective along the front of borders where they can spill over paving or gravel. Some of the best foliage is that of the old-fashioned single or semi-double, clove-scented varieties. Border carnations also have attractive glaucous foliage.

Bergenias, known variously as saxifrages and megaseas, are characterized by bold, glossy, evergreen leaves, which turn rich colours in autumn and winter. Species include *B. crassifolia, cordifolia, delavayi, ligulata, purpurascens* and *stracheyi*, with cultivars such as 'Sunshade' and 'Evening Glow'.

Irises are useful, as the fans of sword-like jade-green leaves persist through the winter and quickly lengthen as the days draw out. The foliage furnishes the border throughout the year, the old outer leaves dying down and the centre ones growing vigorously. The old *Iris pallida dalmatica* has particularly attractive blue-green foliage, which is an asset to any border where contrasting leaf-forms and colours are desirable.

Christmas Roses and Heliotrope

In theory, the long winter months should be poor ones for flowers in our gardens, but several woody shrubs (*see* p. 41) and herbaceous plants are proof to the contrary. They may look a bit cold and naked at moments, but so great is their power of recuperation and so prolific is the quantity of bloom, that they are remarkable stand-bys. I, for one, do not mind their rather bare branches devoid of leaves.

The Christmas rose deserves first mention. Strange-

The blue-green foliage and apple-green, bowl-shaped flowers of *Helleborus argutifolius* in late winter and spring make it an indispensable plant for gardeners who appreciate fine foliage.

ly, it bears the Latin name *Helleborus niger*, which obviously does not refer to the beautifully formed white flower, sometimes flushed with pale pink or spotted red, but to the colour of its roots. It needs rich deep soil, moisture in the growing season and good drainage at all times. Shade is helpful, but it is probably the root-crown that needs protection from the sun rather than the foliage. Plants should be allowed to establish without disturbance. As the flowers are white, they may look bedraggled unless they are protected from rain and mud, preferably with cloches. Contrary to belief, it isn't the protection from cold that they particularly need. Christmas roses vary a lot in character. One form with rather longer stems than some others is known as *H. niger altifolius*, and there is a particularly early form, *praecox*. This begins to flower in November or early December. Plants sold by reliable nurserymen are usually good forms and it is often difficult to find the varietal forms mentioned above. Christmas roses flower well into the New Year, sometimes even to as late as early April. Flowers which are seen in shops are either cloche-grown or are perhaps the blooms of plants that have been lifted and forced commercially, as is done in Holland. Christmas roses, if potted-up and grown in a cool-house, flower superbly and can be used as pot-plants.

The best Christmas roses I have ever seen were grown by my father in his garden about fifty miles from New York. These were planted against the east wall of a garage, where they experienced temperatures in the nineties in summer and even sub-zero ones in winter. They started to flower in the autumn and produced well over a hundred blooms per plant in a single season. Their white flowers peering through the snow was a familiar sight in January and February.

Probably the scarcest of all forms of the Christmas Rose, but surely the finest, is 'Potter's Wheel'. This superb plant, found in a garden in the Potteries district of England in the fifties, was immediately recognized as exceptional. The pure white flowers, often four inches across, are borne on sturdy six-inch stems. This find is a good example of the importance of selecting the best form of a flower, and it illustrates how important it is to search out in small gardens the unusual plants which might so easily be lost to cultivation. 'Potter's Wheel', saved by a stroke of good fortune, is a winner.

The intriguing Corsican hellebore, *Helloborus argutifolius*, is superb for those who like apple-green flowers and striking grey-green foliage. And who does not? *H. foetidus*, a much-neglected plant of great distinction, has dark, finely cut, evergreen foliage and contrasting light green, bell-shaped flowers, edged purple. Both these hellebores should flower in winter and early spring

Helleborus niger, the Christmas Rose, is not only the handsomest of winter-flowering perennials but the bravest, as it defies all weathers.

in Zone 8 and possibly in Zone 7 in favoured positions. If plants are not available commercially, they can be grown from seeds.

One other winter-flowering plant is worthy of mention, in this case the rampant herbaceous *Petasites fragrans*. It is so invasive that it should never be allowed a place in the garden, though its scent of heliotrope, the old-fashioned light purple one, is delightful and I am enchanted when I come upon it, whether in a country lane or along a railway siding. The flowers themselves are unspectacular, but a few stems will scent a room. I know of one garden where it was produced as a treasure by a so-called 'friend'. The results were disastrous as it spread under a wall and took over a large area. Its scent, lovely as it is, came at too high a price.

10 Water-gardens and Bog-plants

Early Beauties of The Bog

There is a fascination about water in a garden, whether a trickling fountain, formal pool, natural pond, gurgling stream, old ditch or bog. What is of more interest to the gardener than the sound and glitter of water is the range of exciting plants made possible by ground that is constantly moist and cool. The first stirrings of spring are manifest in the boggy margins of pools and streams, where the waving winter catkins of alders, the silver silken fur of pussy-willows and the tender greens of weeping willows shelter the flaunting gold of marsh cowslips and the strange yellow or white spathes of lysichitums.

But a word of warning – the mere presence of water is not enough to ensure moisture, for the surrounding soil may be bone-dry if the pond is contained by masonry walls or plastic, as is so often the case in modern gardens. Of course, you can overcome these difficulties by providing pockets of soil built up with stones or bricks within the pool, by a gentle trickle from the overflow or by underground irrigation. In my old London garden the area beyond the pond looked lush and moist, but in reality the pond was entirely contained by cement margins. The planting was partly in pockets of soil within the pool and partly in specially prepared, moisture-retentive soil into which the water gradually seeped. Many gardeners are blessed with natural features which provide ideal conditions for bog-plants, such as pools, streams, old ditches or natural swamp land. These may partially dry up in summer but they still offer rich rewards for a little ingenuity and effort.

Careful selection of plants is necessary, as some are true aquatics, growing in water of various depths, while others are moisture-loving perennials for banks and marginal plantings. Some will even thrive in rich, relatively moist garden soil if pampered in infancy and again during periods of drought. Plants in this last group will not tolerate water over the crowns and they require plenty of soil for a clear root-run. True aquatics include water-lilies, *Iris laevigata*, the wild yellow *I. pseudacorus*, water-forget-me-nots *(Myosotis palustris)* and the lovely blue-flowered *Pontaderia cordata*. To the latter group belong the numerous candelabra primulas, Japanese and Siberian irises, and the feathery astilbes and filipendulas (formerly spiraeas). Perhaps the most satisfying of all treasures are the foliage plants, ranging from giant-leaved *Gunnera manicata*, glaucous hostas and rodgersias to feathery ferns, fragrant mints and rushes.

The earliest flowers for the bog-garden are indispensable and must claim our attention. The Marsh Marigold or Cowslip, one of the earliest and best-loved moisture-loving herbaceous plants, is equally happy in the shallow water of a pond or its muddy margins. In Britain, where Cowslips are also indigenous, they are generally known as King Cups. They rival celandines and buttercups, the gleaming yellow flowers carpeting bogs and the grassy banks of streams with sheets of gold. The rounded, heavy-textured leaves are bronze-green in early spring, but the flower clusters on twelve-inch stems can be so profusely produced in March and early April that the leaves are almost completely masked. I prefer the single-flowered *Caltha palustris*, but the double *flora pleno* with tightly-packed buttons of glistening egg-yellow are more popular. Then there is the much rarer Himalayan Marsh Marigold *(C. palustris* var. *alba)*, single and creamy white. From the Balkans and Asia Minor comes the giant golden *C. polypetala*, which reaches a height of as much as thirty inches with leaves a foot across. This species is easily propagated by its long stoloniferous stems. Other species are increased by root-division or by seeds, which, I am told, germinate quickly if they are sown as soon as they are gathered. This is true of other genera, including primulas and meconopsis. Calthas are easy spectacular plants for every bog-garden, whether on alkaline, neutral or acid soil.

A striking companion for the garden with deep, moist soil and plenty of space is the spectacular but

Richardia 'Crowborough', the hardier form of the white arum, growing with thalictrums and the lovely leaves of boccania.

curious western North American *Lysichitum americanum*, with its pointed yellow spathes, closely related to Skunk Cabbage. These at once identify it as an arum. The bright green leaves, sometimes over two feet long, follow the flowers. The Japanese *L. camtschatcense*, its only relative in this genus, is even more striking, with its hooded white spathes and glaucous leaves. It flowers a few weeks later and is not as robust as the yellow one. There are gardens where *L. americanum* seeds itself freely, the seeds being carried downstream by the running water, but the white-flowered species is less accommodating. Both can be propagated by divisions of the rhizomes. Visitors to the Savill Gardens at Windsor in March and April will have noticed with wonder these strange, rather exotic flowers growing at the water's edge among the Marsh Marigolds and sheets of *Primula rosea*.

This last plant, another Himalayan treasure, is perfect for those who like patches of brilliant colour. Its vivid rose colouring has a fascination at a time when so many spring bulbs favour blue, white and yellow. It is dwarf in habit, seldom exceeding three to eight inches, with upright sessile leaves which develop after the appearance of the short scapes bearing the clusters of bright rosy-red flowers. It likes lots of moisture and will even survive flooding in spring and

frost, which, strangely, do not bother its seemingly fragile beauty. There are two forms readily available, *P. rosea grandiflora* and 'Delight' ('Micia Visser de Geer'), the latter being a more intense carmine-red. Plants of *Primula rosea* are available or it can be grown from seed.

Foliage for Bog-gardens

Although the water- or bog-garden derives much of its interest from colourful flowers, it is the plants with handsome foliage that are most telling, as they furnish the margins of ponds and streams over a very long season, creating a luxuriant setting under the frame of willows, red-stemmed dogwoods and alders. True, candelabra primulas, astilbes, lobelias and a number of the water-loving irises have their periods of glory, but it is the foliage plants that are indispensable. Fortunately irises, including Siberian, Japanese, and the native yellow flag, are dual-purpose plants and we treasure them as much for their leaves as for their flowers. Pools and slow-moving streams are almost unthinkable without their graceful sword-like foliage. My real favourites are the large-leaved hostas, ferns, rheums and, most dramatic of all for extensive gardens, the giant *Gunnera manicata*, with leaves as much as six to eight feet across. The last in fact bears the distinction of having the largest leaves of any hardy plant in this country. Common as gunneras may be, there is always a feeling of incredulity and wonder when I am confronted by them.

There is, then, a very wide choice of foliage for moist positions, with an infinite variety of leaf-shapes, textures and shades of green, ranging from those tinged with coppery-red and clear light yellow to misty blue and glaucous greys, all of which are a wonderful foil for the predominantly green summer landscape. Moreover, when mirrored in still water, they assume an even more subtle beauty.

Hostas stand supreme. Beautiful as the mauve, violet or white spikes of lily-like flowers may be, it is for the foliage that they are generally grown. Their requirements are relatively simple – shade, semi-shade or even sun, good deep soil and plenty of moisture. For size and delicate colouration of leaf, moist, partly shaded positions are best. For an abundance of flower, sunshine is advantageous but leaves will be smaller. The genus *Hosta* is large and complicated, but several species are so handsome and so ideally suited to the shady bog-garden that they stand out.

Pride of place on my short list goes to *H. sieboldiana*,

The giant leaves and curious greenish-brown flower-heads of the Brazilian *Gunnera manicata*, growing in a very moist position. It is doubtfully hardy north of Washington, D.C.

The bold foliage of *Rodgersia aesculifolia* by the waterside contrasts pleasantly with the broad green blades of bog irises and colours a deep reddish-bronze in autumn.

with broad heart-shaped leaves as much as eight or nine inches across, crinkled and deeply veined. The best forms are a rich blue-grey with a subtle grape-like bloom. These leaves are wonderful for flower-arrangements, as are the rather dense heads of flaring tubular flowers, white suffused with lilac, in July. This fine plant, Japanese in origin, as are so many hostas, is sometimes known as *H. glauca*. Another splendid species, *H. fortunei*, has broad leaves, less glaucous than *H. sieboldiana*, and lilac flowers. Its varietal form *albo-picta* is of unrivalled beauty in May and early June, when the leaves are a clear butter-yellow with an uneven margin of vibrant green. This intriguing contrast is, of course, too good to last and by midsummer the leaves are a uniform soft green. *Hosta undulata* has smaller, pointed leaves with undulated margins, often twisted in a gentle spiral. Even more startling is the colour and pattern of the leaves, which have wide, rather irregular patches of creamy-white in the middle of the blades with dark green margins to accentuate them. Few plants are more striking in borders and shrubberies. In late July and August there are tall graceful spikes of rich lilac flowers. Pots of this species are good short-term house-plants in spring. I like to

keep them for a month or two and then plant them out in the border.

Hostas are invaluable in large pots or tubs for shady town gardens. If the soil is rich in humus or peat and the pots are liberally watered, results are excellent. Old and established hostas benefit by division. After the flowers, the decorative spikes of seeds are useful for winter bouquets. As the seeds germinate relatively easily, species can be grown from seeds as well as from division. Confusion in nomenclature adds greatly to the complications of ordering hostas. I select forms at flower-shows, ordering them there and then. Hostas are widely exhibited because they make such superb bold underplanting.

For dynamic effect, *Gunnera manicata* has no equal. The enormous bristly leaves with prominent ribbing are borne on equally bristly stems. Here is a subject for gardens or parks where there is plenty of room, a developed clump often measuring twelve to fourteen feet across. In spring, the great fat leaf-buds are covered with a tawny-brown reticulated tunic, and later the leaves, unfolding like little furry paws, are remarkable in their intricate beauty. In summer a large flower spike two or three feet long, brownish-green at first but

the ground around the plants to provide much-needed humus. Although water-rats sometimes disturb the roots with their underground tunnels, on the whole gunnera are easy plants when established.

Planting Pools

A water feature has always been important in the charm of a garden, partly for the beauty of the reflections, partly for the movement and sound and, of course, for the delightful flowers and foliage effects that are possible, not only in the damp margins but in the water itself.

If there is a natural pond or lake, plant boldly with red-stemmed cornuses, water irises, low-growing willows such as the purple willow *(Salix purpurea nana)*, the hoary willow *(S. incana)* or the taller violet willow *(S. daphnoides)*. Birches and alders are fast-growing. I particularly like the grey cut-leafed alder *(Alnus incana acuminata)*. Beware of rushes and certain decorative grasses which may be invasive, especially if the water is shallow. Much as I like water lilies, they too can take over a large area if planted in the bottom of the pond and not in tubs or baskets. If there is a stream, find out if it floods in winter. If so, primulas, choice irises and ferns may be washed away, especially when recently planted.

Polythene, fibre-glass, vinyl, plastolene and other compositions have revolutionized the making of garden-pools and the days when concrete had to be mixed and poured are at an end. So too are the agonizing hours spent trying to locate the leaks in the cement after a hard winter. Concrete pools are still widely used, but the prefabricated ones fill a wide role, especially in town and suburban gardens. Plants do not take kindly to newly-constructed pools because of the excessive amount of free lime. Fill the pool and let the water stand for a month or six weeks, if possible. Then drain and refill it. The process can be hastened if the water is changed several times.

The planting of pools is my concern here. With a natural pond or stream, marginal planting along the banks presents no problem. For a concrete pool, shelves with edges of brick or stone can easily be constructed to hold the soil. With plastic and fibre-glass pools this is less easy and polythene boxes or crates are recommended to contain the soil and keep rampant plants in their allotted space.

Beware of growing too much, as a small pool can soon become a jungle. Many water-plants are invasive, such as the Arrowhead *(Sagittaria sagittifolia)* or the

later tinged with rusty red, pushes up among the leaves. The flower-stalks, more interesting than decorative, may be removed to throw further vigour into leaf-development. This exotic plant thrives in deep, rich, boggy soil, preferably in sun or light shade. Soil, well laced with well-rotted manure, should be used at planting time, and mulching has good effects. Gunneras are best planted in spring when the frosts are over, or they can be grown from seeds. Do not make the mistake of planting gunneras too close. Their true beauty is best appreciated if they are used singly or in widely-spaced clumps. Few gardens today have space for the latter.

Gunneras are moderately hardy and grow in Zone 8, but doubtfully in Zone 7. The leaves, for all their leathery texture and apparent strength, collapse with the first frosts, becoming limp and black. Though unsightly, these should not be removed but bent double over the crown of the plant to give winter protection. A mulch of bracken, hay or leaf-mould can also be applied. In spring the old leaves should be trodden into much smaller *S. lancifolia* and *S. latifolia*. Another ramper is the attractive blue *Pontaderia cordata*. There are many lovely plants for marginal planting, including the marsh marigolds *(Caltha)*, irises *(I. laevigata* and *pseudacorus)*, candelabra primulas, water-forget-me-nots, mimulus, mint and a host of others.

Exploit that charming group of plants known as floating aquatics. One of the loveliest is the water-hyacinth *(Eichhornia speciosa major)*. Its beautiful lavender-blue flowers with a dark purple peacock-eye appear in late summer, if it has been a hot, sunny one. As this plant is not hardy, it should be brought under cover in buckets of soil and water in early autumn. It is not an easy plant in northern climates, but it is so lovely that you should accept the challenge. Another charmer is the bladderwort *(Utricularia vulgaris)*, with small clusters of clear yellow flowers which seem to hover like butterflies a few inches above the water. This one submerges after blooming and hence is hardy. Beware of the well-known duckweed, particularly the lesser form *(Lemna minor)*, as it can become a pest in natural lakes and ponds. I struggled with it for

years but never succeeded in getting rid of it. In small pools it is an excellent food for fish.

Submerged oxygenating aquatics are useful as they help to keep a pool in balance, so that the water remains clear. They should be used in conjunction with floating aquatics and snails. There are a number of these submerged aquatics and if planted in plastic pots they will not become invasive. Use a heavy fibrous loam. Light, sandy soils are not satisfactory, nor are those rich in peat or leaf-mould. Also avoid manure, except for water-lilies. Fertilizers are not needed.

One of the loveliest oxygenators is the Water Violet *(Hottonia palustris)* because of its soft green fern-like foliage and pale lavender, violet-like flowers borne six to eight inches above the surface. I am very fond of the feathery fern-like *Myriophyllum*, which is a lovely green. Another charmer is *Ranunculus aquatilis*, with small snow-white flowers borne above the surface leaves, which are often likened to tiny clover-shaped lily-pads. Water lobelia *(Lobelia dortmanna)* produces flowers above the surface of the pool, in this case fragile and lavender-blue. These oxygenators, though

The romantic fascination of a small lake in a setting of trees and moisture-loving plants is enhanced by the shimmering reflections among the water-lilies.

unspectacular, are attractive as well as useful in providing oxygen by a miraculous process which puts back what fish and water animals absorb.

Put Out More Flags

Almost every garden boasts a clump or two of irises, while others may have iris borders of rainbow colours or even iris gardens as a special feature. These are usually planted with the bearded irises or, as they are variously known, the flag or German irises. There are many other types, including the bulbous Dutch, Spanish and English irises which begin to flower in late spring, but our concern for the moment is with that very handsome group of giant irises suited to the border, the stream or the bog-garden.

One of the great delights of long summer days is the vision of water-meadows traversed by a meandering stream, the margins crowded with colonies of the blue *Iris versicolor* and the taller golden-yellow *Iris pseudacorus*. The flowers of the latter are borne in quantity on three-foot stems above the tips of the graceful sword-like leaves. This vigorous iris always makes me a little envious on a hot summer day when I see it standing cool and splendid, its feet immersed in water. Daisies, forget-me-nots, pink campions and buttercups in the meadows nearby may not indicate good farming, but meadows in full bloom are to my mind more lovely than many gardens.

Iris pseudacorus grew happily in the margins of a shallow reflecting pool in not more than six to eight inches of soil on top of the cement bottom. It always flowered both in full sun or half-shade and was virtually trouble-free. Even the rigours of very bad winters did not discourage it. This iris seeded freely and came up in shady borders where the soil was left undisturbed. Surprisingly enough, it even seeded in a very dry unpromising position under a Lombardy poplar. The clumps developed and reached flowering size, but I must admit that a bucket of water from the pool nearby helped them over the dry periods.

There are various colour forms. The variety 'Bastardi' is a clear primrose-yellow, effective in positions where deep yellow is too strong a colour. There is a variety with much larger flowers called 'Golden Queen', but supplies are limited and it is rather more expensive. I particularly like the variegated form, which has leaves strongly streaked with gold in spring and early summer. Unfortunately, the colour deepens to the usual green by August. Much more effective and lasting throughout the summer is the beautiful variegated sweet rush, *Acorus calamus variegatus*, with markings of white with glints of rose and gold. It grows to two and a half feet and is effective with the glistening white of water lilies.

Iris pseudacorus, the wild yellow flag, with its handsome golden flowers and spiky foliage, is actually an immigrant from Europe.

Iris monnieri has large, soft yellow, lightly fragrant flowers in clusters on three- to four-foot stems in late June or early July. It requires a dampish position or a rich moisture-retentive soil. Like *Iris pseudacorus* it is lime-tolerant. *Iris ochroleuca* is a lovely white species with orange markings in the centre of each petal. It grows to about the same height and shows up particularly well in the border. It is also useful for cutting when long stems are needed. Of course, the individual flowers last only for a day or two, but there are more to follow. The foliage is handsome when cut for big vases, and this is true of all the large species and their hybrids.

Iris ochraurea, a large, clear yellow with long stems, needs plenty of moisture. There is a lavender-purple form of *Iris spuria* known as 'Notha', which is useful where a tall one is required in another colour-range, and there are others listed in catalogues variously under *Iris monspur*, such as 'A. J. Balfour', with clear blue flowers; 'Cambridge Blue' and 'Juno', a paler blue. There is confusion about some of these irises and several nurseries list 'Cambridge Blue' as a form of *I. monnieri*. It matters little, as the important thing is to have splendid plants for bold groups. Because of their vigour they can be relied on to stand alone and they do not leave gaps in the border, as so many June and early July-flowering herbaceous plants are prone to do.

180

Dwarf daffodils and blue grape hyacinths in a pocket on a rock garden
carry out the blue and gold theme of spring.

These irises take a little time to establish and should be kept well watered if the summer is dry.

Clematis-flowered Irises

The most spectacular of the moisture-loving irises are the clematis-flowered Japanese irises, usually known as *I. kaempferi*. They are similar in appearance to *I. laevigata*, but there are certain definite differences. Both are very beautiful and one or other, preferably both, should be grown in all gardens where conditions permit.

Iris kaempferi require a rich, lime-free soil and plenty of moisture. They grow well at the edge of a pond or stream where they will not be subjected to winter flooding, and are definitely not plants for positions where the roots will be submerged in winter. Ideally, a pool or stream which can be flooded in summer, so that there is an inch or so of water above the roots, is the answer if, in turn, the water-table can be lowered in winter. This is often possible by controlling the level of the overflow of a pool or pond. Japanese irises do not like the edges of swiftly-moving streams. They are heavy feeders, reacting well to rich loam or peaty soils which have been laced with well-rotted manure. They thrive in borders which can be kept damp in dry summers but, on the other hand, do not become water-logged during a wet winter.

In some gardens wooden tubs are sunk in a dry border or at the edge of a cement pool. Coarse drainage should be provided at the bottom with rich compost above it. These tubs provide excellent sites for Japanese irises, as the soil can be kept very damp. I used to grow them successfully in this way in a very dry border. It is also possible to grow them in tubs or boxes placed in a pool so that the water comes just about to the top of the roots. In autumn the tubs should be moved to a frame or sunk in the ground for the winter to keep the roots relatively dry.

The flowers of *I. kaempferi* are freely borne above the graceful sword-like leaves. These have a distinct ridge down the centre of the blade, which serves to distinguish them from *I. laevigata*. The flowers are spectacular and include both singles and doubles, the latter having twice the number of broad falls. The poise of the flowers is one of the great charms and explains both the description 'clematis-flowered' and the many comparisons to butterflies. The colours are varied and rich and some of the falls have wonderful velvety textures and ruffled edges. Self-colours include white, rich blues, claret-reds, deep purples and misty blues. Others are stippled or veined in intricate patterns.

A wide number of named varieties are available, some with Japanese names and others with English vernacular names, obviously translations from the former, and others are available as strains. Those, raised from seedlings produce excellent results. The loveliest of the Japanese irises are the singles, which have such elegance and beauty of form. The double ones are to me monsters by comparison. As I have said before, this is a matter of individual taste. When planting do not crowd them, as they increase relatively quickly and the individual flowers are so beautiful in shape they should be seen to full advantage. Japanese irises cut well, and although the blooms do not last for more than a day or two, the buds will open in water. Plant them in spring in cold areas so that they can establish. They usually flower with roses in June and July. Of course, Japanese irises do well in areas where rainfall is high, making waterside or bog conditions unnecessary. *Iris kaempferi* can be grown from seed, as can *I. laevigata*, but named clones will not come true.

Iris laevigata usually reaches its peak of bloom in June, while the Kaempferis are definitely best in July. The former are more tolerant of lime and therefore adaptable to gardens in areas where Kaempferis are impossible. They like rich soil and in areas of high lime content, peat or leaf-mould and well-rotted manure should be worked into the compost. They are true water-plants, growing happily with their roots in water throughout the year. They will, of course, grow happily in bogs as well as in gardens where the ground is always moist. The true *I. laevigata* is a plant about two feet tall with standards and falls of a striking clear blue with delicate gold lines at the bases of the petals. There is a fine white variety *alba* which produces a wealth of blooms, as well as a deep violet-purple *(atropurpurea)* and others flecked and mottled with blue or mauve on a light ground. Nurseries that specialize in Kaempferi varieties obviously list *I. laevigata* as well.

For varied conditions by far the most adaptable iris is *I. sibirica*, which will grow in almost any soil, acid or alkaline, wet or moderate; it flowers from early June throughout July, depending on the locality. Among good varieties are 'The Emperor', a large deep blue (three feet); 'Caesar's Brother', a deep pansy-violet; 'Snowcrest', a fine tall white (two and a half feet); 'Gatineau', Cambridge-blue standards with china-blue falls (three feet); 'Snow Queen', ivory-white; 'Perry's Blue'; 'Tycoon', large violet-blue (three and a half feet); 'Emperor', violet-blue (four feet) and 'Helen Astor', rosy red (two and a half feet).

There is a charming water-garden with fine Japanese irises in the gardens at Bagatelle on the outskirts of Paris; those who go to see the wonderful rose collections should not miss it. There are good groups of *I. laevigata* and *I. kaempferi* at Winterthur and Longwood Gardens near Wilmington and in most private and botanic gardens where water is a feature.

181

11 Bulbs and Corms

General Principles for Planting Bulbs

Late summer and autumn are interesting times of the year for the gardener, as he must look ahead to spring, sensing the delicious fragrance of hyacinths drifting in through the windows and visualizing the sheets of daffodils, the clumps of stately tulips in the borders, and the endless possibilities for small bulbs to be tucked into odd nooks and corners – at the foot of hedges, around the bottom of trees, in window-boxes, tubs and urns, and as underplanting for shrubs or roses. I spend many happy hours with bulb-catalogues, planning and scheming, adding up the figures, knocking out an item here to cut the total, but always finding something else to be included.

Bulbs are essential for good spring gardens as they guarantee splendid results the first year. As the flowers are already formed within the bulb, success is assured. For new gardens and for town gardens where space is limited, no other flowers yield such dividends for so little effort, while in larger gardens where bulbs can be left to naturalize under good conditions, the increasing yield with the years is astonishing, particularly of aconites, snowdrops, scillas, chionodoxas, anemones, daffodils and crocuses. Bulbs are relatively cheap in view of the returns in beauty and pleasure, although newer daffodils can be astronomically expensive because of their novelty, scarcity and their own intrinsic merits. There are, however, many fine, less expensive, tried-and-true favourites which the average gardener wants.

Daffodils, Dutch crocuses, the large bluebells *(Scilla campanulata)*, hyacinths and the dwarf bulbs should take priority of planting in September and October over tulips, which are far better planted in late October, or November or after frost. Planting large quantities is time-consuming, and if advance preparation can be done, so much the better. Buy good-quality bulbs from reliable sources. Be sure that they are firm and in

Snowdrops, naturalized at the foot of a tree, carpet the ground with white in the late winter or early spring.

healthy condition. A firm, heavy bulb is better than a larger light one. Tulips may have lost their brown tunics, but no matter if they are clean and sound. If you cannot deal with bulbs on delivery, open the containers so that there is a circulation of air and store them in a cool, dry place.

Try to get the best effect possible with your bulbs. A common fault is crowding, so that clumps of tulips are so tight that their individual grace cannot be enjoyed. Tulips should be planted three to four inches deep and five to eight inches apart, depending on variety, the smaller tulip species, of course, being closer. Hyacinths should be put in at a depth of three inches, but allow eight to nine inches between them for good effect and four to five inches for Cynthella hyacinths, which are smaller and more graceful. Don't forget that hyacinths used for forcing are enchanting if grown the next year in grass or at the edge of shrubberies.

As a rule, no special preparation is required when naturalizing bulbs in grass on reasonably good soils. If, however, you are planting in prepared positions in beds or borders, it is well to make up the soil, adding leaf-mould or peat to light, dry soils and sand or ash to heavy, wet clay. Avoid manure with bulbs, unless it is very old indeed or you are using a dehydrated product. Bone-meal is an ideal long-term food, and a balanced organic fertilizer helps on hungry soils. Humus to retain moisture is highly important for the future life of the bulb, which, after flowering, stores up reserves and makes the flower-bud for another year. Peat, garden compost, spent hops or some of the special organic plant-mulches are ideal. For large tubs and containers I suggest the use of a generous layer of several inches of vermiculite to cover the crocks and stones used for drainage. This helps to prevent the soil above from drying out.

Dwarf bulbs such as crocuses, scillas, tulip species, chionodoxas, grape hyacinths, aconites and snowdrops grow well on acid, neutral or chalky soils, particularly the last. This is explained by the fact that many of them are native to the lime soil of the Mediterranean and the Middle East. It is in spring that the

Daffodils growing in round beds under apple trees in a country garden solve the mowing problem in an orchard as their foliage must not be cut until it withers.

gardener on chalk has his greatest opportunity. Obviously, hyacinths and large-flowered tulips, which are in any case shorter-term bulbs, need richer soil and do not naturalize.

When planting bulbs such as narcissi or crocuses in drifts, throw down the bulbs with a sweeping gesture and plant them as they fall, avoiding even spacing and spreading them out further if they seem too close. Edges should be blurred and non-geometric. Don't plant a circle or triangle of crocuses in the lawn but a soft, pleasing drift. In places where there is a circle cut out under a tree or formal geometric borders or beds, the problem is quite different. Try to make informal groups bear relation to permanent landscape features, such as walls, trees, shrubberies, streams, rocks, slopes and banks. Don't plant isolated groups for no reason. When selecting bulbs, choose those that are suited to the position. For example, it is madness to plant a very

tall, heavy-headed daffodil, no matter how beautiful, in a windy, exposed position.

In some gardens established plantings of bulbs are far too geometric in shape and may even have been planted in lines. If so, lift a few here and there and interplant to break the ranks and to blur the outline of the groups, thus achieving a more natural effect. Above all, make notes in spring in other gardens and trial-grounds of varieties you particularly favour, so that you can order them later in the season. It is best to record such notes in a book, so that they will not be mislaid.

Each season I am further impressed by the beauty and usefulness of the Lent Lily, the early wild European daffodil, with the amusing name *Narcissus pseudo-narcissus*. It is one of the most enchanting of all dwarf daffodils. It naturalizes beautifully, and as it is not heavy-headed, it stands up to wind. The wonderful slope where tens of thousands have naturalized at Nymans, the National Trust Garden, at Handcross in Sussex, is well worth a visit in April, and so are the fine daffodil meadows of dwarf *N. cyclamineus* and *N. bulbocodium* (Hoop Petticoat) in the Savill Gardens at Windsor and at Wisley. One of the secrets in these gardens is to allow the plants to seed undisturbed in summer and to mow the grass in the autumn, so that the short stems of the daffodils do not have to compete with old grasses in spring.

Blue and Gold for Spring

The wealth of spring bulbs is bewildering, and for the owner of the small garden in town or village it is remarkable what a transformation a small but careful selection can make over a long period, from February until well into May. Of course, localities and seasons vary enormously.

The earliest are, of course, the snowdrops *(Galanthus)* and the aconites *(Eranthis)*, which literally appear with the melting snows. These establish happily in shady places under trees, on banks and in shrubberies where they can be left undisturbed. They are tolerant of alkaline soil, yet equally happy in dark rich loam or even clay. Plenty of moisture is a great help. Both these charming harbingers of spring are too well known to need further description and they are readily available from bulb-merchants, though it must be admitted that snowdrops will take a season to establish and be a disappointment the first spring. Far better to divide them immediately after they have flowered or obtain them in clumps from friends. However, many of us are forced to buy the dried bulbs and plant them in the autumn.

September and October are the ideal month for planting daffodils. Early planting is always preferable, as bulbs are then firm and in good condition, so that they root quickly, not having to wait until the ground warms up in spring, as bulbs planted very late would have to do. I must in fairness say that I have experimented with bulbs planted in a mild winter in November and even December with good results though the flowers have been later, a little smaller and not as plentiful the following year. Therefore, if you acquire a new garden in late autumn or have been unable to plant daffodils earlier, it doesn't follow that you must forego one of the gayest pleasures of spring, but there are several 'ifs' involved: one, if you can obtain good firm bulbs; two, if the ground is frost-free; and three, if you don't expect superb results. Most of us probably order bulbs when we see them in flower in the spring or when the bulb-catalogues arrive in summer.

I always enjoy autumn planting. There is excitement in projecting one's thoughts to spring as the golden leaves swirl down and the pungent smell of bonfires fills the air. The materials to have in readiness for planting bulbs will depend on your soil and the site. Daffodils like good drainage, but need moisture both in spring and after flowering, when they are building up for the following year. Certain types in particular need moist conditions at these times. I have found vast fields of *N. peoticus* growing with terrestial orchids in very damp conditions at fairly high altitudes in south-west France in May, where later on the ground would be sun-baked and dry. This tells the story. *Narcissus cyclamineus* also favours plenty of moisture in spring. But on the whole, daffodils are delightfully adaptable flowers. Lime or chalk does not worry them, nor does an acid soil, as long as drainage is good. On light, dry soils the addition of leaf-mould, garden compost or peat provides much-needed humus to retain moisture. On heavy clay or badly drained land, coarse sand or coal-ash can be worked into the soil, and a little sand at the base of each bulb is useful for daffodils as well as hyacinths, tulips and lilies.

As far as feeding is concerned, the flower for next spring is already formed when the bulb is planted. Bone-meal worked into the ground at planting time

'Beryl' is an enchanting little hybrid of *Narcissus cyclamineus*, with pale yellow petals, slightly reflexed from the gold-and-orange cup.

and again after flowering is a good long-range measure. Hoof and horn is also useful; sulphate of potash is recommended by some growers, but on good sturdy soil this should not be necessary. Some firms offer special bulb-fertilizers.

Methods of planting will vary according to position. In shrubberies, borders or in cutting-gardens, pockets or trenches can be dug out and prepared, the bulbs placed in position and then covered over. In grass (mow long grass first) bulb-planters may be used to take out a circle of sod and earth to the required depth, and then the soil replaced on top of the bulb. Many gardeners prefer to plant with a trowel or spade. Depth of planting will depend on both the nature of the soil and the size of the bulb. On light soils it is sound practice to plant more deeply than on heavy ones – five to six inches of soil from the neck of the bulb to the surface on light ones and on heavy soil three to four for large bulbs. Very small bulbs, such as those of *N. triandrus, bulbocodium* and *cyclamineus*, should, of course, be more shallowly planted, three inches being ample. The distance between bulbs will vary. For large-flowered daffodils six to nine inches is suggested; for smaller ones decrease the interval, according to the size of the flower and the effect desired. Remember that the dwarf species, if happy, will seed freely, in moist rich soil, if the seed pods can ripen without disturbance. It means untidy grass for some weeks.

The choice of varieties is wide, as there are so many different types of modern hybrids. Some people like the bright yellows or those with vivid red or orange cups. Others prefer the whites, ivories and very pale creams, or even the newer pinks. Some like trumpets; others prefer shallow cups. This is a matter of personal taste, coupled with the purpose for which the bulbs are needed. Certainly, for flower-arrangements the selection would be different from those for naturalizing. Catalogues from reliable bulb-merchants are good guides, as flowers are well described and in some catalogues are divided into nine numbered Divisions, based on their form and colouring.

I want particularly to call attention to some of the early-flowering varieties with which to start the season, such as 'February Gold', 'March Sunshine' and 'Peeping Tom', all of which are hybrids of *N. cyclamineus* and may be found listed in catalogues under Division VI, or possibly among bulbs for the rock-garden. I have a weakness for the hybrids of *N. triandrus* (Division V), which have clusters of scented pendulous flowers. Fine ones include 'Thalia', 'Tresamble', 'Shot Silk', 'Silver Chimes' and 'Moonshine'. I am also fond of the Poeticus Hybrids (Division IX), which are generally late-flowering and very fragrant, with gleaming white perianths and shallow cups or eyes, often of yellow

with a rim of red. Good varieties include 'Queen of Narcissi', the very large 'Actaea', the all-white 'Polar Ice' and, of course, the very late, old-fashioned Pheasant Eye *(N. poeticus recurvus)*, with recurving perianth segments.

The doubles (Division IV) are popular, especially for cutting, but not with me. I love, perhaps inconsistently, the May-flowering *N. albus plenus odoratus*, with double, pure white, exquisitely scented, gardenia-like flowers. My defence is that it is a double Poeticus. It is far from easy to grow, requiring very early planting, deep rich soil, moisture and partial shade – conditions that many gardens do not provide. Popular doubles include the pale yellow, very large 'Gardenia', the creamy-white and orange 'Mary Copeland', the paler 'Mrs William Copeland', and the well-known spectacular 'Texas' and 'Twink'.

Tazettas with multiple flowers such as 'Geranium', 'Cheerfulness', 'Scarlet Gem', and 'St Agnes' are useful, showy and sturdy.

For scent the true jonquil *(N. jonquilla)* with clusters of small, golden-yellow, short-cupped flowers on twelve-inch stems among dark rush-like foliage takes pride of place. It is a flower of refinement and its orange-blossom scent is intoxicating.

When ordering daffodils be sure to include some of the delightful, dwarf, blue-flowered, spring bulbs which are such a wonderful foil in late March and April to the yellows and whites. Snowdrops and winter aconites will already have spread the palette of spring with the same colour as the daffodils, and blue is welcome as a contrast. These bulbs include scillas, chionodoxas, muscari, and the blue forms of *Anemone blanda* and *apennina*.

Scilla bifolia has clusters of starry turquoise-blue flowers, while *S. sibirica* has deeper, very rich, cobalt-blue ones. Chionodoxas, charmingly named Glory of the Snows, are perhaps even lovelier and have larger flowers. Three species are *C. luciliae*, Cambridge-blue with a white eye, *gigantea* with larger flowers of deeper blue washed with mauve, and the darker blue *sardensis*. All these require sun, good drainage, and any reasonable garden soil, including chalk. Plant them about three inches deep in drifts or pockets. They are charming as underplanting for early pink cherries or forsythias; they can be used in pockets in paving or at the base of a hedge, if planted on the sunny side. They can be scattered through borders where they will seed, and they do not resent occasional disturbance. In our old garden they increased very rapidly over a few years and were particularly lovely interplanted with drifts of yellow polyanthus.

Grape Hyacinths *(Muscari)*, another lovely dwarf blue bulb, should be copiously planted in full sun, and they, too, are tolerant of lime. A few dozen or a few

A colony of the large-flowered *Crocus vernus* 'Vanguard', with its globular silvery-grey and lavender flowers, growing at the base of shrubs in a woodland garden.

hundred of any or all of these early bulbs will add immeasurably to the interest of the spring garden.

Crocuses for Naturalizing

Of the spring bulbs I suppose the daffodil is the most loved, but certainly hyacinths and tulips are runners-up in many of our gardens. I am devoted to the great variety of small bulbs that grow so happily and look so natural in groups under trees, in narrow borders along paths or under hedges, in sunny situations among shrubs, in pockets in the rock-garden and in window-boxes, tubs or vases. Their uses are indeed legion and they can be relied upon to make patches of brilliant colour.

Crocuses are one of the surest signs of spring. The great sheets of large-flowered Dutch hybrids, with their fat buds opening to large chalice-shaped flowers in colours ranging from white and gold to silvery mauve and deepest purple, are a feature of almost every park and many gardens, both in town and country. The corms should be planted in the autumn about three inches deep. It is advisable to plant early, certainly not later than the first weeks of November, as the buds

break into growth and start sprouting in the bag. Scatter them in loose drifts in the grass, if they are to be naturalized, making sure that they are not too close together and that the outlines of the groups are sufficiently blurred to look natural. Patches in shrubberies or along the base of hedges should be equally informal.

Whether you plant drifts of a single colour or whether you mix two or more, such as yellows with purples or mauves, is a matter for personal preference. I usually favour one variety to a group. Good whites include 'Snowdrift', 'Katherine Parlow' and 'Snowstorm'. The best yellow is 'Dutch Yellow', which appears variously as 'Yellow Giant' or 'Large Yellow'. These are earlier than the rest. Purples are numerous, including 'Negro Boy', 'Purple Beauty', 'Purpureus Grandiflorus', 'Ivanhoe', 'Remembrance', 'The Bishop' and a number of others. Mauves and lilacs, so subtle in their colouring, include 'Enchantress', 'Excelsior', 'Jubilee', 'Queen of the Blues' and 'Little Dorrit'. Striped crocuses, which have a rather bizarre, harlequin quality, are often attractive if planted in smaller numbers with one of the self-coloured varieties which repeats the striping. For example, 'Striped Beauty', which has rich purple markings on a silvery-white ground, looks

187

charming with a deep purple or a pure white. Some bulb-merchants list Dutch crocuses by colour, rather than by name.

When planting crocuses in grass, remember that the foliage must die down before it is cut off, if the corms are to build up strength to flower for the next season. This may well not happen before June, so do not naturalize them in grass that must be mown and tidy.

Far lovelier than the large Dutch hybrids for the rock-garden or choice positions are the seedlings of *Corcus chrysanthus*, a winter-flowering species, native to Greece and Asia Minor. These commence to bloom in late winter or early spring and often last for weeks. This enchanting crocus will always be associated for me with the late Mr. E. A. Bowles, whose remarkable garden at Enfield near London was the scene of origin of so many varieties, charmingly named for birds – 'Snow Bunting', 'Yellow Hammer', 'Blue Bird', etc. There are also a number of varieties of Dutch origin that are equally enchanting, including 'E. A. Bowles', 'Moonlight' and 'Zwanenburg'. Surely these are among the most lovely of all crocuses, and as they come so early, they are doubly welcome. They are tolerant of a variety of soils and excellent on chalk or in alkaline areas. Give them a well-drained sunny position where they can ripen undisturbed after flowering. Plant them at about the same depth as the size of the corm. Crocuses, like many other bulbs, don't require manure. In fact, it is harmful. Bone-meal and perhaps a little dried blood after flowering make an excellent long-term tonic.

Several other crocuses deserve particular attention, especially the obliging species, *C. tomasinianus*, which seeds and spreads rapidly, almost becoming a weed in some gardens. It flowers in late winter or very early spring, painting the grass a delicate lilac and mauve. There are lovely deeper forms that have been selected and named, such as 'Barr's Purple', 'Taplow Ruby' and 'Whitewell Purple'. These are, of course, more expensive, but I particularly like to mix a few of these deeper tones of reddish-purple and lilac-purple with the paler type. Remember that full sun is essential if crocuses are to open their flowers and give the best effect.

Tulipomania

I have always suffered from Tulipomania. I love tulips of every variety, from the gay early bedders such as 'Keizerskroon', a gaudy scarlet, deeply edged with gold, and the elegant species such as the Lady Tulip (*Tulipa clusiana*), with small pointed buds of white, striped pink, to the large Paeony-flowered doubles, so superb for flower-decorations, the exquisitely graceful Lily-flowered singles, and the traditional goblet-shaped Darwins and Cottage tulips. The problem is to

select the right type for the role it is to fulfil and then to blend the colours with their surroundings. The large bulb-houses offer a bewildering range, including old favourites such as the salmon-rose 'Clara Butt', the lilac-mauve 'Rev. Ewbank' or the sulphur-yellow 'Niphetos' on the one hand, and novelties like the ever-increasing range of brilliant hybrids derived from *T. fosteriana* and *greigii* on the other.

One of the endearing things about tulips is the fact that they change so much and so quickly, whether in the garden or in a vase. They open and shut, twist and turn, and change colour, perhaps deepening or paling, as they develop, as every flower-arranger has discovered. This is part of their special charm, as is the enormous range of colours, the subtle blendings, and the stipplings and shadings. The species are particularly attractive in the garden, as so many of them open flat, like a daisy, with the sun, losing their familiar cup-shaped form, only to close up tight again as shadows fall.

The charming wild species are appropriate for the rock-garden or pockets in shrubberies. Of these, the Water-lily Tulip, *Tulipa kaufmanniana*, is perhaps the favourite, with its unusual shape and rich reddish markings on the outside, in contrast to the clear creamy-white or yellow on the inside. There are many hybrids of it, as the result of crosses, which vary in colour and size, but all have the marked characteristics of *T. kaufmanniana*. These flower in mid-spring.

Another favourite is *Tulipa chrysantha (T. stellata chrysantha)*, a Himalayan species six to nine inches tall, which flowers in April. The three outer petals are flushed on the outside with carmine and rose, while the inner surfaces are a clear butter-yellow. The multiple-flowered *T. tarda (dasystemon)* has special charm, bearing on six-inch stems as many as four to six star-like flowers in early spring. The outsides of the petals are flushed with yellowish-green and purple, while the insides are bright yellow with pure white tips. In bright sun this tulip has a luminous quality.

I am always amused by people who ask me what tulips to grow. The answer is difficult; there are questions of season, type, shape and colour to take into account. Moreover, we all have our likes and dislikes, some of mine being very strong. Gardeners are lucky today, as they have access to flower-shows, trial-grounds, parks, botanical gardens, nurseries and an increasing number of the better private gardens which, when at their best are open for different causes. Here they can observe at first hand an almost complete range of plants without relying entirely on catalogues, which, though good on the whole, are often over-enthusiastic about new varieties, which may not necessarily be improvements on older ones. Catalogues don't mean to mislead, but descriptions of colour and shadings

Chionodoxas and Kaufmaniana hybrid tulips are enchanting in their subtle colouring,
which is enhanced by the grey of the paving stones. The bulbs like
the sharp drainage of the foundations.

are difficult, as we all tend to see colours slightly differently.

For dazzling brilliance what can equal the oriental scarlet 'Madame Lefeber' ('Holland's Glory'), the brilliance of which puts to shame the guardsman's scarlet tunic, the lacquered gleam of the dwarf 'Red Riding Hood', with its black anthers and the dusky base to the petals, or the huge and equally fiery blooms of 'General Eisenhower', borne on stately stems over two feet in height? Colours such as these must be treated with reverence, as they will kill more subtle colours which may be around them. They are best in pockets on the rock-garden, where they are isolated among the grey stones, or are equally effective in groups in shrubberies or mixed borders where they can have full honour.

For the lover of strong colour, *T. praestans* takes some beating. Only about six inches high, with two to four flowers on a stem, it is a species of unrivalled brilliance, with its uncompromising orange-scarlet above distinctive foliage of apple-green, edged with dark red. It is early-flowering, often opening at the end of March or early April. Again, it should be isolated because of its strident colour.

But the fun of planting tulips is the reverse of this principle of isolation. Instead of segregating varieties, there is the art of blending the pinks and mauves, the blues and yellows, into ravishing rainbows. Tulips, planted on a very generous scale in public parks and squares throughout the country, furnish good examples of effective mass planting. Here, by careful juxtaposition, wonderful palettes of colour are achieved. Some individual flowers are already subtle blends or contrasts of colour and we have the extraordinary striped and stippled Bybloemens and Bizarres. These are most effective when planted with a tulip that picks up the base-colour of creamy-yellow or purple-black as a foil to accentuate the markings. Some firms offer 'Black Boy', a mahogany ground with veining and flashes of gold; 'Absalon', a bright yellow flamed and feathered with mahogany; or the fine heavy-textured 'American Flag', a rosy-red, overlaid with white striping. Others offer mixtures which will give the flower-arranger a scope undreamed of if bulbs are grown in quantity for cutting.

Similarly, Parrot tulips are useful for the same purpose, but to my mind are less satisfactory as good garden plants, as they are heavy-headed and usually require staking. The twisted, crested petals often have a base-rib of green, which gradually fades to rose, orange or purple, depending on the variety. 'Fantasy' is the best known, and how enchanting it is, with its green background, gradually reduced as the bright pink works ever deeper towards the centre of the petals until only faint green ribs and streaks remain. Mean-

Dwarf tulip species, such as *Tulipa tarda*, with its clusters of yellow and greenish-purple flowers on six-inch stems, are real treasures.

while the petals expand wider and wider until the open flower is almost flat, with its white centre margined with blue. 'Firebird' is a scarlet-red form of 'Fantasy' with attractive green cresting. One of the best is 'Blue Parrot'. This has the merits of great vigour of constitution combined with strong stems and exceptionally large flowers, even for a Parrot tulip. It is a curious blend of lavender and mauve with streaks of pale green. 'Orange Favourite' is arresting, its brilliant orange being touched with clear green; better still, it is scented. There are many other varieties in a range of colours which include white, yellow ('Sunshine Gold' and 'Texas Gold') and deep maroon (the so-called 'Black Parrot').

One other type must be mentioned, again with the enthusiasts for flower-decoration in mind – the green-flowered tulips, developed from *T. viridiflora*. One of the loveliest is *T. viridiflora praecox*. It is an extraordinary combination of greens – a strong green outside with a yellow, lime-green inside. The wonderfully frilled flowers have a strange twist to the petals, rather like a flame. They are far from cheap but well worth the cost.

May-flowering tulips with drifts of blue and pink forget-me-nots and herbaceous plants are typical of informal planting in a country garden.

'Artist' combines green with soft purple and rose on the outside of the petals and within a subtle shading of green to apricot and rose. Again, the petals are twisted and rather tapered, so that the flowers have a remarkable feeling of rhythm. 'Greenland' is a remarkable flower, characterized by a blaze of true green in the centre of each petal outlined with yellowish-green, lilac and pink. These last two varieties are much cheaper.

The dwarf pale yellow *Tulipa batalinii* has pointed petals and lovely long tapered leaves. Its variety, 'Bronze Charm' has warm yellow flowers flushed with rich reddish brown. Both grow well in light soil. They are treasures suited to the rock-garden, or, better still, to a raised bed where their delicacy and refinement are nearer eye-level.

The early singles and doubles and May-flowering Cottage and Darwin types are so well known that I can pass over them, except to say that I still think that the Darwin 'Sweet Harmony', with its beautifully shaped butter-yellow flowers paling to silvery-white at the margins, and the clear salmon-pink globular flowers of 'Queen of Bartigons' are as satisfactory as any tulips I know. They are excellent for garden decoration as well as for cutting, as they are vigorous and sturdy.

Lily-flowering tulips have a special appeal, being less rigid, with their subtly recurved petals forming a taller, narrower flower than the goblets and chalices of other tulips. They are perhaps a little earlier than the Darwins, but all are May-flowering. Their unusual grace and elegance make them ideal in the house or in clumps or drifts in borders and shrubberies, though perhaps they are less suitable for formal bedding. I am particularly fond of 'China Pink' and the deeper pink 'Mariette', planted in association with the reddish-purple 'Capt. Fryatt'. There are good yellows, including 'Ellen Willmott', 'Golden Duchess', 'Philemon', and 'Yellow Marvel'. Good whites include 'White Duchess', 'Picotee', white edged with a tinge of pink, and 'White Triumphator'.

For rich, dark colours there are, of course, Darwins such as 'La Tulipe Noire', 'Queen of the Night' and 'Black Swan', and the neglected Breeder Tulips which provide wonderful deep colour-notes, rather like Wagnerian music. A clump or two is the perfect foil for brighter, lighter colours. These tulips feature copper, bronze, purple and mahogany tones, sometimes with orange, straw-yellow or crimson flushes. 'Indian Chief' (mahogany-brown suffused with purple), 'Southern Cross' (straw-yellow shaded bronze) and 'Louis XIV' (deep purple flushed with golden-bronze suffused lilac), all large-sized on very sturdy stems, should excite flower-arrangers and gardeners alike to investigate other lovely varieties of the Breeder group.

Tulips should not be planted until the latter part of October or November, and they may be planted even as late as December in an open winter. In other words, the planting season of daffodils and tulips is nicely staggered, as the former should be planted in September and October. Tulips are sun-lovers and tolerant as to soil, so gardeners on chalk need have no fears. Moreover, success with tulips is generally assured if good clean bulbs are obtained and the dreaded Tulip Fire *(Botrytis tulipae)* is not already present in the soil.

Tulip Fire is serious in that it spreads rapidly and infected bulbs should be destroyed. The spores fall into the soil and the ground is subsequently infected, making it impossible to grow tulips on the same soil for a number of years. In many gardens, as a result of Tulip Fire, schemes involving tulips have had to be altered, the tulip-garden becoming a rose-garden, a spring-garden or an iris-garden. Soil in tulip-beds can be changed, but this, of course, is a big undertaking. I don't want to labour this danger, but there is always the temptation to say to oneself that although there was trouble last year, perhaps with new bulbs and better weather, conditions will be different this season. The answer is that they probably won't be. Change of location, late planting, mulching the ground in the spring, and good stocks of healthy bulbs are important factors for success. Several bulb firms recommend a non-poisonous powder called Botrilex, which they advocate for dusting bulbs before planting to help combat tulip fire.

Bulbs must be protected from moles, which often tunnel through newly prepared beds, followed in turn by field-mice, which nibble the delectable plump bulbs. Every means in the way of traps and deterrents should be used where mice or moles are prevalent. Camphor-balls or napthalene-flakes placed near the bulbs at planting time are said to be effective by some people, though scorned by others. When I gardened in America, field-mice played havoc with the tulips. I used to love Darwin and May-flowering tulips in shades of pink, pale yellow and purple and they were so much a feature, with lilacs, blue *Phlox divaricata* and deep purple and mauve violas, that I made baskets of small, square wire mesh in which the bulbs were planted and these were staggered through the borders. It was a great labour, but the field-mice were defeated.

Erythroniums and Camassias

Perhaps you have procrastinated for a long time about trying a new plant, as I have done for the last few years about erythroniums. There are few more rewarding flowers when established in colonies.

The tubers of erythroniums are best planted in early autumn before they dry out. If dried ones are purchased, plant them immediately they arrive. Sometimes pot-grown plants can be obtained, but supplies of these are very limited. Plant the tubers about three inches deep and they will find their own level. I remember when I was a boy, trying to dig up *E. americanum*, a pale yellow species with mottled leaves, which grew prolifically under trees on a shady lawn where we did not want them, so that I could move them to my newly-made rock-garden. To my surprise and annoyance, the treasured roots were as much as nine inches to a foot down, joined to the flower by a long, very fragile, thin, white stem that invariably broke.

The European *E. dens-canis*, commonly known as Dog's-tooth Violet, is a charmer for any well-drained soil in sun or light shade. Alkaline soils should be well laced with leaf-mould or peat. The marbled leaves and delicate recurved petals of the single nodding flowers in late March and April have a subtle grace that makes them ideal for pockets on the rock-garden or for naturalizing in the woodland garden in light shade. Colours range from purplish rose to white and pink. 'Rose Queen' is a clear pink, 'Congo' a rosy-purple, and whites are listed variously as 'Blanca', 'Album' and 'Snowflake'.

Then there are our fine native species. I think my favourite is the Californian *E. tuolumnense*, which has yellowish-green mottled leaves and usually bears several golden-yellow flowers on twelve-inch stems. This plant requires plenty of leaf-mould and a dampish, semi-shaded position. It tends to increase freely by offsets in rich soil in semi-shade. An even larger and perhaps finer, clear yellow is the hybrid of it, known

The airy grace of Erythronium 'White Beauty' is effective for shady pockets on the rock garden or for broad drifts in light woodland.

Camassia esculenta with its eighteen-inch spikes of rich blue flowers is an unusual May-flowering bulb for semi-shady positions.

as 'Pagoda'. This is still scarce and hence rather expensive. Another lovely erythronium of West Coast origin is *E. revolutum*, which is a rose-pink with mottled leaves, from which it gets the name Trout Lily. There are various lovely hybrid erythroniums, including 'White Beauty', with widely flaring white petals; it is a welcome addition to any woodland garden. Erythroniums are also effective in pockets on the rock-garden where special conditions can be provided, and they are particularly lovely when seen at eye level or from below.

Another American favourite of mine, and a very neglected one, is worth mentioning. This is the *Camassia*, a liliaceous bulbous genus, known by its Indian name Quamash. It is a little like a blue eremurus. There are various species, but the three showiest are

C. esculenta, with spikes of starry blue flowers on two-foot stems above a whorl of strap-like leaves, common to all species; the taller (three to four feet) *C. cusickii*, with flowers of a similar shape but of a paler lavender-blue as much as one and a half inches across; and *C. leichtlinii* (three to four feet) of stout sturdy growth and with broad-petalled flowers. The finest form is var. *atroviolacea (atrocaerulea)*, with very showy, brilliant blue flowers on huge spikes. All are relatively cheap.

Camassias should be planted about four inches deep and six inches apart in rich, moist soil. They will not flourish in light, sandy soil or in hot positions. I like to plant them in broad masses in dampish meadows or wild gardens in full sun or light dappled shade, where the clouds of blue spikes make a charming picture in June or early July. They can also be grown in shrubberies or borders were there is moist, heavy loam or even moderate clay. The bulbs do not seem to mind wet in winter months, so they can even be planted with safety in meadows along streams that overflow their banks.

Most gardens boast clumps of Grape Hyacinths. An oddity of which I am fond is the well-named Feather or Tassel Hyacinth, *Muscari comosum* var. *monstrosum*, known also as *M. plumosum*. Even the Latin name has something a little comic about it. The flowers appear in late May or June, rather later than most other species, and grow from twelve to fifteen inches tall. There are only sterile flowers, with feathery tufts of bluish-mauve, hence its vernacular name. Clumps of this strange bulb flourished in raised beds in our garden for a number of years and always came as a surprise, as they were so much later than other dwarf bulbs.

Splendid Grows the Lily

Certain lilies seem consistently good in a number of localities, and these merit special consideration. In both Scotland and Ireland I have been particularly struck by fine vigorous groups of orange, upright-facing lilies, which seemed to grow with ease; they appeared in quantities in cottage gardens, in beds or station platforms, and in suburban and town gardens. Often four or five houses in a row boasted the same lily, clearly indicating that bulbs had changed hands and settled down in their homes to grow as happily as in the garden from which they came. I tried to learn the name and source of one particularly good clone, but was always told that it was known only as the 'Orange Lily' and that it had come from another village nearby.

Now this state of affairs cheered me enormously, for this is exactly how I should like other types of lilies to behave. There is no doubt that *Lilium umbellatum* is a first-class garden plant. It establishes easily, flowers copiously and does not seem to be as prone to disease as are so many other lilies. This happy state of affairs, I hasten to add, is not true of many of the species, as they are difficult to establish. Fortunately a number of the splendid new hybrids raised in the Northwest are proving easier garden plants.

There are a number of good named clones of *L. umbellatum*, *grandiflorum* being one of the best. Its colour is a rich orange-red, and there is also *splendidum*, a brilliant deep vermilion. These fine lilies bloom in late June and July, depending on the area, and they like full sun or light shade. Soil should be well drained and rich, but avoid using fresh manure. Bone-meal worked into the soil at planting time is beneficial, and sieved leaf-mould or peat helps to make light soils

more retentive of moisture. Autumn-planting is preferable, but very early spring-planting is often necessary if the ground is frozen when the bulbs arrive. Plant at a depth of about five inches to the top of the bulb. This lily is stem-rooting, so it helps to top-dress established bulbs with sieved compost or leaf-mould. Staking is usually unnecessary as the sturdy vigorous stems rarely exceed two and a half to three feet in height.

I like their bright colours, particularly against a grey stone wall, the dark, glistening green of box, or the purple-green of yew. The blues of the hardy geraniums and the various campanulas, including *C. persicifolia* varieties, the rich purple of *C. glomerata*, and the taller *C. lactiflora* or *C. latiloba* are splendid foils. A foreground of blue nepeta is also effective. Another excellent foil for the bright orange-reds are any of the silvery-grey foliage plants, such as artemisias, *Stachys lanata*, *Senecio maritima* or clumps of hardy pinks. Blue delphiniums and the delicate mauve flowers of *Thalictrum dipterocarpum* or the fine form known as 'Hewitt's Double', with their charming glaucous foliage, are also effective with orange lilies.

Another remarkable lily is Jan de Graaff's outstanding hybrid clone, charmingly named 'Enchantment'. Of all recent introductions it seems the most reliable, as it thrives in gardens under very varied conditions, increasing rapidly and providing a spectacular July display of upright flowers of a vivid and unusual shade – a blend of red, orange and nasturtium-pink. For intensity of colour it has few equals. This lily stands up well to dry climates, as well as to those where there is heavy rainfall, and it has become one of the star turns in gardens throughout the country. Moreover, it has been established long enough in some gardens to prove its consistent performance. 'Enchantment' is easily increased from scales or from the bulbils which form in the leaf-axils.

Because of its vivid colouring, 'Enchantment' must be carefully placed. It is striking in shrubberies, especially with the glossy leaves of rhododendrons, camellias and grey foliage. I like the combination of it with broad clumps of the black-eyed, violent magenta *Geranium armenum*, but this is not a plant-association for everyone. If 'Enchantment' has a fault, it is the rather close bunching of the flower-heads, so that the shape of the individual flowers cannot be seen to the best advantage. I have been much struck with a similar lily called 'Firecrown'. It is a little more reddish in tone and the flowers are better spaced, but it remains to be seen whether it has the same fine constitution. 'Enchantment' should be planted in the same way and under similar conditions as those described for *Lilium umbellatum*. On heavy clay or wet soils, it often helps to raise the planting pockets a few inches about

Regales are surely the best-loved of the lilies, and one of the easiest to grow successfully in sun or semi-shade on well-drained soils.

the surrounding ground-level, and where slugs are prevalent to scatter the surface with coarse sand or sifted coal-ash.

For outdoor planting, the Madonna lily *(Lilium candidum)* should be ordered in late summer and if possible planted in the first half of September, so that the bulbs will make their autumn growth of basal leaves. This, the loveliest of white lilies and the lily of the Annunciation, should be planted so that the bulb is barely covered, in light well-drained soil, with or without lime, and in a hot sunny position. Candidums are not the easiest of lilies. They flourish in cottage gardens, where they grow undisturbed and unmolested, while they may languish where given every care. The combination of Madonna lilies with delphiniums is unforgettable and with roses or pinks they are equally lovely. Bulbs at one time were largely imported from France, but an increasing number are being grown here. Several grades are available, and every gardener with suitable positions for this enchanting, heavily fragrant, satiny-white, recurved lily should try a few bulbs. Be sure to plant your bulbs early and in full sun.

The Lily, Queen of Flowers

After each lily season, I find that I am more enthusiastic than ever about these stately flowers. A few well-placed clumps can transform a rather pedestrian garden into a place of magical charm. Lilies are unpredictable; some of them, fickle. Yet to most good gardeners certain varieties are indispensable.

Madonna lilies, *Lilium henryi, szovitzianum, martagon, tigrinum* and various of the *aurelianense* hybrids, are lime-tolerant and compensate in part for the many splendid lilies, including *L. auratum, speciosum, japonicum, rubellum* and a number of others, which insist on an acid soil, languishing and soon disappearing if they do not have it.

All lilies like good drainage. They do not like to grow with their feet in stagnant water or even in damp, although many of our lovely North-American species and their hybrids don't mind considerable moisture as long as they have drainage and therefore air at the roots. It is true that *L. canadense, pardalinum, superbum, philadelphicum* and *parryi* grow wild in moist positions in the United States, but often the places where they flourish, though wet in the growing and flowering seasons, are relatively dry as the summer progresses, in accordance with the North-American pattern.

Generally, rich well-drained garden soil is suitable for lilies. Fresh manure is murder. Very well-rotted dung is suitable, but use it well below the level of the bulb or as a top-dressing in winter. Bone-meal is excellent, as it cannot damage the bulbs and is available when and if the plant requires it. What lilies really like is plenty of leaf-mould, well rotted, so that it can be sieved to produce a loose, feathery mass to lighten the soil, retain moisture and feed the roots with its rich organic matter. Well-made compost is also ideal. If leaf-mould or compost are not available, peat is the next best thing, but be sure to dampen it before use.

Lilies deserve all the love and care we can lavish on them. Site them carefully, remembering that most of them are fond of light shade and grow well with the lower part of their stems shielded from the sun. On the other hand, at the Oregon Bulb Farm Mr Jan de Graaff, the most successful raiser of lilies in the world, grows hundreds of acres of lilies in full sun under field conditions.

Planting-depth is important. For lilies such as

194

regales, *L. davidii*, the Mid-Century Hybrids, including 'Enchantment', and both the 'Backhouse' and the 'Preston Hybrids', three to four inches is sufficient. If the soil is damp and heavy, it can be lightened with coarse sand or coal-ash. Often it is advisable to mound up the bed so that the bulbs are lifted above the sodden earth and there is better drainage. Planting on a slope is also advisable. If the soil is very heavy, it may be necessary to excavate it to a considerable depth and to put very coarse drainage-material at the bottom. Relatively few gardeners, however. will want to go to such lengths.

Among the good growers there is a generous choice. Fortunately, largely thanks to Mr de Graaff, lily bulbs are far less expensive than they used to be and good bulbs are readily available throughout the country. I consider *Lilium regale* indispensable for gardens. Its white trumpets, backed with purple and pink, are freely produced and heavily fragrant. Regales are lovely in the border with delphiniums, roses and any of the midsummer herbaceous flowers, such as paeonies and verbascums. The bulbs are relatively cheap and plentiful. Regales are also wonderful for large pots and tubs for penthouse or terrace gardens, as well as for country ones.

Besides the nasturtium-red 'Enchantment', which I have praised earlier, there are other Mid-Century Hybrids well worth growing, such as the clear yellow 'Destiny', with its brown markings, the crimson-red 'Fireflame', and the apricot-orange 'Harmony', with broad overlapping petals. These varieties flower in early or mid-July for a fairly long season and reach a height of three to four feet.

There are a few trumpets of exceptional merit. I particularly like 'Green Dragon' and 'Black Dragon', which are vigorous growers with heavy textured trumpets, shaded with the colouring from which they take their name. Under good conditions they will grow to four or five feet. 'Golden Clarion' is a wonderful yellow trumpet of fine form. The bulbs are often sold under the label 'Golden Clarion Strain'. These will have similar flowers but without complete uniformity as to colour, some being golden, others a soft lemon or primrose, often with a hint of green. These variations can be attractive and there are few finer lilies for cutting.

At lily shows and in gardens I always single out 'Limelight', a widely flaring trumpet of gleaming lime-yellow, flushed on the outside with green. Even lovelier, though similar, is 'Honeydew', perfectly named for its shape and a subtle harmony of mimosa-yellow and

Lilium martagon var. *album* naturalizes happily in a number of localities, in sun or semi-shade. It is lime-tolerant and hardy.

The Madonna Lily *(Lilium candidum)* is early, very fragrant and lime-tolerant, as well as being one of the most beautiful of the family.

Subtle Elegance of the New Gladioli

The enormous popularity of gladioli is understandable. They are the easiest and most reliable of summer bulbs and corms, growing in any reasonable soil, as long as there is good drainage and sunshine. Their merits as a cut flower are well known, and although some people find them stiff in habit and hence not to their liking, summer flowers in most houses would be very different without them. In recent years great strides have been made not only in the devolopment of new shades and colour harmonies, but in the size, type and shape of flower. For years, size was all too often the criterion, but now with modern conditions this has changed. Gardens are smaller and so are houses and apartments, with the result that smaller flowers are needed. Giant spikes of gladioli are out of scale in many modern rooms. Furthermore, increased interest in flower-arrangement has stimulated demand for smaller blooms of subtle colouring.

Gladioli fall into four groups. The earliest to flower are the graceful hybrids of *Gladiolus nanus*, which grow from eighteen to twenty-four inches tall, with strong wiry stems bearing graceful delicate flowers in a wide range of colours. The corms of these should be planted in the autumn in well-prepared, rich soil in a sheltered position at a depth of three inches. In cool areas a winter-mulch is advisable. Good varieties include 'Blushing Bride', a pure white flecked carmine; 'Nymph', of similar colouring; 'Charm', soft lilac; 'Peach Blossom', soft rose; 'The Bride', early pure white; and 'Spitfire', scarlet with purple blotches. Spring is not the season to plant this type, and I emphasize this fact because so many gardeners think that they are choosing these when they order the Butterfly-flowered varieties. Note that they are rather tender.

Butterfly gladioli are characterized by small flowers of delicate form with waved and crimped petals, which have an almost sculptural quality. They have become extremely popular for indoor decoration because of their scale, delicacy and colouring. There is a prevalent misconception that they are dwarf. This is not true; they grow to three feet or even a little more under good conditions. It is only in size of flower that they differ. One of the loveliest is 'Green Woodpecker', with slender tapered spikes of greenish buds which open to soft yellow flowers flushed with green and orchid and with an orchid-purple throat. 'Green Bird' has even greener buds and delicate greenish-yellow flowers, with a rosy flush and striking dark blue-black anthers. 'Elf', a delicate oyster-pink, is suffused at the base with pale yellow, while 'Gypsy Love' is a symphony of orange and carmine with a tongue of crimson on the central gold band of the lower petal. 'Donald Duck', which has been a prize-winner, has pale creamy-yellow

pale green. Then there is the dynamic 'Thunderbolt', with widely flared flat flowers of rich orange and apricot borne on five- to six-foot stems. 'Stardust' is another that pleases my fancy; it is one of a group of open, chalice-shaped lilies with the tips of the petals recurved, but to a lesser degree, rather like a fine *L. speciosum*. Ivory and white suffused with apricot at the centre sounds attractive, and it is. 'Bright Star' is a similar type with rather wavy white petals and a broad bright orange flash at the base of each petal, making a star of colour in the centre. All are late-flowering and heavily fragrant.

flowers, delicately flushed with pink at the throat and accented with a scarlet blotch. 'Atom' is scarlet with a crisp white edge, and 'Polar Beauty' presents a symphony of greenish-white and ivory with a clear green throat. It is these subtle shades coupled with elegance of form that makes these varieties eminently suited to floral displays. There are many other varieties from which to choose, as each firm has its own selected list.

Primulinus gladioli are another attractive group, well worth growing for their charming well-spaced flowers, which again are smaller than the large-flowered types. They grow from two to three feet tall and come in a wide range of colours. Good varieties include 'Candy', a pale apricot with a crimson throat and bold red splashes on the lower petals; 'Harmon', cyclamen-purple with neat, smooth florets; 'Pretoria', a deep apricot flushed red with a golden centre; and 'White City', a creamy-white fading to chalky-white with purple streaks and dark anthers. There are many others in a wide range of colours.

Best known of all are the large-flowered varieties, which are more widely grown than others. Like other types, they are easily grown if planted four to five inches deep in good, rich soil and kept well watered, particularly when flower-buds are forming. Certain catalogues indicate the period of flowering, so if a long season is desired, be sure to spread your choice over the early, middle and later varieties. The time of flowering can also be controlled to a degree by the time of planting. The wealth of colours of large-flowered varieties is unbelievable, and they are so generally listed in catalogues that there is no need for me to single out any particular varieties.

Summer-flowering Corms: an Essentially Orange Trio

As far as the gardener is concerned, the operative factor about the name of a plant is whether or not it can be found in a catalogue. *Montbretia* is a splendid case in point. The lovely South-African montbretias are superb plants for our gardens in late July and August and even into September in mild, moist climates. Books tell us that the garden hybrids grown under that name are really hybrids of *Crocosmia lutea* and *Crocosmia pottsii*. So far so good, but search the spring-bulb catalogues or some of the herbaceous ones for *Crocosmia*, on the fairly obvious assumption that the result of 'Smith' crossed 'Smith' is surely 'Smith'.

But that of *Crocosmia* crossed *Crocosmia* is listed in catalogues as *Montbretia*. It really is like a line from *Alice in Wonderland*. As so often happens, the old name has stuck and the botanists' change has not been generally accepted.

I have always valued montbretias in the garden. Because of their South African origin they are supposed to be on the tender side, but from experience they seem fairly tough. In colder parts of the country they can be generously mulched with peat, leaf mould or bracken, or the corms may be lifted and treated as gladioli or

Crocosmia masonorum, with its large panicles of upward-facing reddish-orange flowers, is proving hardier than was at first believed.

197

other tender bulbs. Montbretias are well suited to the mild climate of the coastal regions of Washington and Oregon. They grow best on light soils. They associate happily with rhododendrons, pernettyas and heathers. In dry sunny positions montbretias flower copiously, but the foliage withers and turns brown by late summer.

They are ideal as cut flowers as the delicate sprays of narrow freesia-like flowers have a natural grace that makes them easy to arrange, and they keep well, as even the smaller buds open in water. A little grooming each day makes a bouquet presentable for a long time. The foliage, sword-like, thin and of a clear light green, is attractive too. Clumps of it in the garden are lovely near the large leathery leaves of bergenias or the bold glaucous leaves of hostas. I love the contrast of form and colour. They are effective on a slope where they form a natural colony, as they do in so many West-Coast gardens, where the moist, peaty soil encourages them to spread to such a degree that they are truly invasive.

Montbretias should be planted in spring in well-prepared soil. A depth of three inches is sufficient, with a three- to five-inch interval. If they are happy they will, after several years, form a thick mass and after three or four years should be divided.

Colours vary from bright orange, certainly the most familiar, to clear yellow ('Rhinegold', 'Citronella'), orange-scarlet ('His Majesty'), pale yellow shaded peach-pink ('Lady Oxford'), bronze-gold with a maroon centre ('Comet'), and the small-flowered delicate pink ('Rosea'). Many gardeners prefer to grow mixed varieties and for them there is the fine large-flowered strain, 'Earlham Hybrids'. These will give a good range of harmonizing colours for cutting. Several of the bulb-houses offer mixtures.

For those who have room, *Curtonus paniculatus* is a dynamic plant. Most of us know it is *Antholyza*, which has earned it the endearing name of Aunt Lizzie, and in catalogues it is still generally listed under *Antholyza*. It is indeed a handsome plant, with its long pleated green leaves, often three to three and half feet tall, with branching flower-spikes rising above them in August and early September. The flower-heads themselves are strange in that the stems have a curious zig-zag habit unlike other flowers. Antholyzas were often used in large groups in old-fashioned borders. I like to plant them in big drifts in a shrubbery, so that their striking foliage is a foil to feathery textures or to broad, rounded leaves. They are handsome by a pool or lake with day-lilies, both for the contrast in the form of the flowers and in the spiky fanned foliage. Their habits are similar to montbretias and they spread rapidly. I like to save the seed-heads for large, dried winter-bouquets, as the curious formation of the flower-stem is amusing. Plant them in the spring at a depth of

three to four inches and they should increase rapidly.

One other flower fits conveniently into this group and that is the showiest of them all – the flame-coloured *Crocosmia masonorum*, and, believe it or not, you can look in catalogues for it under its own name. Graceful arching stems flatten out at the ends to display the long spikes of large upward-facing flowers. These are strangely exotic and their glowing reddish-orange is superb near the silver foliage of *Stachys lanata* or artemisias. Crocosmias are a little more tender than the other genera which I have mentioned and will require a generous mulch in zones where frost gets into the ground to any depth. In Zones 7 and below they should be lifted. A few sprays are very effective in a specimen vase as the poise of the spikes is particularly graceful. The flaming colour is similar to that of some nasturtiums and low bowls of the latter are striking in the same room, especially against a grey or blue background. Butterflies are fond of montbretias and crocosmias and this is always a further inducement.

Success with Hardy Cyclamen

Few flowers have greater charm than the hardy dwarf cyclamen which, like crocuses, have two major flowering seasons – late summer and autumn, and winter and spring. Cyclamen have a distinct advantage over crocuses in that their luxuriant foliage is as great a feature as the flowers and lasts over far longer periods. In fact, the autumn-flowering *C. neapolitanum* is a garden asset for the better part of the year, its variable foliage persisting through the winter and well into spring. In shadowy places the sheets of foliage marbled with white and silvery-grey enhance the darkest days of winter.

Cyclamen are not difficult to grow if certain rules are followed and if only the hardiest and easiest species are attempted on cold or difficult soils. Because of their Mediterranean origin (southern France, Italy, Greece, Turkey, the Greek Islands, etc.) they are splendid on alkaline soils. Although we think of these as warm mild climates, winters can be severe, especially at high altitudes. The altitude at which plants are collected has much to do with their hardiness and plants grown from seeds can often be acclimatized. Good drainage is essential, as they do not like their feet to be wet. They are definitely shade-lovers, growing obligingly under the canopies of forest trees or smaller flowering ones and even under yews and evergreen oaks. This is not as surprising as it may first appear, for cyclamen in their native habitats often grow in the heavy shade of olives, cork oaks and other evergreens. Hence they are particularly useful in shady gardens, where there are few plants suitable for ground-covers that take kindly to such heavy shade and dry conditions, except

Cyclamen neapolitanum start to flower in late July or August, often before the leaves appear, and continue to bloom well into autumn. The handsome foliage is a feature.

ivies and periwinkles. Of course, cyclamen take time to establish as ground-cover and they are relatively expensive unless raised from seeds.

Of the many species (there has been a good deal of regrouping recently) several are outstanding for their hardiness and their ability to give a good account of themselves each year. *Cyclamen neapolitanum* is the most reliable of the autumn-flowering group. The deliciously scented flowers appear in late summer or early autumn, followed soon after by the foliage. After a dry summer the first rains quickly stir them from summer sleep, and it is during the previous dormant period in mid-summer that they are best planted or moved, so that they settle down quickly in their new homes just as they are due to grow afresh. All species, whether spring or autumn-flowering, are best planted at this time, especially if not pot-grown.

What colours are the flowers of this lovely species and what are the characteristics of the foliage? You may well ask, for few plants show greater variations, particularly as to foliage. The graceful little flowers, with petals swept back like a rabbit's ears, resemble a cloud of hovering miniature shuttlecocks ranging in colour from white to deep rose-pink with subtle variations of mauve and pale pink. The leaves are more varied – round, oblong, or tapered like an arrow-head, with smooth or serrated margins and varying in colour from a uniform, polished deep green to silvery-green with complicated patterns of white marbling. It is this variation which makes naturalized colonies of cyclamen so fascinating and at times so perplexing.

Cyclamen europaeum is another excellent summer-flowering cyclamen, though a little more tender than *neopolitanum* and not suitable for cold districts. It has very fragrant flowers in profusion, ranging from pink to deep carmine.

Of the winter and spring-flowering species *C. orbiculatum* is the current name for a group which includes *C. atkinsii, coum* and *hiemale, C. vernum* and *C. ibericum* being considered as synonymous with *C. orbiculatum*. The flowering season will depend a great deal on the area and the actual planting positions and the season. The flowers are compact in form and are borne on short stems not more than a few inches long. Colours include white with shadings of pink or purple, deep reddish-magenta, reddish-purple, pink and mauve. Clumps or large drifts of this charming dwarf species associate happily with the white of Christmas roses *(Helleborus niger), Iris reticulata*, snowdrops and other early bulbs, making pools of colour under the dull gold of witch-hazel *(Hamamelis)*, the bright pink of *Camellia* × *williamsii* or the rich rosy purple of *Rhododendron* 'Praecox'. Rather more tender and flowering later, in April, May and often into June, *C. repandum* has larger flowers with long twisted petals and a delicate fragrance. It needs a warm district if it is to be grown without protection, although, as so often happens, it has become acclimatized in gardens which might be thought too cold. When happy, it naturalizes freely, with an abundance of flowers and masses of marbled foliage.

Cyclamen can be grown from seeds, preferably sown the moment they are ripe, or from established corms. The latter are offered either in a dried state or plump and growing and, if obtainable, growing corms are certainly preferable, as they establish quickly, the dried ones often hanging fire for a year until they can make roots and new growth-buds or 'branches', as they are sometimes called. As it is from these branches that both leaves and flowers spring, it takes a long time for the corm to break into growth if these are rubbed off, damaged or withered.

The corms of *C. neapolitanum* are saucer-shaped and vary in size with age, old ones being as large as the saucer of a coffee-cup. Both the roots and the flowers spring from the top of the corm, which is flattened with a slight indentation or sunken area, the bottom being dome-shaped and rootless, like the cap of a mushroom. Be sure to plant cyclamen the right side up, reversing the usual procedure of planting with the rooting-area at the bottom. If planting is being done in woodland, the soil is probably satisfactory; otherwise the bed must be thoroughly prepared with plenty of fine leaf-mould (a little granulated peat mixed with good garden compost will serve if leaf-mould is not available). Bone-meal is an excellent long-term food. Remember, however, that cyclamen are surface-rooting, and deep preparation is not required if drainage is already satisfactory.

Shallow planting is essential, a depth of two to three inches being the maximum. Firm well and make sure that the birds do not disturb the freshly planted beds. Watering of newly planted corms hastens growth. Established plantings require little attention except an annual top-dressing with sieved leaf-mould or compost to feed the surface-roots and to make a good rooting-medium for the ripened seeds. The seeds of *C. neapolitanum* are borne in a large, round, crimson-purple capsule on the end of an amusing stem, coiled like a spring. Where conditions are favourable, cyclamen spread rapidly. Seeds can be sown in pans and the young plants later pricked out in boxes, prior to planting out. They are not easy to grow in city gardens or areas of high atmospheric pollution.

Cyclamen are effective in clumps at the front of shrubberies, in shady pockets on the rock-garden and as underplanting for shrubs or trees in places where they can grow unmolested by too thick herbage, although I have seen an orchard where *C. repandum* had naturalized in great drifts in the long grass under apple trees. They are, of course, one of the most delightful flowers for pans in the cool greenhouse, as visitors to alpine houses well known. I recently saw an excellent small collection in a private greenhouse on Long Island.

Colchicums and Autumn Crocuses

August is the time to order and plant the lovely autumn-flowering crocuses (Meadow Saffron) and colchicums, which make such a fine show in late summer and autumn. Similar in appearance, though not in size, colchicums have larger, more spectacular flowers, yet belong to different families. To the average gardener the most noticeable difference is in the foliage. Autumn crocuses have narrow, strap-shaped leaves which appear and die down in due course, like the foliage of their spring-flowered relatives; but not so colchicums, which in early spring produce stems with four or five broad gleaming green leaves as much as a foot long. These must be left to ripen and wither before they can be cut back in July. In the wild, on natural slopes and meadows, this does not matter, but in gardens it limits their usefulness as the large, coarse leaves are prominent, and though I rather like them when they are young, I find them a nuisance later on. As a result, colchicums may not be suited to the rock-garden or to prominent positions, such as the front of a border. They are lovely in grass or when used in bold groups in shrubberies or in drifts under old shrub-roses. I know one garden where they have been planted in broad clumps among autumn-flowering heathers, their bold goblet-shaped chalices of purple and amethyst harmonizing with the feathery pinks and mauves of *Erica cinerea* and *E. vagans*, the charming Cornish Heath.

Colchicums can also be grown in blocks or drifts in borders of flowers and herbs in the kitchen-garden or interplanted with narcissus to provide autumn colour. Crocuses are easier to use and are pretty when naturalized in grass, in clumps in the rock-garden, or in borders at the foot of walls. In fact, their uses are legion. As both these flowers have no foliage when in bloom, they look a little naked in bare earth until they are established, but this happens readily where they are left alone on reasonably well-drained soil. As crocuses and colchicums are native to the Mediterranean and the Middle East, they are lime-tolerant and also will flower in semi-shade, though I find them best in full sun.

Autumn crocuses seed freely and hence many varieties increase rapidly if left undisturbed, though light forking will distribute the small corms. Colchicums, on the other hand, grow from large fleshy tubers, and these would easily be damaged by forking.

Some of the best of the crocuses are the various forms of *C. speciosus*, which is a lovely, misty lavender-blue flower of good shape with darker lavender veining and in the centre golden anthers and feathery orange stigmata. Its variety *albus* has very beautiful silvery-white rounded petals, while var. *globosus* produces almost spherical, bluish-purple, delicately scented flowers very late in the season. 'Conqueror' is spectacular – a rounded well-formed violet-blue flower, accented by orange-gold stigmata. Other good ones are 'Cassiope', blue washed with silver, and 'Oxonian', a bright blue with a violet-blue exterior. The latter is a fine free-flowering variety, but rather more expensive. For those who want a few choice bulbs for the rock-garden, I recommend *C. karduchorum* and *C. medius*.

Autumn crocuses should be planted in August or early September at a depth not greater than three inches. Colchicums should be planted in August about two to three inches deep. They will flower on a window-sill without soil or water, but, of course, the bulb becomes expendable after flowering unless it is planted in the garden. This always seems a heartless procedure, but for the city-dweller it may afford amusement and interest to flower them indoors. Good species include *C. byzantinum (autumnale major)*, soft lilac flowers borne early and in great profusion; *autumnale roseum plenum*, late, double, rosy-mauve; *autumnale album*, fine white six inches tall, and *C. bornmuelleri*, enormous rose-lilac flowers with a large white central zone. There are a number of fine, large-flowered hybrids of *C. speciosum*, such as 'Lilac Wonder', 'The Giant', 'Autumn Queen' and 'Waterlily', a very large double-flowered lilac-pink of great beauty. Autumn crocuses are not expensive, but colchicums are a little dearer. Both are a good

investment, however, as they establish in most gardens, though I should point out that game birds find crocus-corms a delightful delicacy in country gardens and this may well prove a real hazard.

Nerines for Autumn Brilliance

In a late flowering season in favoured gardens two lovely South African bulbous plants often linger on in late autumn and in some gardens are even very late in commencing to flower. I refer to *Amaryllis belladonna* and *Nerine bowdenii*, both a little tender, but both highly desirable, if they can be given warm, sheltered positions. They are superb for cutting, and wonderful arrangements can be made with masses of them or with a few spikes or even one combined with foliage and perhaps other flowers.

As *Amaryllis belladonna* comes into flower rather earlier, let us consider it first. The sturdy stalks, often as much as two and a half feet tall, bear umbels of rose-coloured, trumpet-shaped flowers, each with six petal segments. The curious effect of the stems with swollen flower-buds thrusting through the bare earth under the silvery-grey of olive trees in Mediterranean gardens and then bursting into glorious sheets of pink is a sight not to be forgotten. On the island of Corfu lovely groups on lightly wooded slopes, where they have naturalized for years, appear with the first rains in early autumn or when urged on with liberal watering to start them into action. The rosy-pink flowers, slightly tinged with mauve, with their pale throats make a pleasing contrast with the rather deeper unopened buds.

Belladonna lilies are not fully hardy and should only be attempted without winter protection in mild southern climates. The selection of the planting position is important. They do particularly well at the base of a sunny south wall, where they can establish and grow for some years without disturbance. If the wall is a heated one, such as a house wall, or, better still, that of a greenhouse, the position is ideal. One friend of mine grows them at the base of her conservatory and they are charming when seen from the sitting-area within. Where very protected positions cannot be provided, a cloche in winter, particularly in areas of heavy rain-fall, or a few inches of coal-ash or a layer of dried leaves are useful. This will protect the rather tender leaves, which appear after the flower, as well as the large, fleshy bulbs.

The soil should be preferably a good sandy loam with adequate drainage enriched with leaf-mould and bone-meal. The latter is an ideal food for bulbs as it breaks down slowly and the bulbs absorb it in accordance with their needs. Don't use fine bone-flour, but a moderately coarse meal. The bulbs should be planted in early summer (June or the first half of July) about six

Of all the autumn-flowering bulbs. *Sternbergia lutea*, with its bright yellow, crocus-like flowers and bold strap-shaped leaves, is my favourite. It is of easy cultivation on well-drained soils.

inches deep. Let them establish and multiply. If you are lucky and they are happy, it may be necessary to divide them after about five years, when they may have become overcrowded and started to deteriorate in size. Best results can be expected after a hot, dry summer. In periods of prolonged summer drought it may be necessary to water them in late August to start them into growth. Liquid manure in some form is helpful when they have started to grow, but this is rarely necessary. Dried blood may also be used on established bulbs and a top-dressing of bone-meal and a little leaf-mould is a useful pick-me-up after flowering, especially on light soils.

Belladonna lilies are particularly attractive in association with grey foliage. They are charming in front of the slightly tender *Teucrium fruticans*, a silver-leaved, blue-flowered shrub which enjoys similar conditions. Artemisias, *Senecio (Cineraria) maritima*, *Senecio leucostachys*, *Stachys lanata* and similar plants are attractive in front of the border or in clumps. Belladonna lilies are

sold by some of the good bulb-merchants, but they will probably be listed in spring-bulb catalogues and not the autumn ones.

There are a number of fine nerines, both species and modern hybrids, for the cool greenhouse. A great deal has been done in the hybridization of these exquisite flowers, both in this country and in Great Britain. They are increasingly popular as they make a welcome change from chrysanthemums. Some have a distinct smell of chocolate. The glistening mauves, scarlets, rich purples and delicate shrimp-pinks, some with an iridescent quality like a sprinkling of gold-dust, are only suitable for the cool-house. For outdoor cultivation *Nerine bowdenii* is a reliable stand-by. The umbels of from six to twelve flowers are borne on sturdy stems. The petals, an even pink with a darker central streak, are delightfully reflexed. As cut flowers, they last a long time in water. Do not expect bulbs to flower the first season. They must become crowded.

Crinums are useful summer-flowering bulbs with

wide strap-shaped leaves and huge umbels of pink or white lily-shaped flowers. The best is *Crinum powellii*, hardy in Zone 7, in a warm position with a winter mulch.

One other late autumn-flowering bulb should claim our attention, the cheerful, yellow, crocus-like *Sternbergia lutea*, an enchanting flower which has the added charm of reproducing its heavy-textured golden chalices simultaneously with the dark green, strap-shaped leaves, so that it does not have the nakedness of autumn crocuses or colchicums. I shall never forget my excite-ment when I found it growing wild for the first time on a brilliant sunny September day in Greece. Its golden flowers seemed to catch and intensify the sunlight. Plant them five to six inches deep in late summer or early autumn in warm, sunny positions on light, well-drained soil. They are effective at the base of a sunny wall, in drifts at the front of borders or in sheltered pockets on rock-gardens or raised beds. They will not flower the first year, so once again be patient until the following fall.

There are spring-flowering colchicums, but the autumn-flowering ones are far more spectacular and useful in gardens. Colours include mauve, purple, lilac and white. There are also a few doubles.

12 Town Gardens

Solace for Town Gardeners

I have no doubt that the gardens of the future will inevitably be more closely associated with bricks and mortar. The pattern of urban life, the shortage of labour, the desire for gardens which provide attractive settings for our houses throughout the year, the availability of a large number of new techniques and materials, are all relevant factors. In many gardens, both private and public, the architecture and structural side is in the ascendancy. As areas of planting and grass become more restricted, the challenge of successful planting is the greater. I am always amazed by what remarkable results are achieved in town gardens with relatively little in the way of plants.

Small lawns are a doubtful blessing, especially in shaded gardens. I have seen some pretty sorry ones as a result of poor soil, heavy shade and drip from trees. Mowing is also a bind. White pebbles or gravel in the manner of French gardens make a practical surface and can be freshened up by raking. Edgings can be formal of clipped box or ivy, or plants in borders can be allowed to spill over the gravel. Paving of bricks, set in interesting patterns of herring-bone or basket weave, are even more practical. If paving is pointed, there is no weed problem. Leave a few pockets for blue campanulas, London Pride or pinks. A small graceful tree planted off centre at the back in the gravel or paved area is often very effective. I have used fruit trees, laburnum, birch and false acacia in this way. Those with delicate light foliage are preferable. A few rings of granite setts or dark pools of ivy or periwinkle under the tree is practical and it softens a large hard-surfaced area. Be sure the paving is laid with a proper fall so water does not collect.

The term 'patio' has become so popular and so misapplied that today, alas, it is seldon used in the true Spanish sense to describe 'a court of a house: an inner court open to the sky in a Spanish and Spanish-American house'. It has come to be used for any back-yard, terrace or small garden adjoining a house. This is, of course, a wrong application of the term, but it has been generally accepted by the gardening and architectural press.

Our cities and towns are full of pretty, small gardens where quite enchanting results have been achieved with attractively laid paving, narrow borders, and a few tubs, urns or boxes of flowers. Plants for a border against a wall must be carefully chosen to create the right effect and to grow with abandon, either to soften or to accentuate the architectural features. If there can be but one or two roses, we must weigh their habit, length of blooming season, freedom of flower, fragrance, colour and ease of cultivation. For example, 'Albertine' is very vigorous, with fragrant, salmon-pink flowers shaded carmine and fine lustrous dark foliage, but it tends to be early with a very short blooming period, while 'New Dawn' is a fragrant, perpetual-flowering, soft silvery-pink with clean foliage. Then there is 'Mermaid', that fragrant, single, luminous yellow climber with fine, almost evergreen foliage and an extremely long flowering season. In fact, I have picked blooms both in early summer and autumn. It needs little pruning and a warm sheltered aspect as it is somewhat tender, though, strangely enough, it will flower on a north wall. It is a difficult choice, as there are scores of others.

More excellent climbers for walls, either in cities or towns, include *Vitis coignetiae*, vigorous and bold-leaved, or the charming self-clinging *Vitis henryana*, with amethyst leaves veined with silvery-grey; the fragrant white jasmine (*Jasminum officinale*) and the winter-flowering *Jasminum nudiflorum*, which might well have been called 'winter sunshine', and clematis in variety. The early *C. montana* types are useful, particularly the fine fragrant pink 'Elizabeth'. Honeysuckles are good, but subject to aphides, particularly if grown in full sun. *Hydrangea petiolaris* is ideal for a large shaded wall if the border is not too dry, while wistarias are lovely on south and west exposures. So my list grows.

Similarly with shrubs in the garden near the house, we must think of foliage as much as flowers. Evergreens such as mahonias, camellias and pieris are

Fragrant, old-fashioned single pinks grow happily in the paving of this town garden. They like an alkaline soil and good drainage.

205

effective for semi-shaded town gardens on lime-free soil. *Pittosporum tobira* (Zone 8), is evergreen with handsome foliage and fragrant creamy white flowers in late spring. *Fatsia japonica*, which recalls both the fig and the castor-oil plant, is my first choice for a large, bold evergreen. Among deciduous shrubs, the dwarf lilacs are wonderful, particularly the pinkish-mauve *Syringa microphylla superba* and *S. pallibiniana*. The former flowers abundantly in spring with intermittent fragrant trusses through the summer. *S. pallibiniana* is much dwarfer with neat tapered clusters of small flowers, in late spring only. Choose a mock orange that is not too coarse or rampant, if the garden is small. The species *P. microphyllus* is a small shrub of refinement with no equal for fragrance. 'Manteau d'Hermine' is a charmer with fragrant double flowers. Buddleias thrive in cities and attract butterflies.

For easy hardy herbaceous plants, I suggest some of the following for shade: Solomon's Seals, hostas in variety, bergenias, London Pride, the silver-patterned *Lamium maculatum*, ferns and, of course, lilies of the valley. In my old garden the last were almost a weed, as they came up through the cracks in the paving and spread into the lawn. For sun, plant pinks, colourful and clove-scented, with their cushions of silvery-blue foliage; bearded irises, both for their spiky foliage and scented flowers, and all the lovely grey foliage plants, even if some of them suffer in foggy winters. I like to use grey and silver foliage as the equivalent of flowers in a green setting. Don't forget a few lilies, whether in borders or in tubs or pots.

Good Soil for Urban Gardens

The plight of the town gardener who contends with difficult odds and is defeated because he is either too ambitious or too unrealistic is a familiar one. I have enormous sympathy for the town gardener, whether he lives in New York or in the numerous other cities and large towns throughout the United States. His problems are many and often not easy of solution. Newly acquired properties may have all the horrors, which include poor, exhausted soil, crumbling walls corroded with soot and time, swarms of snails, aphis, wood-lice and other insect pests, poor drainage, and an inheritance of doubtfully desirable plants, such as berberis, forsythia that does not flower, an excess of privet, and probably spotted aucubas, a particular hate of mine, which always look as if the painters had forgotten to cover the shrubs with dust-sheets. There are other problems, such as lack of sunshine, but that isn't as serious, for after all, as I have tried to show earlier on,

Hardy ferns such as *Polystichum angulare plumosum* enhance town gardens, as many of them are shade-lovers and are easy to grow in dry or damp positions.

there are lots of good shade-loving plants that can give a charming effect. Marauding cats and dogs are another very real challenge.

Soil is certainly a major problem. In old gardens it is usually exhausted and poor, while in new ones it may be worthless sub-soil or even rubble. At some time or other you have probably been advised to change the soil. This is armchair advice, which is easy to give and sound if feasible, but for most of us there are the practical considerations of time, labour and money. The prospect of carrying sacks or buckets of soil back and forth, all too often through the house itself – up steps, down again and possibly up steps again – fills us with a sense of futility before we start. Moreover, it is very expensive if it is done by outside labour. Even more heartbreaking, I have known cases where, after it was done, the new soil was found to be a doubtful improvement on the old.

Poor soil should be changed if possible, but if this is impractical the existing soil must be revitalized and restored to good health. The problem of manure at once raises its head. I am very 'pro' organic manures. Nature, after all, managed without inorganic ones for centuries, and well-rotted manure has no real substitute. However, we are today faced with the difficulty of procurement, the problems of storage in confined spaces, and expense. What town gardens require most urgently is humus in large quantities. In nature there is the accumulation of falling leaves, the withered herbage and the natural dung in the pastures and grazing slopes. In town gardens all extra potential humus is removed of necessity when the garden is tidied up. How then can we best provide it? There are a number of ways. Garden compost is wonderful stuff. In our old town garden we had three compost piles that were used in rotation. I used to delight in planting tulips in a relatively impoverished border, which I had made up with crumbly, black, sweet-smelling compost, prepared the previous autumn with leaves, lawn-mawings, coarse herbage, all the vegetable and fruit-parings from the kitchen (never fat in any form) and now and then a few spadefuls of already mature compost to impregnate the new heap with bacteria and sometimes an activator to hasten results and a sprinkling of lime. Time had done the rest. It made a lovely compost when well forked into the soil and the tulips sank gratefully into its depth. I also used a liberal sprinkling of coarse bone-meal and some granulated peat at planting time. My plea is to make compost if it is possible to do so, but often, alas there is not room in small gardens.

A good source of enrichment is spent mushroom compost. This is made up with a bulk of horse-manure and often with a lesser proportion of poultry-manure, which is more powerful. These are mixed with peat

Hosta crispula, with its bold green leaves margined with white, is one of the many good species suitable for shaded town gardens.

and chalk to form an open compost. After mushrooms have been grown for a few months the compost is treated and matured before being sold. I have used it with success, as it both feeds the soil and builds up its humus content. There has long been a controversy over the merits of sawdust. There is no doubt that it is better if well aged and a little depends on the variety of tree from which it comes. After long trials it is established that sawdust improves soil texture, adds to the moisture retentive properties of light soils and is useful as a mulch to suppress weeds. There are also a number of excellent organic composts made from dehydrated farm-, stable- and poultry-manure, bulked with peat or humus in other forms and impregnated with other vital foods. These are clean to handle, concentrated, and a great asset to the town gardener.

Peat in its various forms is another easy source of humus. It lightens heavy soil and improves light sandy ones in a miraculous way. Though peat is not a plant food, it retains moisture, and as plants assimilate food in solution, the benefits of peat are obvious. For use as

Regale lilies grow outside the windows of a house in town. They are ideal for cultivation in tubs or pots, if watered regularly and fed to encourage vigorous growth.

a soil-conditioner, granulated or sedge-peat is ideal, although peat in different forms is useful for other garden purposes. It can be purchased in small quantities, but it is much more economical if bought in units of fifty-six pounds, or even by the hundredweight. Peat is clean, easy to apply and does not deteriorate when stored. I like to mix it with compost, or to use it by itself. With bone-meal, hoof and horn and possibly a balanced fertilizer, peat makes an ideal conditioner. The former should be used at the rate of about three ounces to the square yard, the amount of peat depending on the nature of the soil and your purse. In my old garden I used large quantities as a mulch, and when planting trees and shrubs, I worked it through the roots, especially when the ground was wet or heavy. Bracken peat is much coarser, and I do not recommend it for town gardens, although it is ideal for rhododendrons, azaleas and acid-loving plants.

A third source of humus is hop-manure, or spent hops, if you are lucky enough to live near a brewery and can obtain them. Hop-manure is made by partially dehydrating the spent hops and impregnating them with certain elements. Hop-manure is a useful source of nitrogen, phosphoric acid and potash. Again, it is easy and clean to use and comes in various quantities, ranging from about seven pounds to a hundredweight. I have used both natural spent hops and hop-manure with good results. Hungry, impoverished soil can absorb a surprising amount of hops, or, for that matter, of peat or manure. The best source of humus is leaf-mould, which I like to collect in sacks in the country. If you are flush or want to ask for a present, leaf-mould is obtainable at a price. Bulbs and most plants love it and town gardens benefit particularly. Leaves should be composted, if possible, and the country property should provide some leaf-mould or compost, but town gardens may not.

If drainage is poor, first check to see that all drains and down-pipes are functioning properly. I was told recently that nothing would grow in a certain border. When I investigated, the reason was no secret. The overflow from a storage tank was dripping steadily on to the shrub border below and had been doing so for weeks. In our old garden, unless drains were cleared

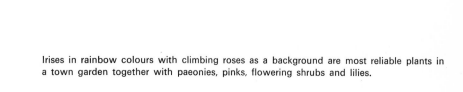

Irises in rainbow colours with climbing roses as a background are most reliable plants in a town garden together with paeonies, pinks, flowering shrubs and lilies.

in autumn of leaves, certain borders became water-logged with seepage. When soil is heavy it can be lightened with sharp sand, coke, coarse coal-ash and by the application of seaweed derivatives which help to improve the structure of heavy clay and to recondition soils generally by increasing the mineral content as well as trace elements.

I have dealt with humus and soil structure in some detail, as they are vital to the success of gardens, particularly urban ones.

Gardening in Pots and Containers

Of great importance, particularly in town gardens, is the use of containers, a term I use to cover all those pots, tubs, vases, urns and boxes which are used for plants. In small paved areas remarkable things can be done with a few flower-tubs and pots. Similarly, on terraces, roof-gardens, in public squares and even in those dreary tarmac stretches between the wings of the old-fashioned isolation hospitals, large tubs or concrete containers are extremely effective. Containers are increasingly widely used as more and more garden areas are paved to eliminate mowing and for practical purposes. Where there is concentration of use, small areas of grass cannot survive. Again scale is paramount. Incidentally, I mourn the all-too-rapid passing of the old type of wood beer-barrel, the source of so many plant-tubs.

Even in country gardens we use vases or tubs to flank steps or gateways, to accentuate the edges of terraces or the corners of pools and in a variety of other positions. The real problem is the selection of suitable plants to fill them.

The most important aspect of any plant-container is the space available for the roots. Some urns and vases, while charming to look at, are impractical in this respect. A close second is the provision for drainage. A generous layer of crocks for drainage and a suitable compost are essential.

Wooden tubs can be either round or square, with vertical or sloping sides. The most durable are made of teak, and these should never be painted. Cedar also stands up well to the dampness of soil. Large square tubs with small knobs at the corners are ideal for orange and lemon trees and in colder areas for bays, clipped box, conifers and Portuguese laurels. These tubs were popular in old orangeries. These tubs must be made to order and this fact, coupled with the cost of teak, cedar or hard wood with a zinc liner, makes them expensive.

Plants grow well in clay pots and, to my mind, look better in them than in almost any other form of container. Italian terracotta lemon-pots are very effective and are now generally available. Terracotta has great charm, as it is an attractive colour and well modelled. It is not cheap, but this is partly explained by the cost of packing and transport. Today there are a number of containers manufactured from cement, clay and reconstituted stone, so that almost every purse is catered for. A recent development is the use of fibre-glass to simulate lead, which has become very expensive. Reproductions, convincing in colour and finish, obviously cost a fraction of the price of eighteenth-century lead ornaments. Actually, when urns or boxes are filled with flowers, one does not stop to think if they are lead or not. One assumes they are. These fibre-glass containers are light in weight, strong and durable and have no bad effects on plants.

Planting can be seasonal or permanent. Seasonal planting is relatively easy as there is a wide choice, starting in early spring with the spring bulbs – hyacinths, daffodils and double early tulips. These are enchanting but of short duration. Herbaceous plants such as the double daisy (Bellis perennis), wall-flowers, myosotis, winter pansies and polyanthus give a far more lasting show in a good season and of course, can be combined with bulbs for an extra dash of colour. Summer in its turn brings a wealth of pelargoniums, including the scented-foliage types, the vivid flowered 'zonals', and ivy-leaved varieties, petunias, white tobacco-plants, heliotropes, and a host of others.

Of a more permanent nature, but requiring protection in cold climates, are such delightful plants as agapanthus, with their umbels of blue flowers and graceful curving strap-shaped leaves, fuchsias and verbenas. Lilies, such as the July-flowering Lilium regale, the most welcome of all lilies, and Lilium speciosum, a superb one for late summer or early autumn-flowering, are most effective. For beauty of shape, sweet scent and a useful flowering season, the lily has few equals. Moreover, cultivation in tubs provides the required drainage, food and isolation that seem to ensure success with lilies.

What some of us want even more than the foregoing are hardy shrubs that can be relied upon for a number of seasons. We want to fill our pots and tubs and then relax with some certainty. To achieve this end there are certain essentials. Containers, whether tubs, pots or vases, must be of sufficient size and have good drainage. Be sure to provide a generous layer of broken crock covered with coarse leaf or fibrous turf. Secondly, use the best commercial compost or other suitable soil to fill the containers so that there is long-term nourishment and perfect drainage. Thirdly, choose suitable plants. Many people seem to ignore one or more of these fundamental principles. For example, there are people who want to grow roses in tubs in heavy shade, hardly likely to prove a success, as

Tubs of *Lilium speciosum* such as these can be grown from a few bulbs, if the soil is good. Division of the bulbs is advisable when they become as crowded as this.

most roses are basically sun-lovers and need the maximum of ventilation and fresh air. Camellias like shelter, acid soil and semi-shade. Obviously these conditions should be provided.

Shrubby potentillas are attractive, particularly *P. arbuscula* which produces a profusion of clear, pale yellow flowers over a very long season and makes a lovely sprawling mat several feet or more in diameter. It is certainly one of the best for pots.

Camellias, rhododendrons and azaleas are well suited to tubs or large pots in shady areas, preferably when sheltered from cold winds. In milder districts (Zone 8) the fragrant evergreen *Pittosporum tobira* is a natural for pots or tubs and in Zone 9 lantanas and oleanders, both single and double, are good choices. They all require good drainage, acid soil rich in peat or leaf-mould, and adequate moisture.

One of the secrets of success with shrubs in pots or tubs is proper watering. Don't over-water, and on the other hand don't ever let tubs or pots dry out completely. Failure can often be traced to a prolonged period of neglect (holiday, illness, business, or even pure forgetfulness) and can explain why the buds of

camellias fall off when half-developed or why foliage withers or suddenly turns yellow. It must be remembered that shrubs and trees in a confined space exhaust the nourishment and that this must be replaced over the years by applications of bone-meal, weak liquid manure, dried blood or balanced fertilizers. Each spring it helps if the surface of the soil in the tub is scraped away and renewed with vigorous fresh compost or sieved leaf-mould.

Other good evergreens for large containers include box bushes, either pyramids or balls, bay trees, Portuguese laurels, yuccas, and the bold gleaming-leaved *Fatsia japonica,* so excellent in shade in London gardens, even under rigorous conditions. Frequent syringeing of the foliage of evergreens helps, but after a foggy winter I wash the individual leaves with a sponge or cloth to dislodge the sticky, sooty deposits that are untouched by a hose. This process is laborious, but with camellias and rhododendrons it pays double dividends, both in the appearance and in the health of the plant.

Other useful evergreens for large containers include well-budded skimmias, pernettyas, covered with a bounty of large pink, white and red berries, which will persist through the winter if carefully handled, sturdy plants of *Mahonia japonica*, and a particularly attractive free-flowering form of laurestinus *(Viburnum tinus)* known as 'Eve Price', with rather smaller, pointed leaves and a dense, compact habit. With ingenuity in combining foliage plants with different leaf-shapes, colours and textures, striking effects can be produced. Trailing ivies and periwinkles are useful to soften the sides of tubs or pots and can be left as part of the permanent planting.

Excellent subjects for tubs include agapanthus, hydrangeas, fuchsias, and in full sun, even roses can be grown successfully, but they are not fully satisfactory, being very dull when out of flower, and especially when bare in the winter.

Town gardeners should use fibre-glass and plastic boxes and containers when planning their spring and autumn planting. They have the great merit of being light and hence easy to lift and move. I have several black fibre-glass tubs made to resemble simple wooden ones (diameter sixteen inches, height eleven inches), which are filled with scented-leaved geraniums for summer and in autumn with skimmias, hyacinths and a few variegated ivies, the frosted silvery foliage making a bright splash against the black.

Remember, when setting out bedding-plants such as fuchsias, pelargoniums, petunias, Morning Glories or chrysanthemums, to be sure that the root-ball is moist before planting it. If you place a dry root-ball in the ground and then water, the moisture very often will not penetrate. I have often found bedding-plants that were badly discoloured, and soon traced this to be the cause. Be particularly careful if using plants in Jiffypots, Root-o-Pots or other similar types where the roots have penetrated the compressed peat or paper. It is essential that the root-ball is moist all the way through. If peat is worked into the soil at planting time, be sure that it, too, is moist. In tubs and boxes and in town gardens peat or garden compost increases the humus content of the soil, and improves water-retention properties.

Geraniums in Happy Clash

There are few plants more useful than the geranium, or for the sake of accuracy, the zonal *Pelargonium*, which is the correct botanical name of our old friend, the window-box geranium. What delightful plants they are, with their abundance of bright flowers, their rapid growth, their capacity to survive adversity, and their enormous variety, ranging from 'Gustav Emich', the splendid, semi-double, scarlet (Buckingham Palace) bedding-plant, to the lovely variegated ivy-leaved 'L'Élégante', with subtle, soft green leaves tinged

with white and purple and its flesh-coloured flowers with dark feathering. Each has its special use, both in the garden and as pot-plants for the terrace, patio or window. I am definitely a geranium-enthusiast and feel that many fascinating varieties, particularly the less familiar scented-leaved ones, are too often overlooked. Moreover, many gardeners don't use them to the best advantage or recognize sufficiently their great merit as cut flowers.

Many inexperienced gardeners are confused by the unfortunate misuse of the term *Geranium*, which is the correct botanical name for the hardy Crane's Bills such as *G. alpinum, pratense, endressii, armenum* and *sanguineum* (Bloody Crane's Bill). Pelargoniums unfortunately are only hardy in milder areas where there is relatively little frost, if any. Secondly, they are never blue in colour, unlike a number of hardy Crane's Bills. Pelargoniums revel in maximum sun and heat, whereas certain varieties of geraniums tolerate or even prefer shade and moist conditions, and are, in face, often woodland plants.

Zonal pelargoniums come in a very wide colour-range which includes whites, pinks, reds, purples and oranges, with subtle blendings, flashings and veinings. The flowers vary in shape and include singles, doubles and semi-doubles. In addition, many varieties have remarkable colouration of foliage, hence the name 'Zonals'. The variations from the usual green include zones of chocolate, yellow, red or even black, and leaf-margins of silver or gold. There are others, often called tricolours, which might just as well be named harlequins, or quadricolours. To this group I am less partial. Their rich tapestry foliage is the delight of those gardeners who like complicated bedding-schemes. I personally prefer to use a plant or two where accent of foliage is needed, particularly as pot-plants to lighten up an all-green corner. Another charming attribute of many pelargoniums is the rich scent of the foliage of certain species and hybrids. Nutmeg, lemon, rose, peppermint, orange and balsam are all represented.

The requirements of pelargoniums are relatively simple. Although their powers of survival are truly remarkable, they like to be well fed, and contrary to popular belief, don't like to be grown too dry. Good drainage and ample moisture are the best rules of thumb. As already hinted, they are sun-lovers, as the geranium-splashed houses of Florida, California and other mild states (Zone 9) bear witness. In the North pelargoniums are at their best in July and August and sometimes into September if it is a warm, dry one, while cherished pots in cottage windows gladden our hearts in the autumn, late winter and early spring. What pelargoniums don't like is too much damp, especially on heavy soils.

Today there is an enormous range of varieties from

which to choose. Alas, some of the loveliest do not stand up to outside conditions of wind and rain, although superb in the greenhouse or as pot-plants for the house. It is hard to draw fast rules as to the suitability of many, as those varieties which prove shy flowerers in a cold district may flower abundantly in warmer ones. Certain well-known varieties are of course, tried and true for bedding; others are definitely for the collector. Among the first group in the pink and salmon colour range are 'Queen of Denmark', 'Salmon Paul Crampel', 'The Speaker', 'Belvedere Glory', 'Mrs Lawrence' and 'King of Denmark'. 'Maxim Kovalesky' is certainly an outstanding clear orange; 'A. M. Mayne', 'Royal Purple' and 'Festiva Maxima' are good double purples, while 'Prince of Wales' is a splendid single; 'Queen of the Whites' is an outstanding single white, while 'Hermine' and 'Ryecroft White' are good double whites, with a constitution that will stand up to weather, although whites are not the most satisfactory in this respect. As for crimson and reds, there is again a choice; 'Paul Crampel' and 'Gustav Emich' need no introduction, and 'Double Henry Jacoby' is one of the darkest double reds for bedding.

The new Irene strain of geraniums, so successful in this country, mark a very real advance. They flower freely, stand up to weather, and have remarkable vigour. They are all semi-doubles unless noted. They include 'Salmon Irene', 'Dark Red Irene', the cerise-pink 'Electra' with a compact and very free-flowering habit, the vivid vermilion 'Irene', the carmine-crimson 'La Jolla', 'Modesty', a white tinged with flesh pink, 'Rose Irene' with a white eye, the light pink 'Party Dress', the brilliant scarlet 'Toyon', the deep coral 'Trulls Hatch', and the fully double 'Orange Fizz', to name a few. The First Lady varieties include 'Mamie', a vigorous, dark red; 'Eleanor', a mauve-pink with a large flowerhead; 'Bess', a clear salmon-pink; and 'Jacqueline', a crimson-scarlet on a compact plant. All are semi-double. Other good varieties include 'Inspiration', a semi-double creamy white flushed light salmon; 'Fanfare', a double salmon-apricot; and 'Radiance', a double salmon-red with a white centre.

As a small plant for a desk, dressing-table, a small flower-bed, trough or pot, few pelargoniums have more charm than 'Black Vesuvius', a well-named miniature with vermilion flowers, enhanced by almost black foliage. Then there is the charming 'Kewense', with delicate lacy flowers of intense crimson, and the salmon-pink *P. salmonea*, from which it is derived.

Of the scented-leaved pelargoniums the most decorative is the species *P. tomentosum*, graceful in its rather lax habit with beautiful velvety green leaves, soft and silky to touch, and smelling, when bruised, of strong peppermint.

Luxuriant Window-boxes for all Seasons

A pressing problem for the owner of window-boxes is the choice of plants to follow the fuchsias, pelargoniums, petunias and other summer plants. Boxes in winter too often look bare and unloved, even though they may presently be teeming with fragrant hyacinths, daffodils and early tulips. We all want something attractive to fill the gap. Evergreen plants are obviously an ideal solution, and they can be combined with dwarf bulbs to give a luxuriant effect, where the texture and form of foliage are as important as the colours.

First let us consider some of the orthodox spring-bedding plants. Polyanthus are an old stand-by and have the great merit of commencing to flower as soon as there is a little sunny weather in early spring, especially in sunny positions, and of continuing to flower for a long period. Another satisfactory feature is their tolerance of shade; they will grow in a north exposure with almost no direct light, but, of course, in this position they will not flower early. If possible, plant a few single or double early tulips among them. Dwarf daffodils are charming if used in a similar fashion. Hybrids of *Narcissus cyclamineus* and *N. triandrus*, are ideal (*see* p. 186). Large purple or yellow Dutch crocuses, followed by chionodoxas or blue scillas, are also attractive mixed with polyanthus in small window boxes, as they are right in scale. Polyanthus and the various bulbs can be planted in September in the North but later in milder districts. Be sure to use good moisture-retentive compost and to keep them well watered.

Wall-flowers are not ideal for window-boxes in cold areas and cities. They do not like the pollution of the atmosphere, and if the winter is severe, they tend to suffer. If the weather is mild, of course, the results are rather better. In country gardens and in sunny protected ones in towns and villages, wall-flowers can be charming, with their deliciously fragrant flowers and rich colouring. Forget-me-nots are not reliable in cold areas. I have tried them at various times, but with mixed results. They are charming in boxes interplanted with dwarf tulips. They should be wintered in frames or sheltered borders and planted out in spring. This goes for pansies and violas too. *Bellis perennis*, the dwarf daisy, is an excellent choice, with its profusion of gay pink, red and white flowers.

Periwinkles are effective in a window-box or garden-vase. The trailing green foliage, starred with blue, white or purple in spring, is charming, and early bulbs growing through this light cover have a splendid dark background. In an urn in our courtyard, for instance, we interplanted periwinkles with combinations of

Roman hyacinths, the charming dwarf Angel's Tears *(Narcissus triandrus)*, snowdrops, scillas and crocuses to ensure a succession. There are lots of other combinations, using chionodoxas, grape hyacinths, *Iris reticulata* or *I. histrioides*. These have such form and grace and such lovely colouring.

For a striking winter effect, dwarf hardy shrubs with evergreen foliage are invaluable. The large family of Veronicas *(Hebe)* offer a number of possibilities, including the glaucous silvery-blue of *V. pagei* and *V. darwiniana*, the rich olive-green of *V. anomala* and *V. subalpina*, with oval apple-green leaves and a nice, broad, low-growing habit. In nurseries and florists' shops various varieties are sold as small pot-plants for the charm of their foliage. Some of these would ultimately grow into large shrubs, but as the planting of window-boxes is only a short-term measure, some of these larger ones could be utilized for a year or two. Other good stand-bys are small plants of variegated varieties of *Elaeagnus pungens*, which include *aureo-variegata*, *simonii*, *maculuta* and *variegata*. Again, these would in time grow too large, but for a winter or two they lend a bright note, with their golden edgings or splashings. Ericas are also useful, but it must be remembered that only *Erica carnea* and *mediterranea* are lime-tolerant. The others require an acid compost. This is easy in the restricted confines of a window-box, vase or tub by the addition of liberal amounts of leaf-mould or peat. Varieties should be selected carefully for foliage as well as winter flower. *Erica carnea* varieties are ideal, as they flower in late winter or early spring. The problem will be to find plants large enough to make an immediate effect. This rather limits the choice to pot-plants, as nursery plants are often too small.

Euonymus is another genus offering broad-leaved evergreens with attractively coloured forms. *Euonymus japonica* has a number of variegated varieties, where silver and gold either rim or zone the leaves. Small, compact plants are striking in window-boxes. *Euonymus radicans* 'Silver Queen' is a good low shrub of recumbent habit with marked silver variegation. Other evergreens that can be used where solid effects are desired include box, holly, sarcococcas and even plants like compact lavenders and santolinas. Dwarf rhododendrons and pernettyas are effective for lime-free composts. There are also a number of conifers, either dwarf or larger ones in their young state, that are suitable.

If you want to plant mixed window boxes, vases or tubs, don't try to fill them with stock ordered from a nursery by mail. Go to your local gardening centre and select the material yourself. The groupings should be composed on the spot by measuring out the size of the box and standing the plants in their pots or balls of sacking side by side to achieve the desired effect. Take the plants home with you and fill the boxes at once. Boxes filled in this way may become very expensive, as you are buying young shrubs and not annuals, but this is counterbalanced by the fact that often large tubs, pots or boxes are being planted permanently for several years or more. Moreover, for those who also have gardens, either in town or country, it is possible later to use the shrubs in permanent shrub-borders. I know various gardens where this system is carried out with complete success.

The last but by no means the least satisfactory stand-by for window-boxes is ivy in some of its many forms. Charming boxes can be arranged with silver or golden variegated ivy or some of the various green ones. They drape themselves gracefully over the edge and can be interplanted with bulbs. I find that stone or lead urns planted with ivies are often far more effective than when filled with flowers. In certain types of gardens this simple permanent solution is so much happier than the usual burst of ivy-leaved geraniums. Select good, sturdy plants with side-shoots and avoid those with a long single stem. Be sure that the plants are acclimatized and have been hardened off to stand cold, as many ivies are grown under glass and will have spent their time in warm shops. Make it quite clear that you intend to use the plants outside if you are buying from a florist instead of a nursery.

Geraniums are perfect for tubs and window-boxes because of their abundance of flowers over a long season and the wide range of colours.

13 Lawns

Grass, God's Gift to Gardens

One of the greatest assets to the British gardener is the relative ease with which grass grows and is maintained. Anyone who has coped with the almost insuperable task of providing good turf in most parts of the United States will understand my use of the word 'ease'. Hot sun and dry weather are the problems.

Grass is generally more important than almost any other feature in our gardens, as it provides the perfect setting for trees, shrubs and flowers, and large areas can be maintained with comparative ease if certain routine procedures are followed. In very small gardens the suppression of all lawn may be desirable. In town gardens where there is insufficient sun, drip from trees, no home for the lawn-mower or no-one to mow, it is often possible to use paved or gravelled areas with combinations of bricks, cobbles or granite setts, to make small patio or courtyard gardens with loose spilling borders. In cottage gardens grass often gives way completely to vegetables and flowers. Better no grass than poor grass maintained by an uneven struggle.

The amount does not matter as much as the open sweep provided for mowing. For efficiency and for successful design, beware of small beds and, above all, of verges. Long ribbon-borders of shrubs, mixes plantings of herbaceous plants with roses, lavender, potentillas, phlomis and similar shrubs are practical and relatively easy to maintain. There is only the front of the border to be cut and edged. Fortunately the popularity of flower-beds in circles, squares, crescents and other geometric shapes has passed. Beware also of verges along paths, drives and terraces. If they are necessary, be sure they are wide enough to be easily mown. Where possible, eliminate them entirely. Loose flowering borders spilling over bricks, paving or gravel are far more delightful and practical than those bands of grass.

If plants encroach on the grass, it is difficult to mow and soon dies back. A flat edging of paving-stones or brick not less than eighteen inches wide along the front edge of a border is practical. Pinks, nepeta, thyme, *Stachys lanata* and rock roses *(Helianthemum)* will cover the stone quickly and the border will look wider and more effective. If the stones are properly laid so that the surface is even, one wheel of the mower can run along them. A similar mowing-stone is often incorporated at the foot of retaining walls.

I have an aversion to the practice of cutting back the turf next to a wall, hard-surfaced path or terrace. Gradually the turf is nibbled farther and farther back until there is a wide gulley. I have seen gardens where the gap has been widened through the years in an attempt to maintain a straight clean edge until it was as much as eight inches or a foot in width. These gaps – or horrors, as I choose to call them – are unnecessary, unattractive, at times dangerous and certainly not labour-saving, as they too must be weeded, edged and cared for.

There are excellent grass-clippers and cutters for verges and edges, but where turf abuts onto paving or brick, it is easy to take an old kitchen-knife and to run the blade along the edge of the stone, cutting off the flat growths nestling on the surface of the stone. The stems of grass come away neat and clean and no gap results. Turf abutting on to stone or a hard surface should be laid so that when it settles, the grass and paving are at the same level. To achieve this, the newly-laid turf should be about an inch 'proud' of the stone. There will be no high edge to cut and no turf to break down if it is stepped on by accident. It is attention to details such as these that makes a garden satisfying to the eye and easy to maintain.

Where a grass verge with a vertical edge is necessary along drives and gravel paths, there are tools to cope with the task, ranging from simple, inexpensive sheep-shears for those with strong backs who don't mind bending, to long-handled, dual-purpose shears, some with wheels. Like all tools and garden machines, you must suit the instrument to the particular job it is to perform, always keeping in mind the cost.

The famous chessmen in box in the topiary garden at Haseley Court in Oxfordshire are enhanced by the setting of smooth, well-kept lawns and the beds of silvery santolinas and lavenders.

The Lawn in Spring

March or early April is the time to start on lawn-renovation, much-needed after the long winter, but it is well to wait until frost and all traces of snow have vanished and the surface is not too wet and soggy. There is no doubt that turf has a bad time of it after an extreme winter, especially where piles of snow from paths and drives have been heaped upon the verges, or even more where pathways have been cleared across the lawns, exposing the grass to wear and extreme cold. I recall several gardens where areas cleared of snow have been heaved by frost three or four inches above the rest, so that there were raised paths running across the turf, though these settled down eventually.

First, a careful brushing with a besom, or raking

215

The even bands of expert mowing make a pattern on a lawn, but isolated specimen trees complicate mowing at the margins. It is advisable not to mow always in the same direction.

and light sacrifying with a flexible metal rake is necessary to remove the accumulated debris, and particularly moss. Make sure that gravel lifted with the snow from drives and paths has not been deposited on the lawns. If so, sweep it off carefully, as it is bad for the mower.

Next, the lawn should be rolled carefully to restore the surface, with a roller that is not too heavy. I always like to roll grass in two directions to level it out, just as I like to mow in different directions from time to time to improve the levels. Rolling should be followed by aerating, either by inserting the prongs of a round-tined fork at four- to five-inch intervals to a depth of at least three inches on small lawns, or with a mechanical aerator, of which there are various sizes and models to meet different requirements, on larger lawns and park areas. This operation, though laborious, pays dividends as it improves drainage and lets air in among the roots. It also is excellent on lawns badly infested with moss, which usually indicates poor drainage and im-

poverished soil, as healthy grass will suppress moss. A long wet season will obviously encourage it, but moss can also appear during a warm dry one. The first appearance of moss is a sign to heed and action should be taken at once before more of the grass is smothered.

Use either lawn-sand, which contains a mercury compound, or proprietary brand of moss-killer. Several of these are applied in liquid form and I usually find this the more satisfactory method. Apply either type in early fall or spring. Be sure not to exceed the prescribed strength. For a few weeks the lawn will be unsightly with dark, dead patches. Next rake or brush it to remove the dead moss and then feed it with a balanced lawn-fertilizer at the rate advised to encourage the growth of the grass.

Many lawns are hungry for humus, and if a dressing was not applied in autumn, a liberal one in spring of sieved compost, loam, fine peat, or a special lawn compost, does wonders. It is even possible to correct slight depressions or hollows by repeated applications

216

over the months when the grass is in vigorous growth. Where the turf is thin or worn, grass-seed can be scattered on the top-dressing, as it makes a good seed-bed. Apply seed at the rate of one to two ounces per square yard. Do not sow seed until the soil begins to warm up. After seeding, roll the areas lightly, or firm with a board or the back of a rake.

A generous feeding of established grass will be appreciated. Lawn-dressings fall into two general groups. There are the straight, balanced fertilizers and those with selective weed-killers added, so that a single application both fertilizes and eliminates the weeds at the same time. For early spring use or on lawns badly infested with weeds I prefer the straight fertilizer to induce healthy, vigorous growth and then to deal with the weeds as required in early summer. If the dual-purpose type is used, I cannot over-emphasize the importance of application on a still, windless day, as clouds of it can so easily be carried down-wind to beds and borders, Also, be careful if applying it on slopes, as there can be seepage to beds, borders and even hedges at the foot.

It is possible to make up your own fertilizer formula, if you know the particular deficiencies of the soil. This should contain a nitrogenous fertilizer, such as sulphate of ammonia, using half an ounce per square yard, and superphosphate in the form of bone-meal or super-phosphate itself at the rate of one ounce for the same basic unit.

The method of application is as important as the lawn-dressing. It is difficult to spread fertilizer evenly unless it is thoroughly mixed with a carrier such as sand or sieved soil. Granulated peat is not very satisfactory. The proportions should be from six to eight ounces of the carrier to one ounce of fertilizer. The dressing can be distributed by hand on a calm day, but for large areas a mechanical distributor is recommended, and in this case the carrier is not necessary. It is essential that the distribution should be even and does not exceed the prescribed rate of application, or scorched patches and uneven colour will result.

In cold northern areas with heavy falls of snow over the long winter months, lawns often suffer from serious invasions of different fungi, including *Fusarium nivale*, or 'Snow Mould', as it is commonly called. This can ruin the appearance of good turf, and unless action is taken it will continue to spread. Small patches several inches in diameter of light yellowish-brown appear first and these gradually change to greyish-white, steadily enlarging at the same time into wider and wider circles as the infection advances. With warm weather the activity slackens but the spores are embedded in the infected turf, ready to revive in the autumn with cooler weather.

Infected areas should be treated when first detected. The remedy is a mercurial fungicide, of which there are various products on the market. These are, of course, poisonous and must be used with care. They should be applied strictly in accordance with the manufacturers' instructions.

A good lawn can do much for even the simplest garden and care in early spring should make possible good turf throughout the summer. Mowing should not be rushed in spring. Let the grass establish itself. Set the mower so that the first several cuttings are not too close. Where creeping crab grass is a problem, a rotary mower is more effective than a roller type.

Be sure that the mower is in good order. If it is worn-out or not satisfactory for the job, inquire about a new one. Choose a mower that will do the job efficiently. If you need a motor-mower, by all means have one. For small areas they are a doubtful blessing. For large lawns they are indispensable. Select wisely and seek expert advice from reliable firms who stock a range of mowers and, if possible, test them. Price is an important factor. The most expensive is not necessarily the best, nor is the cheapest the greatest economy over the years. The advice of friends who have had experience with conditions and problems similar to your own is also helpful.

The Lawn in Autumn

Sometimes, as the result of an exceptionally warm and sunny October, grass will still be growing rapidly in November. In spite of your boast early in October that you were mowing for the last time, you have probably mowed several times since and will, in all probability, do so again. Be sure that the grass is reasonably tidy for winter, as it makes the raking of leaves and subsequent feeding and rolling so much easier. Moreover, if you are planting bulbs in lawns, rough-mown orchards and wild gardens, short grass is an enormous help. Lastly, if you are contemplating any renovation of worn or scruffy patches, mowing is an essential first step.

Autumn and winter are ideal for turfing, if there is no frost in the ground and it is not too wet. In an open winter, turfing may continue throughout the season. Turfing in spring is complicated by the danger of droughts, but if water is available and there is labour to carry out this operation regularly, reasonable success is assured. For the average gardener, who already has too much to do in spring, turfing is better treated as a late summer or autumn operation.

In wet seasons compaction of the soil is a serious problem on new or inadequately drained lawns. If grass is mown when wet and spongy or with too heavy a mower, the soil is gradually amalgamated with the subsoil. Air no longer penetrates to the fine hair-roots and, as the soil becomes increasingly waterlogged, they rot. Turning a heavy mower at the end of each run can wear even well established turf and constant walking on moist areas leaves little grass. So many grass paths, areas of lawns adjoining borders, or short-cuts for the postman, the paper boy or the dog, tell an identical tale. The drip from trees and heavy shade are even worse. Re-turfing of these areas may be necessary annually.

Be careful with heavy rollers. One friend of mine recently had a fairly large one working on his drive. As there were ridges in the lawn, the operator was induced to roll the sodden grass. Alas, the turf, only down for a few years, had been lain on a filled terrace. You can guess the results. Moss grew rapidly on the compacted soil and there were also major problems of drainage. Better a ridge or a depression or two. If there are depressions, it is better to lift the turf by rolling it back in strips and filling evenly beneath it with good soil, rather than to try to roll down the ridges.

Another solution is to scatter an even layer of sifted soil, compost, fine peat or well-rotted manure to build up the level gradually. Several times a year I scatter a liberal dressing over depressed areas and a lighter dressing of the same material over the whole lawn. In towns and on light, sandy soils or on lawns which get heavy wear, this added humus is important for success, as the surface-roots find food and protection against the winter. With a winter or early spring lawn-fertilizer to stimulate growth at the proper time, this works wonders.

In preparation for turfing, the area should first be thoroughly dug and broken up, although a tilth as fine as for seeding is not needed. Add bone-meal, or preferably a balanced fertilizer. A well-known authority on lawns and sports-grounds recommends a mixture of one ounce superphosphate, one ounce bone-meal and half an ounce of sulphate of potash per square yard. This encourages root-action. For seeding, half an ounce of sulphate of ammonia is added. The soil-bed must be even, and good turf, if well cut, should be of uniform thickness. Turves are usually a foot wide and of varying lengths of from one to three feet. The longer turves are rolled up for easy handling and transport. Lay the turf closely and bond it like bricks or paving to make it secure. Sand or sandy compost can be used to build up turves if they are uneven in thickness and it can also be worked through the joints, but well-cut turves properly laid are very close indeed and the joints are not readily discernible. Do not roll freshly laid lawns, but wait until the turf has grown together and started to root in the soil-bed. Never let fresh turf dry out. Top-dress in spring and fertilize to stimulate growth.

Lawns from Seeding

As lawns are one of the most important features of our gardens, it is important that the standard should be high, with weed-free turf of even, rich colour. It is essential, therefore, to prepare the site carefully, and home-owners, embarking on the development of a new garden, should make every effort to ensure that they will have a fine lawn. A sunny, open site is best, and where there are trees a special seed-mixture for shady areas should be used. Autumn-sowing is preferable to spring-sowing; the actual time will vary with your part of the country but if the autumn is very wet it is best to defer sowing until the spring.

On a new site, contouring may be necessary. Two fundamental rules should be followed. First, contouring should be restricted to the sub-soil, and the fertile top-soil should be heaped for even distribution over the contoured surface. Otherwise top-soil will be buried. Second, make sure that banks and slopes around trees are of a gentle gradient that can be easily mown. If they are too steep, it is better to build a retaining wall to give a terraced effect, or, if this is too formal or too expensive, plant the incline with ground-covers to hold the soil. For this purpose *Hypericum calycinum*, ivies, periwinkles, the prostrate junipers, such as *Juniperus sabina tamariscifolia*, *Cotoneaster dammeri*, *conspicua decora* and similar subjects, are useful.

Proper drainage of a lawn is essential for good turf. On heavy clay or soils where there is a hard-pan under the top-soil, it may be necessary to lay a land-drain, possibly with a few laterals. Where poor drainage is localized, it is often possible to lead the water by a drain to a soakaway nearby. Generally, however, these special precautions are not needed.

The lawn-area should be thoroughly cultivated. If there is not a sufficient depth of good top-soil (four to six inches) it will be necessary to bring in more. It is an advantage if the site can be dug or rotavated well in advance, so that it has time to settle. Autumn preparation for spring sowing is excellent. Be sure there is plenty of humus, particularly on light, sandy soils. Add garden compost, well-rotted manure, peat, spent hops, concentrated organic manures, or leaf-mould.

A level seed-bed is essential and so is a fine tilth. This means raking to remove the stones and to even-out the little humps and depressions. This will also break down the lumps and gradually make a fine tilth. If the soil is loose, tread on it to compact it. Rake in different directions and repeat the treading, following this by further raking until the desired surface is attained. Usually, if you tread crosswise and then lengthwise, this will prove adequate. Light rolling is also advisable. Obviously, both treading and raking operations cannot be done when the soil is wet or when frost is coming out of the ground.

A week or two before, if possible, scatter a basic lawn fertilizer at the rate of three ounces per square yard and rake it so as to distribute it in the top inch or two of soil. There are a number of proprietary brands suited to this purpose. Grass prefers a slightly acid soil, so do not over-lime. Before sowing, hoe all annual weeds or apply a paraquat weed-killer which is harmless to the soil.

Grass-seeds should be selected with an eye to the amount of use the turf will have. For very fine grass, select a mixture containing Fescue *(Festuca)* and *Agrostis*, but no Perennial Ryegrass. For tough hard-wearing turf and for shady areas the addition of the last is desirable.

Seeds should be sown at a rate of from one to two ounces per square yard. Usually one and a half ounces will give good results, but patience, weed-suppression and conditions for good germination are factors. Use high-quality seeds and do not try to save on such a fundamental, long-term feature of your garden as the lawn. Seeds should be evenly distributed in a cross-wise direction. Divide the area into strips and allot equal quantities of seed to each.

After sowing, rake the lawn lightly so that the seeds are covered to a depth of about a quarter of an inch. Light rolling will help, but this should not be attempted if there is any moisture, as the roller will collect soil and seeds. In dry periods, common in spring, sprinkling may be necessary after the seed begins to germinate. The spray should be fine and gentle.

When the grass starts to grow, do not attempt to cut it until it is at least three inches tall. Then cut with the blades of the mower set high. Repeat several times before setting the blades lower, to about three quarters of an inch. The following year a setting of half an inch will be excellent for a neat lawn. Perennial weeds can be eliminated with a selective killer, but only after the grass is well established. Annual weeds will to a large extent be checked by mowing.

A broad sweep of lawn leads to a bronze sculpture by Henry Moore, which looks out over a haha to a country landscape.

14 House-plants and Greenhouses

The Care of Christmas Plants

When Christmas is over, many of use are confronted with the care of house-plants received as gifts and each year we resolve to keep them in their prime. Let's consider the most important factors.

More plants are probably lost because of excessive watering in the winter months than for any other reason. Growth obviously slows down with cool, dark days as the evenings draw in and far less water and nourishment is required. In hot, centrally-heated houses, however, the rate of evaporation can be rapid, so the only safe guide is to observe the condition of the soil. It should be damp to the touch but not wet enough to be so clogged that the roots cannot breathe. Look at your plants daily and don't water them unless they need it. Some may not need attention more than once a week. Try to use water at room-temperature, not icy water from the tap. If rainwater is available, so much the better.

Remember that plants vary in their requirements of heat and light. Ivies, *Philodendron scandens*, the charming variegated *Chlorophytum capense variegatum*, and many others do not mind the lack of direct sunshine and therefore are adaptable. Others, such as crotons and the glossy aphelandras with their striking dark leaves handsomely ribbed with white, require more light and higher temperatures.

Poinsettias will have been forced, so will undoubtedly have come from a high temperature. They, like other florist-plants, have probably journeyed first to a wholesale in urban areas, followed by another journey to a retail shop and then have been carried through the streets or placed in a cold delivery-van, before reaching your door. This variation in temperature is not good for plants and often explains the loss of lower leaves.

Don't let plants stand for long in water. If water collects in the saucer or *cache pot*, empty it out. This applies particularly to azaleas and cyclamen. If a plant has dried out, don't go to the other extreme. If a plant is unhealthy, you can ring the death-knell by over-watering or over-feeding.

The type of container has a lot to do with the amount of watering required. Plastic or glazed flower-pots do not have the rapid evaporation that occurs through the walls of clay pots and therefore will require less water. I remember once seeing a lot of begonias, some of which were potted in plastic and others in the usual clay. All had been receiving the same treatment. In every case it was those in the plastic pots that were suffering. There was nothing wrong with the pots; the trouble was that they had been given too much water.

The same problem arises with heating. Don't put plants too near a radiator or fire. The dry heat has damaging effects, as I discovered to my cost when I placed a trailing silver-edged ivy on the mantlepiece above an open log fire. Don't bring bulbs that have been plunged in the cold-frame or an ash-mound into sudden heat: the transition should be gradual. I have seen hyacinths placed near a stove to hasten flowering. Alas, they were partially cooked and had no future. If you have gas fires, forget about trying to grow cyclamen; they are sensitive to sulphur fumes. If you have a very warm room, again cyclamen will have a short life. They are essentially for cooler temperatures, ie, 50–65°F (10–18°C).

Most house-plants do not mind being pot-bound. Do not re-pot them until spring or early summer, when root- and leaf-growth is active. An expert friend of mind even suggests that it is wise to buy the less reliable ones that require cosseting in the late spring or summer so that they acclimatize to your home conditions as winter approaches. Don't pot-on into pots that are too large. It is amazing how well plants will grow in three-inch and five-inch pots. Also, remember that flowering plants are often included in arrangements with the tougher long-term foliage plants. If this is the case, discard the former after flowering and let the others fill their space, as they are bound to do in time.

A fine batch of Zonal Pelargonium 'King of Denmark' shows the possibilities of the small greenhouse for forcing and wintering tender plants.

A practical, well-equipped, working greenhouse is divided into warm and cool sections with a propagating frame. Such a house can be put to a number of uses.

The Small Heated Greenhouse

There is a sadness about the first killing frost, for in its wake we see blackened dahlias, nasturtiums reduced to a soft pulp and drained of their brilliant colours, and pale pink tomatoes hanging heavily from limp stems. Happy is the gardener with a greenhouse, where he can shelter tender treasures and bring on all sorts of beauties through the winter and spring, to say nothing of seeking for himself a warm refuge from the cold winter winds. The greenhouse may be a cool one, always frost-free, in which camellias, tender rhododendrons, lilies, nerines, mimosas, plumbagoes and a host of other delightful shrubs and bulbs can be grown successfully, or it may be a heated greenhouse, where in autumn there are velvety-leaved Smithianthas (Naegelias) with long-lasting spikes of flowers in shades of pink, coral, scarlet and yellow above the exotic foliage, ranging from shades of olive to purple with strange spotting and veining, and later winter-flowering, fibrous-rooted begonias. Gaudy poinsettias can be forced into bloom for Christmas and white trum-

pet-lilies for Easter. The range of plants that can be grown, depending on the minimum winter temperature provided, is impressive. Geraniums flower in successive bursts, and sweet-scented stocks, schizanthus, primulas and cyclamen are among the other favourites.

With modern building techniques, greenhouses have long been an integral part of many American homes, opening off the hall, sitting-room or kitchen, and warmed either by the central heating or by special electrical or oil devices. This arrangement is admirable as it cuts heating costs, and the accessibility of the greenhouse makes it possible to slip in for a few minutes at odd intervals when we would not be tempted to go outside. Lastly, the glass can become a decorative feature in the manner of the old conservatory and can serve as a glorified sun-room. In this case the choice of plants must be limited to those suited to the conditions provided.

In recent years orchids have become a popular hobby for the mystique, so long associated with these exotic flowers, has largely been dispelled. Cypripediums and cymbidiums are relatively easy and do not require high temperatures. In fact, a minimum night temperature of forty-five to fifty-five degrees and fifty-five to sixty-five by day will suffice in winter. They need plenty of light and good ventilation. A lot of trouble with orchids stems from inadequate circulation of air but direct draughts must be avoided. Due to the enormous propagation of orchids, the cost of plants has gradually evened out in recent years. I do not mean that orchids are cheap, but good reliable varieties are less expensive than they used to be, and from a single plant it is possible to propagate others. Obviously clones that have received awards and new colour breaks will be very expensive indeed. The blooms of cymbidiums and cypripediums last for many weeks and hence are particularly good value. Also they tend to flower in autumn, winter and early spring, when they are particularly needed. The new dwarf cymbidiums are ideal for smaller houses. The Rag Orchid *(Coelogyne cristata)* is another lovely easy variety with its abundance of white flowers over a longish season in winter.

Although cymbidiums will require shading from direct sun in spring and summer, sunlight is needed to produce flower buds in fall and winter. Orchids react favourably to artificial light and a great deal is being done along these lines. It makes it possible to grow orchids in sunless positions that several decades ago would have been pronounced as unsuitable.

Correct watering is important. In principle, give them less water in cold weather when the days are short, and never over-water so that air cannot reach the roots. Water that is heavily chlorinated is not suitable. Rainwater is excellent but it must be pure with no trace of oil or tar from the roofing as this is very injurious.

For a cool house at temperatures suitable for cymbidiums, cyclamen are ideal. Grow these from seed in late summer. The seedlings should be transplanted into boxes early in the new year and potted up in three-inch pots in March or April and into larger ones in early summer. By this method plants will flower in the fall and continue until spring. This entails a lot of work so you may prefer to buy young plants from cyclamen specialists in early spring, thereby omitting sowing and pricking out.

Indica azaleas are also happy in a cool house. With these the secret is an open acid compost, rich in leaf mould or peat, and careful watering to keep the root-ball moist but not saturated. Be sure to grow a pot or two of the very fragrant *Jasminum polyanthum*, trained as a pyramid, ball or fan. It likes cool temperatures and plenty of sun. If space permits, a few pots of camellias and fragrant tender rhododendrons are wonderful value in a cool house, but they do need room.

There will inevitably be pots of spring bulbs, some pelargoniums, (regales, scented-leaved and zonals),

Primula x kewensis is a fragrant buttercup-yellow hybrid, excellent for a cool-house and easily grown from seeds.

giant hippeastrums and, I hope, a few personal favourites. Everyone should have his own pet plants.

Successful House-plants

As winter approaches, we think in terms of putting our gardens to bed in readiness for spring, and inevitably of what we can bring into the house to bridge the gap. Fresh flowers more or less come to an end with the first frosts and many of us must fall back on house-plants. Bulbs will, of course, have been planned for by now, and pots of hyacinths, daffodils and bowls of Paper Whites are waiting their turn in cool seclusion.

In the last few years house-plants have entered a new phase in this country. For a long time we relied on azaleas, cyclamen, primulas, including *P. malacoides, P. obconica* and others of the same family, and a limited number of foliage plants as well, but, on the whole, the choice was definitely limited. Now, all this has changed. House-plants, both for foliage-effect and flowers, have come into deserved popularity and there is an ever-increasing choice. This recent vogue is readily understandable for a number of reasons. Perhaps foremost among these is the advancement of heating techniques for houses and apartment blocks. A fairly constant heat with no marked extremes is a requisite for the successful cultivation of many varieties. Secondly, the absence of fumes from gas and coal fires is equally important, as they spell ill-health and even death to many plants. Thirdly, the very nature of modern architecture and interior design with large areas of glass, flat panelling and unbroken wall surface requires the three-dimensional, almost sculptural quality of large house plants with their bold foliage, with contrasting leaf shapes, textures and colours ranging from deep bottle greens to creamy yellows and glaucous blues. Certainly the high cost of flowers has been another factor.

One of the delights of house-plants is their acquisition. By browsing in the florists' shops, nursery-gardens with glass, department stores and even chain stores, we may find delightful surprises. A golden rule is to buy what you want when you see it. Take the coveted plant then and there; the actual selection is half the fun. Ask the florist for tips on successful cultivation, if you are in doubt. Many plants are now sold with a label of instructions, telling you about temperature, sun or shade and, above all, watering. Follow these directions carefully, particularly if the plant is an unfamiliar one. There are today an ever-increasing number of new varieties from which to choose, but a word of warning: some are easy and some are not. Make sure that you can satisfy the conditions required. It is no use putting a plant that requires sun in a room with only a north light. It is no use having plants that require a warm, even temperature in a cold, unheated house. Above all, be realistic. Too many gardeners, alas, are ruled by the heart and not the head. With house-plants this can lead to frustration and costly failures.

Plants fall into two basic groups – flowering plants and foliage plants, which, of course, may have blooms that are purely incidental. To the latter group belong some of the most useful, such as the lovely Rex begonias, with their huge, bold leaves in shades of red, purple, silver and green, the dark, glossy green rubber plants *(Ficus)*, peperomias and the many varieties of ivy *(Helix)*, with leaves varying in size, shape and colour. Philodendrons are relatively easy plants for indoor cultivation and do not need direct sunlight, in fact, are better without it. They like a warm atmosphere, preferably moist. Many of them have aerial roots and can be grown against a support of cork or a moss

covered branch. The easiest is *P. scandens*, which can either be used as a trailing plant, or if the leaders are pinched out, can be made into a bushy mound. The dark gleaming heart-shaped leaves and pale new growths are extremely attractive. *Monstera deliciosa* with its huge leaves patterned with holes is surely one of the most spectacular of all house plants.

A great favourite of mine is the Grape Ivy *(Rhocissus rhomboidea)* or the quick-growing Kangaroo Vine *(Cissus antarctica)*. Both are delightful in the way that they twine and twist as they clamber or trail. They are relatively easy, requiring daylight but not direct sun, a moderate temperature and ample moisture in summer and spring.

Watering very often spells success or failure. Be sure that plants are not allowed to stand for long in water. Beware of decorative bowls that have no outlets. These may be charming, but they are usually short-term homes for most plants. Generally, water should be partially withheld in winter from many house-plants, so that they have enough but are not really moist. When they are growing vigorously in spring and summer in warm temperatures, they obviously require more. No plant likes a direct draught. Be sure to protect plants from open windows, doors and vents. Newly acquired plants should be gradually acclimatized. It may not be possible to provide conditions identical to those under which the plant was reared, but the period of adjustment should be gradual to minimize shock.

Easter Lilies for Pot-cultivation

Few flowers except for the rose are as universally loved as the lily. This word evokes for most of us the white trumpets, which are universally associated with Easter and with festivities such as weddings and parties. This is *Lilium longiflorum*, a native of southern Japan, while the Lily of the Annunciation is the Madonna Lily *(L. candidum)*. At Easter in churches in many parts of the world white trumpet-lilies are the decorative theme for altars and chapels, particularly in the United States, where pots of lilies at Easter are nearly as universal in churches and homes alike, as fir trees to celebrate Christmas. These waxen white lilies, with heavy-textured, glistening petals and a pervasive sweet perfume, are primarily used for pot-culture, as the fleshy buds are too tender to withstand the frosts and winter damp, save in the mildest climates with plenty of sunshine. Great quantities are grown for the florist trade and now, thanks to cold-storage bulbs in off-seasons, there is not a week in the year when cut blooms are not available.

Longiflorum lilies are ideal pot-plants for those who have a conservatory or greenhouse. Bulbs should be

'Purissima' is a lovely white tulip of fine shape and texture. White tulips are always in demand for flower decoration.

Pots of daffodils, hyacinths and tulips are easily forced for the house if bulbs of good quality are used and the basic principles of good cultivation are carefully followed.

Lilium longiflorum or crosses of it are easily forced in pots during the late winter and early spring, and cut sprays last well in water.

potted-up in late summer or early autumn and later as available in six- to seven-inch pots. These must be clean and well crocked to provide sharp drainage. Plant the bulbs in a rich, loose compost consisting of three parts of good loam, one part of sieved leaf-mould and some sharp sand. Some growers suggest replacing the leaf-mould by well rotted, sieved manure. Longiflorums are stem-rooting, so deep pots are an advantage. They should not be filled completely, so as to allow for subsequent top-dressing. Plunge the pots in a cold-frame or out-of-door plunge-bed and cover them with peat, bracken or leaf-mould. When they are thoroughly rooted and when top-growth appears, they should be moved into a cool-house to acclimatize. Subsequently they should be moved into a warmer house, with a night temperature of about 55–60°F (13° to 16°C). Longiflorums will require quite a little heat to force, and timing will depend on temperature and sunlight. Growing plants require liberal watering, and feeding with weak liquid manure is beneficial when flower-buds form. It usually takes five to six weeks for flowers to open after the buds first appear.

Bermuda has long been associated with Easter lilies, and the sight of the fields in full bloom against the brilliant blue skies in spring is unforgettable. The lilies are believed to have been brought to Bermuda in the mid-fifties of the last century by an English missionary returning from Japan, who generously gave bulbs to a clergyman on the island. The bulbs settled down and grew with such vigour that a thriving bulb-industry was in time established.

That superb lily *(L. longiflorum* var. *eximium)* has a long, rather narrow trumpet of fine substance. The tapered greenish buds open to creamy-white flowers, which gradually turn pure white as they expand. The stems are sturdy and the foliage is definitely columnar in habit. One of the endearing characteristics of Easter lilies is the fact that stems can be picked when the lower buds are just ready to burst. In water, with proper care, every bud will open. This makes lilies easier to pack for market, as the petals themselves are brittle and easily bruised when open. Moreover, the yellow pollen is easily smudged and hence the practice has arisen of removing the anthers of all open flowers before packing them.

I have received boxes of Bermuda lilies in New York and in London, shipped by boat or plane, and they have travelled perfectly. Cut stems of lilies may seem expensive. Usually, a charge is made on the basis of the number of blooms or buds, but they may also be sold by the bunch. However, as a stem may last any-thing from a week to fifteen days, lilies are remarkably good value and a few spikes with good foliage, such as that of camellia, eucalyptus or pittosporum, make a large, dynamic arrangement for an important position. Lilies, in fact, outlast most other cut flowers. Other species suitable for pots, tubs and cutting include *L. regale, speciosum, auratum* and the elegant but very rapid-growing *L. formosanum*, which superficially resembles *longiflorum.*

In America, Mr Jan de Graaff, realizing the potential of lilies as florists' flowers, has developed a number of remarkable hybrids adapted to this use. I am glad to say that through his efforts and those of other hybridi-zers new varieties are appearing in increasing quantities on both sides of the Atlantic in the flower-markets and better shops.

There are a number of named varieties of *L. longi-florum*. In the United States, a lily bearing the name *L.* 'Harrisii' appeared in about 1883. This is our old friend the Bermuda lily (var. *eximium*), which was introduced from Bermuda to the trade by a Phila-delphia nurseryman, W. K. Harris. It is still widely sold in the United States under this name. 'Croft' is a very popular named clone with a short stem (thirty to thirty-six inches high) with well-proportioned wide trumpets. Because of its sturdy stature it is particularly suited to pot-work for florists and is well adapted to small houses and rooms. 'Estate' is rather taller and excellent for cutting, but it has shorter trumpets than

'Croft'. A very robust tall strain is the superb 'Holland's Glory', which is rather hardier than other forms. This makes it useful for outdoor planting in milder areas without protection. It has stems five to six feet tall and as many as seven to nine flowers. A fine tetraploid form known as 'Tetrabel' has been developed at the John Innes Horticultural Institute in England.

Violets That Grow in the House

There are a number of house-plants which flower for a short period and then must go back to the greenhouse. These can hardly be called house-plants in the true sense of the word. To this group belong orchids such as cypripediums and cymbidiums. Although the flowers are long-lasting and beautiful both in form and colour, the plants will not survive the conditions in the average house for long. In the same category are plants such as anthuriums, stephanotis and other exotics.

Perhaps the most popular of all flowering house-plants today is the African Violet, or Saintpaulia. The craze for it has spread from this country, where not only is there an active National African Violet Society, but specimens are to be found in the majority of homes where indoor plants are grown.

There is little doubt that good central heating favours their cultivation. My parents and their friends all had good small collections, growing in such diverse positions as sun-porches, living-rooms, bathrooms and kitchens. The humidity of the last two explains the reasons for success. Saintpaulias need sunlight in winter if they are to flower abundantly and in summer they require light but not strong sunlight. Here are a few practical hints for good cultivation. Use relatively small pots, as plants will not flower if they are over-potted. This principle applies to many other genera as well. As the roots are delicate and hair-like, the compost should be open and friable, as well as highly porous and moisture-retentive. Obviously loam, sand, leaf-mould and granulated peat with base-fertilizers

Saintpaulias are today the most coveted of house-plants, with their clusters of single or double flowers, in colours ranging from deep blue and purple to white and clear pink.

are the required ingredients. Any good potting compost plus extra leaf-mould would be satisfactory. Add extra sand if the compost seems heavy.

I always allow the plants to absorb water from the saucers, as the hairy leaves rot easily if water stands on the crowns. Don't over-feed your plants or there will be leaf-growth at the expense of flowers. More 'don'ts': don't expect them to grow where there are gas or coal fumes. In our kitchen in New York they would not grow when we used gas for cooking; when we switched to electricity it was a very different story. Don't expose plants to cold draughts. If you air rooms in cold weather remove the African Violets first. Don't expect them to do well in rooms where temperatures drop below 45°F or at the most 40°F at night (7°–5°C). They like a relatively even temperature and hence central heating suits them.

The varieties today are numerous. Colours include purple, blue, pink, white and mauve, both single and doubles. Nomenclature varies, and some varieties are very similar. Florists' shops and specialist nurseries offer good supplies. African Violets are relatively easy to propagate from leaf-cuttings in either water or a rooting-medium, or from the plantlets which so often form around established plants. I can remember my annoyance when I once found that every small coffee-cup in the pantry had been pressed into service for rooting Saintpaulias.

The propagation of house-plants is enormous fun, and of course there are those endearing plants like outdoor strawberries which make their own progeny in a miraculous way on runners. *Saxifraga sarmentosa*, charmingly dubbed Mother of Thousands, produces small plantlets on long, thin trailing stems, as does the decorative *Chlorophytum elatum variegatum*, with its narrow graceful green-and-white striped leaves, or the amusing Pig-a-back plant *(Tolmiea menziesii)*, with attractive green leaves zoned with bronze, from which the new plantlets spring from the junction of the petiole and the leaf. Layering is the obvious method of propagation for all of these.

Another great favourite, which comes in wonderful shades of pink, red, orange and white, is *Impatiens*, known by the doubtfully attractive vernacular name Busy Lizzie. These grow rapidly in good compost rich in humus, if given plenty of water in the flowering period. They like sun, but also flower in light shade. Propagation is very easy if cuttings are placed in a sandy medium and kept well watered. The wealth of vividly coloured flowers is hard to equal. Plants should be pinched back to keep them compact. In California Impatiens grows out of doors in profusion in borders and small gardens. For that matter, many of our exotic house-plants are common garden plants in that superb, even climate. Pot-grown plants of Im-

patiens can be successfully bedded-out in town gardens.

I have said nothing about cacti. I must admit that I am not an enthusiast, but here I bow to the scores of thousands who are. The extraordinary shapes, the symmetrical forms, the wonderful colours and, in some cases, the brilliant flowers, all excite my interest and admiration, but I don't love them.

Early Bulbs for Indoor Fragrance

As the first few boiling hot days of August make us relax in our gardens, it seems ironic to remind gardeners that then is the time to think of ordering bulbs, especially if there are to be bowls and pans of fragrant hyacinths, freesias, Paper Whites and even daffodils for Christmas. By the time orders go forward and the bulbs are despatched at the end of August or early September, it is not a moment too early. Bulb-houses then have good stocks for immediate delivery for forcing for Christmas and the New Year. Freesias should be planted in August for early flowering, with perhaps another batch or two in September and early October for later flowering.

To my mind, hyacinths are the most rewarding house-plants because of their fine colours and fragrance. They may be potted-up either in soil or bulb-fibre, using a five- or six-inch pot for single bulbs or larger ones for groups. Make sure that the pots are clean and well crocked for good drainage. Use a rich compost, as hyacinths are heavy feeders, and barely cover the bulb with soil. The secret of success is to allow the hyacinths plenty of time in a dark, cool place to establish vigorous root-growth. If possible, plunge the pots in the ground to a depth of six inches, or better still cover them with coarse ashes. This last bit of advice is not so easy to follow in these days of electric and oil heating, as coal-ash is becoming a scarce commodity. Town-dwellers should store the bulbs in a cool, dark cupboard or cellar. Little water is required at this time, but the bulbs must never be allowed to dry out. After eight weeks, probably towards the end of November, examine the root-action by carefully tipping out a pot. If you are satisfied with the quantity of white roots, bring the bulbs gradually into the warmth, increasing the quantity of water and giving them a little liquid food every few weeks. This will not be needed with bulb fibre, as it is already well impregnated with food. Force by gradually increasing the temperature and giving as much sunlight as possible.

If bulbs are placed in a cupboard, the flower-buds should show an inch or two above the leaves before they are brought to the light, as this will take about eight or nine weeks for pre-cooled bulbs. Be sure not to force them too quickly, as the process should be gradual. Bulbs grown in water should be of the largest size and placed in hyacinth-glasses so that the base of the bulb is just on top of the water. If possible, use rainwater with a lump of charcoal to keep it sweet. Charcoal, incidentally, is one of the important ingredients of bulb-fibre.

Now for varieties. The small, heavily scented Roman hyacinths are easiest to force and can be had in bloom by the end of November. The multiple spikes are graceful, with small, relatively widely spaced bells and they flower over a longish period, each bulb usually sending up two, three or even four stems. As the bulbs are much smaller, three to five can be used in a five-inch pot or decorative bowl. Bulbs are relatively scarce and therefore expensive, but the scent is intoxicating and they are in every way enchanting. The light blue miniature hyacinth 'Vanguard' is excellent for forcing, as are 'Fairy Blue' and 'Borah'.

Of the large Dutch hyacinths, good varieties for Christmas include the clear pink 'Rosalie', 'Winter Fragrance', and prepared varieties with colours ranging from white, pale pink and blue to red, dark blue and yellow. 'L'Innocence' is still a remarkable white.

Old stand-bys are the fragrant Narcissus 'Paper White' and 'Soleil d'Or', with its deep yellow petals and shallow orange cup. Both are extremely fragrant and can be grown in soil, bulb-fibre, or pebbles. Paper Whites, unlike other bulbs, can be placed directly in the light of a window after planting. There is a brilliant scarlet Amaryllis (Hippeastrum) called 'Christmas Joy', which should be planted in bulb-fibre and given a minimum temperature of 65° F (18° C) in full sun with plenty of water. If planted in early autumn they should flower for Christmas, but, of course, these are not fragrant.

For later flowering a large number of prepared hyacinths, narcissus and tulips are offered by the good bulb-houses. Crocuses are charming in small pots and force well for late winter, but they should be grown cool. The transition period when they are brought inside is critical, as the buds will dry up and go blind in too much heat. Make haste slowly. Plant them fairly thickly in small pots, just covering the tops with soil, and use light bright colours or mix purple and gold together. Pots should be plunged, as is done with other bulbs.

Pot freesia-corms in a good, open compost, using three parts of loam to one each of leaf-mould and sand to make a loose, open mixture. Stand the pots in a cold-frame and give them very little water until the thin sword-like foliage thrusts through the earth. It is essential to grow freesias cool and to force them gently. When flower-buds are forming, they will require ample moisture and an occasional feeding with liquid fertilizer. Do not attempt to grow them in bulb-fibre or as house-plants. Freesias have wiry stems that need support. Provide this early, or crooked stems will result. I personally prefer the old-fashioned small white Freesia refracta alba, with its creamy petals with purple and gold-stained throats. The scent is intoxicatingly sweet and the flowers have the refinement and beauty characteristic of a species. There are fine, coloured strains in profusion, including large golden yellows. Freesias are easy early-flowering corms of great beauty, and if they are properly dried-off after flowering, they can be used successfully another year. They are also easily grown from seeds, either when ripe or in early March.

After Christmas there is still time to start a pot or two of hippeastrums. This cumbersome word is now the correct name for the magnificent Dutch hybrid amaryllis. The huge, spreading trumpet-shaped flowers are borne on a sturdy stem, the flowers usually appearing in advance of the leaves or of their full development. Bulbs planted in winter will flower in eight to ten weeks, either in a greenhouse or even in a sunny window in a warm room. Bottom-heat promotes rapid root-growth and foliage.

Bulbs should be planted in rich, open compost in a six- to eight-inch pot. I have even had success growing them in bulb-fibre. The top of the bulb should be well above the level of the soil. Only a little water is necessary until the roots have developed and the flower-bud appears. Liquid manure is also beneficial. The individual flowers, often as many as three or four, and measuring six to ten inches across, come in velvety reds, apricots, oranges and, perhaps, loveliest of all, pure whites with cool green throats. There are other flowers with spectacular veining and flushes of rich colour on a lighter ground.

After flowering, hippeastrums must be allowed to grow on to store up food. When the foliage has stopped developing in late August or September, lay the pots on their sides and withhold water to rest the bulbs. In January re-pot or top-dress them as necessary. Very often, bulbs stop flowering because of improper treatment or old age. Obviously, greenhouse conditions produce better long-term results than those of a room.

Index